LAST JUDGMENT ICONOGRAPHY IN THE CARPATHIANS

Few subjects in Christianity have inspired artists as much as the Last Judgment. *Last Judgment Iconography in the Carpathians* examines over 100 images of the Last Judgment, with an emphasis on those from the fifteenth century to the eighteenth century, in the Carpathian mountain region of Ukraine, Poland, Slovakia, and Romania. John-Paul Himka's analysis of these monumental works of art allows him to consider history free from the traditional frameworks and narratives of nations. For nine years, Himka studied Last-Judgment images throughout the Carpathians and found a distinctive and transnational blending of Gothic, Byzantine, and Novgorodian art in the region.

Piecing together the story of how these images were produced and how they developed, Himka traces their origins on linden boards and their evolution on canvas and church walls. Originally painted by monks, these images increased in popularity and eventually came to be commissioned and even painted by peasants and shepherds whose tastes so shocked bishops that they ordered the destruction of depictions of sexual themes and grotesque forms of torture. A richly illustrated and detailed account of history through a style of art, *Last Judgment Iconography in the Carpathians* will find a receptive audience with art historians, religious scholars, and Slavists.

JOHN-PAUL HIMKA is a professor in the Department of History and Classics at the University of Alberta.

JOHN-PAUL HIMKA

Last Judgment Iconography in the Carpathians

UNIVERSITY OF TORONTO PRESS
Toronto Buffalo London

Toronto Buffalo London
utorontopress.com

Reprinted in paperback 2018

ISNB 978-0-8020-9809-2 (cloth)   ISBN 978-1-4875-2341-1 (paper)

Library and Archives Canada Cataloguing in Publication

Himka, John-Paul, 1949–
Last Judgment iconography in the Carpathians / John-Paul Himka.

Includes bibliographical references and index.
ISBN 978-0-8020-9809-2 (case)   ISBN 978-1-4875-2341-1 (softcover)

1. Icons – Carpathian Mountains Region – History. 2. Carpathian Mountains Region – Religious life and customs. 3. Christianity and art – Orthodox Eastern Church. 4. Apocalypse in art. 5. Judgment Day in art. I. Title.

N8120.H54 2009   704.9'482094779   C2009-900440-2

This book has been published with the help of a grant from the Canadian Federation for the Humanities and Social Sciences, through the Aid to Scholarly Publications Program, using funds provided by the Social Sciences and Humanities Research Council of Canada.

University of Toronto Press acknowledges the financial assistance to its publishing program of the Canada Council for the Arts and the Ontario Arts Council, an agency of the Government of Ontario.

Canada Council for the Arts   Conseil des Arts du Canada

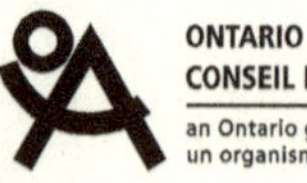
ONTARIO ARTS COUNCIL
CONSEIL DES ARTS DE L'ONTARIO
an Ontario government agency
un organisme du gouvernement de l'Ontario

Funded by the Government of Canada   Financé par le gouvernement du Canada   Canada

This book is dedicated to Drs Peter and Doris Kule,
generous benefactors of Ukrainian studies and religious studies

Contents

Illustrations

Unless otherwise indicated, all photos are the author's.

Maps

Acknowledgments

The research for this book was funded by the International Research and Exchanges Board, the Social Sciences and Humanities Research Council of Canada, and the University of Alberta. I am very grateful for the generous funding that they made available to this project.

Many individuals also helped me with the work. Two anonymous reviewers for the University of Toronto Press made invaluable suggestions for improving the text I submitted. I traded manuscripts and information with Lilya Berezhnaya, who also helped me obtain reproductions of the icons in the Budapest Museum of Ethnography (Néprajzi Múzeum). Oleksandr Bilevych drove me around Transcarpathia and Lviv oblast. His mother, Vira Bilevych, housed me and fed me during my frequent trips to Lviv. Bohdan Bilyj, with whom I have been friends since my first major research trip abroad in 1974–6, put the resources of the Bishop Konstantyn Chekhovych Eparchial Library in Przemyśl at my disposal and also helped me with his knowledge of the Przemyśl environs. Halyna Bilykova took me down to the depository of the National Museum in Kyiv and showed me what they had that related to the Last Judgment. I learned a tremendous amount from the late Romuald Biskupski, the gentlest teacher I ever had; he made me many a cup of tea in Sanok, and Pani Janina Lewandowska hosted me more than once at her table. While attached to the Institute of Art History at Jagiellonian University, I had the privilege of working under the guidance of the late Anna Różycka-Bryzek, who has contributed so much to the field of Byzantine and Rus' art history and trained excellent students. When I was setting out to do research in Poland, Andrzej Chojnowski made inquiries that provided me with a little who's who among Polish scholars of post-Byzantine iconography. Whenever she accompanied me on expeditions, my wife, Chrystia

Chomiak, was everyone's favourite and helped me immeasurably and in many ways; she also read chapters of the first draft of my manuscript. Ron Dutchak was good enough to read the manuscript and tell me whether it could be followed by an educated person outside the field. The maps were drawn by Michael Fisher – highly professional and fun to work with. Michael Flier commented on some of my early work on these icons and answered the occasional query. I am deeply indebted to Jarosław Giemza, who not only devoted much time and energy to me when I visited the Division of Eastern-Church Art at the Castle Museum in Łańcut, invited me to his home several times, and showed me all the literature on icons that he had amassed, but he also followed my work with interest after I left, answered queries, and sent me photos and new publications. Jerzy Ginalski put the resources of the Museum of Folk Architecture in Sanok at my disposal. David Goldfrank was from the first an active reader of, commentator on, and supporter of my work on the icons. Vladislav Grešlík, the leading specialist on the icons of Eastern Slovakia, guided me through the churches and museums of the region, enlisting his brother Mykhailo as chauffeur; extraordinarily generous, even for this part of the world, he continued to provide me with photos and publications in subsequent years. Agnieszka Gronek has been working on a related icon, that of the Passion; she shared her wide knowledge and balanced perspectives with me both in a few illuminating conversations in Kraków and in the dissertations and articles that she made available to me; she also shared photographs and research notes. When I needed six months in Lviv and had not yet secured funding for my project, Father Borys Gudziak graciously hired me to teach at what was then the Lviv Theological Academy (now the Ukrainian Catholic University), and later he took time out of his unenviably busy schedule to write letters of recommendation for me. Volodymyr Haiuk let me photograph the Last Judgment icon in the Museum of the History of Religion in Lviv. Chris Hann set me up with Romuald Biskupski and encouraged my work on icons of the Carpathian region. Valerii Helchuk let me use his photos of the eighteenth-century Pohorilivka icon. As the footnotes will demonstrate, I gained much from consultations with Mariia Helytovych at the National Museum in Lviv. Eva and Mykhailo Himka sketched scenes from an icon for me when they were still children; now Mykhailo has also drawn one of the illustrations for this book. Halyna Holchuk was planning to write a master's thesis in Lviv on the Last Judgment icons and generously shared what she knew with me. Yaroslav Hrytsak arranged for me to teach a course at Ivan Franko Lviv National University when I needed to do research in the city. Renata Kinga Jara guided me through the Museum of Folk Architecture in Sanok. My friend Oleh Kholkovsky accompanied me on a number of short trips around Ukraine in search of the icons, making the bus travel more pleasant. My first research assistant was Hanna Kos, who searched through a large amount of Ukrainian art historical literature looking for references to Last Judgment icons and murals and their locations; this was immensely helpful. Andrii Krawchuk shared his photos of Last Judgment icons. Anatoliy and Natalka Kruglashov hosted me in Chernivtsi, arranged and often accompanied me on trips around Bukovina, and made important connections for me. Mirosław Kruk arranged for me to take photographs in the National Museum in Kraków, shared his erudition on West-Rus' iconography, and travelled with me to Luzhany. Paul Robert Magocsi read the manuscript and made valuable suggestions. Michal Mlynarz helped with preparing the illustrations. Włodzimierz Mokry allowed me to use the resources of the Foundation of St Volodymyr when I was working in Kraków. Myroslav Marynovych provided me with some photos of the Drohobych mural. Yurii Ostrovsky gave me the perspective of a restorer on one of the icons I deal with in this book. Vasyl Otkovych gave me permission to take photographs in the National Museum in Lviv and also offered guidance at an early stage of the project. I had lively discussions with Włodzimierz Pilipowicz in Przemyśl and benefited from his immense private library. Serhii Plokhy and I have shared an interest in icons for some time, and he has helped me out more than once. Robert Pollák allowed me to take photographs in the East Slovakian Museum in Košice. Ioan and Eudochia Pop both drove my wife and me around Maramureş and hosted us in their home. Stefan Purici did the advance reconnaissance of the Moldavian frescoes and then chauffeured my wife and me around to see and photograph them. Ladislav Puškár guided me around the Museum of Ukrainian-Rusyn Culture in Svidník. Alan Rutkowski listened to me talk about this project for many, many hours as we lifted weights or made wine together; he also worked on solving some of the puzzles of the iconography and read chapters with attention to style. Tania Sabodash helped me at the Branch of the Lviv Art Gallery in Olesko; in particular, she showed me what the gallery had in the depository. Father Ioan Sauciuk of Baia Mare heard that I was interested in the murals of Maramureş, sought me out, and gave me two very useful books on the wooden churches of Maramureş. I have been benefiting from the friendship and insights of Mother Sophia Senyk for over twenty years; on this project, too, she shared ideas and bibliography and commented perceptively on drafts. Paul Shore examined some pictures for me and commented from the perspective of a historian of Austrian art. Early on in this work Iryna Shults showed me everything of relevance in the National Kyiv-Caves Historical-Cultural Preserve, allowed me to photograph the icons, guided me to useful literature, and even took me to another museum to check on some things. The librarian Aleksander Siemaszko was a great help at the Institute of Art History, Jagellonian University. Halyna Skop answered questions for me at the Museum of the History of Religion in Lviv. I had one rather intense conversation with the art historian Małgorzata Smorąg Różycka in Kraków, but it clarified a great deal for me. Miroslav Sopoliga gave me permission to take photos at the Museum of Ukrainian-Rusyn Culture in Svidník. In Przemyśl I was attached to the Southeastern Scholarly Institute; its director, Stanisław Stępień, aided me in many ways, including arranging for lodging, mailing my books, and inviting me to speak on my research in the institute. At the National Museum in Lviv, my primary contact was Oleh Sydor, who showed me the most important icons of this rather inaccessible collection. Borys Voznytsky met with me once, but he crammed a lot into that meeting, giving me permission to take photos in the Olesko branch of the Lviv Art Gallery and also many very useful tips and perspectives. Katarzyna Winnicka was my guide at the Historical Museum in Sanok. Michael Yonan answered a query that required expertise in Hungarian art history. Yuriy Zazuliak, who has a detailed knowledge of fifteenth-century Galicia, read a draft of my second chapter and provided me with additional perspectives and information that I incorporated into my text. Tetiana Zubovych helped me in Chernivtsi.

I would also like to thank my research assistants at the University of Alberta: Anne-Laurence Caudano, Natalka Cmoc, Shane Ennest, Krzysztof Lada, Srdja Pavlovic, Oleksandr Shevchenko, and Mykola Soroka.

I was deeply moved when on an expedition in Bukovina. The parishioners of the Church of the Dormition in Roztoky, Putyla raion, Chernivtsi oblast, a mountain village, presented me and my companion Anatoliy Kruglashov with beautiful embroidered towels (*rushnyky*). May God bless them.

Abbreviations

AB GK	Archiwum Państwowe w Przemyślu, Archiwum Biskupstwa grecko-katolickiego w Przemyślu
Akc.	accession number
f.	fond (archival collection)
LNB	L'vivs'ka naukova biblioteka im. V. Stefanyka
NTSh	Naukove tovarystvo im. Shevchenka
op.	opys (archival inventory)
spr.	sprava (archival unit)

LAST JUDGMENT ICONOGRAPHY IN THE CARPATHIANS

1 Introduction

Origin of the Project

My son Mykhailo jokingly said to me while I was researching this book: 'Tato, your book is going to revolutionise the way people think about Carpathian Last Judgment icons.' The joke, of course, is that no one really thinks about this topic anyway. And he knew too that I had set my sights rather higher. What I was trying to do was to find a new way to write history.

It might be helpful if I explain the train of thought that set this project off. I was struck by Ernest Gellner's observation that nationalist intellectuals in the nineteenth century created a modern culture based on elements of traditional culture. They believed that they were merely preserving the heritage of the common people, but in fact they were replacing the old low cultures with an amalgamated high culture that shared the same epistemological base as other, more developed nations. In Gellner's own words:

> Generally speaking, nationalist ideology suffers from pervasive false consciousness. Its myths invert reality: it claims to defend folk culture while in fact it is forging a high culture ... It preaches and defends continuity, but owes everything to a decisive and unutterably profound break in human history. It preaches and defends cultural diversity, when in fact it imposes homogeneity ... Its self-image and its true nature are inversely related, with an ironic neatness seldom equalled even by other successful ideologies.[1]

It followed from this, from the inverse relation between 'its self-image and its true nature,' that the national culture can easily give the fundamentally misleading impression that the pre-existing traditional culture of a certain group is already known within the national culture. But the reality is different: the national culture routinely disguises the nature of the suppressed culture.

I wanted to make an end run around the national historical perspective and see if I could engage the cultural past of Ukraine more on its own terms. I came up with a procedure which I called 'mental archaeology.' I would explore some large complex of the past culture that had nothing to do with the nation and its objectives, something that had not been assimilated into the national narrative. I would explore it like a lost city, trying to deduce from its surviving artefacts what the culture was like that had produced it. I came up with the idea of exploring the culture of the Last Judgment. There is no Last Judgment in national culture, but it used to be quite important in the past.[2]

This was the first time I had ever formulated a research project so abstractly, so conceptually. Much of my original conception was plagued with false assumptions, and I will discuss some of them in the conclusions to this book, because part of the result of the confrontation with sources was to abandon baggage that was not merely useless but detrimental. When I undertook the project, I knew that it would be difficult and that I would have to expand my skill set. I did not foresee, however, just how difficult it would prove to make sense of all the cultural fragments I collected. The reader has before him or her a book in which the arguments are, I hope, clearly laid out. But it took me years to make some order out of the chaos of concrete facts and suppositions that swirled before me. Pieces of evidence do not come marked 'important,' 'less important,' and 'red herring.' The researcher has no choice but to keep as much evidence in his or her head as it can hold and ruminate over the material until some kind of solutions begin to take shape. There is no systematic process for solving complex riddles, and the time it can take is unpredictable. Shedding assumptions, it turned out, was about as important as discovering the facts.

I also had no idea when I came up with this project that it would involve so much arduous work and travel. Over a period of nine years I spent several months most summers on expeditions to gather source material; often I spent a few weeks during the winter in the same way. Of all the research I have conducted in the course of my scholarly career, the research for this book has been the most enjoyable. Much of it involved riding in a car through the Carpathians, searching out the churches with Last Judgment icons or murals. Some of the ideas came from just hiking in the mountains. There was always pleasant company on these expeditions, memorable encounters with villagers, tasty meals, and stimulating scenery. I never missed the archives.

Nature of the Project

This is an investigation of iconographic development, the comparison of discrete elements that constitute a Last Judgment icon or mural. It seeks to do with this material what historians are supposed to do, to pay 'attention to comparison among detailed particulars, all different,' because 'their co-ordination and comparison permits us, by consilience of induction, to explain the past.'[3] Although this is a quotation from an evolutionary biologist, it certainly fits this project.

Another 'found' explanation of what is happening in this monograph comes from religious studies, and it calls the kind of procedure I am following 'cultural sociology':

> The new cultural sociology regards culture as something tangible, explicit, and overtly produced. It consists of texts, discourse, language, music, and the symbolic-expressive dimensions of interpersonal behaviour, organisations, transactions, and so on. Proponents of the view hold that any specific cultural artefact should be examined in terms of questions about its production, its relations with other cultural elements, its internal structure, and the resources that determine how well it becomes institutionalised ... We regard symbolism as a reality, important in its own right, worthy of systematic investigation. Consequently, we attempt to look directly at symbolism – in the case of religion, at the symbolism of meaning – rather than looking through it to see how it functions for the individual or even to give an interpretation of what sort of meaning it conveys. To be sure, we still engage in a hermeneutic process when we attempt this kind of analysis: we ultimately give our own interpretations of how symbols are put together ... What is interesting about this kind of analysis is that it focuses on observable cultural materials: texts, sermons, discourse. It seldom strays into the subjective consciousness of the individual ... or into the collective unconscious of ... a group ... The focus is on patterns among discursive elements, structural relations among these elements – their arrangement, the boundaries that separate them, the connections drawn between them, their variety, the degree of repetition evident, formal properties, the structure that gives them internal coherence.[4]

But what I am writing is not religious studies or cultural sociology, but history. It is a type of history that is necessarily a little complicated and microhistorical, yet which demonstrates, I believe, possibilities that have not been fully realized by the historical profession.

The book examines over a hundred images of the Last Judgment – frescoes, icons on wood and canvas, and murals on the walls of wooden churches – to reconstruct the societies and cultures that fashioned them.[5] The chronological emphasis is on the fifteenth through eighteenth centuries, but I also use comparative material from the twelfth through fourteenth centuries and from the nineteenth century almost to the present. Last Judgments were monumental works. The icons, traditionally painted on linden boards, were as tall as a man, and the frescoes could take up the entire interior of a narthex or, in the case of Moldavian frescoes, an entire exterior wall. Last Judgment iconography was the most complex iconography in the Byzantine and post-Byzantine cultural sphere. An icon or mural of the Last Judgment was composed of dozens of discrete elements. Over time, new ones entered the iconography, others left it, still others were modified, subtly or dramatically. The formation and accretion of elements tell a story. The evolution of the icons reflects the cultural resources in the vicinity, the conditions of material life, and changes in mentality and taste. The icons open up the spiritual world of a semi-literate highland society that left posterity little in the way of ordinary texts. I am hopeful that the method I employ in this study can serve as a model for similar mental archaeologies of other cultures articulate on a plane different from our own.

Although this is a book informed by and speaking to art history, it is not able to incorporate all the tools of art history. I am not qualified to offer a sophisticated analysis of artistic technique or styles, nor do I have anything to say about perspective or the folds of garments or colour. This is a book about tradition and innovation in iconography and in this it bears some relation to one of the classic works of the art history of the Last Judgment, Beat Brenk's *Tradition und Neuerung in der christlichen Kunst des ersten Jahrtausends: Studien zur Geschichte des Weltgerichtsbildes.*

Perhaps because of my historical training, I tend to be more conservative in the acceptance of evidence than are many of the scholars working in Ukrainian art history. I try throughout this book to enunciate a clear distinction between what I consider to be certain and what I construct in my imagination to fit the evidence. I agree with Volodymyr Aleksandrovych, a fellow historian who works on the border with art history, that we should avoid the kind of art history that, 'basing itself on accidental bits of information, unnecessarily formulates wider conclusions and hypotheses, not realising that it is simply creating myths.'[6] He may not always follow his own good advice, but it is good advice nonetheless.

In addition to the larger aspirations of this work, my intention here is also to stimulate more study of these works of sacral art. I make no claim to having authored the definitive monograph on Last Judgment iconography in the Carpathians. If further research proves me wrong about this or that, I will be happy to have provoked further examination of these holy images, from having reintroduced them into discourse. Only by reflecting on the artefacts of the past can we appreciate them and develop a taste for them. These icons have aspects that make me uncomfortable – some xenophobia, some misogyny – but there is much more in them that I respect. Almost all of them are effective as works of art; even the most primitive of them are aesthetically powerful.[7] They also recall to mind the lofty spiritual aspirations of shepherds and farmers, and monks and craftsmen, in the highlands of Eastern Europe. They stand too as testimony to the luxuriant creativity of borderlands, for these icons and murals were produced where Poland, Hungary, and Moldavia once met as well as Austria and Turkey, on the linguistic border between Slavs and Magyars and Vlachs, and on the border connecting Western and Eastern Christendom.

How to Read This Book

The book consists of text and illustrations. It is essential for the understanding of the work to look at the illustrations, since the argument largely proceeds through the consideration of visual evidence.[8] This is not a book for which the illustrations serve as embellishments.

The core of the book's argument is found in three interlocking chapters. Chapter 2 explains the origin of the Last Judgment icons in the Carpathians in the fifteenth century. In the first part of this chapter, I am afraid, the reader may sometimes wonder where some of the laborious comparisons and analyses are headed. I say: be patient and try to enjoy the illustrations and the exegesis of allusions, temporarily for their own sake; suspend your disbelief that this will lead somewhere – it will. The point of the comparisons is to isolate the individuality of the Carpathian icons, and from this individuality to hypothesize about their origins. Chapter 3 follows the further development of icons painted on boards in the sixteenth through eighteenth centuries. It maps the diffusion of the practice, speculates about the painters, and demonstrates how the iconography became ever more elaborate. New themes incorporated into the icons say something about the life and attitudes of the people who created and worshipped with them as well as about currents in the larger social and cultural environment. Chapter 4 concerns the disintegration of this once vibrant artistic tradition. It concentrates on icons painted on canvas and on murals painted directly on the walls of log churches. The geographical focus is expanded, since Last Judgment images in these new forms acquired a larger habitat. The chronological focus is from the mid-seventeenth century onward. This chapter also describes shifts in attitude that undermined the tradition of placing Last Judgments in churches. Each chapter concludes with a summary of the main points, and the overall conclusions of the book are presented in chapter 5.

For the convenience of the reader, the most important Last Judgment images referred to in the book are listed, with the most pertinent information and bibliography, in a catalogue that follows the appendices.

Geography and National Terminology

The region under discussion is a place of cultural contact. Here the ethnographic territories of Poles, Slovaks, Hungarians, Romanians, and Rusyns/Ukrainians came together; and strewn throughout the region were Germans, Jews, and Roma. It is difficult to settle on terminology for such a multiethnic region, at least on a terminology that would satisfy all the national claims that have been made on these territories. I will try to explain the terms I will be using. They are far from perfect.

I will often refer to the Carpathians or the Carpathian region. Sometimes I just mean the mountains (see map 1, Physical Geography of the Carpathian Region and Environs.) Usually, however, I am referring to the specific region where our icons and murals were installed, not to the Carpathian mountain region as a whole. I am really interested in the northern Carpathians. As I have explained elsewhere,[9] the term 'Carpathian icons' is not acceptable to all researchers, but I use it. I use it to indicate the regional character of the set of icons I am studying here. I do not mean all the icons of the northern Carpathians either, but just the ones associated with the Rus' settlements and excluding Bukovina. Therefore, even though the frescoes of Moldavia are located in the Carpathian foothills and the murals of Maramureş are right in the heart of the mountains, I do not include them in the Carpathian region as meant in this book. Sometimes when I think there might be confusion, I refer to 'our Carpathians,' meaning the zone we have been working on, or 'the Ukrainian Carpathians,' meaning the lands inhabited by Rusyns/Ukrainians, but not necessarily located on the territory of the current Ukrainian state.

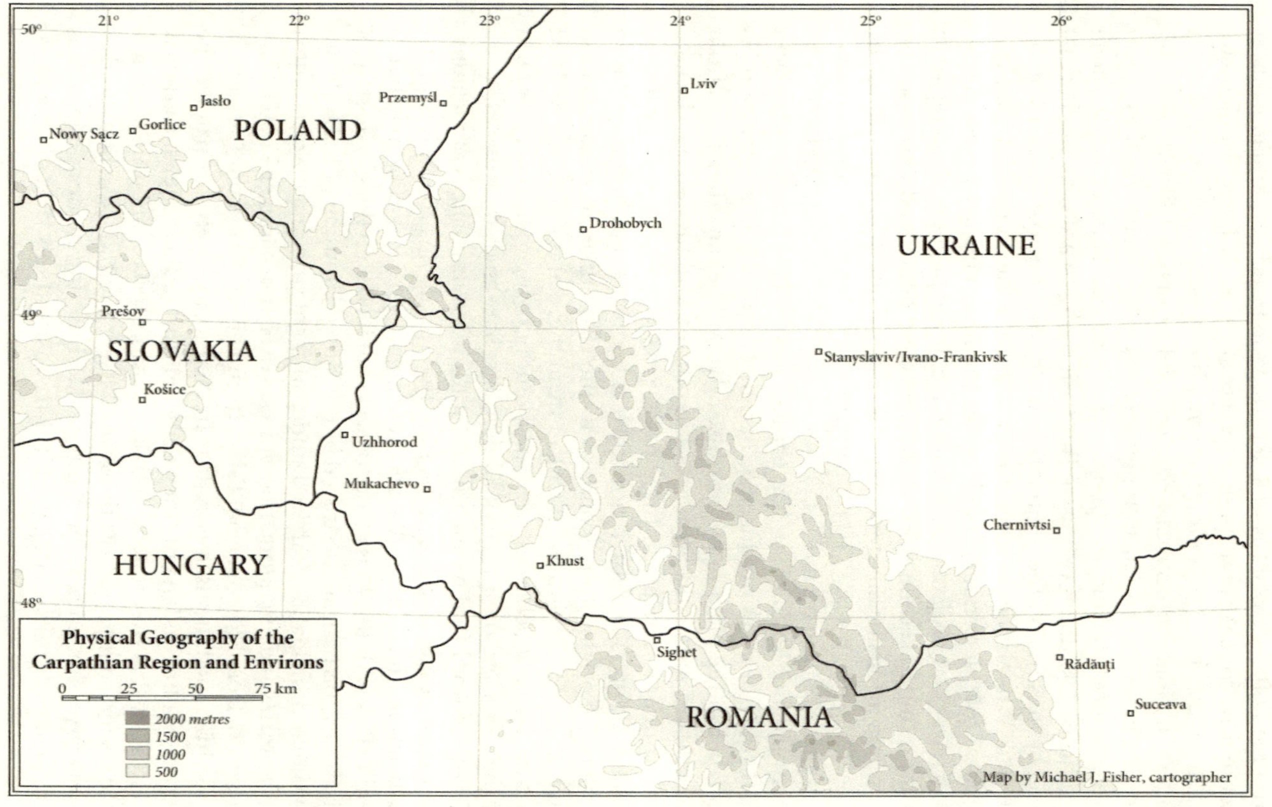

1. Physical Geography of the Carpathian Region and Environs

Here are the objections to this terminology. Many Ukrainian scholars, and some Polish scholars as well, feel that the term 'Carpathian icons' is intended to conceal that these artefacts are part of the Ukrainian cultural heritage. This is not my intention. I have reservations about the way modern nations appropriate past cultural artefacts,[10] but there is no question in my mind that, although there may be exceptions, these icons were produced by and for people whose descendants consider themselves to be Ukrainian or Rusyn. But I am trying to avoid an intellectual pitfall by insisting on the regional character of these icons instead of the national. When they were produced, the local was important, and it is the local that determines much about them. Their incorporation later into a particular projection of a national cultural past is misleading when we are trying to set the context for their emergence and development. Ukrainian art historians generally call all the icons that I refer to by the name 'Carpathian icons' 'Ukrainian icons,' but there are many Ukrainian icons that do not have much in common with the Carpathian icons. The other objection to the term 'Carpathian icons' is that there are icons in this set that were not produced or installed in the mountains or foothills at all, but in the plain to the northeast. We will be including icons from Zhovkva and Kamianka Strumylova in our set, and they are not located close to the mountains. In these cases, yes – the adjective 'Carpathian' does not fit literally. I use it nonetheless because it has become clear to me that the origin of the icons was in the Carpathian mountain region and that the interest in them spread from there also into some lowland districts. I do not believe there is any point in trying to invent a new term for the icons and their region; all signifiers have their weaknesses.

I use the word Rus' frequently and with different nuances of meaning. The origin of the word lies in the state that sprang up around Kyiv in the ninth and tenth centuries. We get our English word Russia from it, but to identify Rus' with Russia is erroneous, even if it is often done. The state of Kyivan Rus' was basically destroyed by the Mongol invasion of 1237–40, but individual principalities survived under Mongol suzerainty over the next few centuries and its cultural traditions survived much longer. People from Novgorod, from Moscow, from Pskov, from Kyiv, and from our Carpathian region identified themselves as Rus'. In their icons, when they painted the nations awaiting judgment, they depicted Turks, Tatars, Jews, Germans, and Rus'. By Rus' they understood themselves. Most often I use Rus' in this sense, as the contemporary ethnonym. I use it as a collective noun and as an adjective. Sometimes, for clarity's sake, I use the modern ethnonyms Ukrainian or Russian, but generally I try to avoid this kind of anachronism. I sometimes use the term Rusyn. There is a movement in eastern Slovakia, in Transcarpathia oblast in Ukraine, among the Lemko population of Poland, and among the descendants of immigrants from these populations in North America to consider themselves a separate, fourth East Slavic nationality alongside the Russians, Belarusians, and Ukrainians. They call themselves Rusyns. Among these same populations many also consider themselves Ukrainians, and this is also the standard view of the Ukrainian identity project as a whole. In a study like this, there is no reason to take sides, so I also refer to Rusyns occasionally.

I often write of northern Rus' instead of Russia, particularly in reference to the fifteenth century. The northern Rus' principalities whose art was influential in Carpathian Rus' – Novgorod, Pskov, and perhaps Tver – were not incorporated into Muscovy until the second half of the fifteenth century. Muscovy, moreover, is not quite Russia. Again, I am opting for a more conservative terminology reflecting the contemporary realia. I also think that Rus' in the fifteenth century still existed as a larger cultural and ecclesiastical community; Rus' was something more than the sum of territories inhabited by people who happened to call themselves by the same name.

I sometimes have to refer to Galicia. This is a historical region that derives ultimately from the Rus' principality of Galicia which existed in the Middle Ages until it was incorporated into Poland at the end of the fourteenth century. The name comes from its first capital, Halych; by the mid-thirteenth century its capital was Lviv. But the real shape of the region in our present consciousness, and in the way I use it in this book, was given to it by the Habsburg monarchy, which acquired it from Poland in 1772. The Habsburg crown land was larger than the historical principality and included much territory inhabited by ethnic Poles. Today, what used to be Habsburg Galicia is divided between Poland and Ukraine, and when Ukrainians say Galicia, they usually mean the part that is in Ukraine, reserving the terms 'San region' (*Nadsiannia*) and 'Lemko region' (*Lemkivshchyna*) for the Ukrainian-inhabited areas of Galicia now in Poland. The part of Galicia that is now in Ukraine roughly corresponds to the oblasts of Lviv, Ivano-Frankivsk, and Ternopil (see map 2, Historical Map of the Carpathian Region and Environs, and map 3, Current Administrative Boundaries, Carpathian Region and Environs.)

Transcarpathia is the region across the Carpathian mountains from the standpoint of the rest of Ukraine. This area had been part of Hungary (or Transylvania) for over nine hundred years until it was joined to Czechoslovakia after the collapse of Austria-Hungary in 1918. In 1945 it

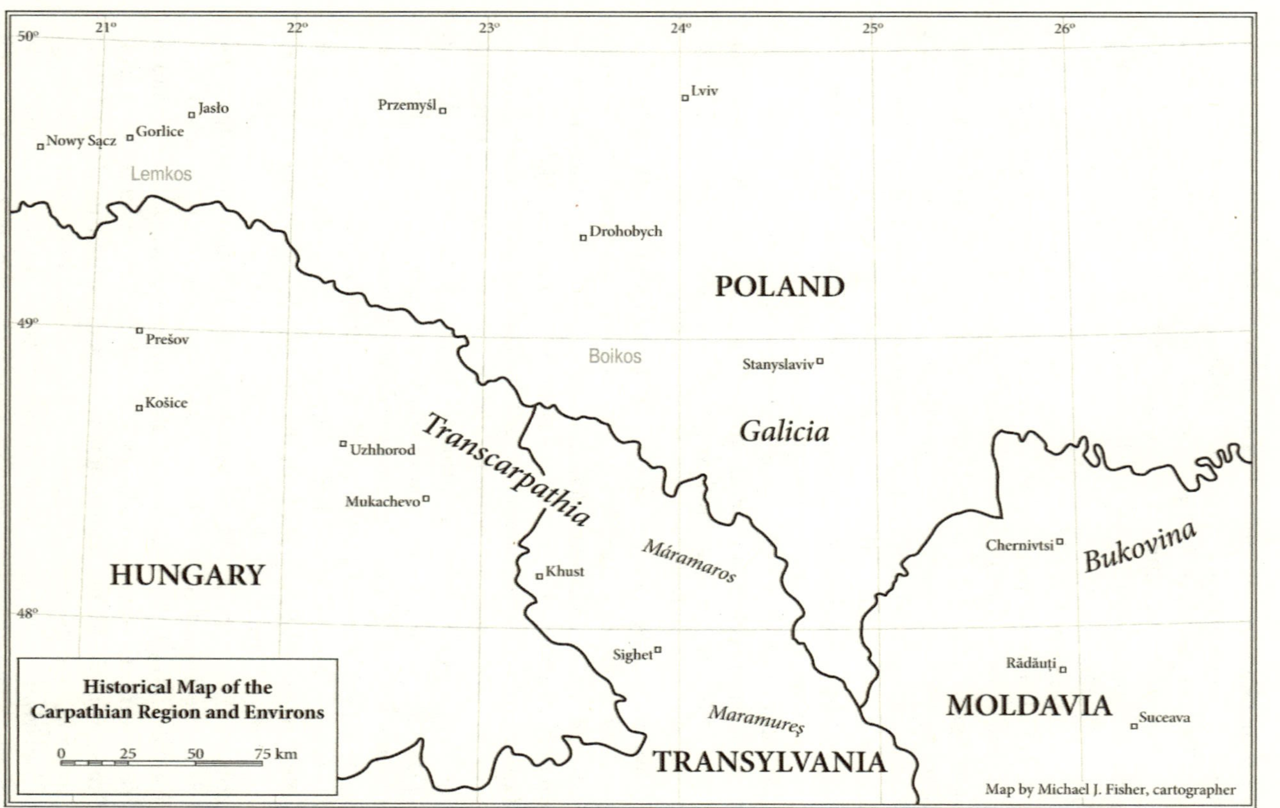

2. Historical Map of the Carpathian Region and Environs

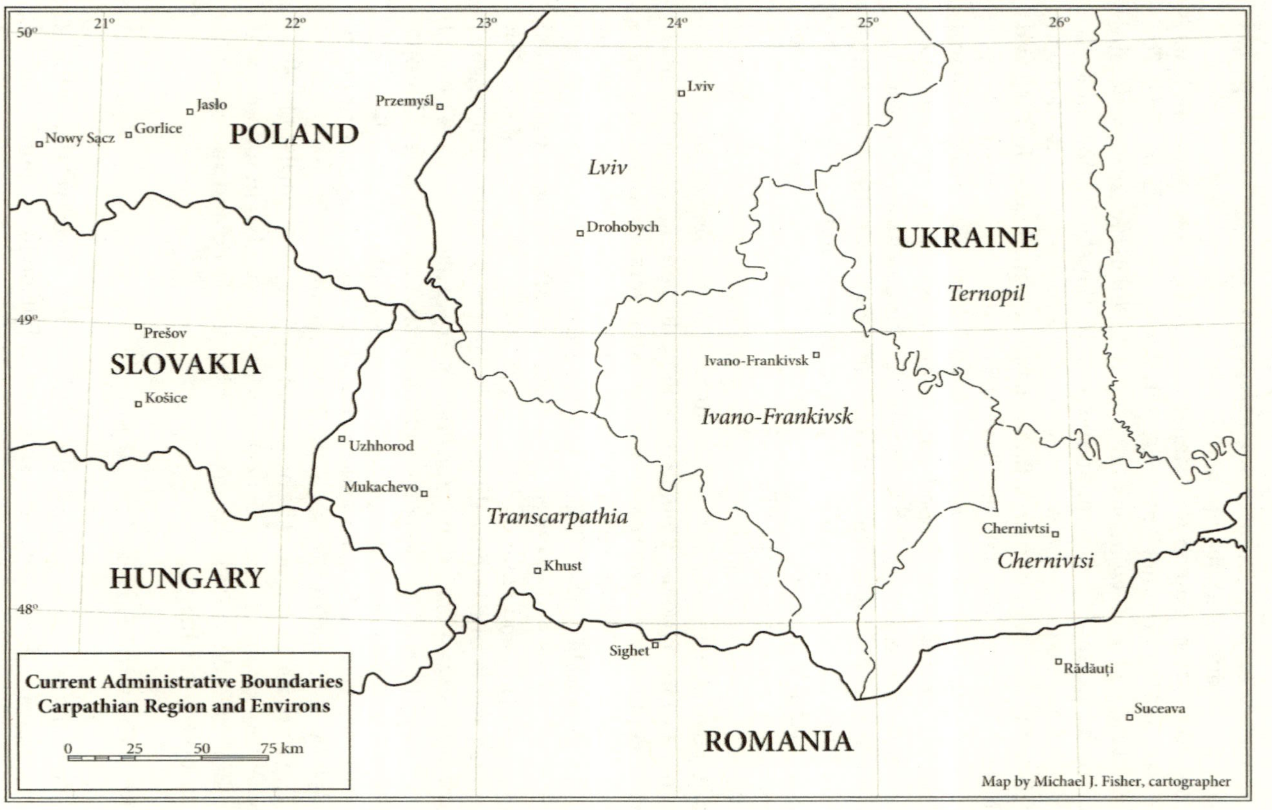

3. Current Administrative Boundaries, Carpathian Region and Environs

was annexed to Soviet Ukraine. It corresponds to today's Transcarpathia oblast in Ukraine, with its capital in Uzhhorod.

Bukovina[11] first came into existence as an Austrian crown land. It was the part of Moldavia that Austria acquired from the Turks in 1774. The crown land had a mixed population, with Ukrainian-speakers predominant in the north and Romanian-speakers in the south. Bukovina disappeared as an administrative entity after it became a part of Romania in 1918. Stalin annexed northern Bukovina to Soviet Ukraine in 1940 and today it constitutes the bulk of Chernivtsi oblast.

There was a county in Hungary, and from 1526 to 1733 in Transylvania, called Máramaros. It developed some distinctive cultural characteristics. The northern part was inhabited by Ukrainian/Rusyn-speakers, the southern part by Romanian-speakers. I refer to it by either Máramaros, when I mean the Ukrainian/Rusyn part of the old county, or Maramureş, when I mean the Romanian part. The Ukrainian/Rusyn part of Máramaros makes up the eastern part of Transcarpathia.

When I speak of Moldavia in this book, I mean the principality that existed from the fourteenth century until it became one of the constituent parts of the modern Romanian state in the second half of the nineteenth century. Moldavia was under Turkish suzerainty as of 1512. Parts of this historical Moldavia were annexed by Austria (Bukovina) and by Russia (Bessarabia) when Turkey was in decline.

For most of the early modern period our Carpathian region was divided between Poland and Hungary/Transylvania. Today the part of this region that once was Poland is divided between Poland and Ukraine. The original Ukrainian/Rusyn population in the Polish part was removed in 1947, one of the episodes of wartime and postwar ethnic cleansing in this part of Europe. The southern part of the Carpathian region, what used to be Hungary, is now divided between Slovakia and Ukraine. The Rusyn/Ukrainian population is located in eastern Slovakia in the Prešov region.

The Carpathian region that produced our icons was inhabited primarily by two subethnic or dialectical groups, the Lemkos in the west and the Boikos in the east. Today most Lemkos live in Poland and Slovakia, most Boikos in Ukraine.

A Brief Historical Survey of the Region

In the early fifteenth century, the ridge of the northern Carpathians formed the border between the kingdom of Poland in the north and the kingdom of Hungary and principality of Moldavia in the south. Poland

and Hungary were Catholic countries, but with large Orthodox populations, while Moldavia was predominantly Orthodox. In the mountainous border regions the rural population was largely Orthodox and spoke Slav and Vlach dialects. Much of this population had settled here only within the previous century and engaged in mixed farming. Sheep and other livestock grazed in the highlands, and their manure enriched the farms and gardens in the lowlands. The settlements benefited from the abundance of land, from the protection of states, and from systems of local self-government (especially the so-called Vlach law).

By the late fifteenth century, both Hungary and Moldavia were fighting the ascendant power of the Ottoman Turks. Moldavia became a tributary of the sultan in 1512, but Moldavian princes still retained considerable autonomy. Hungary was defeated by the Ottomans at Mohács in 1526 and lost its independence. Western Hungary, including much of the western Carpathian region, was inherited by the Habsburgs, who waged war against the Turks until the end of the seventeenth century to gain the rest of the country. Máramaros county was incorporated into Transylvania, which enjoyed virtual independence under Ottoman suzerainty. Austria formally acquired Transylvania by the treaty of Karlovci of 1699, but it had to pacify anti-Habsburg rebels there until the 1730s. It was at that time that Máramaros county was finally joined with the rest of historical Hungary under the Habsburg sceptre. In addition to Austrian and Turkish military campaigns in the region, Tatars frequently raided southern Poland and northern Hungary to capture slaves for the Ottoman market.

The situation of the free peasantry deteriorated in the later fifteenth century in the Polish Carpathians, and the population there was completely enserfed by the middle of the sixteenth century. Enserfment went hand in hand with the weakening of state authority and the disintegration of legality. In Poland the chief form of rents was in labour – peasants worked three or even more days a week on a landlord's estate (*folwark*) or in forestry. The oppressive demands on peasant labour, and also the exhaustion of the agricultural land, caused many peasants to move illegally across the mountains to Hungary or Transylvania.

Although in the fifteenth century Hungary was the scene of some ferocious peasant uprisings, the warfare of the sixteenth and seventeenth centuries reduced the population so much that landlords attracted immigrant peasants with reduced rents or temporary exemptions from rents. Moreover, in Hungary the chief form of rents was in kind rather than in labour. The emigration of peasants from the Polish to the

Hungarian/Transylvanian Carpathians then reduced the population north of the border so that in the late seventeenth century serfdom there was not so onerous; the low mountain crests and passes along what is today the Polish-Slovak border facilitated this emigration from the Lemko region. Labour rents also existed in Hungary, but a day and a half per week was considered very high. Rents in kind also existed in Poland; in mountain villages peasants might have had to pay a tithe in sheep. Money rents were small in both Hungary and Poland. The migration of peasants across the mountain borders helps to explain certain similar cultural tastes and practices in the Carpathian region as a whole.

The period covered in this book was one of religious strife. The sixteenth century saw the diffusion of the Reformation – Calvinism spread among the Polish and Hungarian nobility, and almost all the Germans of the region converted to Lutheranism. The late sixteenth and seventeenth centuries witnessed the Catholic Counter-Reformation, which had a profound effect on culture and religious politics in our region well into the eighteenth century. Our whole period, furthermore, was a time when unions were attempted between the Roman Catholic and Eastern Orthodox churches. These were accompanied by controversies and strife. The church unions of Florence (1439) and, especially, Brest (1596) had repercussions in our region, but did not take root. Our region remained Orthodox until the mid-seventeenth century, when the Rus' Orthodox in Habsburg Hungary began to enter into communion with Rome after the union of Uzhhorod of 1646. At first only the westernmost Rus' in Hungary became Uniate, but then the union spread east in the 1650s, stopping at the borders of Transylvania. Máramaros county was integrated into the union in 1721. The union was established in the Polish part of our region at the turn of the eighteenth century. The eparchy of Przemyśl united with Rome in 1692; the eparchy of Lviv, in 1700. The last Orthodox holdout north of the old Polish-Hungarian border was a monastery, Maniava Skete; it was dissolved in 1786 by the Austrian emperor, Joseph II.

In the eighteenth century all the rest of the territory examined in this monograph came under Habsburg rule. The Carpathian region that had been part of Poland was acquired by Austria in 1772 and constituted a major part of the crown land of Galicia. In 1774 Turkey ceded a portion of Moldavia to Austria, which the Austrians named Bukovina. The southern part of Bukovina included the Moldavian monasteries and churches with frescoes of the Last Judgment.[12]

The Theology of the Last Judgment

The idea of a judgment of the dead is found in many cultures. In Christianity this idea is linked with the second coming of Christ. The doctrine is tersely formulated in the Nicene Creed, which says that Jesus 'will come again to judge the living and the dead.' The most extensive account of this notion in the gospels can be found in chapter 25 of the Gospel of Matthew. The relevant text, Matthew 25:31–46, is the Gospel for Meatfare Sunday, the second Sunday before Great Lent. (The Sunday is called Meatfare because it is the last day one may eat meat until Easter; one bids farewell to meat, in Latin: *carnevale.*) It describes how the 'Son of man' will appear in glory and divide humankind into the righteous, whom he will place to his right, and the iniquitous, whom he will place to his left. The former will enter a heavenly kingdom, the latter will be consigned to everlasting fire. The major criterion for this division is whether or not individuals performed works of mercy for the 'least of these my brethren.'

Judgment is also a theme in the book of Revelation, which contains many obscure prophecies about the end of the world. It draws heavily on the vision of Daniel (chapter 7) in the Old Testament. In these accounts, the emphases are on the throne of judgment and the books in which all human actions are recorded.

A Greek writer took the information in these texts and in many other scattered passages in scripture to develop an overall vision of how this Second Coming and Last Judgment would transpire. He attributed his works on the subject to the great fourth-century father of the church Ephraim the Syrian. The real Ephraim the Syrian was a Syriac writer who left, as far as we know, no original text in Greek.[13] The one text on the Last Judgment that can be genuinely attributed to Ephraim is brilliant, but it had no direct influence on Eastern Orthodox teaching or iconography.[14] The Last Judgment texts of Ephraim the Syrian Graecus, which perhaps originated in the decades after the death of the real Ephraim Syrus, exist in many variants, and there are many Slavonic translations.[15] I have included a summary translation of one of Ephraim Graecus's sermons in Appendix 2. Ephraim's account was not a work of systematic theology, but a description of the last events based on his understanding of scriptural revelation.

In this account, signs will portend the Last Judgment. In particular, a cross will appear in the sky. Angels will roll up the heavens like a scroll, and a river of fire will consume the earth. A new heaven and a new earth will replace these. Christ will descend in glory to judge humanity. The dead will crawl out from their graves and assume their bodies. Woe to the sinners, who will be punished with horrible torments. The whole tone of Ephraim's description is one of terror. Under the influence of his writings, the Orthodox Slavs refer to the Last Judgment as *strashnyi sud*, literally 'fearful judgment.'

Ephraim the Syrian's description served as the basis for the liturgical poetry of Meatfare Sunday composed by Roman the Melodist in the sixth century.[16] The verses speak of the river of fire, the throne of glory, the opening of the books, the fearful sound of lamentation, the sounding of trumpets, the emptying of the tombs, the outer darkness, the nether world, and the like. 'I tremble with fear when I ponder and foresee the dread day of Thine ineffable coming, when Thou shalt sit and judge the living and the dead, O my God all-powerful.'[17]

In the writings of the Greek Ephraim, the dead seem to lie in some dormant state until reawakened to life and rejoined with their bodies at the Last Judgment. And the classical Byzantine iconography of the Last Judgment appears to share this outlook. At least there is no iconographic reflection of what is known as particular judgment, that is, the disposition of the soul in the period between an individual's death and the universal resurrection at the end of time.

In the Last Judgment iconography of Rus' from the fifteenth century on, however, elements were incorporated that referred to the particular judgment. Much of the thinking on that subject derived from a tenth-century text, the Life of St Basil the New. The text was originally written in Greek, but it was known in Slavonic translation from perhaps as early as the eleventh century.[18] I have also included a very abridged summary of the work in Appendix 3.

The Life took an old idea attributed to St Cyril of Alexandria, that of the aerial tollbooths, and developed it in more detail. In one of the visions that Basil's disciple Gregory has, Gregory saw Basil's late servant Theodora in the aftermath of her death. She had to travel through various tollbooths in the air. Each tollbooth represented a certain sin, and Theodora had to pass all the tollbooths in order to achieve salvation. In Slavonic these tollbooths are known as *mytarstva*, and they have come to mean 'ordeals' in modern Russian. If a soul successfully passed the tollbooths, it was conducted to paradise. Otherwise it was sent to hell. This disposition was not finalized until the Last Judgment, but the relationship between the latter and the particular judgment was never well clarified.

Building on certain scriptural texts, the later Orthodox iconography of the Last Judgment also incorporated scenes of the death of a righteous man and the death of a sinner. The former's soul was accepted by an angel while King David sat nearby and played the lute. The sinner, however, was slain by a demon or a monstrous personification of death while a demon accepted his soul.

These thoughts about death and the Last Judgment constituted the mental framework in which the icon painters worked. The iconography of the Last Judgment did not include references to the Antichrist.

Historiography

Of works treating the subject of Last Judgment iconography as a whole, pride of place belongs to Beat Brenk's fundamental monograph, already mentioned, *Tradition und Neuerung in der christlichen Kunst des ersten Jahrtausends: Studien zur Geschichte des Weltgerichtsbildes* (Tradition and Innovation in Christian Art of the First Millennium: Studies on the History of the Image of the Last Judgment).[19] This is a study that encompasses Western as well as Eastern Christian iconography, although more attention is devoted to the East, where the basic elements of the Last Judgment composition came together. The dynamic of accretion that he describes seems to have continued in later Last Judgment images, including ours. A late nineteenth-century work that covers some of the same territory, but also surveys later, particularly Russian, images is N.V. Pokrovskii's 'Strashnyi sud v pamiatnikakh vizantiiskago i russkago iskusstva' (The Last Judgment in Monuments of Byzantine and Russian Art). A good overview of Orthodox iconography of the Last Judgment was written by Desanka Milošević, but unfortunately it appeared a few years before the publication of Brenk's important contribution. Miltiadis K. Garidis wrote a study of post-Byzantine Last Judgments with special attention to the depiction of sinners and demons. None of these works, however, take into account icons of Carpathian Rus'. The region has in general been poorly incorporated into the scholarship on icons. For example, Kurt Weitzmann and six other authors published a monumental collection on the icon tradition, *The Icon*, which reproduced and analysed icons of Byzantium, Georgia, the Balkan peninsula and Greek islands, Russia, Wallachia, and Moldavia. It does not mention the icons of our Carpathians.

Although there were earlier publications that mentioned the Carpathian icons, the first major contribution was published as a monograph and an album in the late 1920s by the first director of the National

Museum in Lviv, Ilarion Svientsits'kyi. His work was limited to the icons in his museum's collection, which constitutes the richest collection of Carpathian iconography anywhere. Six Last Judgment icons were illustrated. Svientsits'kyi assumed that the icons collected in the Carpathians were products of a tradition that spread from Byzantium to Kyiv and from Kyiv to Halych and Lviv and from there into the mountains.

Almost half a century was to pass before another work of importance appeared on the Carpathian icons – Janina Kłosińska's *Ikony*. Kłosińska was the curator of the icon collection of the National Museum in Kraków and the volume she published concerned that collection alone. Three Last Judgment icons were included with detailed commentary. Kłosińska had earlier written an article on Carpathian iconography of the Last Judgment, and so her discussion of these icons was well informed. She was the first to coin the term 'Carpathian icon.' She also rejected Svientsits'kyi's view that this iconography had its roots in the medieval Galician principality. She instead connected it with influences from the south, suggesting that Vlach migrants had brought with them the artistic culture of Moldavia. Her usage 'Carpathian icons' and suggestion of their Romanian origins were criticized by Ukrainian art historians decades later, in the 1990s,[20] when a freer discourse entered scholarship in Ukraine. They suspected that her positions reflected Polish chauvinism. I am doubtful of that in Kłosińska's case, but I think it is true about an album entitled *Ikona karpacka* [The Carpathian Icon] put out by the Museum of Folk Architecture in Sanok in 1998.[21]

Kłosińska's successor as curator of Kraków's icon collection is Mirosław P. Kruk. He has moved away from the term 'Carpathian icon' and instead finds it more useful to talk of 'West Ruthenian' (*zachodnioruskie*) icons. His works on iconography reflect high standards of scholarship,[22] and his presentation of the arguments about the origins of the icons is careful and measured. He is a student of the late Professor Anna Różycka-Bryzek, who taught Byzantine art at Jagiellonian University and authored valuable studies of the Byzantine-style frescoes commissioned by Polish kings in the fifteenth century. Other students of Professor Różycka-Bryzek include Agnieszka Gronek, who has written two dissertations (one of which is now a book) and a series of articles on the Carpathian icon of the Passion, and Małgorzata Smorąg Różycka, who has worked on the Byzantine-inspired art of medieval Rus'.

One of the most erudite researchers on the Carpathian icons was Romuald Biskupski of Sanok. He spent many years working in Sanok's Historical Museum and had a wide knowledge of the culture of early modern Carpathian Rus'. He clearly connected the icons of the Carpathians with Ukrainian culture and referred to them as 'Ukrainian icons.' He was also an excellent photographer of the icons. From a much younger generation than Biskupski, but of a similar profile is Jarosław Giemza, curator of the icon collection at the Castle Museum in Łańcut. In addition to writing his own interesting contributions on the icons, he has been active as an editor of collected papers on the same subject.

The icons that are now within the borders of Slovakia, which include many of the Last Judgment, have been known to researchers from albums put together by Heinz Skrobucha in 1971 and by Štefan Tkáč in 1982. Tkáč's album is particularly detailed. Since the mid-1990s the icons in Slovakia have benefited from the attention of Vladislav Grešlík of Prešov University. He has published many excellent photographs accompanied by detailed, reliable analysis. A scholar in Budapest, Bernadett Puskás, specializes in a related area: the icons of Mukachevo eparchy from the sixteenth century on.

In Soviet Ukraine good scholarship on the icons was hobbled by communist ideological restrictions. For the first two decades of Soviet rule in Western Ukraine no scholarly work on the icons appeared. A major breakthrough was the six-volume series *Istoriia ukrains'koho mystetstva* (History of Ukrainian Art) published in the late 1960s. Three volumes were devoted to the history of Ukrainian art before the nineteenth century, and many reproductions of sacral art were included. The works were interpreted in a strictly Soviet framework. The icons were ransacked for indications of social and national conflict, popular aesthetics, and democratic attitudes. Last Judgment icons figured prominently in these volumes because they lent themselves well to populist exegesis.[23]

The authors of the sections on icons in the multivolume history were Vira Svientsits'ka and Pavlo Zholtovs'kyi. Vira Svientsits'ka was the daughter of Ilarion Svientsits'kyi and worked in the National Museum in Lviv. She was also a member of the Organization of Ukrainian Nationalists. She was imprisoned by the Polish authorities between the wars and arrested at the outbreak of the Second World War; she was also arrested by the Soviet authorities in 1948. She spent eight years in the gulag. After her release she returned to work at the National Museum. Pavlo Zholtovs'kyi had also been repressed by the Soviets; in the later 1950s he went to work for the Lviv branch of the Institute of Fine Arts, Folklore, and Ethnography of the Academy of Sciences. Although the works of both of these scholars contain valuable material, they wrote about icons with exaggerated attention to social and national elements. They had no interest in the sacral character of the art and searched the icons instead for elements of realism and folk creativity. Their approach to the icons has remained influential on the generation of Ukrainian scholars that followed.

With the decline and collapse of communist rule, scholars associated with the National Museum in Lviv produced more scholarship on the icons. Among other publications, Vasyl' Otkovych wrote a book with Svientsits'ka on Ukrainian folk painting in which many icons were reproduced and commented upon.[24] Stronger as scholars are Oleh Sydor and Mariia Helytovych; Sydor served as curator of the icon collection at the museum, and Helytovych was his replacement. Sydor has written directly on Last Judgment iconography and also compiled a register of all the Last Judgment icons in the possession of the National Museum. Helytovych has published two excellent albums of icons in the museum's collection and numerous specialized articles on iconography.

Information on Last Judgment iconography was included in the publications of Hryhorii Lohvyn. He published a number of guides to the artistic monuments in various regions of Ukraine as well as a synthetic work covering all Ukraine. His books were written in Soviet times, but remain important.

Volodymyr Aleksandrovych's publications are the result of carefully sifting diverse archives to find references to West Ukrainian painters. For the most part, these archival references concern mundane matters like debts, wills, and court cases. Only in a few instances has it been possible to link the names and skeletal biographies of painters to any extant works. Aleksandrovych's more creative attempts to bridge the gap between painters identified from the archives and particular works of art are not always convincing.

Dmytro Stepovyk, an art historian based in Kyiv, has written a volume that surveys the entire spectrum of Ukrainian iconography, *Istoriia ukrains'koi ikony, X–XX st.* (The History of the Ukrainian Icon from the Tenth to the Twentieth Century). What I call Carpathian icons figure significantly. Although the book makes for lively reading, it is marred by nationalist mythologizing and also by poor reproductions.[25] A better balanced overall survey was published earlier in the diaspora by the painter and art historian Sviatoslav Hordyns'kyi, but this work is nowhere near as detailed as Stepovyk's.

Patriarch Dymytrii (Iarema) of the Ukrainian Autocephalous Orthodox Church, who had published on Ukrainian art history before becoming a bishop, wrote a survey of the iconography of Western Ukraine from the twelfth through fifteenth century that was published posthumously.

Unfortunately, it is of little scholarly value, although the illustrations are useful. The Lviv art historian Hanna Kos has also written a brief survey of Last Judgment iconography.

There have been some stimulating studies comparing Last Judgment iconography in the Carpathians with that of northern Rus'/Russia. Heinz Skrobucha was the first to engage in this comparison. His relatively early article contains a number of errors and has been superseded by subsequent literature. In particular, David Goldfrank wrote a provocative piece on the two iconographies, focusing on the figure of a serpent with rings on its body that represent tollbooths of sin. Lilya Berezhnaya, originally from Zaporizhzhia but now living in Germany, compared sinners. V.K. Tsodikovich published many reproductions of both Carpathian and northern Rus' icons of the Last Judgment, but the text that accompanies them proposes a pagan origin to the tollbooths that has not convinced other scholars. Some studies of Russian iconography of the Last Judgment have been useful for interpreting Carpathian icons, particularly works by Eva Haustein-Bartsch and Levon Nersesian.

Technical Matters

When I discuss Last Judgment iconography, right and left are the reverse of the viewer's perspective. Much of the iconography is developed from the Gospel of Matthew, which makes a clear division between left and right: 'And he shall set the sheep on his right hand, but the goats on the left' (Mt 25:33). But this is left and right from the perspective of the Son of man who is performing the judgment. Thus in the icons, hell is on the left, heaven on the right, sinners on the left, and saints on the right, but only from the perspective of the icon itself. Although it may be a little difficult for readers to get used to, left and right in this book, when referring to Last Judgment iconography, proceeds from the icon's, not the viewer's, perspective.

Unless otherwise noted, all translations are my own. For translations from the New Testament, I use the King James Version. For the Old Testament I also use the King James Version, but checked against the Septuagint and, as necessary, against the Slavonic translation of the same (the Ostrih Bible); I modify the King James Version wherever it is required in order to render the sense of the Septuagint. I also number verses according to the Septuagint. The major discrepancy here is in the Book of Psalms. The Septuagint combines what the Masoretic Text, on which King James is based, counts as separate psalms, 9 and 10, and the

Masoretic Text combines what the Septuagint counts as separate psalms, 146 and 147. Thus the numbering is the same for psalms 1–8 and 148–50, but the Septuagint is one number lower for the psalms in between 9/10 and 146/47.

Partly for technical reasons and partly in order not to encumber an already complicated text, I will transliterate from Cyrillic and Greek. Transliterations from Ukrainian and Russian will follow a modified version of the Library of Congress system. Rusyn place names in Appendix 1 will follow the system of transliteration used by Paul R. Magocsi.[26] Names in the text (except for the section on historiography in chapter 1) will be spelled without indicating soft signs, and endings such as -s'kyi and -skii will be spelled with -sky; in the section on historiography, in citations, and in the bibliography, however, names will be transliterated without these modifications. Place names will be transliterated without indicating soft signs. In transliterating Church Slavonic and its variants, I will use the liturgical pronunciation that was universal in Western Ukraine until the late twentieth century, imagining that it was written in modern Ukrainian characters, and then following the modified Library of Congress system. Thus I would transliterate the first verse of John's gospel as: *V nachali bi Slovo, i Slovo bi k Bohu, i Boh bi Slovo.* Specialist readers should have no trouble with this, and it will make no difference to the non-specialist. I will write out in full all abbreviations and ligatures in Slavonic and Greek. I will transliterate all Greek according to the usual practice for classical Greek, even though the pronunciation was different in Byzantine Greek. I will also spell the Greek as if it were classical.

Place names are given in the language of the state in which they are now located, although not always in their modern form. Appendix 1 contains a list of localities with their names in different languages.

Bibliographical citations in the notes are provided in shortened form, but all the relevant particulars can be found in the bibliography. All attempts have been made to contact rights holders of illustrations.

2 Origins

The Earliest Last Judgment Icons in the Carpathians

It is one of the mysteries of East European art history that in the fourteenth and fifteenth centuries Rus' churches in the Carpathians were suddenly adorned with numerous icons of high quality and distinctive composition, the antecedents of which are unclear. Ukrainian scholars generally argue that these icons are but the continuation of the iconographic tradition of Kyiv and Halych; they are unable, however, to marshal sufficient evidence. Many Polish scholars argue that the icons are Balkan or Moldavian in origin, but they also are unable to produce convincing proofs.[1] In this chapter, I will propose a different solution of the origins question, at least as far as Last Judgment icons are concerned. The argument will proceed by a close, comparative analysis of the elements that comprise the oldest examples of Carpathian Last Judgment icons to survive to our times; then I will survey the environment in which they were created.

The three earliest extant Ukrainian icons of the Last Judgment are Vanivka, Polana, and Mshanets (figs 2.1, 2.2, 2.3). Vanivka is the old Ukrainian name for a village now in Poland, Węglówka. Polana is the Polish name for a village now in Ukraine, Poliana.[2] Both Poliana and Mshanets are today in Staryi Sambir raion, Lviv oblast, Ukraine, not far from the Polish border (map 5). All three localities are in the foothills of the northern slopes of the Carpathians. Węglówka, north of Krosno, is one of the northernmost localities inhabited by the Lemkos, while both Poliana and Mshanets are in Boiko territory. These villages were located in Poland in the fifteenth century.

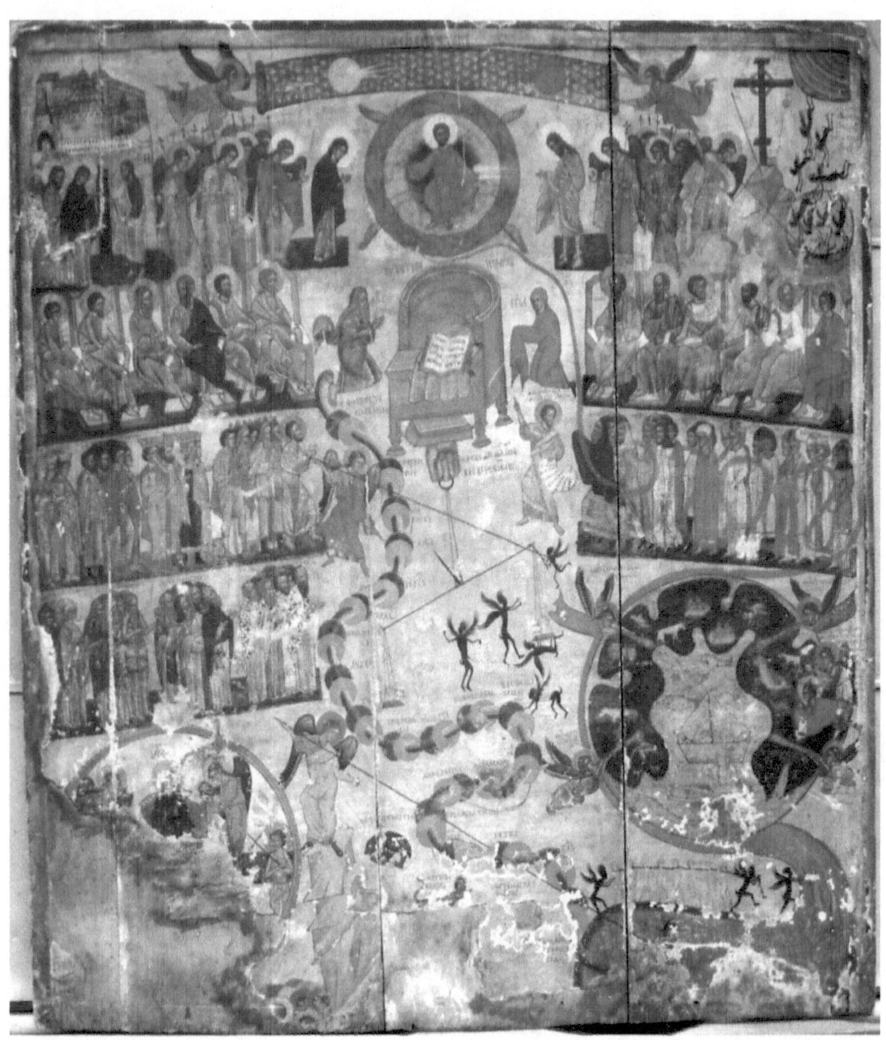

2.1 Vanivka overview

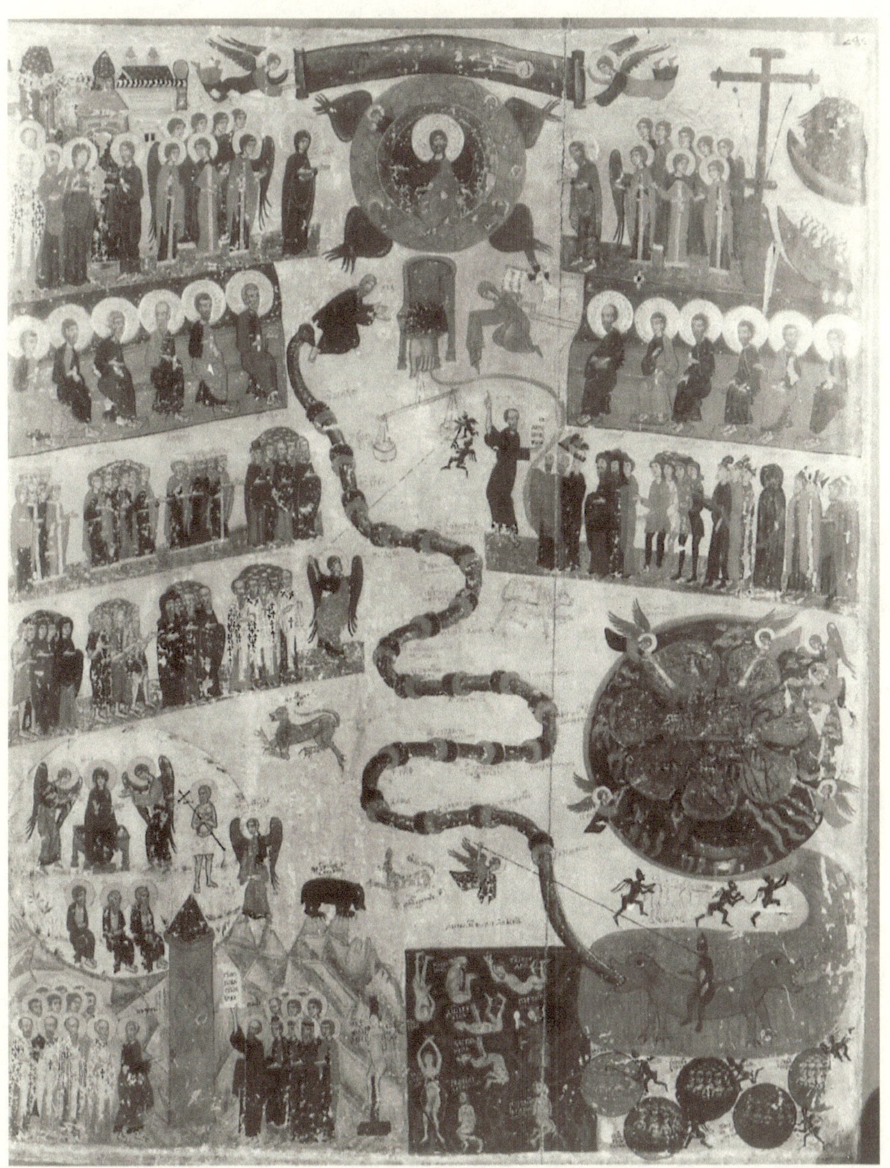

2.2 Polana overview

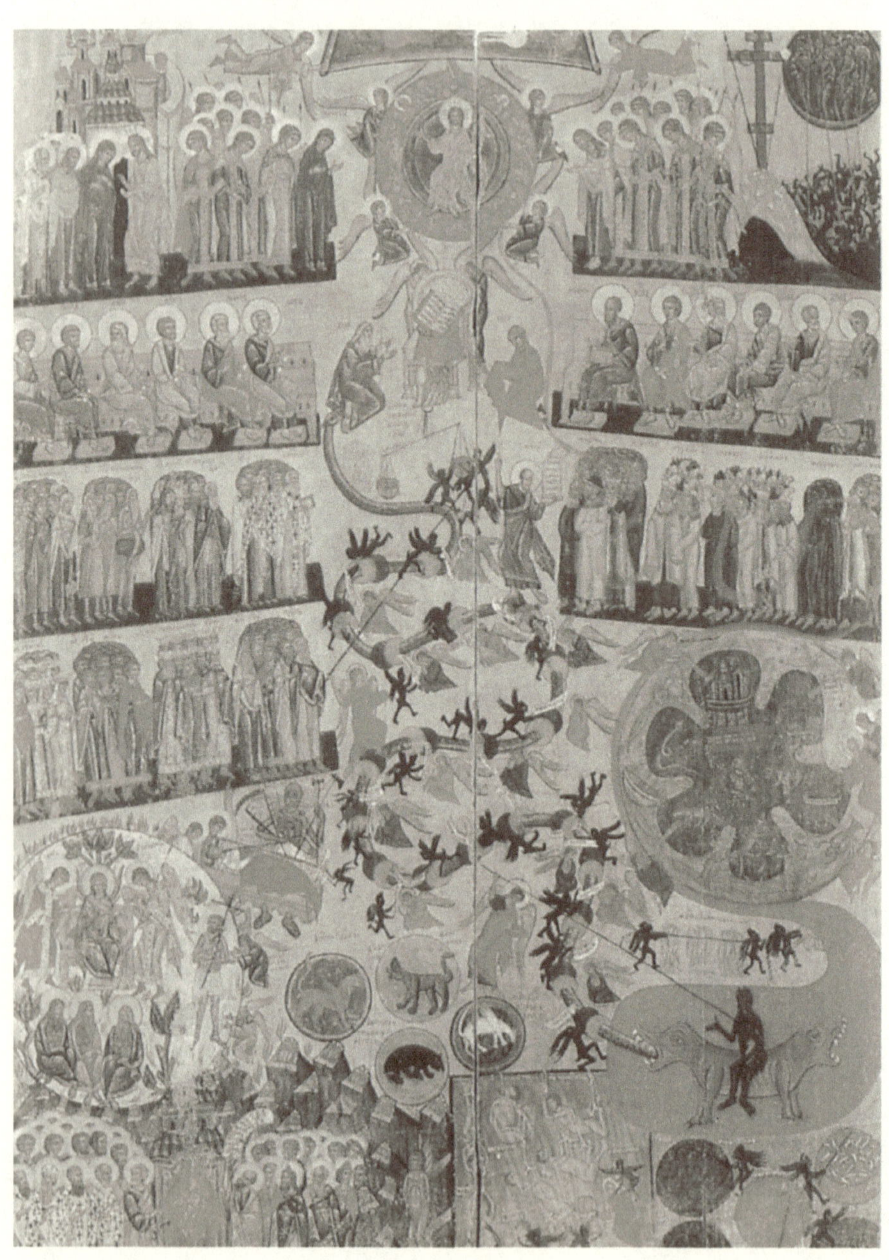

2.3 Mshanets overview

Art historians date the icons to the fifteenth century. They generally consider that Vanivka is the oldest, Polana the next oldest, and Mshanets somewhat younger than the other two.[3] Oleh Sydor, the former curator of the icon collection at the National Museum in Lviv, which holds both Vanivka and Mshanets, dates Vanivka to the first third of the fifteenth century and Mshanets to the second half of the fifteenth century.[4] Heinz Skrobucha, however, ascribed Mshanets to the sixteenth century.[5] For the moment, until serious dendrochronological and other scientific methods are applied, all dating is provisional. We know that these three icons come at the beginning of a longer tradition of Last Judgment icons in the Carpathian and neighbouring regions, but the first dated icon of any kind from the Carpathian region stems from 1547 and the first dated icon of a Last Judgment (from Kamianka Strumylova, a town at some distance north of the Carpathians) from 1587.[6] David Goldfrank has suggested that the icons are from no earlier than the 1520s or 1530s, arguing that the model for them was formulated in northern Rus' at that time by followers of Iosif Volotsky in response to controversies then raging in Muscovy.[7] Goldfrank's argument is thought-provoking, but without direct evidence to connect the evolution of Last Judgment iconography with Volotsky's movement, I am inclined to reserve judgment. Further along in this chapter, I will make an argument for a fifteenth-century dating, but what is really important for this work is that they constitute the beginning of a sequence, irrespective of when exactly they were painted. The three villages of the icons' provenance were themselves all founded in the fifteenth century[8] in the course of the Vlach migration.

These were large icons, painted with egg tempera on vertical linden boards. Part of Vanivka has been cut off on the bottom, but it was probably about 175 cm high and 135 cm wide; it was painted on four boards.[9] Polana measures 182 cm x 144 cm and was painted on three linden boards with some canvas on the surface.[10] Mshanets is 190 cm x 136 cm on four linden boards.[11] These are fairly typical of the kind of Last Judgment icon that was painted in the Carpathians through the middle of the seventeenth century: egg tempera on several, usually three, vertical linden boards about the height of an adult. Most of the later Last Judgments were a bit taller than the first three, usually over 200 cm.

From the very beginning of Last Judgment iconography in Byzantium, the image, whether fresco or icon, was constructed through the compilation of diverse elements, and the evolution of the image proceeded through the incorporation of additional elements or modification of existing ones.[12] It is a complex image, the most complex in Byzantine and post-Byzantine sacral art. There are other images that have many parts: for example, the calendar icons frequently found in Moldavian churches and in Russia that illustrate all the saints for a particular month or the icons of the Passion, frequently paired with Last Judgments in Carpathian churches, that illustrate the events surrounding the crucifixion of the Saviour, beginning with the raising of Lazarus in Bethany or the entry into Jerusalem and ending with the Resurrection. In the case of the calendars, there is no logical connection among the parts, and in the case of the Passions, the connection is serial, chronological. The Last Judgment image is more like a many-sided theological interpretation of Christian eschatology and the judgment of the dead. In fact, there is no text in the normal sense that has as much to say about Orthodox Last Judgment theology as the image does. To present its subject, it draws on scripture, especially Daniel 7 and Matthew 25:31–46 (the Gospel of Meatfare Sunday), apocrypha, liturgical texts for Meatfare Sunday, and the teachings of the Fathers, especially Ephraim the Syrian (Graecus). Different times and different places are combined into a complex image, with its own iconographic logic and internal geography. The complexity of the Last Judgment image produces considerable creative tension, which helps explain the image's evolution in the Carpathians. The evolution proceeds, as stated at the outset of this paragraph, through the incorporation and modification of various elements.

The analysis of the evolution of the elements will provide us with clues about the icons' origins in the Carpathian foothills and, in subsequent chapters, about changes in the culture and mentality of the people who produced them and worshipped through them. Some of these elements were passed on from the original Byzantine models of the eighth through twelfth centuries, while others appear for the first time in the fifteenth century far from Constantinople, in Carpathian Rus' or in the more distant northern Rus'. We will begin our analysis by examining the Byzantine elements imbedded in the first three Carpathian icons of the Last Judgment.

Vanivka has been cut off at the bottom, and the lower part of what survived is damaged. Fortunately, it is possible to have a good idea of what was contained in the missing portions, because a very close, though not exact, copy of the icon was made in the first half of the sixteenth century for the Church of Ss Cosmas and Damian in the village of Lukov-Venecia (Prešov region, Slovakia). For some of the discussion below it will be necessary to refer to the lower portions of the Lukov-Venecia icon, even though it was painted after the fifteenth century (fig. 2.4).

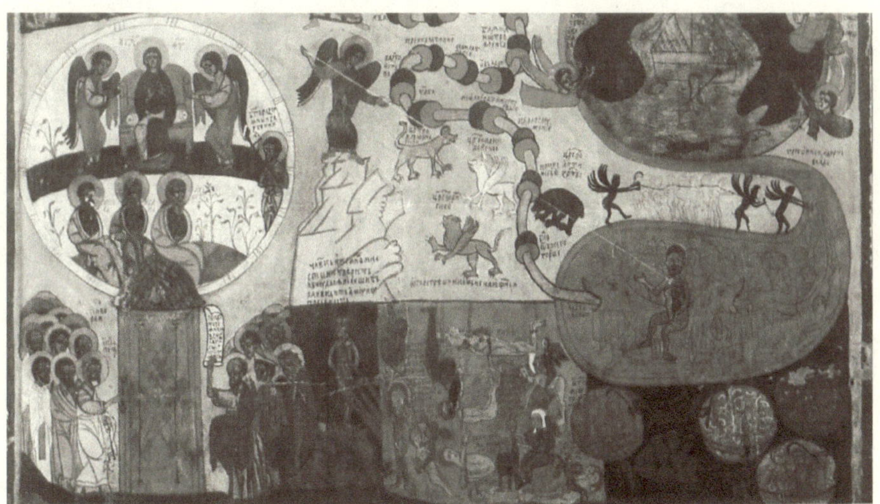

2.4 Lower portion of Lukov-Venecia. Source: Štefan Tkáč, *Ikony zo 16.–19. storočia na severovýchodnom Slovensku* (Bratislava: Tatran, 1982), 138, pl. 58.

Byzantine Elements

We will start by comparing our three Carpathian icons with an icon of the Last Judgment from Mount Sinai painted in the second half of the twelfth century (fig. 2.5).[13] At the very top of the Mount Sinai are angels, because 'the Son of man shall come in his glory, and all the holy angels with him' (Mt 25:31). The angels are also represented in our three earliest as well as all subsequent Carpathian icons of the Last Judgment, but their placement is usually different. They stand behind the Mother of God, at the Saviour's right hand, and behind John the Baptist, at his left.

Also, all images of the Last Judgment contained the so-called deesis or trimorphion, that is, the figure of the returning Saviour in a mandorla flanked by his mother and John the Baptist (fig. 2.6).[14] In the Mount Sinai icon, the deesis is placed amid the apostles, six on each side, while in the Carpathian icons the apostles, though arranged the same way, are positioned one row down. The apostles are present in the icon because Jesus promised them that 'in the regeneration when the Son of man shall sit in the throne of his glory, ye also shall sit upon twelve thrones, judging the twelve tribes of Israel' (Mt 19:28; see also Lk 22:30) (see fig. 2.7).

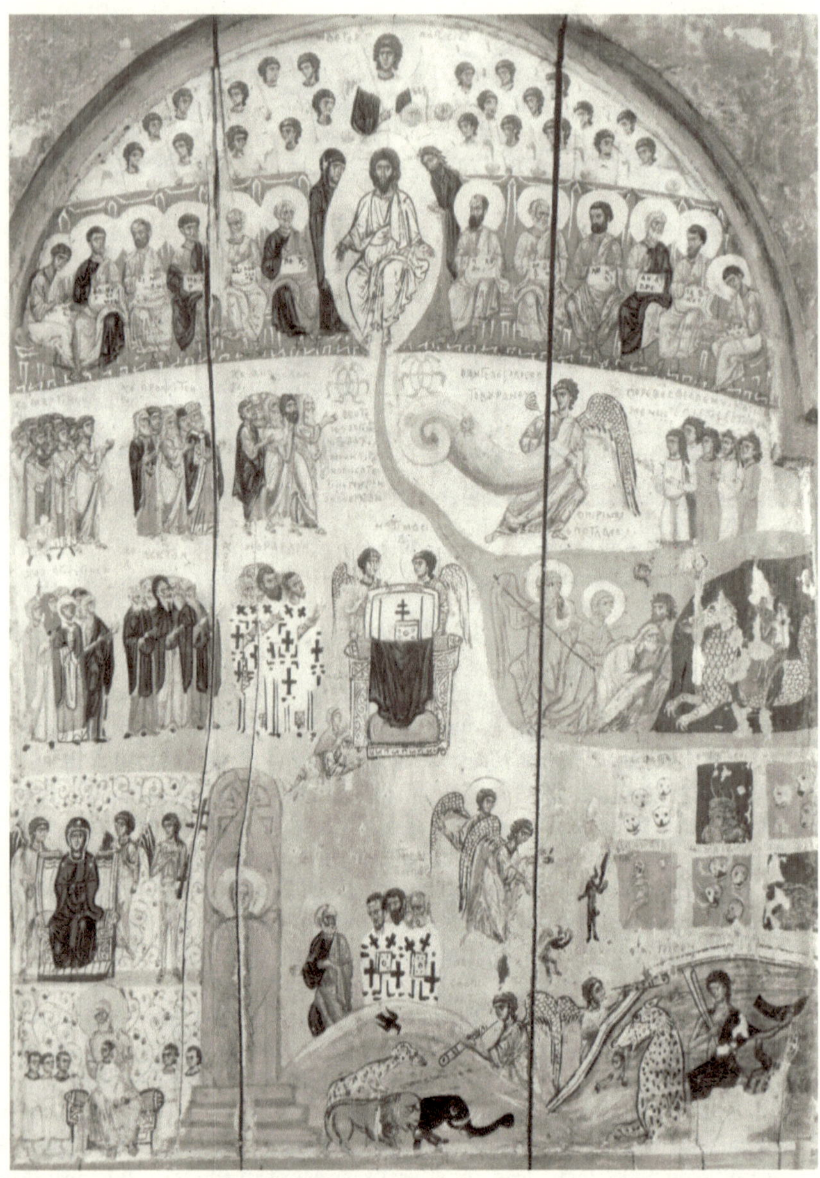

2.5 A Byzantine Last Judgment from Mount Sinai. Source: Selma Jónsdóttir, *An 11th Century Byzantine Last Judgment in Iceland* (Reykjavik: Almenna Bókafélagið, 1959), ill. 6.

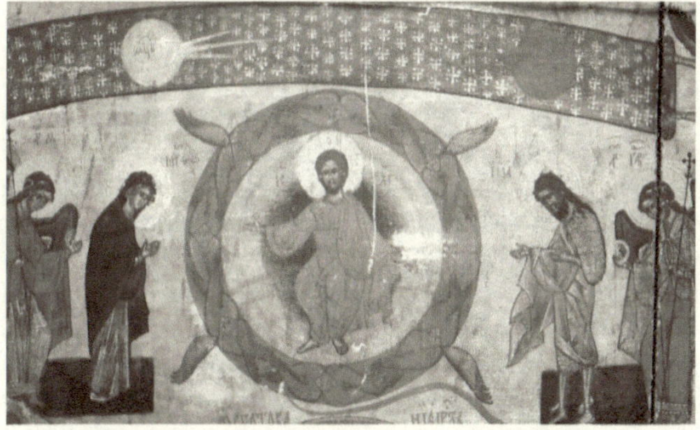

2.6 Deesis and Scroll of Heaven, Vanivka

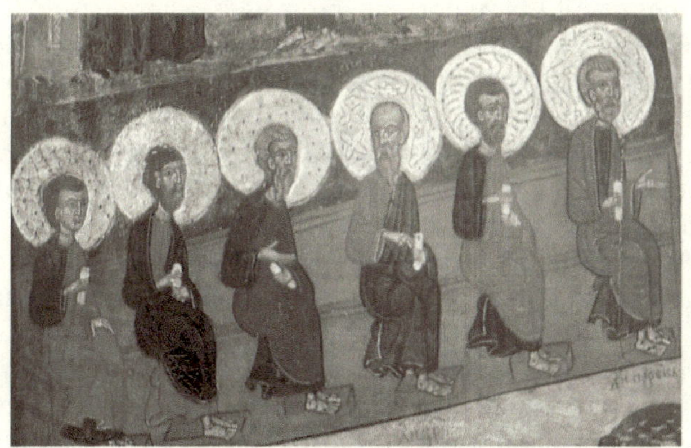

2.7 Six of the Apostles, Polana

Below the apostles on the right hand side of the Son of man, in both the Mount Sinai and the Carpathian icons, are choirs of various saints in two rows, including saintly women, martyrs, and holy hierarchs. Perhaps the textual origin of this motif is from canticle four of the matins of Meatfare Sunday: 'In their order will monk and hierarch, old man and young, slave and master be interrogated. Widow and virgin will be put right.'

In all four icons except Polana, a stream of fire exits from the foot of the Saviour, turns into a river, and empties into the lake of Gehenna. In Polana too the river of fire is present, but it starts from the throne instead of the foot of Christ. The origin of this element is to be found in the book of Daniel: 'A fiery stream issued and came forth from before him' (Dn 7:10).

Just across the river from the apostles in Mount Sinai is an angel fulfilling the words of the prophet Isaiah that 'the heavens shall be rolled together as a scroll' (Is 34:4; see also Rv 6:14). In the Carpathian icons, the scroll is placed above the deesis and decorated with the sun and moon; two angels roll it together.

An interesting feature of the Mount Sinai icon is the group of five condemned sinners[15] to the left of the angel rolling up the scroll. (I remind the reader that in describing Last Judgment images, the left and right refer not to the viewer's perspective, but to the perspective of the Son of man, i.e., as if one were looking out from the icon.) The sinners are there as compositional balance to the saints on the right. Nothing like this can be found in other contemporary Byzantine images of the Last Judgment, and I have not run across it elsewhere either. It looks as if this element is contained in the Carpathian icons, but not quite. As we shall see below, the figures in the Carpathian icons represent various nations coming to judgment. But what is interesting is that the Mount Sinai iconographer introduced this group of figures to create balance, and the same thought evidently lay behind the placement of different figures here in the Carpathian icons.

Below the angel with the scroll and the condemned sinners in Mount Sinai, angels can be seen driving sinners into hell. In the three Carpathian icons (as well as in Moldavian frescoes and even in Gothic images),[16] a related scene is found above the lake of Gehenna at the bottom left: sinners with chains around their neck being led into the fire by devils. This variant was known already in early fourteenth-century Constantinople.[17] All our icons – Mount Sinai, Vanivka/Lukov-Venecia, Polana, and Mshanets – include the same visual image inside the lake of Gehenna: Satan or the personification of Hades sits astride a two-headed beast of the apocalypse, holding the soul of Judas Iscariot or perhaps the Antichrist in his hands. (In Carpathian icons it is almost always Satan rather than Hades and Judas rather than the Antichrist.)

Below Gehenna in the Mount Sinai icon as well as in the Carpathian icons are the chambers of the traditional torments, some mentioned in the Gospels, such as outer darkness, weeping, and gnashing of teeth (Mt 25:30), everlasting fire (Mt 25:41), and the worm that dieth not (Mk 9:44, 48), and others that were inferred from scriptural references, such as 'the fierce fire' (*ohn' liuta*) and 'the fierce cold' (*studen liuta*) in Polana

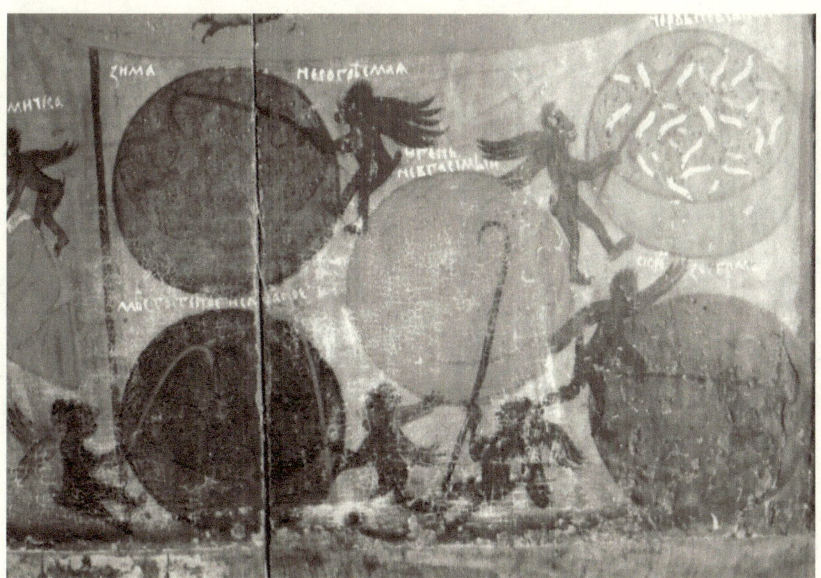

2.8 Traditional Torments, Mshanets

and 'the unheatable winter' (*zyma nesohrivaiemaia*) and 'the dark and smelly place' (*misto temnoie i smradnoie*) in Mshanets (fig. 2.8). These must be the 'infernal prisons and dungeons of Hades' that Cyril of Alexandria believed were in the 'lower parts.'[18]

In the Mount Sinai icon, one of the six chambers, the one on the bottom left, is occupied by the rich man of the Lazarus tale. 'And in hell he lift up his eyes, being in torments, and seeth Abraham afar off, and Lazarus in his bosom. And he cried and said, Father Abraham, have mercy on me, and send Lazarus, that he may dip the tip of his finger in water, and cool my tongue; for I am tormented in this flame' (Lk 16:23-4). The figure of the rich man, sitting in hell, with a hand near his mouth to indicate thirst, was a regular feature of Byzantine and much post-Byzantine iconography of the Last Judgment, including the exquisite eleventh-century ivory carving owned by the Victoria and Albert (fig. 2.9). The rich man does not appear in the three earliest Carpathian icons, but he is in one of the the next earliest, Vilshanytsia, from the first half of the sixteenth century as well as in a number of later icons (fig. 2.10).[19]

Near the traditional torments in the Mount Sinai icon are two angels, one of whom is spearing a devil. In the three Carpathian icons, the motif

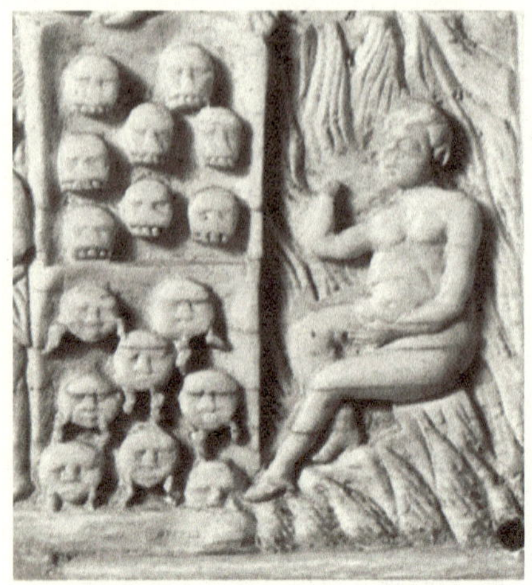

2.9 Traditional Torments and Rich Man from an eleventh-century Byzantine ivory carving in the Victoria and Albert Museum. Source: Kurt Weitzmann et al., *The Icon* (New York: Dorset Press, 1987), 39.

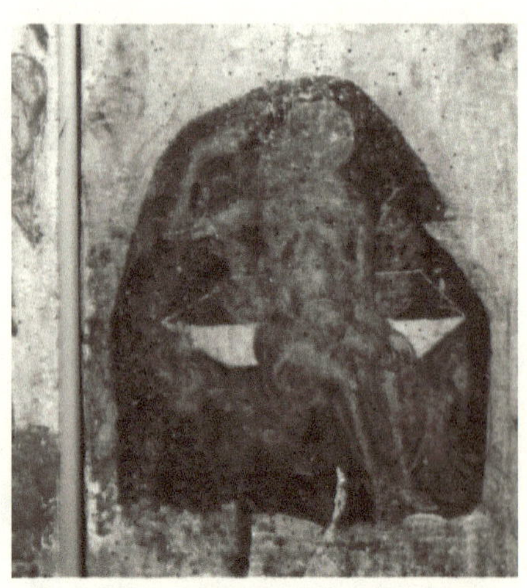

2.10 Rich Man from Vilshanytsia, first half of the sixteenth century

appears twice: once near the bottom, where an angel spears Satan riding on the beast, and once in the middle, where an angel spears a small devil trying to tip the scales.

The resurrection of the dead is depicted at the bottom left in the Mount Sinai icon. Two angels are trumpeting, 'for the trumpet shall sound, and the dead shall be raised incorruptible' (1 Cor 15:52; see also 1 Thes 4:16). At the far left a sea monster, with the personification of the sea on its back, is throwing up body parts for the resurrection. Towards the centre, land animals do the same. The origin of this scene is in Revelation 20:13 ('and the sea gave up the dead which were in it') and in the apocryphal Apocalypse of Peter from the first half of the second century.[20] In the Carpathian icons the resurrection of the dead takes place in a circle on the bottom half of the left side of the icon. There are four angels trumpeting. Among these early icons, only Vanivka has a personification of the sea, but later icons sometimes include both that figure and the personification of the land (fig. 2.11).[21]

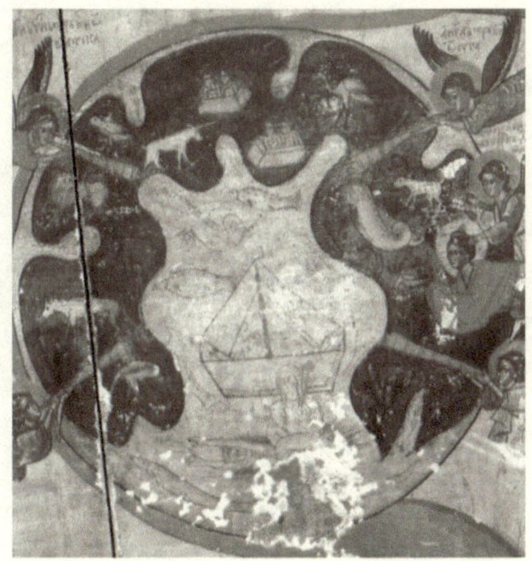

2.11 The Resurrection of the Dead, Vanivka

In the centre of the Mount Sinai icon is the throne or 'preparation' (*hetoimasia* in Greek) – 'he hath prepared his throne for judgment' (Ps 9:8; see also Ps 102:19) and 'justice and judgment are the preparation of thy throne' (Ps 88:14).[22] The inscription above the throne in Vanivka reads: 'preparation of the throne' (*uhotovaniie prestolu*). The Gospel of Matthew says that the Son of man shall 'sit upon the throne of his glory' (25: 31). The imagery of a throne with a book comes from Daniel (Dn 7:9–10) and Revelation (Rv 4:2–5:14). Most Carpathian icons have the same figure of a throne with a book, and often a cross too, as in the Mount Sinai icon. Of the three earliest, only Polana does not have a book on it, just a cloth, but there is a book to the left of the throne between Eve and a lamb (fig. 2.12). The books on Vanivka and Polana are opened to Matthew 25:34: 'Come, ye blessed of my Father, inherit the kingdom prepared for you from the foundation of the world.' This inscription is the most common one on Carpathian icons, but there are other variants. Mshanets, for instance, has the book open to Matthew 11:28: 'Come unto me, all ye that labour and are heavy laden, and I will give you rest.'

At the right bottom corner of the throne in the Mount Sinai icon, Adam and Eve are interceding for their progeny. Adam and Eve are also present in Carpathian icons, including the first three, but Adam is positioned on the right of the throne and Eve on the left.

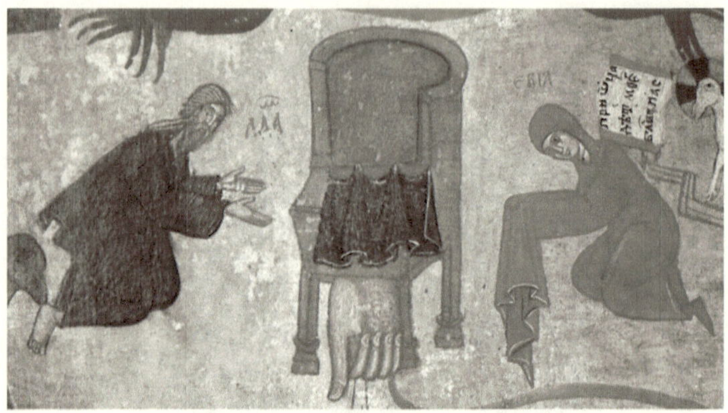

2.12 Adam and Eve Kneeling by the Throne, Polana

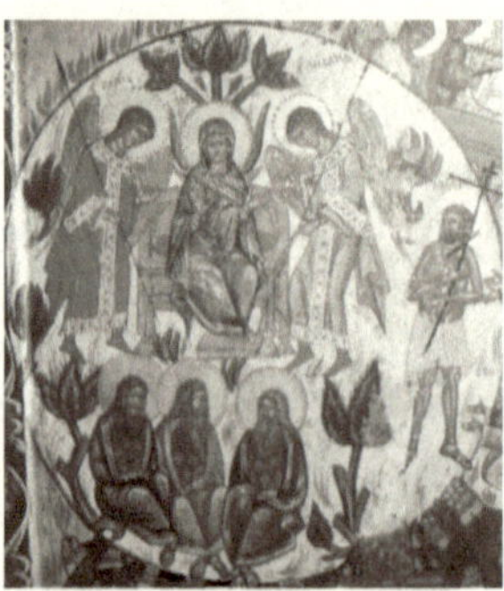

2.13 Paradise and the Bosom of Abraham, Mshanets

In the Mount Sinai icon on the extreme bottom right is paradise, represented by the Mother of God flanked by angels and accompanied by the good thief. The same can be found in the three Carpathian icons, although enclosed in a circle. In both the Mount Sinai and the Carpathian icons the bosom of Abraham[23] is placed just below paradise. In the classic Byzantine tradition, as in the Mount Sinai icon, only Abraham was depicted holding a soul. In the Carpathian and Russian iconography the bosom of Abraham was represented by the three patriarchs Jacob, Isaac, and Abraham, each holding many souls on his breast. The latter version was inspired by Luke 13:28: '... ye shall see Abraham, and Isaac, and Jacob, and all the prophets, in the kingdom of God' (fig. 2.13).

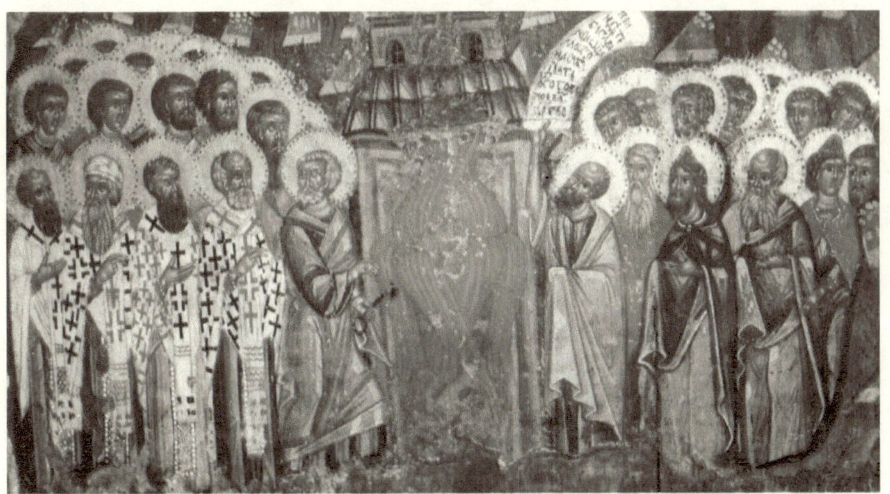

2.14 Saints Entering Paradise, Mshanets

In the Mount Sinai icon, to the immediate left of paradise and the bosom of Abraham, and in the Carpathian icons, below them, is the gate to paradise, guarded by a fiery cherub. In all the icons, St Peter is opening the gates for the saints to enter. In the Carpathian icons Peter is shown with 'the keys of the kingdom of heaven' promised to him by Jesus (Mt 16:19) (fig. 2.14).

All the elements described above, and common to the Mount Sinai and the three early Carpathian icons, form part of the universal patrimony of post-Byzantine depictions of the Last Judgment. They can be found, with local variations, of course, throughout the Orthodox world, of which Carpathian Rus' was an integral part (figs 2.15, 2.16, 2.17).

The First Carpathian Elaboration

In the Carpathian icons, however, there were elements that were not part of the general Byzantine legacy, that were limited in range. Some of these elements were common to the entire territory of Rus' and later also spread to Moldavia and other Romanian-inhabited lands; some elements were specific to the Carpathian region exclusively. The set of features that are common to the three fifteenth-century icons, but not part of the traditional Byzantine iconography, I call 'the first Carpathian elaboration.'

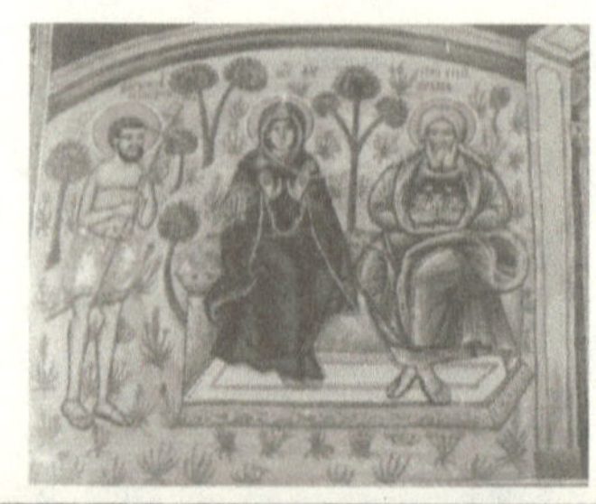

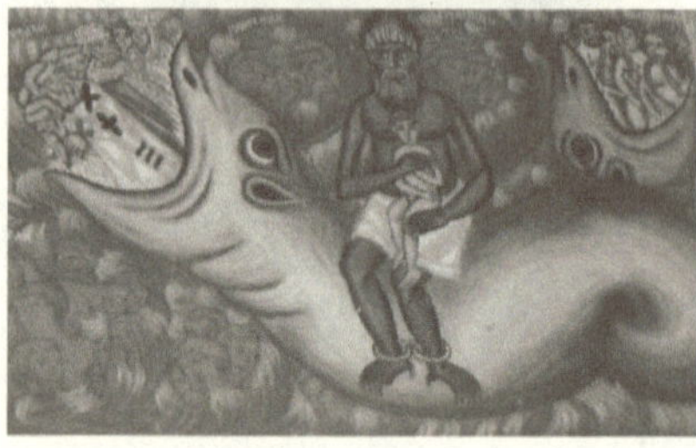

2.15 Paradise and the Bosom of Abraham, Satan on the Two-Headed Beast, Morača Monastery, Montenegro, 1577–8. Photo: Srdja Pavlovic.

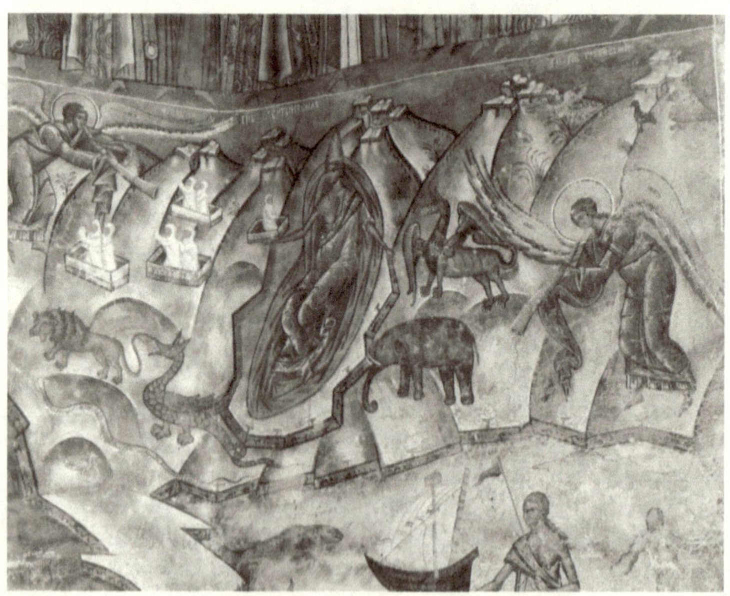

2.16 The Resurrection of the Dead, Voroneţ, Romania, mid-sixteenth century

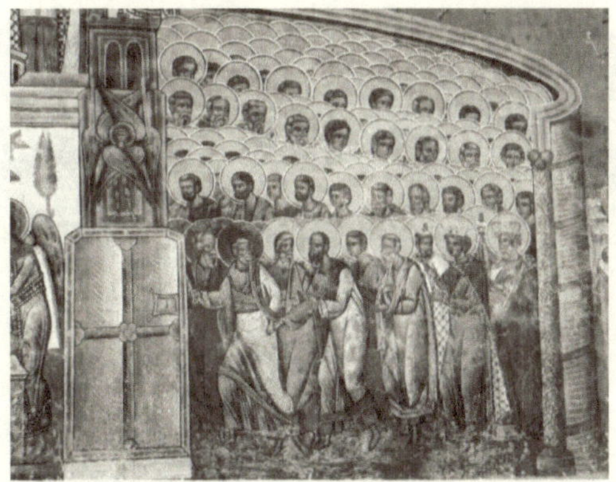

2.17 Saints Entering Paradise, Voroneț, Romania, mid-sixteenth century

In the illustration 'Mshanets with the Byzantine Elements Removed' (fig. 2.18), I have reproduced the Mshanets icon, but erased all the Byzantine elements that were discussed in the preceding section. The elements remaining, which may be considered the elements that are characteristic of the first Carpathian elaboration are as follows:

1 the heavenly Jerusalem, in the upper right-hand side of the icon;
2 the fall of the rebel angels, in the upper left side of the icon;
3 near the latter, the crucifix and instruments of Christ's Passion;
4 the hand of God, holding the souls of the righteous and also
5 some scales with souls in them;
6 a serpent running the length of the icon, from Adam's heel to the mouth of the beast, upon which are
7 tollbooths, about twenty of them, each labelled with a particular sin and flanked by a devil and an angel;
8 on the left, Moses, pointing to the Saviour, holding a scroll telling 'the wretched Jews,' to see whom they have crucified and near him Jews and other peoples in costume;
9 to the left of the resurrection of the dead, the prophet Daniel accompanied by an angel;
10 in the nether regions, four beasts representing four evil kingdoms;
11 to the right of the beasts, tight against paradise, monks flying into paradise;
12 above them, near a bed, Death, carrying various tools, including a scythe and an hourglass (only Mshanets);

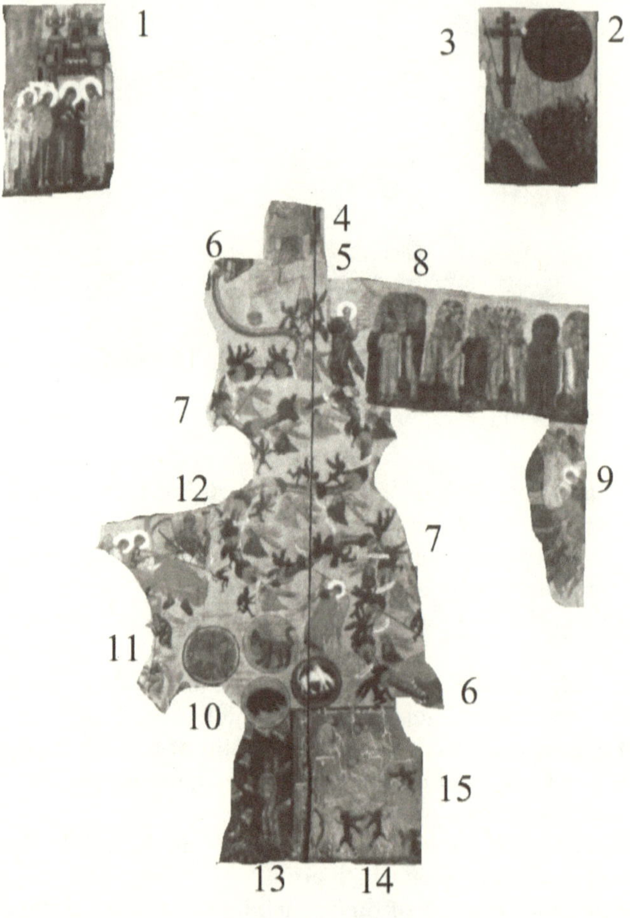

2.18 Mshanets with the Byzantine elements removed

13 near the bottom, between paradise and the torments of the damned, tied to a pillar, the almsgiving fornicator;
14 just behind him, what I call 'the new hell,' because various sinners are being punished in a squarish area with torments that did not appear in the standard Byzantine iconography;
15 standing near the mouth of hell with a barrel in front of her and a devil behind, a tavernmaid;
16 near the throne, a lamb (only Polana).

Let us examine these elements with the aim of determining their textual origin, their compositional function, and their iconographic origin and range.

1–2) The Heavenly Jerusalem and Fall of the Rebel Angels

The terminology of the heavenly Jerusalem, or the 'Jerusalem which is above' (Gal 4:25), derives from St Paul: 'But ye are come unto mount Sion, and unto the city of the living God, the heavenly Jerusalem, and to an innumerable company of angels' (Heb 12:22). The concept, however, may be rooted in Daniel's vision of an everlasting kingdom for 'the saints of the most High' (Dn 7:22, 27). The heavenly Jerusalem found its most extensive New Testament elaboration in Revelation 21. The defeat of the devil and his angels is also elaborated in Revelation (12:7–9): 'And there was war in heaven: Michael and his angels fought against the dragon; and the dragon fought and his angels, And prevailed not; neither was their place found any more in heaven. And the great dragon was cast out, that old serpent, called the Devil, and Satan, which deceiveth the whole world: he was cast out into the earth, and his angels were cast out with him.' These scriptural passages clearly inform the iconography in the three Carpathian icons. The inscriptions on Vanivka are: 'The Lord invites his saints into the upper city of Jerusalem (*hornyi hrad Ierusalym*)' and 'The tenth order of angels fell from the heavens into the abyss' (figs 2.19, 2.20). (According to Pseudo-Dionysius the Areopagite there are nine orders of angels. The devils once formed a tenth order.)

These two elements are closely related and correspond to the alternatives put forward in Matthew 25:34–46. To the blessed, the righteous, standing to his right, the Son of man offers 'the kingdom prepared ... from the foundation of the world.' For those on his left, however, there is 'everlasting fire, prepared for the devil and his angels.'[24] The inclusion of these two complementary subjects in the upper corners of the icon enhanced the compositional balance.

The only other images of the Last Judgment in which the heavenly Jerusalem and the fall of the rebel angels appear are in the icons of northern Rus'. They first appear in a fifteenth-century icon of the Novgorod school held by the Tretiakov Gallery in Moscow (hereafter Novgorod-Tretiakov) (fig. 2.21).[25] They remained a common feature in Russian icons thereafter; they are present, for example, in the Recklinghausen icon of the second half of the seventeenth century.[26]

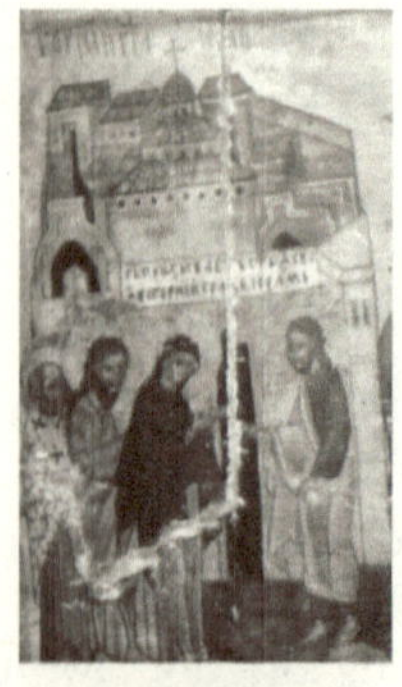

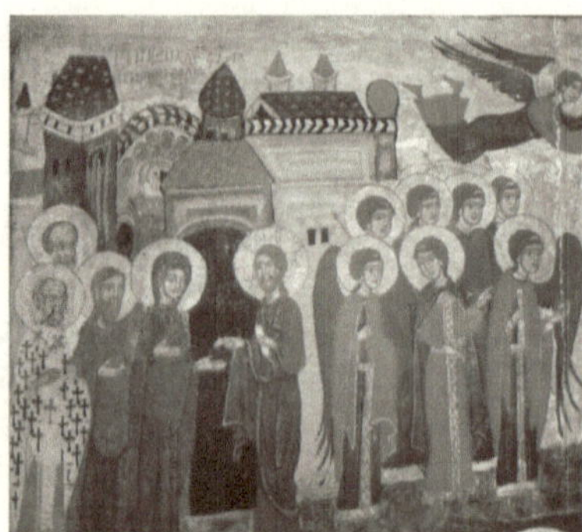

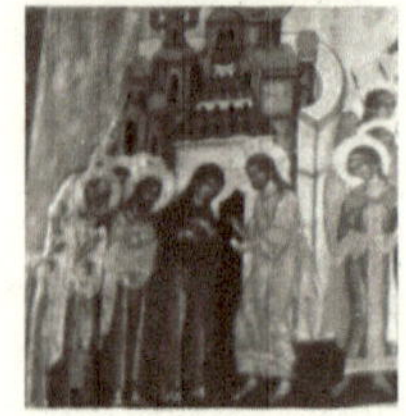

2.19 The Heavenly Jerusalem: Vanivka, Polana, Mshanets

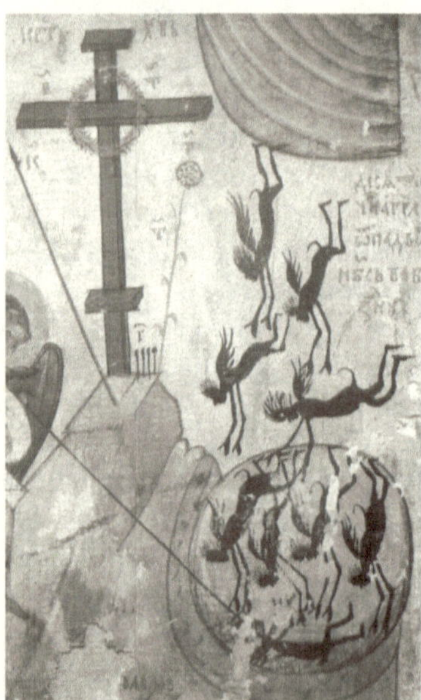

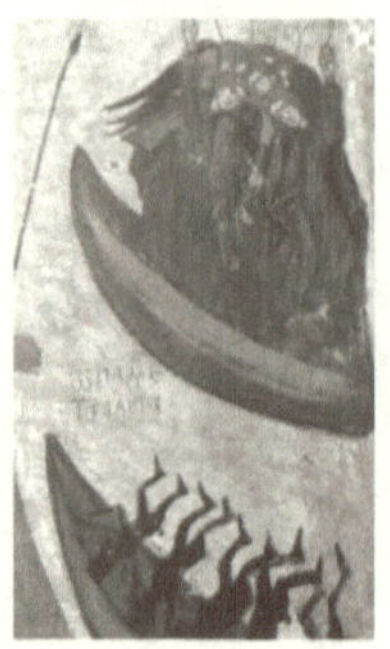

2.20 The Fall of the Rebel Angels: Vanivka, Polana

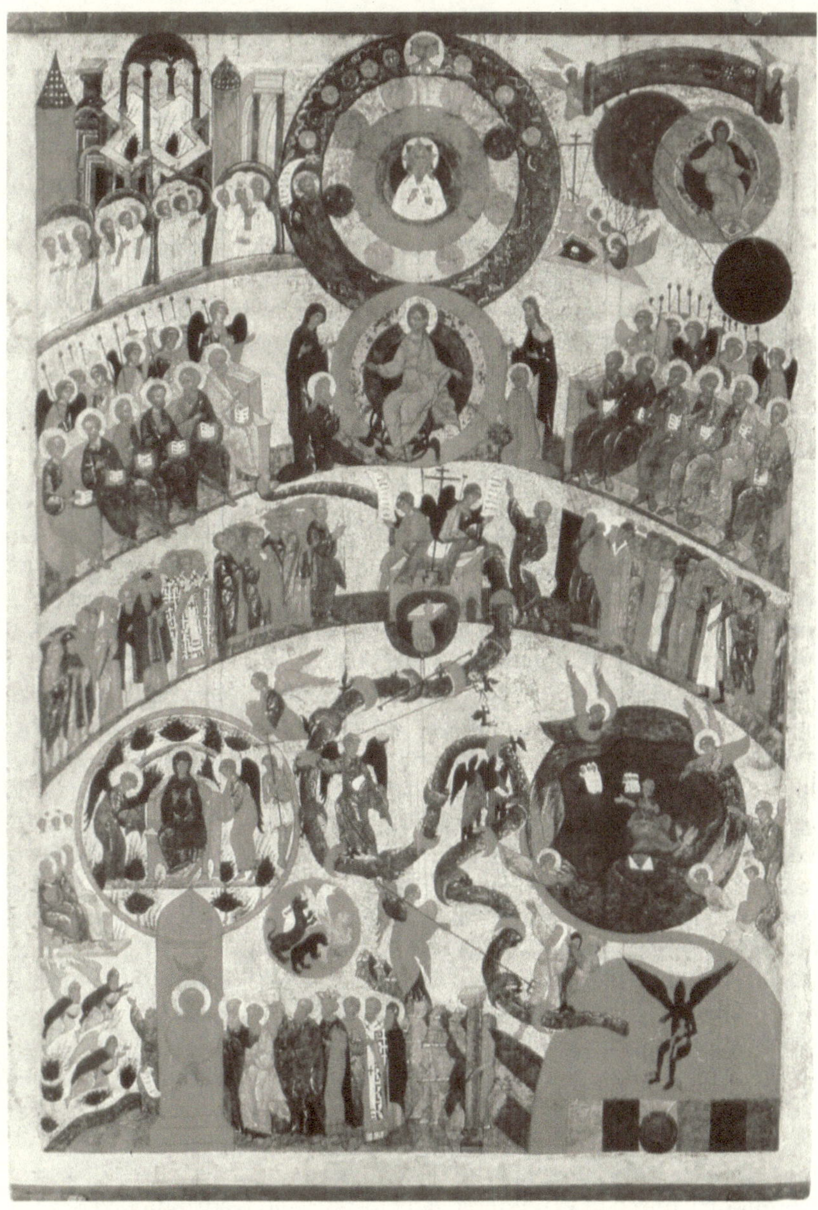

2.21 Novgorod-Tretiakov. Source: Kurt Weitzmann et al., *The Icon* (New York: Dorset Press, 1987), 281.

3) The Crucifix and Instruments

The textual origin of this element, placed in the heavens near to the right of the fall of the rebel angels, is in the Gospel of Matthew, in a passage describing the last days: 'And then shall appear the sign of the Son of man in heaven ...' (24:30). Ephraim the Syrian interpreted this sign to be the cross upon which Christ was crucified.[27] The crucifix in Vanivka is accompanied by the following instruments, each identified by its initial: the crown of thorns (*t[ernov vinets]*), the sponge (*h[uba]*), the reed (*t[rost']*), the nails (*h[vozdy]*), and the lance (*k[opiie]*). Compositionally, this element is attached to the fall of the rebel angels and serves the same function of balancing the painting. The crucifix and instruments appear on Novgorod-Tretiakov and other Russian icons.

4–5) The Hand of God and Scales

The Wisdom of Solomon is the textual origin of the depiction of the hand of God holding souls: 'The souls of the righteous are in the hand of God, and no torment shall touch them' (3:1). The verse was well known in monastic milieus, since it is the opening of an Old Testament reading at vespers several times a year.[28] Its connection with the afterlife was recognized in a fifth-century work attributed to St Cyril of Alexandria: 'The righteous are in the hand of God, the sinners in the place of the devil.'[29] The notion of weighing souls in scales is ancient and widespread.[30] The scriptural basis for including the image in Christian iconography may derive from from Job 31:6 ('I stood on a true scale, and the Lord saw my lack of malice') and Daniel 5:27 ('He was weighed in the balances, and was found wanting'). Both Vanivka and Mshanets near the hand of God bear the inscription 'The souls of the righteous in the hand of God.' (Polana has no inscription here.) Compositionally, these elements extend further the central vertical line that begins with the figure of the Son of man and the throne. The scales, not balanced, add a certain dynamism to the centre.

The souls of the righteous in the hand of God appeared in Orthodox iconography in the early fourteenth century, both in association with the Last Judgment[31] and in other contexts.[32] The first appearance in Rus' of this motif in assocation with the Last Judgment is in a fresco in the Dormition Church in Vladimir; it dates to 1408 and is attributed to Andrei Rublev (fig. 2.22). The hand of God became fully integrated into Last Judgment iconography in the fifteenth-century icons of Carpathian and northern Rus'. It can be found in Vanivka, Polana, Mshanets, Novgorod-Tretiakov, and also the more archaic icon from the Moscow Dormition Church (fig. 2.23).[33] All of these, moreover, show the hand of God holding scales (fig. 2.24). The hand of God holding scales also appears, although rarely, in medieval Last Judgment iconography in the West.[34]

Scales to weigh souls appeared in Last Judgment iconography during the very formation of the classical Byzantine image. They are difficult to see in our reproduction, but scales are being held by an angel near the traditional torments in the Mount Sinai icon. Scales are to be found in other classical Byzantine images as well,[35] usually held by an angel (fig. 2.25). Angels with scales are also found in a number of Rus' Last Judgment images prior to the fifteenth century. The Chora monastery in Constantinople, painted with frescoes in the early fourteenth century, shows the scales descending from the throne.[36] This depiction is close to the image that developed in Rus', but only there, in the fifteenth century, did the scales appear in the hand of God.

As to Moldavian frescoes of the Last Judgment, the following frescoes depicted only an angel with scales without the hand of God: Luzhany[37] (1453–9), Pătrăuţi (1483), Probota (1532), and Râşca (1552). The hand of God with scales as in the Rus' icons of the fifteenth century appeared in Humor (1535), Suceava: St Demetrius (1535), Moldoviţa (1537), Arbore (1541), Voroneţ (1550), and Suceviţa (1595–6) (fig. 2.26). Except for the instance of Râşca, which was painted by a Greek artist, the hand of God replaced the angel in the 1530s. The element is unknown in Greek and South Slavic images of the Last Judgment.[38]

6–7) Serpent and Tollbooths

The textual origin of the serpent is the 'subtil' beast of Genesis 3, which initiated humanity into sin.[39] The connection with Genesis is brought out iconographically by the serpent's biting Adam's heel. The serpent is an appropriate setting for the tollbooths, which take the form of rings on the serpent's body, each of which is labelled with a sin.[40]

The tollbooths do not have a scriptural origin. The idea of tollbooths, at which souls were tried for particular sins, with demons and angels contesting the souls' innocence and guilt, was developed in 'On the Exit of the Soul and on the Second Coming,' attributed to Cyril of Alexandria.[41] This fifth-century work, however, did not specify the number of tollbooths or name all the sins that later became associated with them. A more detailed and influential work on the tollbooths was the Life of St Basil the

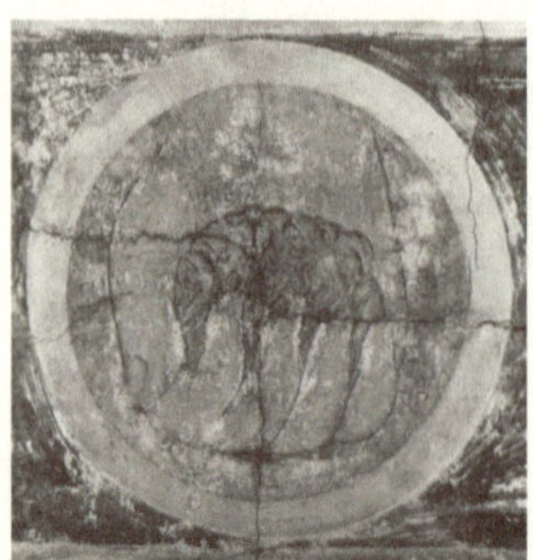

2.22 Hand of God, Dormition Church, Vladimir, 1408. Source: V.N. Lazarev, *Drevnerusskie mozaiki i freski XI–XV vv.* (Moscow: Iskusstvo, 1973), ill. 416.

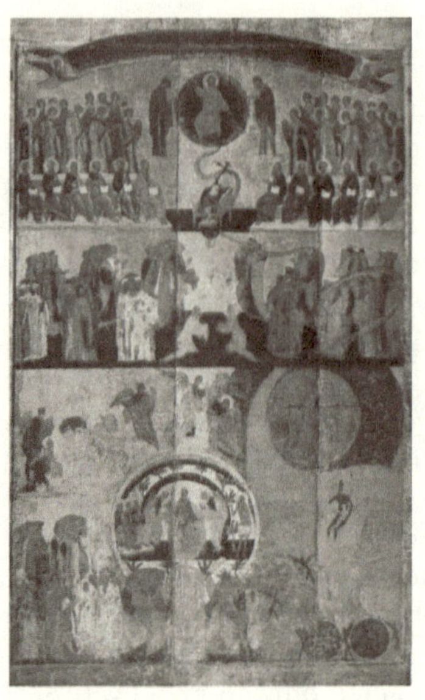

2.23 Icon of the Moscow Dormition Church. Source: E.S. Smirnova, *Moskovskaia ikona XIV–XVII vekov* (Leningrad: Avrora, 1988), pl. 113.

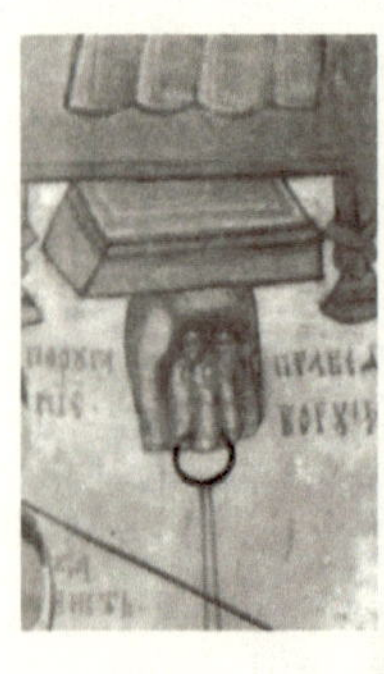

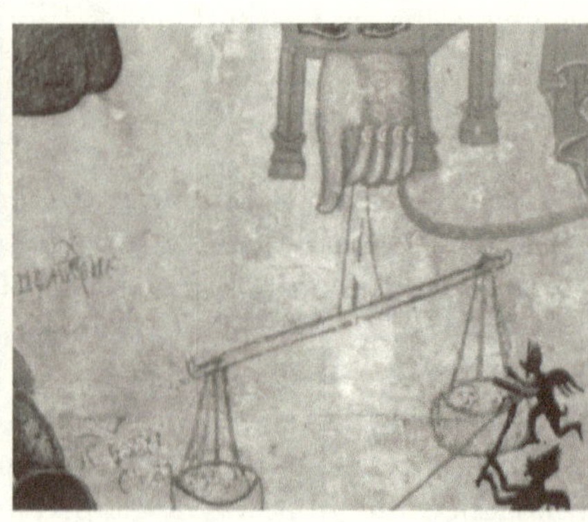

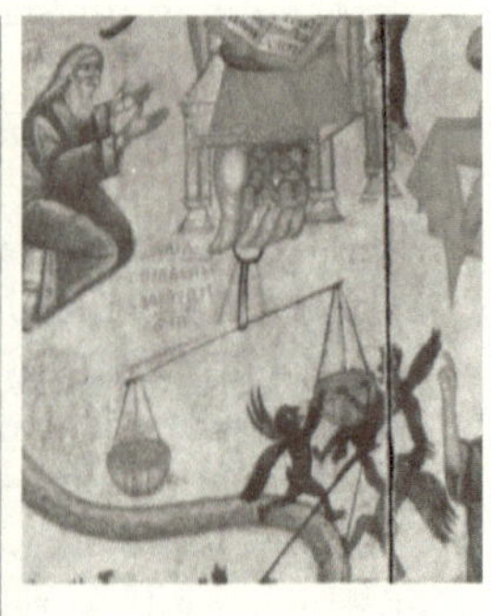

2.24 Hand of God with Scales, Vanivka, Polana, Mshanets

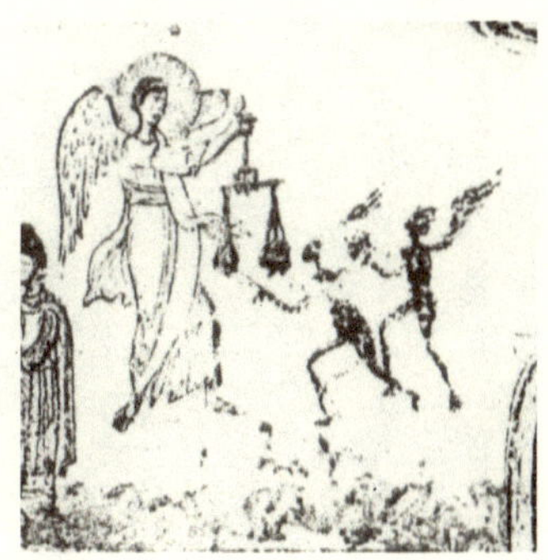

2.25 Angel with Scales, illustration to Matthew 25 in an eleventh-century Greek Gospel book. Source: Bibliothèque Nationale, Département des manuscrits, *Évangiles avec peintures byzantines di XIe siècle: Reproduction des 361 miniatures du manuscrit grec 74 de la Bibliothèque Nationale*, 2 vols (Paris: Imprimerie Berthaud frères, n.d.), pl. 41.

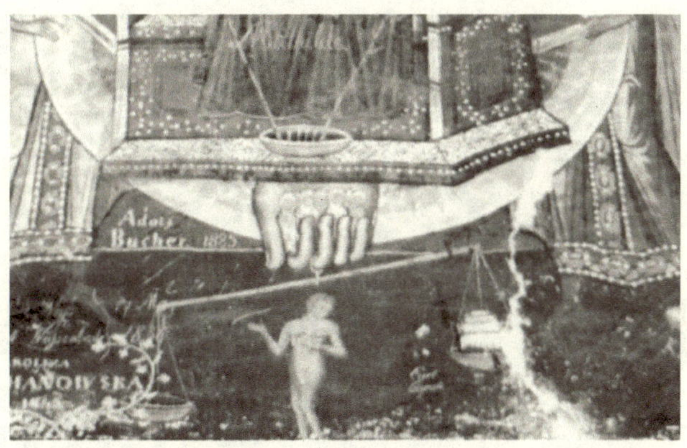

2.26 Hand of God with Scales, Moldoviţa

New, which was known in Rus' in two redactions.[42] The Life of St Basil the New was also the source of a late twelfth- or early thirteenth-century Rus' eschatological work, 'The Sermon on the Heavenly Powers' (*Slovo o sylakh nebesnykh*), which also discussed the tollbooths.[43] Various redactions of the Life of St Basil the New had twenty or twenty-one tollbooths.[44] A comparison of the sins listed on the tollbooths in the Carpathian icons and in the Life of St Basil the New demonstrates beyond any doubt that this text was the source that directly or indirectly placed the tollbooths on the icons (table 2.1). Earlier investigators had also identified the crucial

Table 2.1
Tollbooth Sins on the Earliest Carpathian Icons and in the Life of St Basil the New

Vanika	Polana	Mshanets	Life of St Basil the New, First Rus' Redaction
tollbooth of slander (*mytarstvo klevetnoie*)	slander (*kleveta*)	slander (*kleveta*)	false witness (*obolhaniie*)
mockery (*poruhaniie*)	mockery (*poruhaniie*)	mockery (*poruhaniie*)	slandering (*oklevetaniie*)
envy (*zavyst'*)	envy (*zavyst'*)	envy? (*[zavys]t'*) PRIDE (*HORDOST'*)	envy (*zavyst'*)
lying (*lzha*)	lying (*lzha*)	hatred (*nenavyst'*)	tollbooth of the liars (*mytartsvo lzhyvykh*)
rage (*iarost'*)	anger (*hniv*)	(illegible) RAGE AND ANGER (*IAROST' I HNIV*)	rage and anger (*iarost' i hniv*)
pride (*hordost'*)	pride and vainglory (*hordost' i velychaniie*)	(illegible) ACQUISITIVENESS (*STIAZHANIIE*)	pride (*hordyni*)
empty talk (*praznosloviie*)	obscene, empty talk (*sramosloviie praznosloviie*)	empty talk (*praznosloviie*)	idle and obscene talk (*buiesloviie i sramosloviie*)
usury (*lykhva*)	usuries and deceit (*lykhvy i lest'*)	usury and deceit (*likhva i lest'*)	usury and deceit (*lykhva i lest'*)
vain (talk?) (*tshche[sloviie]*)	vain talk and falsehood (*tshchesloviie i neprav[d]a*)	vain talk (*[tshch]esloviie*) VAINGLORY (*TSHCHESLAVIIE*)	despondency, that is, vainglory (*unyniie syrich' tshcheslaviie*)
love of silver (*srebroliubiie*)	love of silver (*srebroliubiie*)	love of silver (*srebroliubiie*)	love of silver (*srebroliubiie*)
drunkenness (*pian'stvo*)	drunkenness (*p'ian'stvo*)	drunkenness (*pianstvo*)	tollbooth of drunkenness (*pianstvennoie mytarstvo*)
harbouring grudges (*pomneniie zlu*)	harbouring grudges (*pomneniie zlu*)	harbouring grudges (*pom[ne]niie zla*) DOING EVIL (*TVORENIIE ZLA*)	harbouring grudges (*zlovspomynaniie*)

incantations and poisonings (*baianiia i otrovleniia*)	incantation, poisoning, magic (*baianiie otravleniie volkhvovaniie*)	gluttony (*obiadeniie*)	sorcery (*charodiistvo*)
gluttony (*[obiad]eniie*)	gluttony (*ob'iadeniie*)	incantation, poisoning, magic (*baianiie otravleniie volkhvovaniie*)	gluttony (*chrevoobiadeniie*)
idolatry (*idolosluzheniie*)	idolatry, every kind of heresy (*idolosluzheniie vsiaka ieres'*)	idolatry, all kinds of heresies (*idolosluzheniie vsiakiia ieresi*)	idolatry (*kumyrosluzheniie*)
lying with men (*muzhelihaniie*)	lying with men, infanticide (*muzhelihaniie ditohubleniie*)	lying with men, infanticide (*[muzhel]ihaniie [ditoh]ubleniie*)	adultery (*preliubodiistvo*)
adultery (*preliubodiianiie*)	adultery and fornication (*preliubodiistvo i blud*)	adultery (*prel[iubodiianiie]*)	murder (*ubiistvo*)
robbery/assault (*razboi*)	robbery/assault (*razboi*)	thievery (*tatba*)	thievery (*tat'ba*)
thievery (*tatba*)	thievery (*tatba*)	murder (*ub[i]istvo*)	tollbooth of fornication (*mytartsvo bludnoie*)
fornication (*blud*)	murder? (*[ubii]stvo*)	mercilessness (*nemyloserdiie*)	mercilessness (*nemyloserdiie*)
mercilessness and hardness of heart (*nemyloserdiie i zhestokoserdiie*)	mercilessness (*nemyloserdiie*)	and robbery/assault (*i razboi*)	

Source for the Variant Readings of Mshanets' (small caps): Dymytrii, *Ikonopys Zakhidnoi Ukrainy*, 246.
Source for the Tollbooth Sins in the Life of S. Basil the New, First Rus' Redaction: Vilinskii, *Zhitie sv. Vasiliia Novago*, 2:418–29.

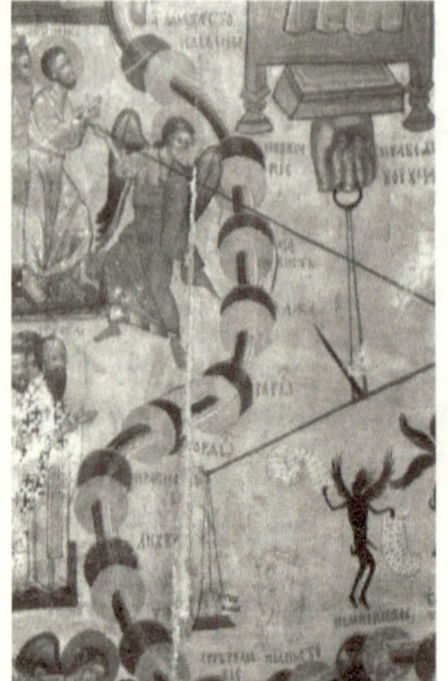

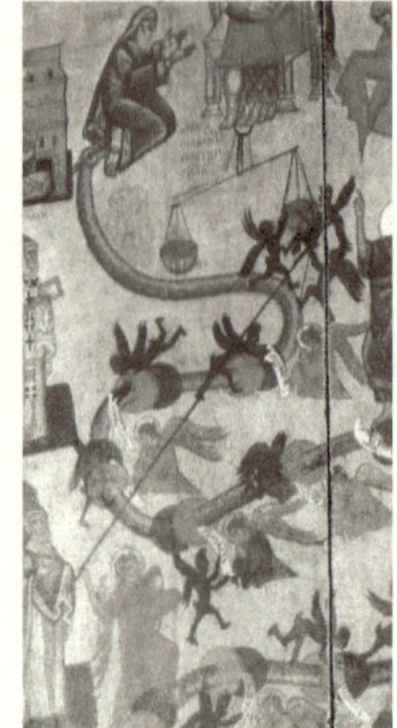

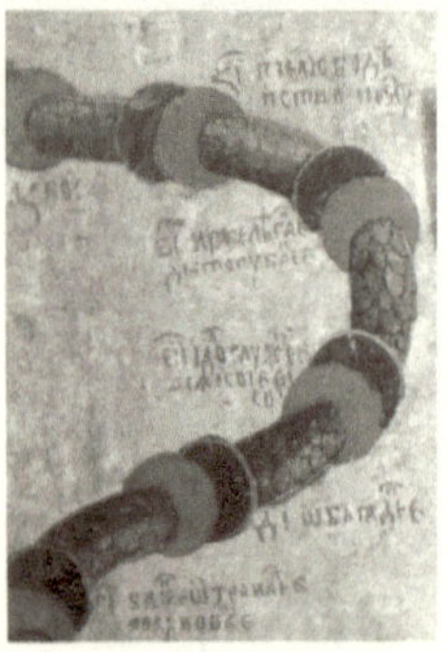

2.27 Serpent and Tollbooths, Vanivka, Polana, Mshanets

role of this text in Rus' iconography of the Last Judgment (fig. 2.27).[45] The addition of the serpent and tollbooths continued the central vertical line of the icon below the hand of God and the scales. Even more than the scales they contribute to creating a dynamic space in the centre, without disturbing the overall symmetry.

Prior to the fifteenth century we know of no Last Judgment image containing a large serpent such as we find in our three Carpathian icons, but of course, since 'the serpent ... serves most frequently of all animals as the personification of evil,'[46] it has a long presence in Christian iconography. Around the same time as the appearance of the 'Sermon on the Heavenly Powers,' St Avraamii of Smolensk (c. 1150–1220) was said to have painted 'two icons: one depicted the Last Judgment and the Second

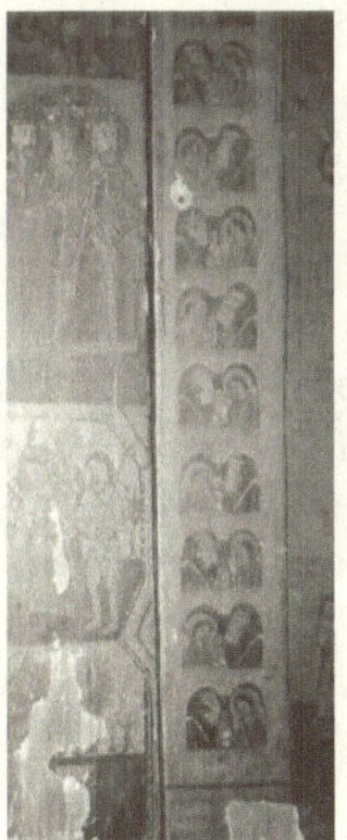

2.28 Tollbooths, Budeşti-Josani

Coming, and the other showed the trial of the aerial tollgates which no one can avoid.'[47] There is, however, no surviving Rus' icon of the Last Judgment from before the fifteenth century, let alone Avraamii's, and none of the frescoes or the manuscript illuminations on this theme contain tollbooths. In the Munich Serbian psalter of the late fourteenth or early fifteenth century there are one or two booths (it is hard to be sure) and two demons, one of whom personifies death; on the right margin, below the booth(s) and the smaller of the demons is inscribed the word 'tollbooth' (*mytarstvo*).[48]

The serpent and tollbooths do appear on the Novgorod-Tretiakov icon and on many Russian icons thereafter. They are absent altogether from the Moldavian frescoes. In fact, tollbooths appear nowhere outside Carpathian and northern Rus' except for those I found on an icon in the village of Budeşti-Josani in Romanian Maramureş. The icon seems to date from the seventeenth century. The tollbooths are placed not on a serpent, but in booths arranged vertically (fig. 2.28). This form of the tollbooths was common at that time also on the Rus' icons of the Carpathians, as we shall see in the next chapter.

8) Moses and the Jews and the Peoples

Typically for the compilatory character of Last Judgment iconography, this element is a combination of two elements that had previously existed separately: (1) Moses and the Jews, and (2) diverse peoples.[49] The first of these elements singled the Jews out for condemnation for refusing to accept Jesus as the Messiah and for crucifying him. The second of these elements expressed the universality of the judgment.

The scriptural origin of Moses and the Jews is John 5:45–6: 'Do not think that I will accuse you to the Father: there is one that accuseth you, even Moses, in whom ye trust. For had ye believed Moses, ye would have believed me: for he wrote of me.' The motif was subsequently developed at length in the Life of St Basil the New, in which the Jews at judgment summon Moses to their defence, only to be told by him that they have ignored his prophecies and crucified the Messiah.[50] The scroll Moses holds in Vanivka reads: 'Wretched, cruel, severe, hateful Jews.' Polana: 'Look wretched Jews.' Mshanets: 'Moses said: Wretched Jews, look whom you have crucified.'

As to the other peoples besides the Jews, their presence is derived from the key Gospel passage, the Gospel of Meatfare Sunday: 'When the Son of man shall come in his glory, and all the holy angels with him, then shall he sit upon the throne of his glory: And before him shall be gathered all nations' (Mt 25:31–2). But this in turn probably derives from the book of Daniel: 'I saw in a dream at night, and, behold, one like the Son of man came with the clouds of heaven ... And there was given him dominion, and honour, and a kingdom, that all people, tribes, and tongues (*liudiie, plemena, iazytsy*) shall labour for him' (Dn 7:13–14).[51] The formula 'all people ... ' appears also elsewhere in Daniel (3:29, 5:19). The Life of St Basil the New reiterated the message of these passages: at the final judgment all mankind will appear divided by ethnos (*rod*), tongue (*iazyk*), and nation (*narod*).[52] The peoples in the three Carpathian icons are identified by inscriptions. In Vanivka they are Jews, Greeks, Poles, Tatars, Moors, Turks, Rus', and Germans. In Polana they are the same with a minor difference in order: Jews, Greeks, Poles, Germans, Tatars, Moors, Turks, and Rus'. In Mshanets they are Jews, Greeks, Turks, Tatars, Armenians, Moors, Rus', and Germans (fig. 2.29).

It is probable that Jews were depicted in Byzantine iconography of the Last Judgment, but they were not so identified in the inscriptions.[53] Moses, labelled, and the Jews, unlabelled, can be found in a fresco from the mid-1450s in the Moldavian Church of the Ascension in Luzhany, near Chernivtsi, on the fringes of Carpathian Rus' (fig. 2.30). (This church may have been painted by Rus' artists.)[54] Jews, identified by insciption but without Moses, are also depicted on their way to hell in an illumination of the Last Judgment in the Kyivan psalter of 1397.[55]

Moses appears with Jews, but again without inscriptions, in the early fourteenth-century frescoes of the Last Judgment in the Snetogorsk

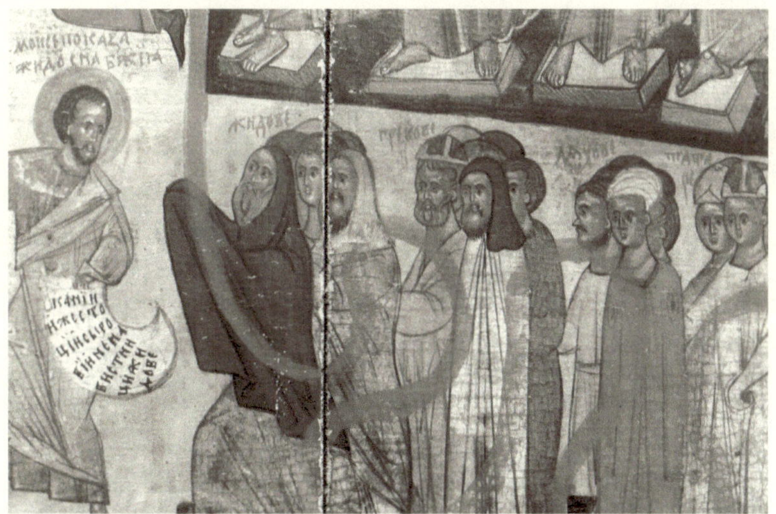

2.29 Moses, Jews, Greeks, Poles, and Tatars, Vanivka

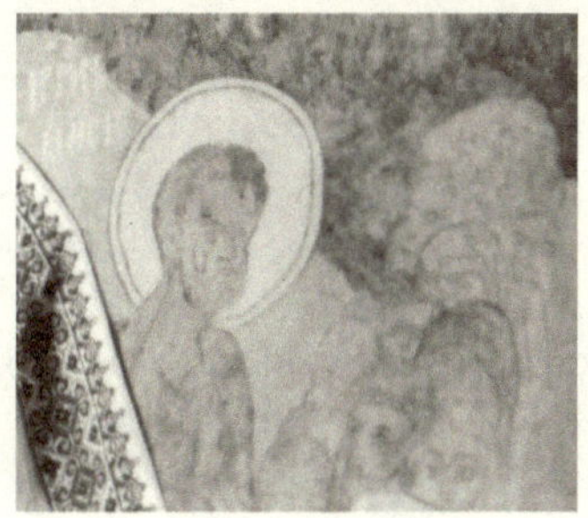

2.30 Moses and Jews, Luzhany, 1453–9

Monastery in Pskov.[56] The composition of this element looks remarkably like the scene of Moses and the Jews when this became part of the combined scene of Moses and the peoples in the fifteenth century. With reference to this particular element, the Snetogorsk fresco can be considered a direct compositional ancestor of the fifteenth-century icons (fig. 2.31).

None of the texts identified above contain phrases closely related to any of the texts found on Moses' scroll in the fifteenth-century Carpathian icons. There is one Greek fresco of the Last Judgment, in the monastery on the island of Salamine, that is closer to the Moses-and-Jews element as it appears in the Carpathian icons. In fact, Moses even holds a scroll with a similar text: 'This is he whom you have crucified.' However, it was

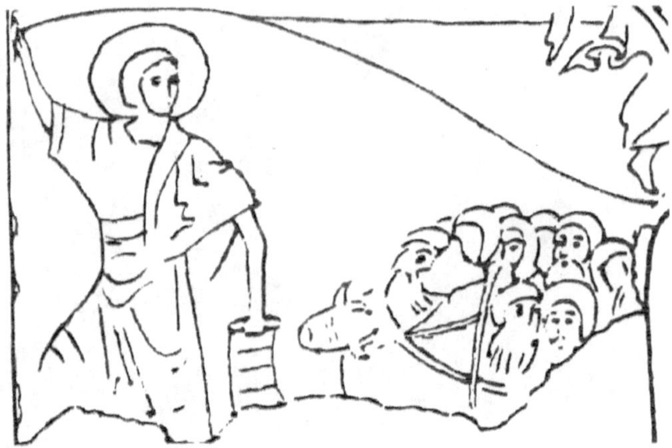

2.31 Moses and Jews, Snetogorsk Monastery, early fourteenth century. Source: Vladimir Sarab'ianov, '"Strashnyi Sud" v rospisiakh sobora Snetogorskogo monastyria v Pskove i ego istoricheskaia osnova,' *Problemy na izkustvoto* 30, no. 2 (1996): 25.

painted in 1735 and, at this late date, testifies to the influence of Russian iconography rather than to the re-emergence of a lost Greek tradition.[57]

Troupes of differently costumed peoples, expressing universalism and diversity, figured in Byzantine icons of the Pentecost in the eleventh and twelfth centuries and in icons of the Tower of Babel,[58] but not in Byzantine icons of the Last Judgment. The earliest surviving depiction of the peoples in a Last Judgment icon is in the Moscow Dormition from the fifteenth century. Importantly, it does not also depict Moses and the Jews, thus confirming that 'the peoples' had existed as a separate element in Last Judgment iconography in northern Rus' before it was combined with Moses and the Jews.[59]

I believe that the reason for the combination was primarily compositional. The two elements could be put together because both were inspired by the same text, the Life of St Basil the New, which had also inspired the new dynamic centre of the icon with the serpent and tollbooths. Also, both elements had a certain commonality in that the Jews were a people as well as the others. These factors permitted the combination, but what made it so desirable was that it established a better balance between the left and right flanks of the icon. What had been gained was a symmetrical counterpart on the left to the choirs of the saints on the right. In many later Carpathian icons there would be exactly as many rows of people on the left as there were choirs of saints on the right. This combination would later, as we shall see in the next chapter, confuse the iconographers who followed, because it did not visually mark the difference between a people that was condemned to eternal damnation (the Jews) and other peoples who were simply approaching judgment.

The combined Moses-Jews-peoples element can be found also in the fifteenth-century Novgorod-Tretiakov icon. Aside from the Jews, the other peoples cannot be identified here with certainty, since the inscriptions are faded.[60] Later Russian icons also depicted the combined element. The peoples in the Russian icons of the sixteenth century and later include some of the same as in the Carpathian icons, such as Jews, Turks, Rus', Poles, and Germans, but also some different ones, such as Lithuanians, Persians, and Indians.[61]

It is possible that the element appeared in the Last Judgment fresco at Wawel Castle, which was destroyed, but has recently been undergoing restoration.[62] These frescoes were completed in 1470 and probably painted by artists from Pskov.[63]

Moses and the Jews and the other peoples first appear in the Moldavian frescoes in 1532 (Probota) and remain thereafter. The Moldavian version of the element differs from the Carpathian and northern Rus' versions in that it never includes Greeks or Rus' or any other Orthodox people. Moses and the peoples also appear in the eighteenth-century frescoes of Romanian Maramureş and in other Romanian images of the Last Judgment. The combined element was unknown among the Greeks and South Slavs.

9) The Prophet Daniel

Since so much of the Last Judgment iconography is informed by chapter 7 of the book of Daniel, it is not surprising to find that prophet depicted in the icon. In the Carpathian icons he is placed on the left of the circle in which the resurrection of the dead is taking place. At the resurrection scene are four angels trumpeting. They are probably associated with 'the four winds of the heaven' creating turmoil 'upon the great sea' (Dn 7:2). The angels in Vanivka, according to the inscriptions, blow from the north, south, east, and west. The sea, of course, is depicted within the resurrection scene. Daniel is shown accompanied by an angel, certainly Gabriel, who took on the appearance of a man and helped him understand his visions (Dn 8:15–16). The inscription is damaged, but what can be deciphered with certainty reads: 'The angel of the Lord reveals to

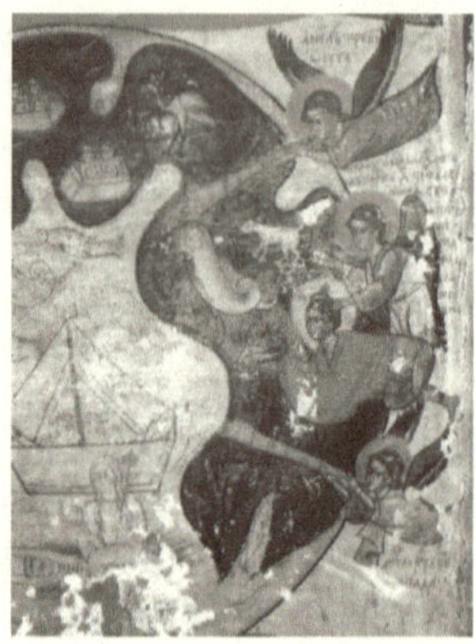

2.32 Daniel, Vanivka

Daniel the prophet the four kingdoms of the earth, the beast and birds ...' We will discuss Daniel's vision of the four beasts/kingdoms separately, after we finish with the examination of the depiction of Daniel the prophet with an angel. The inscription on Mshanets is also largely illegible, but it opens with the words: 'I, Daniel, saw a vision ...' (fig. 2.32).

As far as composition is concerned, Daniel does not add anything to the Carpathian icons. The element is placed tight against the circle in which the resurrection of the dead takes place. In the Novgorod-Tretiakov icon, however, the Daniel scene does balance the composition. Here there are two circles: paradise on the right and the resurrection, earth, and sea on the left. Just to the lower right of the paradise circle are the three Old Testament patriarchs of the bosom of Abraham. Daniel and the angel balance them perfectly to the lower left of the resurrection.

The figures of Daniel and the angel first appeared in the Snetogorsk frescoes of 1313.[64] They are absent from Moscow Dormition, but present in Novgorod-Tretiakov. They remained a regular feature of Russian Last Judgment iconography,[65] but they are not to be found on Moldavian frescoes or in Maramureş.

10) The Four Beasts/Kingdoms

The four beasts identified with evil kingdoms have their origin in Daniel. According to the biblical narrative, Daniel saw four great beasts: one like a lion with an eagle's wings, another like a bear, another like a four-headed leopard that had on its back the wings of a fowl, and a ten-horned

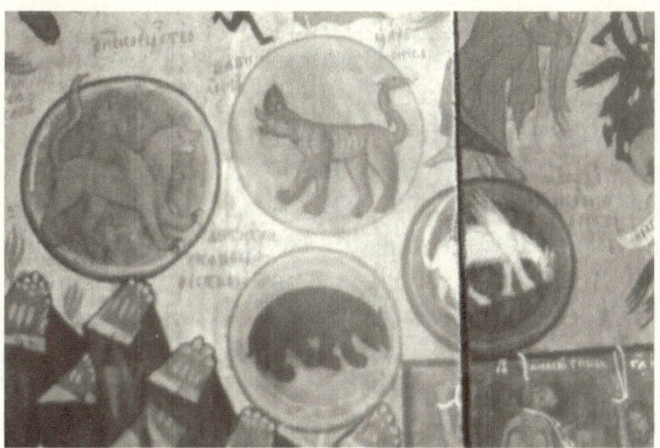

2.33 The Four Beasts/Kingdoms, Mshanets

monster. He learned that the four beasts are four kings that shall arise upon the earth (Dn 7:3–7, 17). In a later vision he saw a two-horned ram and a he-goat with one horn between his eyes. The angel Gabriel later explained to him that the two horns on the ram were the kings of Media and Persia, while the horn on the goat was the king of Grecia. After the latter horn was broken, four new ones appeared that represented four kingdoms. In the last days, one of the kings will be evil and destroy the mighty and the holy people (Dn 8:3–6, 20–4). These obscure passages became the object of interpretation and prophecy in the Byzantine empire.[66] Interpretations of the meaning of the four beasts circulated also in Rus'.[67]

On Vanivka, the inscriptions of only three kingdoms are still visible: 'the kingdom of the anti-Christ' over a bear, 'the Babylonian kingdom' over a partly destroyed beast, and 'Macedonian kingdom' over a completely destroyed beast. If we supplement this with the Lukov-Venecia icon we learn that the fourth kingdom was 'the Roman kingdom,' with the inscription over a brown winged beast. Babylonia was represented by a beast with no wings and two heads, one of them human, and Macedonia by a white winged beast. Polana identifies 'the Roman kingdom of the anti-Christ' with a bear, the Persian kingdom with a winged unicorn, and the Babylonian kingdom with the two-headed, unwinged beast; the inscription on the fourth, also unwinged beast is largely erased, but it may indicate Macedonia. On Mshanets the four beasts appear in medallions. The bear is the kingdom of the Antichrist, the Roman empire is a brown winged beast, Macedonia a white winged beast, and Babylonia the two-headed, unwinged beast (fig. 2.33).

The beasts representing the evil kingdoms can be found in tenth- and eleventh-century Greek manuscript illuminations as well as in a Serbian fresco from the 1250s, but they first became a part of Last Judgment iconography in the early fourteenth-century frescoes of the Snetogorsk Monastery in Pskov. Three of the kingdoms are legible: a winged lion is the Persian kingdom; a bear, the Greek kingdom; and a horned beast, the kingdom of the Antichrist. In the fresco in the Dormition Church in Vladimir (1408–10), a winged lion represented the Roman empire; a bear, Babylonia; a leopard, Macedonia; and a seven-horned beast with a human head on one of its horns, the kingdom of the Antichrist.[68] The four beasts are absent in Moscow Dormition, but present in the Novgorod-Tretiakov icon. From then on, the beasts/kingdoms are included in Russian iconography of the Last Judgment,[69] but they are found nowhere else in Orthodox Last Judgment iconography outside Rus'.

The beasts/kingdoms do not play a strong role in the Carpathian composition, only filling in the space around the lower parts of the serpent. In Novgorod-Tretiakov, the beasts in a circle play a somewhat more effective role, serving to balance the angel on their left.

11) Monks Flying into Paradise

I link this image ultimately with verses in the vespers for two or more saintly monks:[70] 'Now you live rejoicing in the heavenly habitations, where the angels celebrate,'[71] and 'You have achieved the ranks of angels.'[72] More proximately, however, the element may owe its presence in the icon to a reworking of one of the most popular apocrypha in Rus', 'The Journey of the Mother of God among the Torments.'[73] In 1743–52, an Orthodox priest in Moldavia, Father Illia Yaremetsky-Bilakhovych compiled a manuscript collection of apocrypha in Slavonic that he had found in the monastery of Putna and in parishes in the region.[74] One of the stories in the collection was a reworking of the 'Journey.' 'The Mother of God,' it related, 'saw souls flying through the purgatorial fiery river.' Her guide on the journey, the Archangel Michael explained: 'Those are the souls of monks, monks who have received the great schema (*skhymnytsi*), hieromonks, priests, who on earth are called angels, and holy laymen, who truly in this world in the monastic order did please the Lord God by fasting, prayers, purity, poverty, obedience, and other monastic deeds.'[75] Unfortunately, it is not possible to date this particular reworking. The oldest Slavonic version of the 'Journey,' dating to the twelfth century, does not contain the passage cited, but there is another passage in it (actually

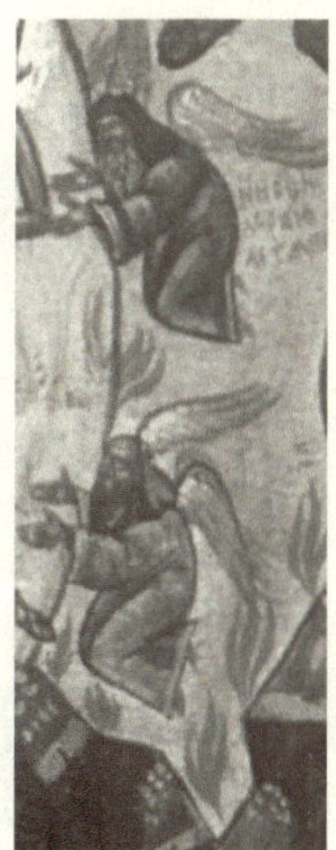

2.34 Monks Flying into Paradise, Mshanets. Photo: Orest Krukovsky.

in a reconstruction of it) that might have provided the impetus for the later elaboration: a description of the torment of those unworthy of 'the order of angels and of apostles,' namely 'patriarchs and bishops' who lacked sanctity.[76] The 'Journey' was frequently recopied and reworked in Russia and Ukraine; in Ukraine, in particular, it became a popular vehicle for speculation about the torments of hell and life beyond the grave.

Levon Nersesian connects the appearance of this element with debates in late fifteenth-century Muscovy about eschatological questions. Some were trying to divine the precise date of the second coming. Others said that this attempt at precision was foolish and, citing a late eleventh-century work known as the *Dioptra,* they argued that one had to wait until the heavens were filled before the world would end. Nesersian sees the emptying of heaven in the fall of the rebel angels, thus creating the necessity for it to be refilled with the righteous, namely the monks ascending into heaven.[77]

The element first appeared in the fifteenth century.[78] It did not appear in all three of the earliest Carpathian icons, only in the Mshanets icon (fig. 2.34). The inscription near the winged monks on the Mshanets icon reads: 'Monks are flying to paradise.' The element continued to appear in many later Carpathian Last Judgment icons. The element is also in the Novgorod-Tretiakov (fig. 2.35). A modified version of this element continued to survive in Russian iconography. This motif is not known outside

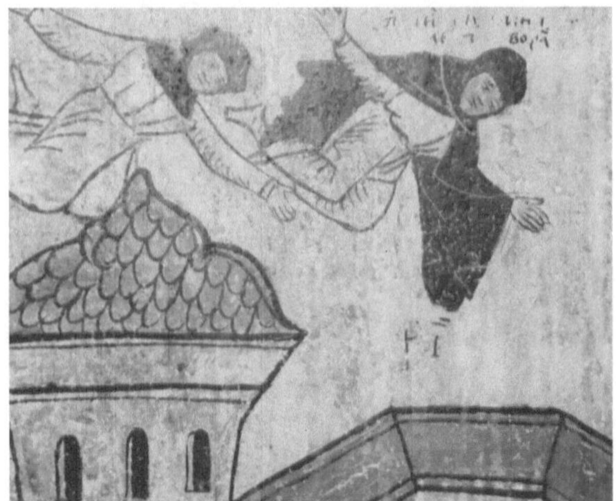

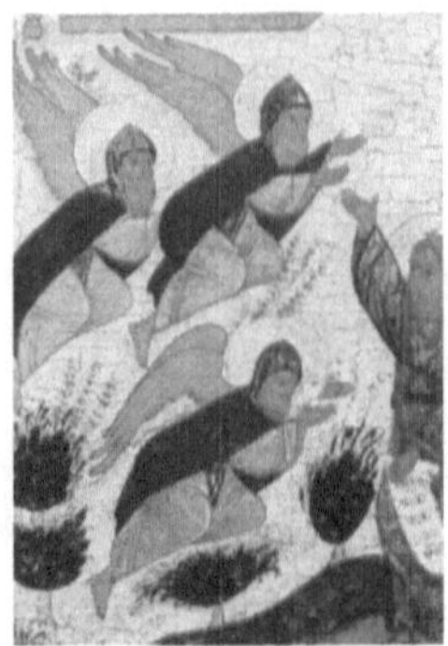

2.35 Monks Flying into Paradise, Tiushka, seventeenth century, and Novgorod-Tretiakov. Source of Novgorod-Tretiakov: Kurt Weitzmann et al., *The Icon* (New York: Dorset Press, 1987), 280.

Carpathian and northern Rus'. The flying monks do not contribute much to the composition in Mshanets but, again, they do contribute to the symmetry in Novgorod-Tretiakov.

12) Death

There may be no textual source for the appearance of a personification of Death on Carpathian Last Judgment icons. It is also possible, however, that it derives from a line in the 'Sermon on the Exit of the Soul' of Cyril the Philosopher: 'And then death appears.'[79] This sermon is not to be confused with the similarly titled work attributed to Cyril of Alexandria. It is instead a work composed somewhere in Rus' and known in numerous manuscripts from Russia and Ukraine from the sixteenth century on. Perhaps it was already being circulated when Mshanets was painted. The 'Sermon' made mention of two other elements that could be found in the first Carpathian elaboration: the heavenly Jerusalem and twenty tollbooths. Perhaps it inspired an iconographer to include Death in his icon. Whether there was a textual source or not, the figure of Death became standard in Carpathian icons after Mshanets; the figure is absent in Vanivka and Polana (fig. 2.36). The inscription around death in Mshanets

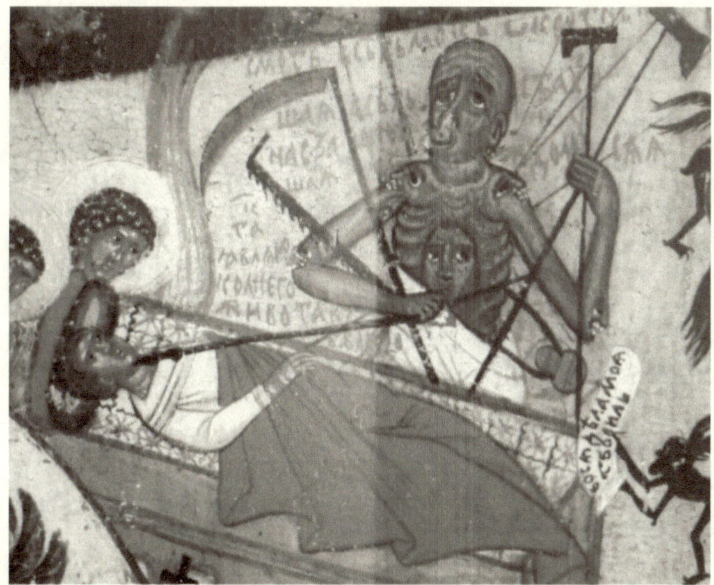

2.36 Death, Mshanets

reads: 'Death is the cruellest of all tortures, the most terrible of all fears, I appear thus to each person when I deprive him of his life.' In the Slavonic this rhymes:

Smert' vsikh muk okrutniishaia,
vsikh strakhov naistrashniishaia,
kozhdomu sia ia tak iavliaiu
koly ieho zhyvota izabavliaiu.

I have been unable to identify a source for this verse, and I suspect it lies outside the Byzantine and post-Byzantine corpus.

Personifications of death were not unknown in late and post-Byzantine art,[80] but I agree with Janina Kłosińska and Lilya Berezhnaya that the portrayal of Death in Mshanets and other Carpathian icons, with his tools and the many faces on his body, borrows from Western models.[81] The instruments that Death holds in Mshanets are a lance, a saw, a scythe, two axes, and an hourglass. There is a related Greek image, but it is late and probably itself reflects Western influence: a mural in the Dionysiou Monastery on Mount Athos, dated to 1603, depicts Death as a black

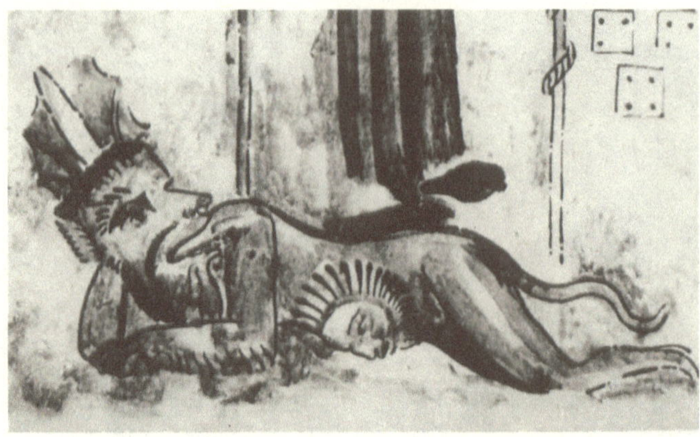

2.37 Gothic Satan with a Face on His Belly, Królewiec, eastern Pomerania, 1340–60. Source: Jerzy Domasłowski et al., *Malarstwo gotyckie na Pomorzu Wschodnim* (Warsaw and Poznań: Państwowe Wydawnictwo Naukowe, 1990), pl. 5.

figure, a skeleton, with a bow and arrow in his left hand and a scythe in his right; on his side he carries a whetstone and a dagger.[82] I should note too that a twelfth-century Byzantine sermon, which was known in Slavonic translation since the fourteenth century and was particularly popular in Rus' in the late sixteenth and seventeenth centuries, spoke of 'death's scythe' (*kosa smertnaia*).[83] Still, I do not doubt that the manner of painting Death in the Carpathian icons was inspired by Western depictions of Death and devils rather than by any Byzantine or post-Byzantine source (fig. 2.37).

The figure of Death does not appear in the Russian iconography of the Last Judgment at all, although some personifications of death appear in other Russian icons.[84] Nor does Death appear in the Moldavian frescoes or Greek and South Slavic images of the Last Judgment. The only place outside of Ukrainian Carpathian icons where I have found Death is, not surprisingly, in Budeşti-Josani. Here Death rides a donkey, a form that can also be found in three seventeenth-century Ukrainian Carpathian icons.[85] The death scene in Mshanets does not seem to improve the composition.

13) The Almsgiving Fornicator

The figure of the almsgiving fornicator (*mylostyvyi bludnyk*) is positioned between paradise and hell. This is a man who gave alms, but continued

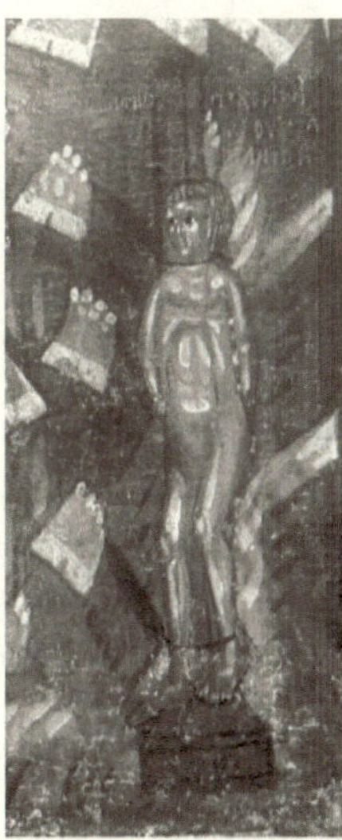

2.38 Almsgiving Fornicator, Mshanets. Photo: Orest Krukovsky.

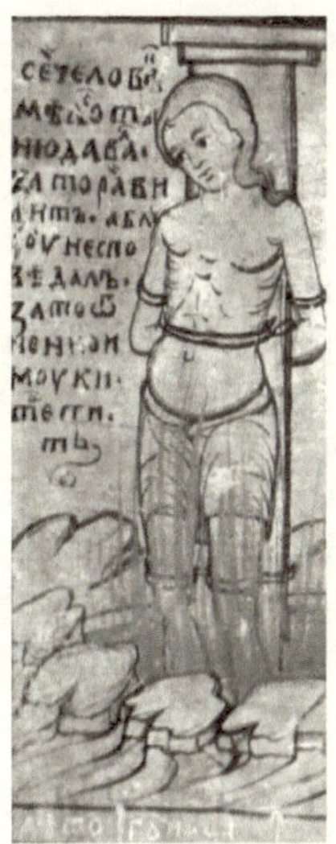

2.39 Almsgiving Fornicator, Bahnovate, second third of sixteenth century

to engage in fornication; thus in the afterlife he could see paradise, but felt the torments of hell. He is almost always accompanied by a text explaining his situation. The figure and its inscription have been destroyed in Vanivka, but the inscription in Lukov-Venecia reads: 'A man who does much almsgiving, but he does not abandon his fornication; he sees paradise, but bears torment.' The inscription in Polana is partly illegible, but it begins: 'A man was giving alms ...' Mshanets reads: 'This man performed almsgiving, he did not give up fornication' (fig. 2.38). The tale ultimately derives from a Byzantine chronograph, but it was also a popular inclusion in West Ukrainian miscellanies in the sixteenth century.[86]

The almsgiving fornicator first appeared in the fifteenth century, in our three Carpathian icons and in Novgorod-Tretiakov. For centuries later in both Ukrainian Carpathian and Russian iconography, he remained tied to a pillar between hell and paradise (fig. 2.38). The only place he can be found outside these two iconographies is in Budeşti-Josani.

In Mshanets the fornicator is right in the centre of the icon at the bottom, renewing the vertical line that started with the Son of man, throne, and hand of God and that was interrupted by the serpent. In the other three icons the figure is off to one side or the other and thus does not enhance the composition.

14) The New Hell

The presentation will be clearer if we begin with a description of the new hell as it appears in the oldest Carpathian icons. The new hell in Vanivka has not survived, so we have to examine Lukov-Venecia instead. In the upper right corner a sinner is being hung by the neck and feet in a distorted position. The inscription above him reads 'accuser' (*sok*). Beneath him is a woman, an infanticide. She is covered with serpents who suck her breasts. The inscription above her reads: 'Woe to this woman who spoils the fruit of her womb, for this reason the serpents drink her.' Below her a devil is sitting astride a woman and forcing a funnel into her mouth. 'And look,' says the inscription, 'a devil feeds a sorceress.' Hanging upside down above her, at the top of hell, is a figure whose inscription has been mostly destroyed (all that remains legible is the suffix *nyk*). To the left of him, hanging horizontally, is a thief. Below him is a murderer, and below him is one person described as 'an envious man and a glutton.' Below him, lying on the floor of hell, is a tavernkeeper. To his left a devil is sitting astride two figures and pouring the contents of a pitcher into one of their mouths. The inscription reads: 'A devil is giving drink to drunkards.' In this area, appropriately, is a tavernmaid, but she is fully dressed,[87] unlike the other figures in hell, and I will deal with her separately in the next section. Directly above her is a naked priest, with a head covering and a devil riding on his back, apparently slicing him with a blade. The inscription reads: 'O woe to such a priest who does not himself act according to the law and does not teach his people' (fig. 2.40).

Polana's hell has a robber (*razboinyk*) hanging upside down in the upper right corner. Below him is another woman with serpents attached to both of her breasts. She is identified as a sorceress. To her left squats a 'usurer (*rizoimets*) and lover of silver.' Above him hangs an envious man, above him a murderer, and above him, in a contorted position and with his tongue sticking out, a slanderer. In the upper left corner hangs a 'thief and fornicator.' Below him again is the fully clothed tavernmaid. Below her is one figure who is identified as 'a tavernkeeper and all drunkards' (fig. 2.41).

Mshanets again has a robber hanging over a sorceress tormented by serpents. And, also as in Polana, there is a usurer and lover of silver to her left and an envious man hanging above him. At the top is an accuser (*sok*) and slanderer, this time hanging by his tongue. To his left is a thief and fornicator, below him a murderer, then the tavernmaid, and near her a drunk (fig. 2.42).

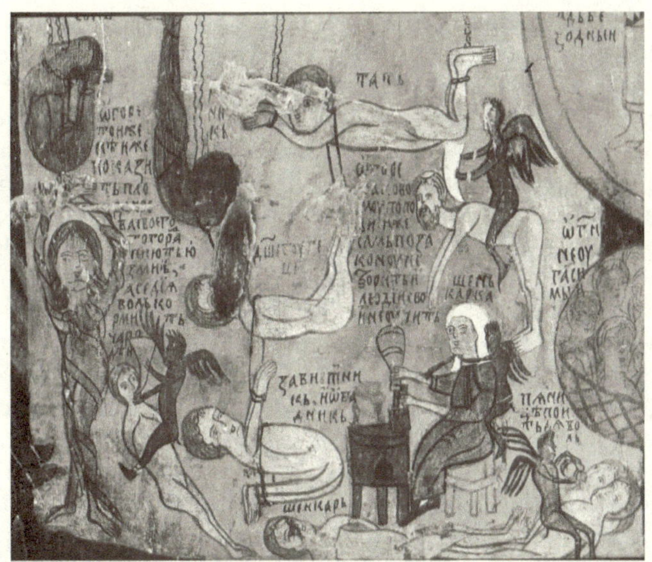

2.40 The New Hell, Lukov-Venecia. Source: Štefan Tkáč, *Ikony zo 16.–19. storočia na severovýchodnom Slovensku* (Bratislava: Tatran, 1982), 138, pl. 66.

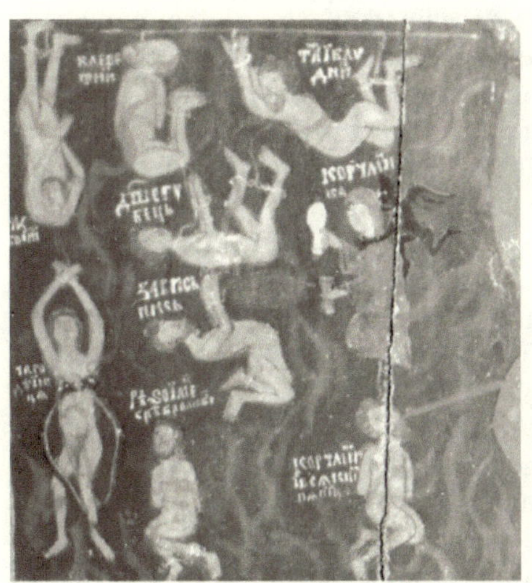

2.41 The New Hell, Polana

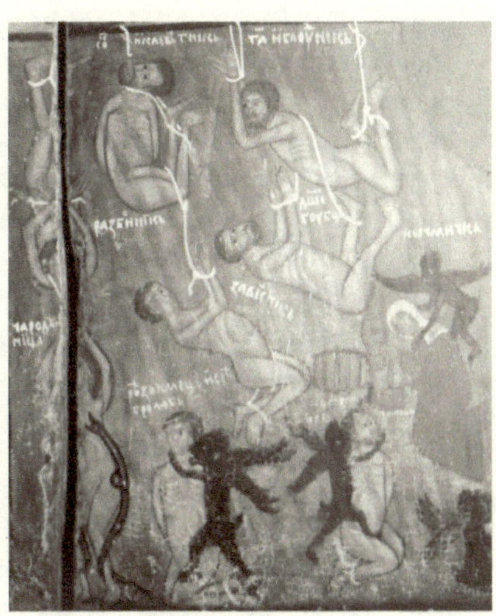

2.42 The New Hell, Mshanets

The new hell in these three icons is rather simple compared to the new hells that will be painted later with many more and more diversified sinners. A perhaps remote textual origin is the 'The Journey of the Mother of God among the Torments.' In this apocryphal text there is a differentiation of sinners and their punishments. Specific mention is made of slanderers hanging by their tongues,[88] women tormented by serpents,[89] and priests who do not perform the will of God.[90] On the other hand, the 'Journey' mentions numerous, more exotic damned that do not figure in our three icons, including those cursed by their parents, cannibals,[91] those who broke an oath made on the cross, and priests who dropped some crumbs of communion bread. Moreover, the women with serpents sucking their breasts in our icons are sorceresses and an infanticide, while in the 'Journey' the women being tormented by serpents are gossips or priests' widows who remarried, and nothing in the text specifically puts the serpents on the women's breasts. (Another apocryphal text, the Apocalypse of Paul, does relate that dragons and serpents tormented infanticides.)[92] All the sinners in the early Carpathian icons, with the exception of the bad priest, committed sins that are identified in the tollbooths, thus connecting the depiction ultimately with the Life of St Basil the New or 'The Sermon on the Heavenly Powers.'

I do not think, however, that we need to posit a particular text as the source of the new hell. It could have developed on a purely iconographical, visual level. Greek and South Slavic depictions of the Last Judgment began to differentiate sinners and their punishments already in the twelfth century.[93] Naked sinners with differentiated punishments can be seen in the Dečani frescoes of 1327–48.[94] The motif of a serpent sucking the breast of a naked female figure is on a fresco painted before 1040 in St Stephan's in Kastoria.[95] A woman with two serpents on her breasts and other women tortured by serpents can also be found in a Cappadocian image from the ninth or tenth century (Yilanli Kilissé).[96] The 'femme au serpents' was also known in Western art from the eleventh century on.[97]

All that said, there is nothing quite like the Carpathian new, square space for hell in other Orthodox iconography. There are, however, clear Gothic models for this (figs 2.43 and 2.44).

In composition, the new hell extends the territory of the lake of Gehenna and traditional torments, providing balance to the also extensive territory of paradise at the bottom of the icon. In our three icons, however, the territory of hell now takes over more than half of the bottom of the icon, making all the icons somewhat out of balance (Lukov-Venecia the most, Mshanets the least).

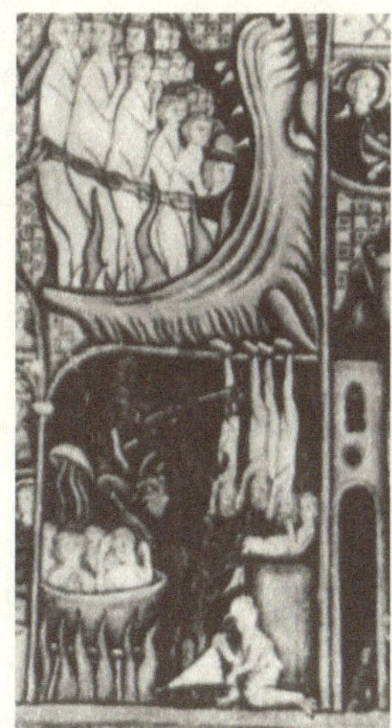

2.43 Scenes from the Apocalypse with a Place Like the 'New Hell,' manuscript from eastern Pomerania, mid-fourteenth century. Source: Jerzy Domasłowski et al., *Malarstwo gotyckie na Pomorzu Wschodnim* (Warsaw and Poznań: Państwowe Wydawnictwo Naukowe, 1990), pl. 110.

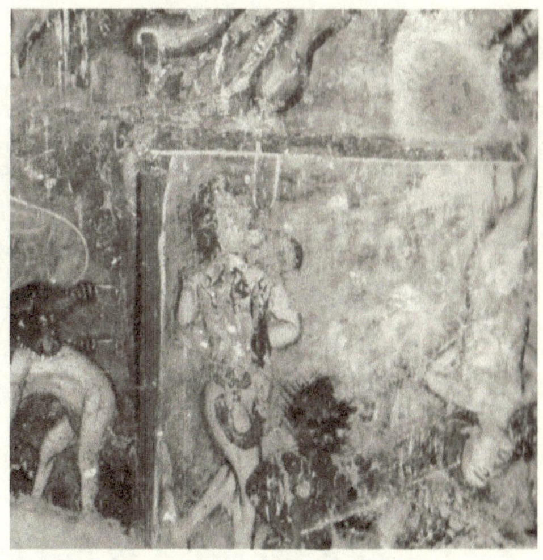

2.44 Last Judgment Detail with a Place Like the 'New Hell,' Svinica, southeastern Slovakia, before the middle of the fourteenth century. Source: Vlasta Dvořáková et al., *Středkověká ná stěnná malba na Slovensku*, photographs by Alexandr Paul st. (Prague and Bratislava: Odeon, Tatran, 1978), pl. 40.

15) The Tavernmaid

There is no text that explains the presence of the tavernmaid in the Last Judgment icons. But there is an iconographic source: Gothic, Roman Catholic Last Judgments. The resemblance between the tavernmaid in the fifteenth-century Carpathian icons and the tavernmaid in a fourteenth-century Silesian fresco leaves no room for doubt. The Silesian Last Judgment was painted in the third quarter of the fourteenth century[98] in Strzelce pod Sobótką, a German settlement about fifty kilometres west of Wrocław (fig. 2.45). As in our early Carpathian icons, the tavernmaid is positioned on the left of hell, a devil is at her back, she has a horizontal barrel in front of her (Mshanets and Polana), and she holds a pitcher in her hand. The differences between the Carpathian image and

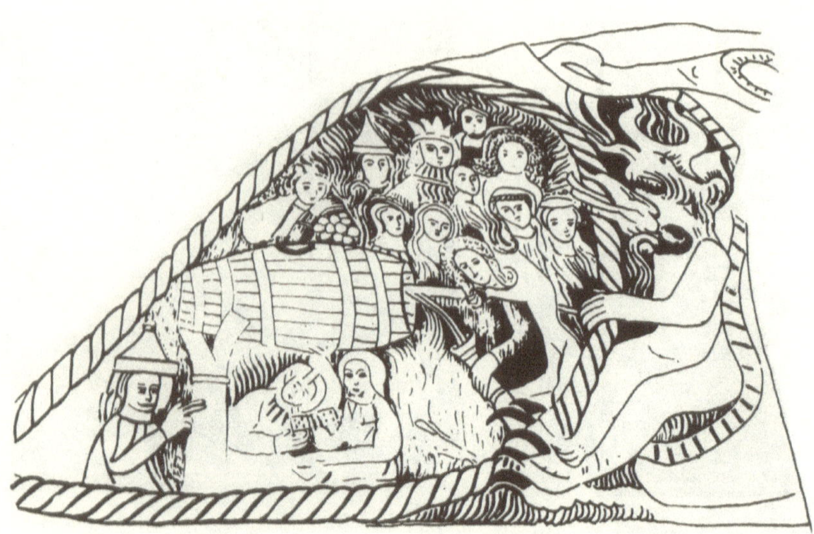

2.45 Hell with Tavernmaid, Strzelce pod Sobótką. Source: Klára Benešková, ed., *King John of Luxembourg (1296–1346) and the Art of His Era* (Prague: Koniasch Latin Press, 1998), pl. 166.

the Silesian image are minor: the Silesian tavernmaid is not wearing a kerchief (although her hair is close in shape to the kerchief in the Carpathian icons), and the Carpathian tavernmaids are pouring beer from a jug into a cup, while the Silesian tavernmaid is filling her jug from the barrel. If the artist who first introduced the tavernmaid into the Carpathian icons did not see this particular Silesian fresco, then he saw something like it. As Anna Orosz has noted, 'Iconographic motifs were spread in the early Middle Ages by wandering monks; their source was also illuminated codices; and perhaps there were some books in which they were collected, something like guides for painters and carvers. Testifying in favour of this is the extraordinary similarity of motifs repeated sometimes in localities very distant from one another.'[99] The borrowing explains why the figure of the tavernmaid is the only clothed figure in the new hell – she was taken as she was from a Western, not a Byzantine or post-Byzantine model.

It is interesting to note, too, how similar are the tavernkeepers in the Carpathian icons, especially in the Polana and Mshanets icons, which are the only ones actually painted in the fifteenth century (the Lukov-Venecia icon, though based on the fifteenth-century Vanivka icon, was painted somewhat later). All three have a similar-looking jug in the same position,

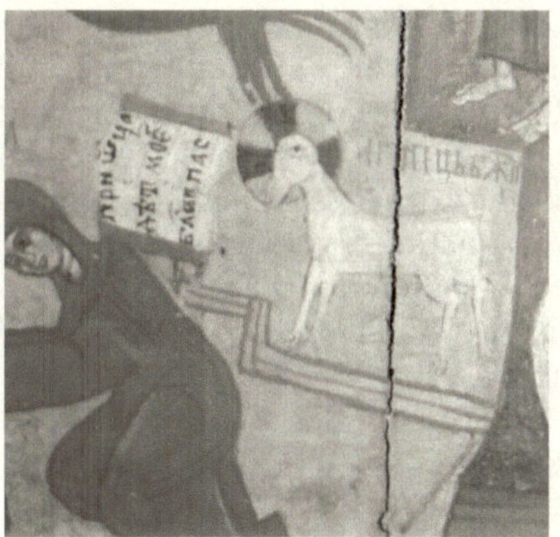

2.46 The Lamb, Polana

and Polana and Mshanets have the tavernmaid kneeling in the same position before the barrel. All three icons label the tavernmaid as such (*shen'karka* in Lukov-Venecia and *korchmychka* in Polana and Mshanets). This element is unique to the Ukrainian Carpathian icons; it is found nowhere else in the post-Byzantine iconography of the Last Judgment.

The compositional impact of the tavernmaid is minimal: she is one of the figures arranged within the new hell.

16) The Lamb

The Polana icon has a lamb next to an open Gospel Book near the throne behind Eve (fig. 2.46). The Gospel Book is open, as was mentioned earlier, to Matthew 25:34. The lamb is identified with Christ because an inscription tells us he is the Lamb of God. This is what John the Baptist called Jesus in the Gospel of John (Jn 1:29, 36). The lamb is also clearly the lamb of Revelation. Although the lamb of Revelation is described as slain and having seven horns and seven eyes (Rv 5:6), we have seen above in the case of the four evil beasts/kingdoms that the complicated animals of visions are simplified in these paintings. But we can be sure this is the lamb of Revelation because he is bringing the Gospel Book. 'And he came and took the book out of the right hand of him that sat upon the throne' (Rv 5:7). There is a reference later in Revelation to 'the Lamb's book of life' (Rv 21:27). A striking feature of the Polana lamb is that he is wearing a halo with a cross. As Janina Kłosińska has pointed out, the lamb with this halo is inspired by Western models and unknown in the iconography of the Eastern church.[100] It is well known in Gothic art.

The lamb appears on Vilshanytsia, painted in the early sixteenth century. Here the lamb is on the throne, just to the left of the drapery. The lamb is small and is wearing no halo. A similar lamb, standing in the middle of the throne, can be found in Volosianka, painted in the seventeenth century. Outside Carpathian iconography a lamb near the throne does not appear in Orthodox Last Judgment images.

The addition of the lamb to Polana does not at all enhance the composition. Instead it throws off the balance between Adam and Eve on either side of the throne.

Results of the Analysis

The detailed analysis of the elements of the three earliest Carpathian icons of the Last Judgment allows us to draw conclusions that contribute towards an explanation of their origins.

1 The model for the first Carpathian elaboration was a type of icon of the Last Judgment that originated in northern Rus' (Novgorod, Pskov).[101]

Several of the elements were first worked out in northern Rus' frescoes before they appeared on Last Judgment icons in the fifteenth century: the hand of God (Dormition Church Vladimir, 1408), the vision of Daniel (Snetogorsk, early fourteenth century), and the four beasts/kingdoms (also Snetogorsk). The peoples, representing the idea of the universality of the judgment, existed as a separate element in the Moscow Dormition icon before it was combined with Moses and the Jews in the Carpathian icons and Novgorod-Tretiakov. Moreover, the form of the Moses and peoples element was first crystallized in the Snetogorsk fresco. To my mind, these facts constitute incontrovertible evidence that the basic prototype of the Carpathian icon arose in northern Rus', not in the Carpathian region itself, nor in some third centre that influenced both Carpathian and northern Rus' art.

There is also circumstantial evidence for this conclusion. An icon similar to Novogorod-Tretiakov was the prototype. Almost all the compositional elements work better in Novgorod-Tretiakov than in the Carpathian icons. Novgorod-Tretiakov is both more symmetrical and less elaborated. The Carpathian icons were elaborated by the accretion of elements, which did not always work as well compositionally as the sparer original model. That Novgorod-Tretiakov was not the exact model for the Carpathian icons is indicated by the former's inclusion of the Ancient of Days motif, which only entered Carpathian Last Judgment iconography in the sixteenth century. The inclusion of this motif in Novgorod-Tretiakov may have displaced the scroll to the left upper corner; in Carpathian icons, the scroll is at the top centre of the icon.[102]

Two major features of both the first Carpathian elaboration and Novgorod-Tretiakov and subsequent Russian iconography derive from the Life of St Basil the New – the tollbooths on the serpent dominating the centre and the row of figures on the left depicting Moses, the Jews, and other peoples. This was a work better known in the north than in the south of Rus'. The great student of the Life and its impact on Rus', S.G. Vilinskii, counted seventy-six surviving manuscripts; seventy-three of these were preserved in Russia proper, only three on the territory of Ukraine.[103]

The link between Carpathian and northern Rus' iconography is not limited to the Last Judgment. There are also well documented connections between Carpathian and northern Rus' icons of 'the Saviour among the powers,' also known as 'the Saviour in glory.'[104] Northern Rus' icons of the Deposition from the cross and the Resurrection (descent into Hades) are also similar to the scenes that appear in early Ukrainian icons of the Passion.[105]

2 There are undeniable borrowings from Western, Gothic sacral art in the Carpathian elaboration.

The tavernmaid is copied from a Western model, even to the point of being retained fully clothed in hell, the only such figure there. Other Western iconographical influences are recognizable in the new hell, the personification of death (Mshanets), and the halo on the lamb (Polana). The borrowings seem mainly to have come from fourteenth-century Gothic art, which was not at such a distant remove from the Byzantine iconographic tradition as later Western art and therefore more assimilable to the spiritual and aesthetic tastes of the Carpathian iconographers. The northern Carpathians are dotted with German and Polish settlements, and, as we shall see, Rus' iconographers worked extensively on the territory that was predominantly inhabited by Poles.

3 We may eliminate the hypothesis that the major influence on the Carpathian icons of the Last Judgment was Moldavian iconography.

The elements of the first Carpathian elaboration appeared in the Rus' icons before they were incorporated, if they were incorporated at all, into Moldavian images of the Last Judgment. Moreover, there is no Moldavian icon as such, distinct from a fresco, of the Last Judgment that has the same antiquity.

4 We may also dismiss the possibility that there was a lost or hidden tradition from Kyiv or Halych that informed these icons.

Every element of these icons can be identified as being either a part of the common Byzantine legacy, or else a feature taken from an icon prototype worked out in northern Rus' in the fifteenth century, or else a borrowing from Gothic sacral art.[106]

5 This particular composition is unique to the region.

Nowhere else are all these features of the three traditions combined.

6 The textual work on the elements was all done elsewhere, in Byzantium or northern Rus'. The additions made by the Carpathian painters were purely visual, taken from local Catholic sacral art.

This is consistent with the modest endowment of the local monasteries; it was not possible for them to maintain libraries and scholars on a par with monasteries in the Orthodox states.

7 The three earliest Carpathian icons exhibit a high degree of iconographic uniformity, which suggests that a basic model was prepared that all the icons followed in this early period.

There are only two elements that are not shared by all three icons – Death and the lamb. The way the tavernmaid is drawn in the icons shows how closely dependent they were on some single model.

8 The three earliest Carpathian icons were produced after 1408 and before c. 1500.

Although many features of the first Carpathian elaboration were already present in the Snetogorsk frescoes of the early fourteenth century, the earliest known association of the hand of God with Last Judgment iconography in Rus' dates to 1408 (a fresco in the Dormition Church, Vladimir).

In the 1530s Moldavian frescoes of the Last Judgment began to include the scene of Moses and the Jews and the peoples, and so the appearance of this element in the Carpathian icons must have been earlier. The Moldavians no longer understood the original meaning of the element and 'corrected' it to exclude Orthodox peoples such as the Greeks and Rus'. This indicates that some time, at least a generation, had elapsed since the element first appeared on the icons.

Icons instead of Frescoes or Murals

By no means do all Orthodox churches contain an icon or mural or fresco of the Last Judgment. Throughout most of the Orthodox realm and throughout most of the history of Orthodoxy, Last Judgment images are few and far between, especially when compared to the ubiquitous images of the Mother of God, the Pantocrator, the archangels, the twelve major feasts, and popular saints such as Nicholas and Paraskeva. The Last Judgment did not form part of the traditional iconostasis of Eastern Orthodox churches. But the theme was unusually popular in the general vicinity of the Carpathians. In Carpathian Rus', the icons and murals that are the subject of our study flourished in the fifteenth through eighteenth centuries. To the southwest, Romanian Maramureş was thick with Last Judgment murals in the eighteenth century and also had some icons earlier. (Most of the evidence was destroyed in the devastating Tatar raid of 1717, but we do still have Budeşti-Josani.) To the southwest, in northern Bukovina, Last Judgment oil paintings and less frequently frescoes became popular adornments to churches from the late eighteenth century on, and at least one mural was painted there in the second half of the seventeenth century. Further to the south, in northern Moldavia, many churches were decorated with Last Judgment frescoes on the exterior and interior beginning in the second half of the fifteenth century and particularly in the first half of the sixteenth century. There were other Last Judgment frescoes in the vicinity as well, and Rus' outside the Carpathians had an old tradition of such frescoes. One may think of the region around the Carpathians as an archipelago of the Last Judgment, a place where that visual theme was particularly appreciated.

In this section, I will first survey the population of Last Judgment frescoes in Rus' and in the Carpathian region from the eleventh through the sixteenth century. Then I will consider what the change from frescoes to icons implied. Throughout the territory of Rus', particularly in the twelfth century under Byzantine influence, major churches and monasteries were decorated with frescoes of the Last Judgment. Not all that were painted would have left evidence, so the actual list of old Rus' frescoes is longer than what I am able to provide here (table 2.2). Although these frescoes are quite distant spatially from the Ukrainian Carpathians, nonetheless, as the links between the Carpathian icons and that of Novgorod-Tretiakov demonstrate, the sacral art of northern Rus' was not so distant culturally from that of the Carpathians. Also, as I will show later in this chapter, painters and churchmen from elsewhere in Rus' could be found in the vicinity of the Carpathians.

Closer geographically, the Moldavian frescoes are much younger, mostly dating from the second half of the fifteenth and especially the first half of the sixteenth century (table 2.3). The large number of them in a

Table 2.2
Rus' Frescoes of the Last Judgment (Arranged Chronologically)

Location	Date
Vydubychi Monastery, Church of St Michael, Kyiv	eleventh century
Nikolai-Dvorishchenskii Church, Novgorod	1130
St Cyril's, Kyiv	1140–6
Yeletskyi Monastery, Church of the Dormition, Chernihiv	mid-twelfth century
Transfiguration Church, Pereiaslavl-Zaleskii	1157
Ascension Church, Vladimir	1161
Dormition Church, Vladimir	1189
St George's, Staraia Ladoga	end of the twelfth century
St Demetrius', Vladimir	1196
Nereditsa near Novgorod	1199
Snetogorsk Monastery, Pskov	1313
Dormition Church, Vladimir	1408

Sources: Asieiev, *Mystetstvo Kyivs'koi Rusi*. Karger, *Drevnerusskaia monumental'naia zhivopis'*. Grabar, *Die Freskomalerei der Dimitrij Kathedrale in Wladimir*. Kilesso, *Vydubyts'kyi monastyr.* Latukha, 'Fresky Uspens'koho soboru v Chernihovi.' Lazarev, *Drevnerusskie mozaiki i freski XI–XV vv.* Miloševič, *Das Jüngste Gericht*, 30. Sarab'ianov, '"Strashnyi Sud" v rospisiakh sobora Snetogorskogo monastyria.' Skrobucha, 'Zur Ikonographie des "Jüngsten Gerichts."'

relatively compact territory of northern Moldavia testifies to the very lively interest in Last Judgment imagery in this region, which is also in the Carpathian foothills. As the crow flies, the localities where the Moldavian frescoes can be found are about 250–300 kilometres southeast of Mshanets and Poliana. It should be noted too that the northern Carpathian communities where the first Last Judgment icons appeared had been recently founded in the course of the Vlach migration and that among the inhabitants were Romanian-speaking Vlachs as well as Slavs.[107]

To the northwest of the Ukrainian Carpathians, in Kraków, a Last Judgment fresco adorned the Holy Cross Chapel in Wawel Castle. It was completed in 1470, probably by artists from Pskov. The king of Poland at that time, Kazimierz Jagiellończyk, whose preferences in sacral art were Eastern Orthodox, had commissioned the Byzantine-style frescoes for this chapel.[108]

Right near Mshanets and Poliana stood the monastery of Lavriv, first mentioned in documents in 1407. The Last Judgment on the west wall has not survived to our time, but traces of paint indicate that one was

Table 2.3
Moldavian Frescoes of the Last Judgment (Arranged Chronologically)

Location	Date
Luzhany	1453–9
Pătrăuţi	1483
Şcheia (nothing visible anymore)	after 1488
Bălineşti, reign of Stefan the Great (nothing visible anymore)	1457–1504
Baia (nothing visible anymore)	1532
Probota	1532
Suceava: St George	1534
Humor	1535
Suceava: St Demetrius	1535
Moldoviţa	1537
Arbore	1541
Voroneţ	1550
Râşca	1552
Suceviţa	1595–6

Sources: I studied these sites in expeditions to Luzhany 12 June 2001 and 27 August 2002 and to the Suceava region in Romania 30 May – 1 June 2005. Drăguţ and Lupan, *Pictura murală din Moldova*. Miclea and Florescu, *Probota*. Şandru and Viţega, *Made by Man, Created by God*. Sinigalia and Puşcaşu, *Mânăstirea Probota*. Ştefănescu, *L'évolution de la peinture religieuse en Bucovine et en Moldavie*.

there.[109] On the basis of a chemical analysis conducted before the First World War, the surviving frescoes were dated to the end of the fifteenth or early sixteenth century.[110] A visually gifted art historian, Mariia Helytovych, on the basis of a comparison of the stylistic features of the frescoes and Ukrainian icons from the region, dates the frescoes to the 1540s.[111] This dating makes sense also because of the many features in common between the Lavriv frescoes and those of Humor, painted in 1535.[112]

Aside from the Orthodox depictions of the Last Judgment, in the vicinity were also Roman Catholic, Gothic frescoes. There was a mid-fourteenth-century Last Judgment in Svinica, for example (fig. 2.44 above).[113] Svinica is located south of the Carpathians, about fifteen kilometres east of Košice, on the periphery of Rus' settlement. In the early nineteenth century it contained a mixed population of Catholics and Greek Catholics.[114]

In such an environment, it is not surprising that those who were building churches in the northern foothills would have considered an image of the Last Judgment to be an appropriate inclusion in their church's visual program. The settlements here were undoubtedly prosperous in the fifteenth century. The region was relatively uninhabited, with plenty of room for sheep and other livestock to graze. There would have been money to commission a finely decorated church. The people of the villages were also mobile, since they traded their livestock over long distances[115] and they were still migrating into the territory from south of the Carpathians (from the Maramureş-Transcarpathian side, not the Moldavian side). They also may have made pilgrimages to the monasteries where the frescoes were. Even if they themselves had not seen the monumental Last Judgments in their environs, their clergymen and painters certainly had. Once one village had put up a Last Judgment, others would have taken notice and perhaps been inclined to do the same. In the course of an expedition to Bukovina, I visited Vyviz, a *khutir* near Kosovanka (9 June 2005). In St George's Church there I saw recently executed oil paintings of the Last Judgment and the Passion. The church elder who commissioned them for the church said he wanted them because he had seen such icons in nearby Lukivtsi.

Although the mixed farmers who settled these regions were relatively well off, they would not have been able to afford to erect stone churches that could support frescoes. Indeed, almost all the Orthodox Last Judgment frescoes listed above were the result of the patronage of the highest elites: Orthodox princes of Rus' and Moldavia, a few of the wealthier, more powerful boyars, and a king of Poland.

The question arises, however: Why were the churches not decorated with murals painted directly on the wood if frescoes were beyond their means? Why were icons used instead? Beginning in the seventeenth century, in both the Ukrainian Carpathians and Romanian Maramureş[116] murals were indeed painted right on the walls of the wooden churches. Why was this not done in the fifteenth century or in the sixteenth?

I have asked those who should know whether there were technical impediments to murals before the seventeenth century. The guide to St George's Church in Drohobych, a spectacular example of a seventeenth-century wooden church decorated with murals, told me that there were no impediments, and that traces of paint have been found on the interiors of wooden churches outside Rus' at least as far back as the twelfth century.[117] Mariia Helytovych also saw no impediments to murals before the seventeenth century.[118] In her doctoral dissertation on Passion icons, however, Agnieszka Gronek has argued that icons were preferred to murals for climatic and technical reasons. Covering the uneven surfaces of the wooden walls of a church with murals required much more effort and therefore was more costly than producing an icon. Also, the image would not endure well on the walls, especially given a climate that fostered dampness and mildew. 'Icons were more accessible, more durable, and in addition they covered all the defects of the crooked walls.'[119]

But this explanation is belied by later developments, when murals were indeed painted on the walls, and that at a time when the region was much more depressed economically.[120] One of the earliest Western Ukrainian wooden churches to be painted with murals was the Church of the Holy Spirit in Potelych, north of our region. It was painted in the 1620s–1640s. In fact, the preparation of the surface was nowhere near as time-consuming as for icons. The tempera was applied directly to a thin layer of gesso and the gaps between logs were covered with bits of cloth or even paper glued on. The artists painting murals did not spend the time to produce a polished surface that hid the texture of the wood as icon painters did.[121] I therefore agree with the Ukrainian art historians who saw no technical impediment to the painting of murals in the fifteenth century.

My own thinking is that this choice of icons over the more fresco-like murals indicates that these were images commissioned from workshops elsewhere, from painters who did not stay and work in the villages themselves; when the icons were completed, they were dismantled into three or four boards and conveyed by cart to the churches they were intended for. I think this also indicates that in the earlier period, the painters were unwilling to spend a year or two living in a village and painting its church, while in the later period painters were glad enough to get that work. I will unfold more of the argument later, but here is where it is heading: in the early phase, in the fifteenth century and also to some extent in the sixteenth century, the painters lived in monasteries and took commissions from the villages; afterwards, men of middle station, such as craftsmen and sons of priests, painted the icons and were also quite willing to work in a village on a longer-term contract for room and board and wages. Also, it is probable that the monks would not paint directly on the walls, as became common later, because the work required to bring the surface of these walls to the quality necessary for icons was extremely demanding, and they were not willing to lower their standards as the laymen painters did later on.

The switch from fresco to icon may explain why the northern Rus' model was so influential in the Carpathian region. Work in frescoes, and in murals as well, was compositionally looser. As Igor Grabar pointed out when writing about old Rus' frescoes of the Last Judgment, there was not enough room to fit the entire composition on the west wall, so it had to be divided up with individual episodes in various corners of the western part of the church.[122] An icon, however, was a restraining form, and painters looked for the best way to fit the episodes on a few pieces of wood. Hence the elegant and ready-made composition from northern Rus' would have appealed to them.

Monasteries and Painting Projects

A characteristic, if counterintuitive, feature of the iconography of Carpathian Rus' was that the quality of the artistry deteriorated rather than improved over time. There are some striking examples of this in other themes besides the Last Judgment. Compare the delicately painted crucifixion of Owczary from the fifteenth century with the seventeenth-century crucifixion of Pielgrzymka (figs 2.47 and 2.48). These two Lemko villages are just twenty kilometres apart. Not far southwest of them is Krempna. The fifteenth-century *acheiropoiētos* (icon not made by human hands) from here is considered a masterpiece of Carpathian iconography.[123] But an *acheiropoiētos* from the same village executed in 1664 is not of the same quality (fig. 2.49).

The Last Judgment icon of Lukov-Venecia from the early sixteenth century was also not nearly as well executed as the original it copied. Occasionally, the artist had to omit features that were present in Vanivka because he did not plan well enough and ran out of room, e.g., he left out the crucifix and instruments.[124] The draughtsmanship and painting technique are both superior in the older of the two icons. Moreover, there is a different proportion between the head and the rest of the body in these icons. The figures are relatively elongated in Vanivka, but shortened in Lukov-Venecia. The head of John the Baptist in Vanivka is in the proportion 1:6, taken in relation to the entire body. The proportion is 1:4.5 in Lukov-Vanivka(fig. 2.50). Agnieszka Gronek has taken measurements of the faces in Passion icons and placed them in relation to the entire bodies. On the whole, the older icons have a proportion of 1:9–1:11, the later ones a proportion of 1:6–1:8.[125] It is reasonable to assume that the older painters were better trained in iconography than the later ones. I believe that those older, more skilled painters were professional iconographers, usually monks. The later painters may have picked up the basic technique of creating icons from them, but they were never able to develop the same level of mastery.

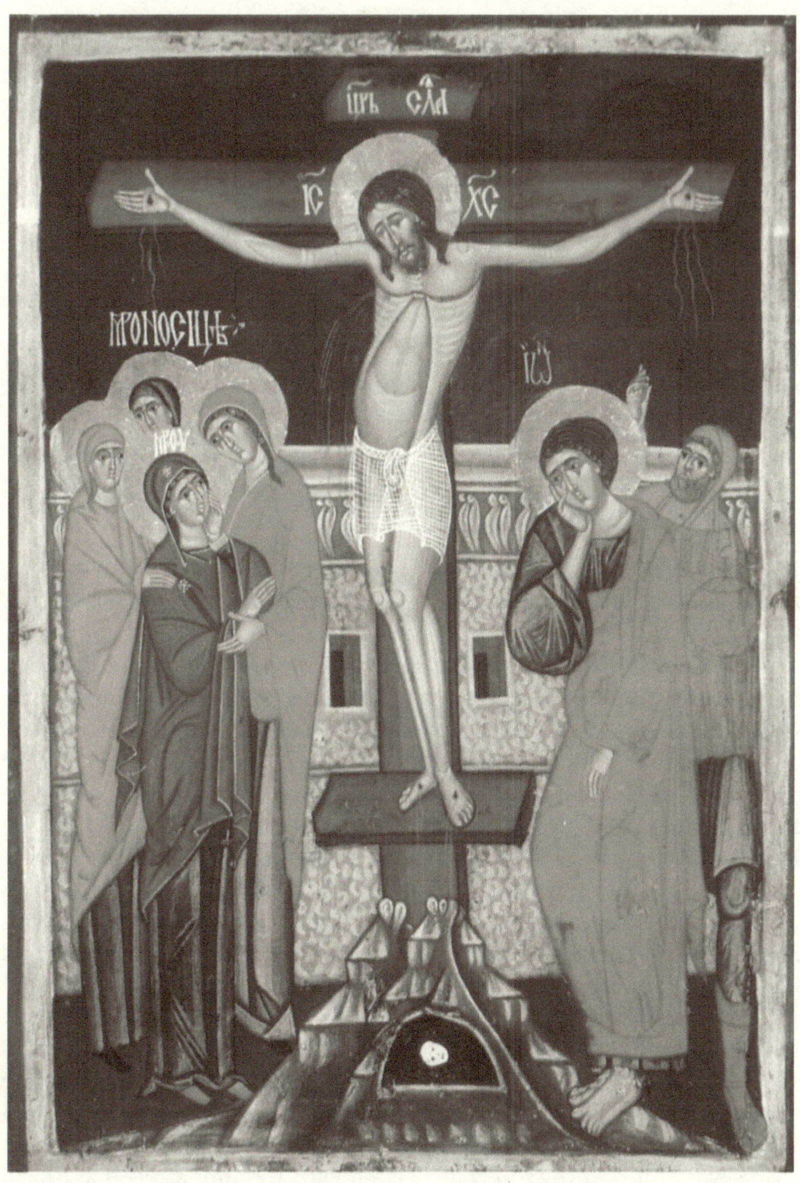

2.47 Crucifixion, Owczary, fifteenth century. Source: Romuald Biskupski, *Ikony ze zbiorów Muzeum Historycznego w Sanoku*, reproductions by Marek Brniak (Warsaw: Krajowa Spoldzielnia Artystyczno-Techniczna, 1991), pl. 15.

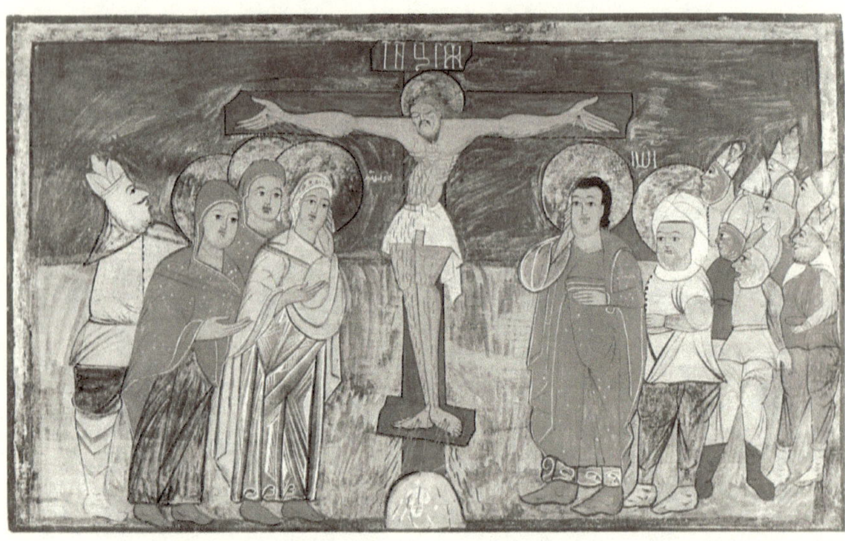

2.48 Crucifixion, Pielgrzymka, seventeenth century. Source: Jerzy Czajkowski et al., *Ikona karpacka* (Sanok: Muzeum Budownictwa Ludowego w Sanoku, 1998), pl. 31.

As we have already seen in our survey of the Last Judgment frescoes, there were numerous monasteries in the general vicinity. Ivan Krypiakevych counted fifty-seven localities in Galicia that had monasteries at some time from the twelfth through the fifteenth centuries. These were men's monasteries; women's monasteries only began to flourish in the late sixteenth century.[126] In the hilly environs of Poliana and Mshanets were six monasteries that existed by the early fifteenth century: not only Lavriv, but another important monastery in Spas, and also monasteries in Smilnytsia, Sozan, Terlo, and Tershiv. A monastery in nearby Stariava was also in existence by 1500.[127] In the sixteenth century monks lived and built a small church on the slope of a hill in Dobromyl, close to Poliana, but a monastery was not built until after 1613 (see map 4).[128] The most significant of these were Spas and Lavriv,[129] but most of these monasteries, which did not enjoy the patronage of Orthodox rulers, were humble establishments.[130] The highest social class that patronised the Carpathian Rus' monasteries were the Orthodox gentry. Indeed, the Sozansky and Terletsky families were closely associated with the monasteries at Sozan and Terlo and some of the members made clerical careers.[131] The Rus' gentry of these mountain regions was not wealthy enough to build imposing monastic centres.

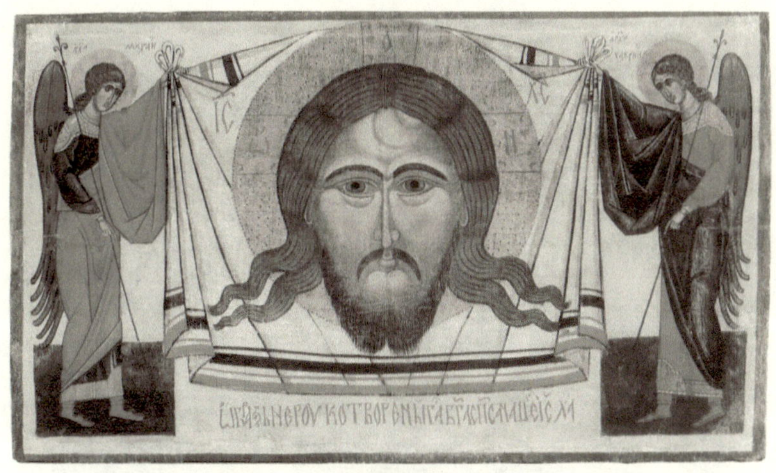

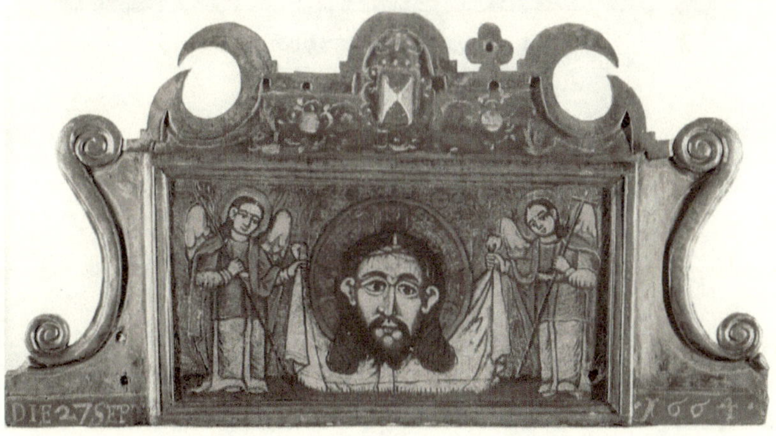

2.49 *Acheiropoiētoi*, Krempna, fifteenth century and 1664. Source: Jerzy Czajkowski et al., *Ikona karpacka* (Sanok: Muzeum Budownictwa Ludowego w Sanoku, 1998), pl. 11 and pl. 28.

The situation was quite different in northern Moldavia, where the Orthodox princes, especially Stefan the Great (1457–1504) and his son Petru Rareş (1541–6), seriously invested in monasteries as holy places, centres of learning, economic enterprises, and fortifications. Princes and prominent boyars built Putna in 1466–9, Pătrăuţi in 1483, Voroneţ in 1488, Humor and Probota in 1530, Moldoviţa in 1532, Râşca in 1542, Slatina in the 1560s, and Suceviţa in 1581–1601. For the most part, these

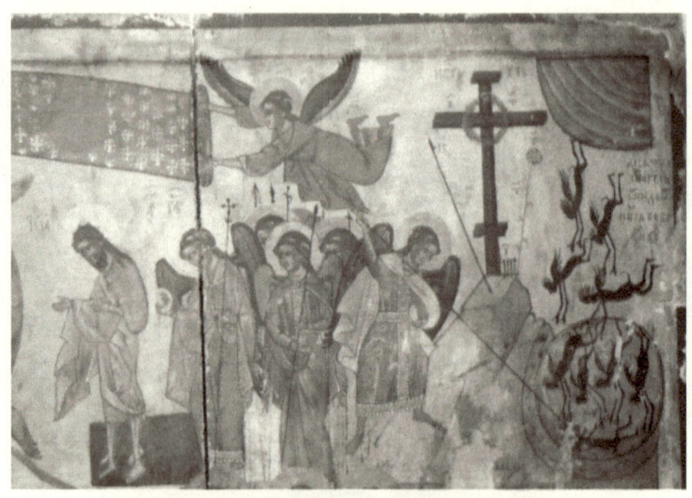

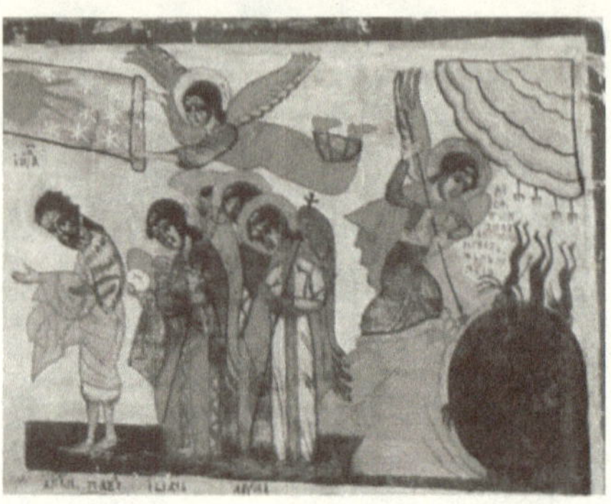

2.50 Upper left corner of Vanivka and Lukov-Venecia. Source of Lukov-Venecia: Štefan Tkáč, *Ikony zo 16.–19. storočia na severovýchodnom Slovensku* (Bratislava: Tatran, 1982), 138, pl. 58.

monasteries were built after the first Last Judgment icons were painted in the Carpathians, but some of them existed as communities of monks before the massive building projects were undertaken, notably Humor and Putna.[132]

The other important monastery in the region was Hrushovo, called by the Romanians Peri. It is located in Transcarpathia, east of the town of Tiachiv. The first written evidence of a monastery at Hrushovo dates from 1391. It was destroyed in the late seventeenth century.[133] While it flourished it exercised spiritual and cultural influence among the Rus' of Transcarpathia and the Romanians of Maramureş. Also in Maramureş

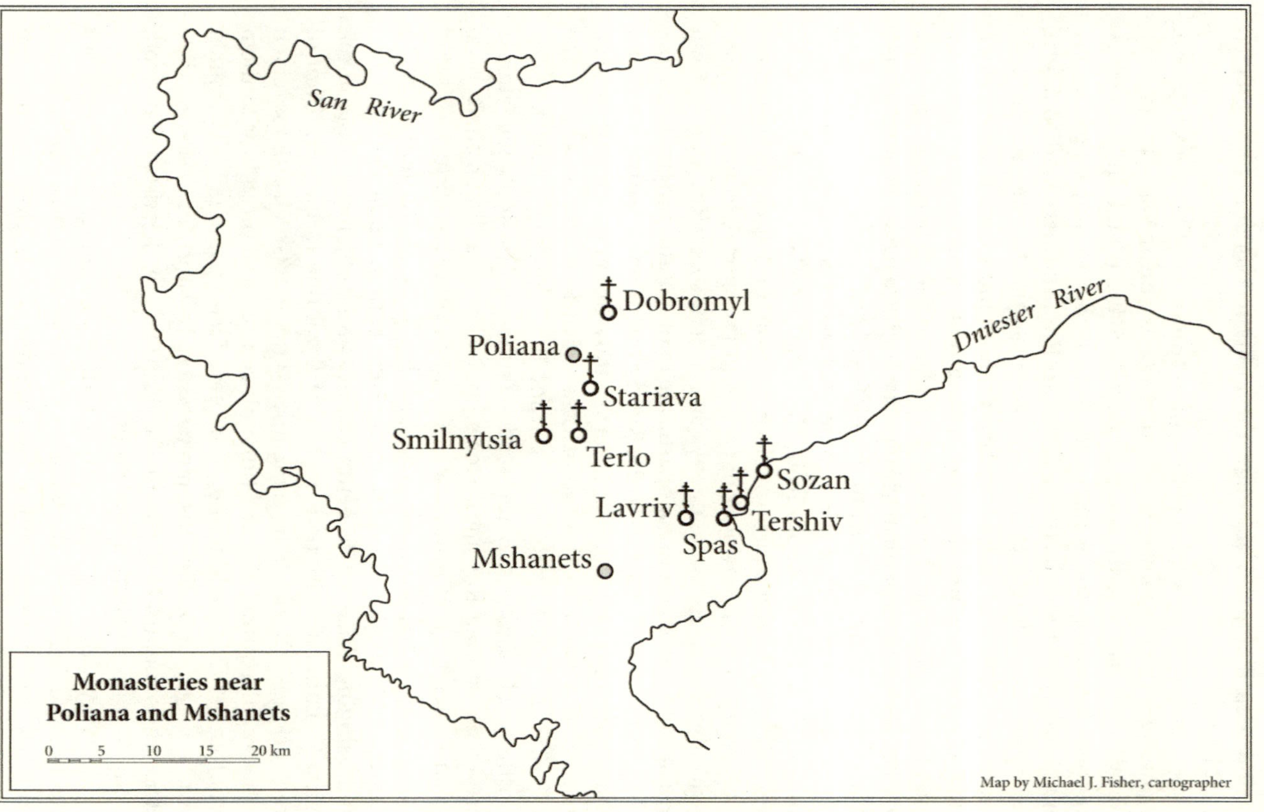

4. Monasteries near Poliana and Mshanets

was the monastery at Bârsana. This was a monastic site since the end of the fourteenth century, although the monastery building was erected much later.[134]

The monasteries were centres of a universal Orthodox culture. Beginning in the late fourteenth century monasteries in Wallachia (Cozia), central Moldavia (Neamţ), and northern Moldavia (Putna and others) established scriptoria where manuscripts from Serbia and Bulgaria were copied. Many of these made their way to Rus', northern and southern, where they contributed to what is known as the 'second South Slavic influence.'[135] For that to have occurred, there must have been considerable traffic between Moldavia and the South Slavs, on the one hand, and Moldavia and Rus', on the other. A scholar of the Rus' manuscript tradition has also noted a particularly rapid cultural exchange between Polish-Lithuanian Rus' and Muscovy in the 1460s–1490s.[136]

Moldavia was on the land route between Moscow and Constantinople[137] and therefore Athos. Monks from Novgorod or Vladimir who were on their way south would pass through our region, perhaps wintering in the monasteries or even staying longer.[138] And the monks from our region would also travel. As Sophia Senyk has noted, some Rus' monks from here desired 'to experience monastic life in one of the generally acknowledged centres of monasticism, the Kiev Lavra, or outside Rus', on Mount Athos, pausing for longer or shorter stays at other monasteries en route.'[139] The Latin archbishop of Lviv was ordered by the king in the early sixteenth century to watch out for Rus' clergymen travelling frequently to Moldavia.[140] In the seventeenth century Romanian monks were in Carpathian Rus' monasteries and vice versa,[141] and there is no reason to believe that it was any different in previous centuries.[142] Rus' cantors and clergymen studied singing in Putna in the mid-sixteenth century. Perhaps they studied there even earlier, because Putna had taught singing since the fifteenth century and influenced music in the region.[143] Putna also housed 'monks of Byzantine formation, if not of Greek origin.'[144] It should be remembered too that Greek bishops served in Rus' regularly until the mid-fifteenth century and brought with them an entourage that could well have included icon painters;[145] they would have been guests of the Rus' monasteries. In short, monasteries were places where cultural trends, including trends in the visual arts, from throughout the Orthodox world met.

Familiarity with universal trends in Orthodox iconography would also have been facilitated by the massive painting projects of the fifteenth and early sixteenth centuries, which drew artists from around the

Byzantine commonwealth. Polish King Władysław Jagiełło (1386–1434) funded eight large Byzantine-style fresco projects in Gniezno, Sandomierz, Wiślica, Łysa Góra, Lublin, and Kraków.[146] The artists were brought from somewhere in Rus', perhaps Tver.[147] As we have already seen, his son Kazimierz Jagiellończyk brought artists from Pskov to paint in Kraków in the late 1460s. I suspect that it was in connection with this particular project that the oldest of the Carpathian Last Judgment icons was painted, probably for the monastery at Lavriv.

The great Moldavian projects of the late fifteenth and sixteenth century attracted Greek artists, notably in Pătrăuţi (1483)[148] and Râşca (1552). The first of these Moldavian projects, in Luzhany, may have employed artists from Volhynia, and we are certain that icons by Moldavian artists were commissioned in Volhynia in the sixteenth century.[149] This international movement of artists explains why monks in the Carpathians would have been aware of iconographic developments in northern Rus' and elsewhere in the Orthodox world.

Conclusions

In the fifteenth century the northern slopes of the Carpathians were being settled by migrants coming in from Transcarpathia and points south. They were largely Orthodox and mainly Slavic-speaking, though some were ethnic Vlachs who spoke Romanian; bilingualism was probably not uncommon. They combined animal husbandry – grazing sheep and other livestock in the hills and mountain meadows – with farming in the valleys. Their animals sold well, and the farming in the rich and largely virgin soil readily sustained their relatively small population.

They had been Christianized for some time and had developed spiritual and aesthetic needs. They, and the local Rus' gentry, supported the monasteries that grew up in their region. Their more talented and spiritually gifted sons would enter these monasteries and develop in the tradition of Rus' monasticism. The monasteries provided pastoral care for neighbouring villages, and men and women in the wider vicinity would visit them in pilgrimage and to meet their spiritual needs. Larger monastic communities like Lavriv and Spas would be particularly influential and respected.

Although the monasteries were not rich, nor rich in cultural attainments, the monks who lived there would travel in the Orthodox world and would also host monks from north and south. Monks from elsewhere in Rus' would be among the visitors who stayed in Lavriv and Spas, and the proximity of traditions and language would lead to a closer relationship with them. Among the monks, local and visitors, would be icon painters, and they would exchange information on the production of sacral art.

As the farmers in the Carpathians prospered, and perhaps with the help of the Rus' gentry, they began to erect their own churches. Although they were doing well, they could not afford the masonry for a church that could support frescoes. They built their churches out of wood. They decorated the churches with icons which they purchased from the local monasteries. The monasteries themselves had wooden churches, and therefore these were embellished with icons rather than frescoes. Among these icons were some of the Last Judgment , since the monks/painters, and probably the villagers/commissioners too, understood the Last Judgment to be an important, impressive, spiritually powerful component of a church.

The monks in the Carpathians put together an icon of the Last Judgment for the churches in the region. It was based on the general Byzantine iconography, but more particularly on a northern Rus' variant of elegant composition. To this they added some features from Gothic models, since in this part of Rus' the influence of the West was very strong.

3 Further Elaboration

This chapter, like the previous chapter, concentrates on icons painted on wood, leaving icons on canvas and murals on the walls of churches for the next chapter.

Geographical Diffusion

Here I outline the geography of the surviving icons of the Last Judgment. Of course, this is not identical with establishing the range of the icons when they were originally painted since the rate of destruction was probably not equal across the territory where they existed, and probably some regions were better collected than others. The extant icons, nonetheless, are the best evidence we have to indicate their diffusion over time, and they do provide useful information (map 5). I should specify that the data do not indicate where the icons were painted, but where they were installed. This is a geography of a particular taste. We will discuss the geography of provenance in the next section.

I divide the icons here into two large chronological periods: (1) the sixteenth and first half of the seventeenth century, and (2) the second half of the seventeenth and the eighteenth century. For the first period we can see an arc of Last Judgment icons sweeping southeast from just south of Przemyśl along the northern slopes of the Carpathians to the town of Dolyna. The arc starts from Trushevychi, proceeds down to Velyke (near Poliana and Dobromyl), to Vovche (south of Mshanets and Lavriv), through Yasinka Masova, Bahnovate, Zavadka, and Sukhyi Potik. There is then a barren stretch to Dolyna. For the second period we can also find icons in this region, in Lipie (near Mshanets), in Smilna (north of Yasinka Masova), in Moldavsko (between Bahnovate and Zavadka).

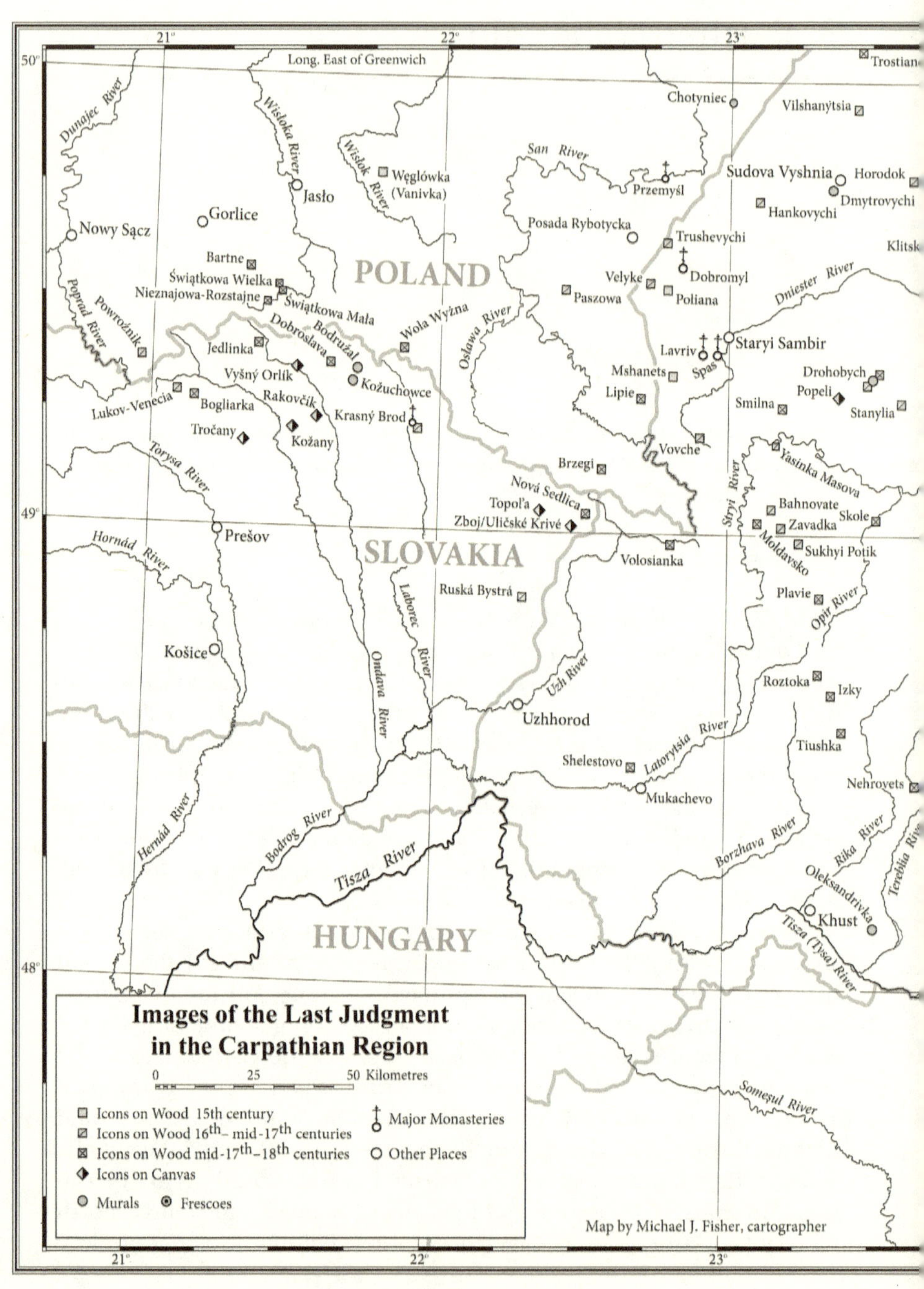

5. Images of the Last Judgment in the Carpathian Region

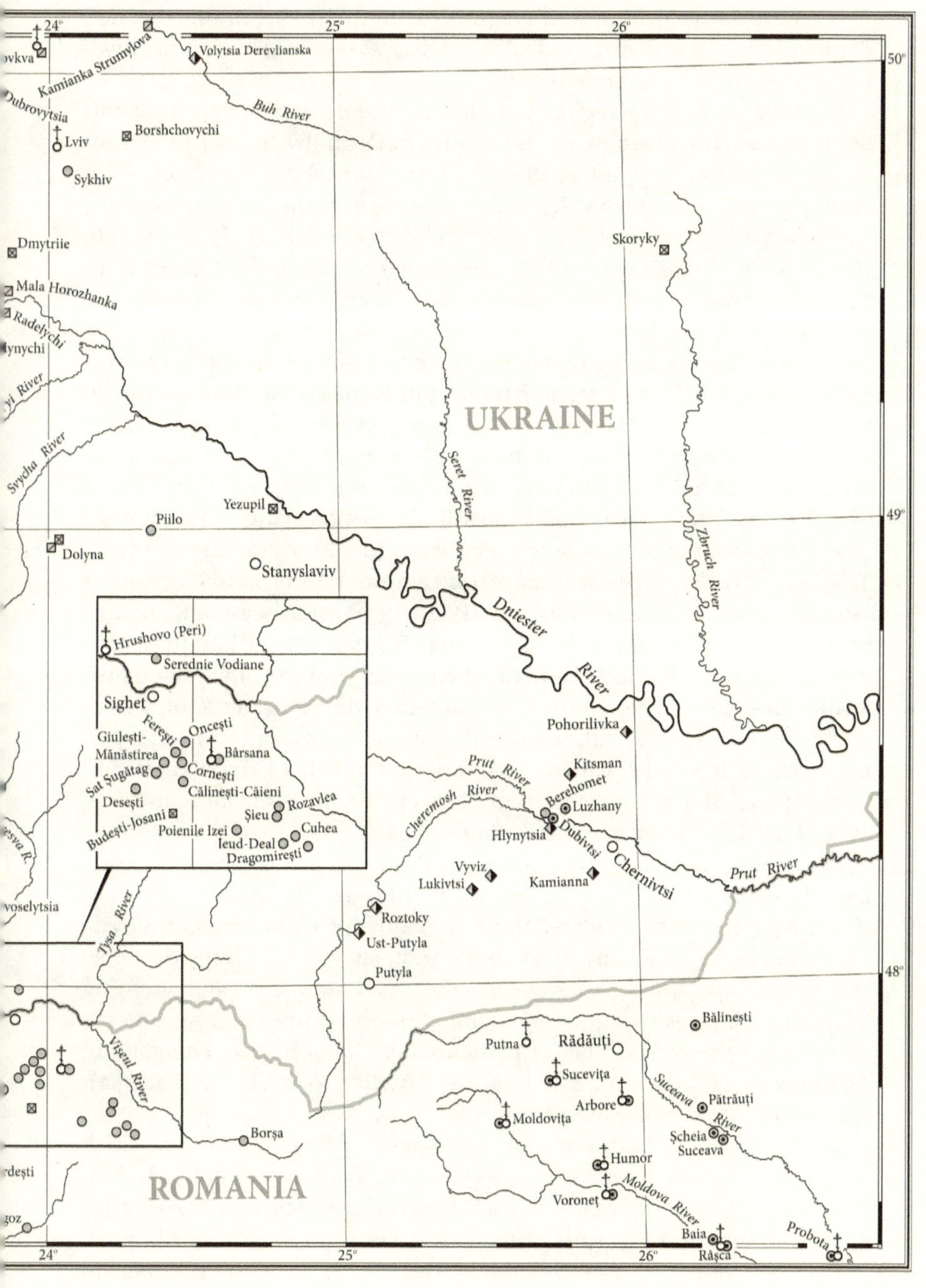
UKRAINE
ROMANIA
Lviv
Sykhiv
Borshchovychi
Volytsia Derevlianska
Kamianka Strumylova
Buh River
Dubrovytsia
Dmytriie
Mala Horozhanka
Radelychi
Skoryky
Seret River
Zbruch River
Dniester River
Yezupil
Piilo
Dolyna
Stanyslaviv
Svycha River
Hrushovo (Peri)
Serednie Vodiane
Sighet
Fereşti
Onceşti
Giuleşti-
Mănăstirea
Bârsana
Sat Şugătag
Corneşti
Deseşti
Călineşti-Căieni
Rozavlea
Budeşti-Josani
Şieu
Poienile Izei
Cuhea
Ieud-Deal
Dragomireşti
Pohorilivka
Kitsman
Prut River
Berehomet
Luzhany
Cheremosh River
Hlynytsia
Dubivtsi
Chernivtsi
Vyviz
Lukivtsi
Kamianna
Roztoky
Ust-Putyla
Putyla
Tysa River
Vişeul River
Borşa
Bălineşti
Putna
Rădăuţi
Suceviţa
Arbore
Suceava River
Pătrăuţi
Moldoviţa
Şcheia
Suceava
Humor
Voroneţ
Moldova River
Baia
Râşca
Probota
24°
25°
26°
50°
49°
48°

The arc in the second period extends further east and south, through Plavie and Skole and again to Dolyna. This was one of the most productive regions for Last Judgment icons.

Another productive region was along a line from the centre of this mountain arc northeast through the town of Drohobych. Yasinka Masova and Smilna already point in the direction. Drohobych had icons from both periods. A little south of Drohobych is Stanylia (first period). Northeast of Drohobych are Medynychi (second period), Radelychi (first), Mala Horozhanka (first), and Dmytriie (second). Not far away is Klitsko (first). There was also an icon from another village in the Drohobych region.[1]

There were icons in the first period on either side of Przemyśl: Paszowa to the southwest (but closer to Sanok) and Hankovychi (Hankowice) to the east. Icons from the first period also appeared in scattered larger towns rather far north of the mountains: Horodok, Zhovkva, and Kamianka Strumylova. Other localities with Last Judgment icons are dispersed over what is today Lviv oblast without any easily discernible pattern: Vilshanytsia (located about halfway between Przemyśl and Zhovkva, first period), Trostianets (north of Vilshanytsia, second period?), Dubrovytsia (betweeen Horodok and Zhovkva, second period), Torky (far northeast of Kamianka Strumylova, second period; it is not on map 5, Images of the Last Judgment in the Carpathian Region),[2] and Borshchovychi (quite south of Kamianka Strumylova, second period). There are surviving fragments of a mid-sixteenth century icon with the features of the Carpathian icons that perhaps comes from the Chełm eparchy, thus north of Trostianets and Vilshanytsia.[3] Skoryky, an icon from 1754, came from quite far to the east, about forty kilometres east of Ternopil.

In the first period there were relatively few icons west of Przemyśl. Aside from Paszowa, which has already been mentioned, there were only four: Ruská Bystrá (rather south of the mountains, near the current Slovak-Ukrainian border); Krásny Brod, to the west, also on the Hungarian side; and Powroźnik and Lukov-Venecia, the westernmost of any surviving Carpathian images of the Last Judgment, situated not far from one another across the crest of the Carpathians, i.e., the old Polish-Hungarian/Transylvanian border. None of these are very close to Węglówka (Vanivka), although Paszowa is the least distant.

In the second period, the settlements west of Przemyśl became thick with Last Judgment icons. They are clustered, like Powroźnik and Lukov-Venecia, on both sides of the border. Proceeding from west to east, they are as follows: Bogliarka (just east of Lukov-Venecia) south of the border; Bartne, Świątkowa Wielka, Świątkowa Mała, and Nieznajowa/Rozstajne

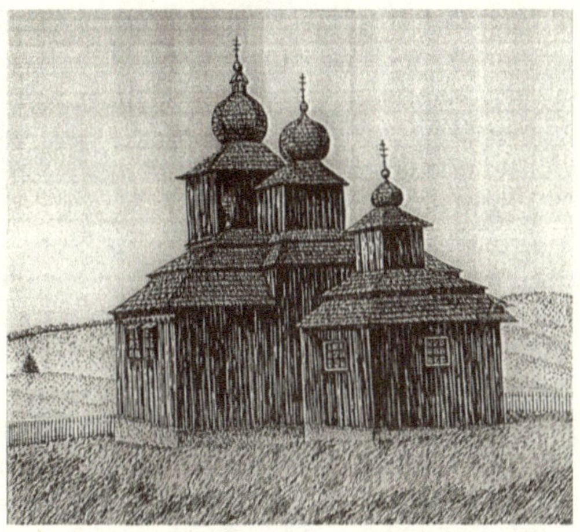

3.1 Wooden church in Dobroslava. Drawing: H. Grešlíková.

(all closely related iconographically) on the north of the border, with Jedlinka just to the south; Dobroslava to the south (fig. 3.1) and Wola Wyżna to the north; Brzegi (a highly atypical icon) to the north and Nová Sedlica to the south; and Volosianka to the south (actually a little west of Przemyśl, but far to the south).

There are also second-period icons in what is today Transcarpathia. There are four icons in the northeast of what was once Máramoros county: Roztoka, Izky, Tiushka, and Nehrovets. These villages actually continue into the southern slopes the line that led from Przemyśl to Plavie. There is a fifth icon (Máramaros-Néprajzi) from the same region, but we cannot be more specific about the locality. Features of a sixth icon (Museum of the History of Religion) also suggest an origin in Máramaros county. The icon of Shelestovo, just east of Mukachiv, comes from outside Máramaros but bears similarities with the others.

Some additional information is available from the records of eighteenth-century parish visitations. I have not attempted to survey them comprehensively but have gathered some data, relying heavily on the work of Agnieszka Gronek (see table 6.1). Most of these images were murals and icons on canvas, but five were our traditional large icons on boards. Two were near Dolyna (Trościaniec and Raków) and three near Zhovkva and Kamianka Strumylova (Wola Kunińska, Remenów, and Glińsk). Marian Radwan published visitation records from over 160 Uniate parishes in Bratslav and Kyiv palatinates, about three or four hundred kilometres east of our zone. None of the descriptions noted the presence in churches of icons of the Last Judgment painted on wood.[4] The utilization of visitation records for Ukrainian art history is only in its infancy, so the information they provide is, at present, very fragmentary. In the future, however, it should be possible to plot the iconographic landscape of much of Ukraine, establishing what kind of icons and murals were where during the eighteenth century.[5]

There are two surviving pre–nineteenth-century Last Judgment icons on wood from the eastern regions of Ukraine: a seventeenth-century icon that originally hung in the hospice of the Golden-Domed St Michael Monastery in Kyiv and is now held by the National Art Museum of Ukraine in that same city[6] and a 'South Russian' icon from the end of the eighteenth century in the Icon Museum in Recklinghausen.[7] Neither look anything like the Carpathian icons of the Last Judgment. Neither the Museum of the Volhynian Icon in Lutsk nor the Regional Museum in Rivne, both with large icon collections, have a Last Judgment.[8] In 1994 the Pereiaslav-Khmelnytskyi Historical-Cultural Preserve exhibited 103 icons, but none was a Last Judgment.[9]

Surprisingly perhaps, none of the surviving Last Judgment icons came from the most important city in the region, Lviv, even though an Orthodox monastery had existed there from the thirteenth century. A survey of all the icons in Lviv churches conducted in 1854 did not mention any icon of the Last Judgment.[10] Nor has any icon or mural of the Last Judgment been traced to that other historically important city, Przemyśl.

Can any generalizations be made from the diffusion as described here? I believe so, even given the various reservations expressed above. We can see that the northern slopes of the Carpathians, where Polana and Mshanets appeared in the fifteenth century, remained the heartland of the Last Judgment icons. From here the icons spread scattershot to the northeast, past Lviv, and in a concentrated way towards Drohobych, towards Dolyna,[11] and to the south, into Máramoros county. In this southward migration, the icons followed the path of the sheep the Boikos herded in the Carpathians.[12] Especially from the mid-seventeenth century on, the icons also spread intensively along both sides of the ridge of the Carpathians, the old Polish-Hungarian border. They were particularly thick in the westernmost areas of Rus' settlement. Perhaps there is a connection between the diffusion to these areas and the establishment and development of the monastery in Krásny Brod. The monastery was founded in the sixteenth century, and by the seventeenth century it ran a school sophisticated enough to teach philosophy.[13] The location of Węglówka in relation to these patterns is anomalous. The large distinctive icons of the Carpathian region did not spread from or beyond the territory described here. Furthermore, examination of these localities on a detailed topographical map reveals many connections between the geology and the diffusion and clustering of the icons. The diffusion of the icons on both sides of the Polish-Hungarian border reflects the relative ease of travel along mountain ridges. Clusters of icons are usually linked by rivers and valleys (e.g., Roztoka, Izky, and Tiushka).

The Painters

The three Last Judgment icons from the fifteenth century were not attributable to any particular individuals, but for the following three centuries we are able to link six icons with named painters. Probably the earliest of these is Ruská Bystrá from the mid-sixteenth century, attributed to a certain Oleksii.[14] He did not sign the Ruská Bystrá Last Judgment, but he signed two other icons as 'the very sinful servant of God Oleksii.' One of these bears an inscription that fixes it as painted in 1547. Of the six icons ascribed to him, only the Ruská Bystrá Last Judgment ended up on the Hungarian side of the mountains. All the others were from localities in Poland: Smolnik, south of Sanok, not far from the Hungarian border (two icons); Liskowate, a village just southwest of Dobromyl and Poliana; and Ustianova Horishnia, just west of the midpoint between Poliana and Mshanets. One other icon is said to be from a village called Roven in the Lesko district, but I was unable to locate it and suspect this is an error.[15] Mariia Helytovych sees similarities between the style and lettering on Oleksii's icons and on the frescoes in Lavriv.[16] My own impression is that the 'very sinful' Oleksii, much of whose work was commissioned in the Last Judgment heartland around Lavriv, Spas, and Dobromyl, was a monk. Certainly the refinement of his style does not belie this (fig. 3.2).

The next icon painter whom we can identify with a Last Judgment is also known only by his first name: 'the very sinful Dymytrii.' Perhaps he too was a monk, but I am less certain about this. It is not even entirely certain that the name here referred to the painter and not to the donor of the icon. Dymytrii left a body of work in one church in Dolyna, including a Last Judgment. His one signed icon is dated 1565. Oleh Sydor speculates that Dymytrii might have been connected with Volhynia, but the evidence is far from conclusive.[17]

The third individual who signed a Last Judgment icon was 'the very sinful servant of God Pavlentii Radymsky,' who painted Powroźnik in 1623. All we know about Pavlentii is what his signature tells us. From the

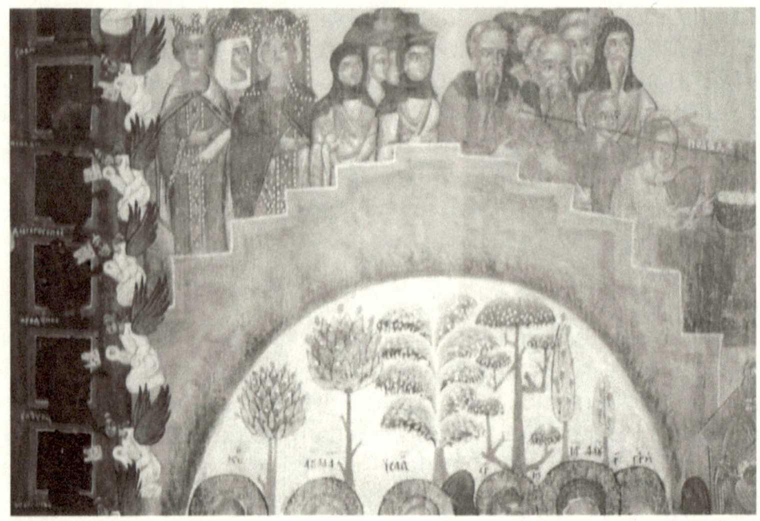

3.2 Saints above Paradise and Tollbooths, Ruská Bystrá

last name we know that he came from Radymno, which is a small town north of Przemyśl and quite far from Powroźnik. The first name, Pavlentii, is a distinctively Rus' first name. The formula of his signature links him to the monastic tradition, although his identification with Radymno suggests a small-town craftsman.

The fourth painter is 'the very sinful servant of God, Pavel, painter, Mushynsky,' i.e., of Muszyna, who painted Jedlinka (1650s). Muszyna, at least in the nineteenth century, was a small market town with a minuscule Rus' minority. Nearby, however, were many Rus' villages, including Powroźnik. Muszyna was on the Polish side of the border, Jedlinka about forty kilometres to the east on the Hungarian side.

The fifth painter is a certain Yakov, who painted Świątkowa Mała in 1687.[18] Nothing is known of him. And the final named painter of a Last Judgment icon is Marko Domazhyrsky Shestakovych, who painted Moldavsko in 1720. He did not sign the Last Judgment, but his authorship is identified by the distinctive style of his lettering, shared by icons he did sign. The Domazhyrsky in his name referred to his origin in the village of Domazhyr, located about halfway between Yavoriv and Lviv. An inscription on the icon tells us that it was commissioned by 'the priest of Domazhyr and presbyter of Moldavsko, Teodor and Bazylii.' The village of Moldavsko was far to the south of Domazhyr, in the arc sweeping down from the Mshanets-Poliana region. Evidently Shestakovych began or

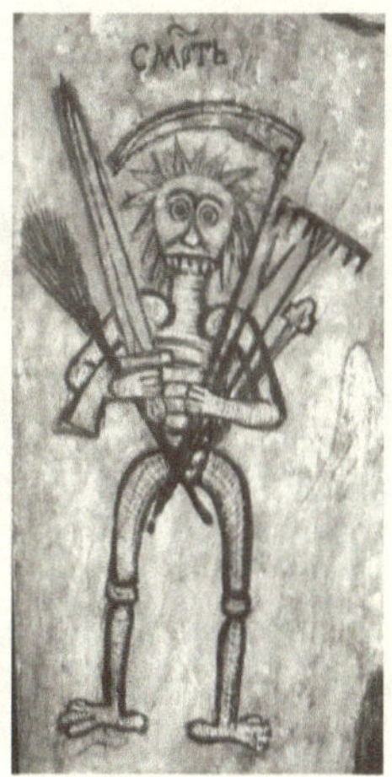

3.3 Death, Moldavsko

conceived this icon in his native village, but finished it in Moldavsko. In his signatures, Shestakovych referred to himself as 'a painter,' and in one icon he called himself 'noble born,' i.e., born into the stratum of Rus' petty gentry. Aside from the Last Judgment and a Passion in Moldavsko, he painted an iconostasis in Rykiv, less than five kilometres northeast of Moldavsko, and a number of icons in Sukhyi Potik, less than fifteen kilometres to the southeast.[19] His work is striking, but not refined (fig. 3.3).

Although this exhausts artists whom we know by name, there is an interesting case in which a single unidentified artist produced several Last Judgment icons. The Last Judgments of Bartne (mid-eighteenth century), Nieznajowa/Rozstajne (1737), and Świątkowa Wielka (mid-eighteenth century) were the work of the same individual. The stylistic similarities are readily apparent, even though Świątkowa Wielka has been partially repainted, and all share the otherwise unique feature that they appear to have been composed originally without a paradise and a hell (fig. 3.4).[20] The same artist also painted the Passion in Świątkowa Wielka (fig. 3.5). Agnieszka Gronek has attributed the latter, on the basis of stylistic features, to 'the circle of Rybotycze painters.'[21] The reference is to a small town, Posada Rybotycka, about halfway between Sanok and Przemyśl. There were many craftsmen here, some of whom specialized in work for Orthodox/Greek Catholic churches. In the late seventeenth century a number of icon painters worked here too, although the significance of the Rybotycze school has been greatly exaggerated and too many anonymous works have been too carelessly attributed to it.[22] I believe in this

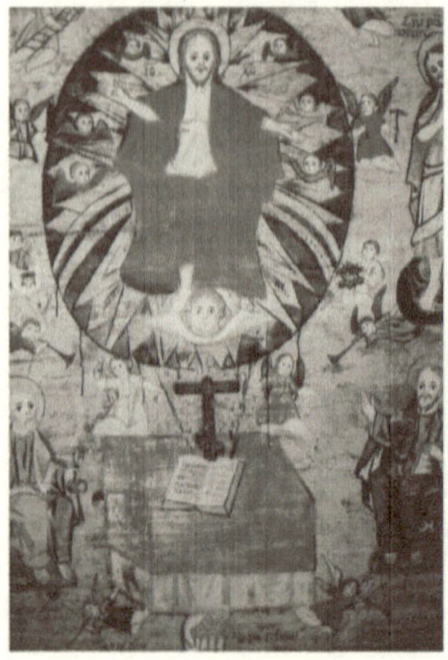

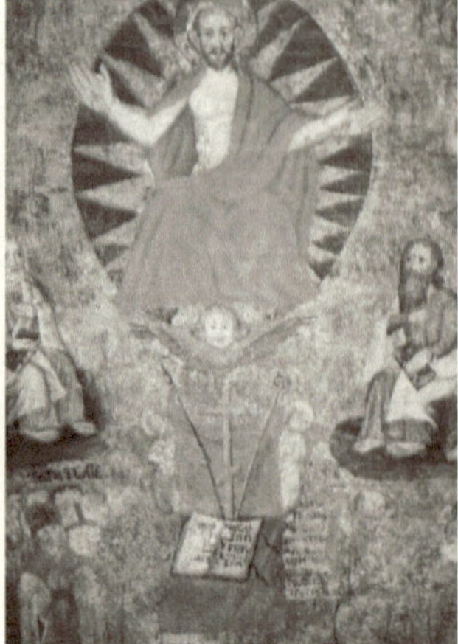

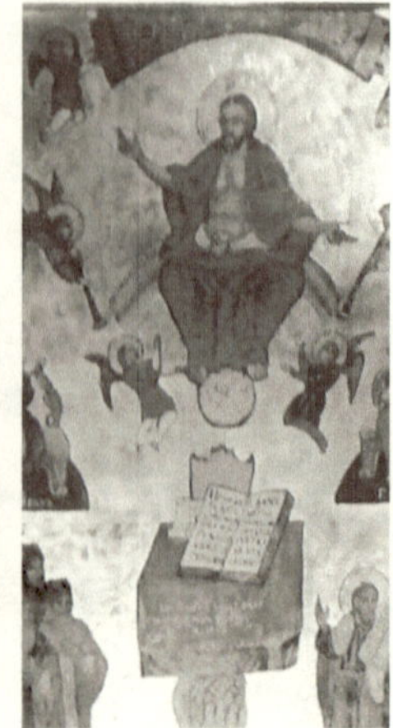

3.4 Son of Man in Mandorla, Bartne, Nieznajowa/Rozstajne, and Świątkowa Wielka. Photo of Świątkowa Wielka: Vladislav Grešlík.

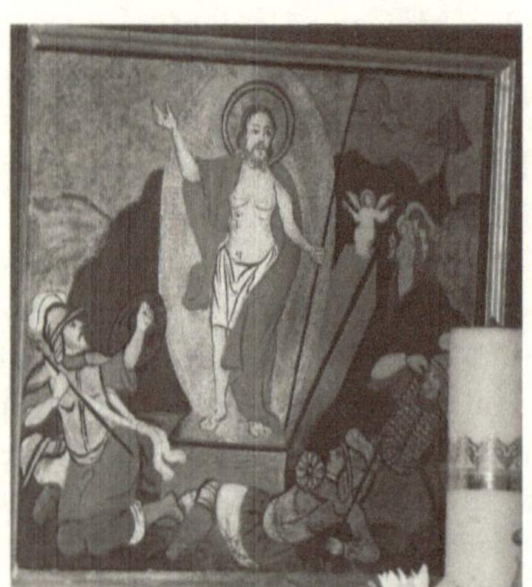

3.5 Resurrected Christ, detail of Passion, Świątkowa Wielka. Source: Agnieszka Gronek, 'Ikony Męki Pańskiej: O przemianach w malarstwie ukraińskim w wiekach XVI–XIX' (PhD diss., Jagiellonian University, 2003), Katalog no. 21.

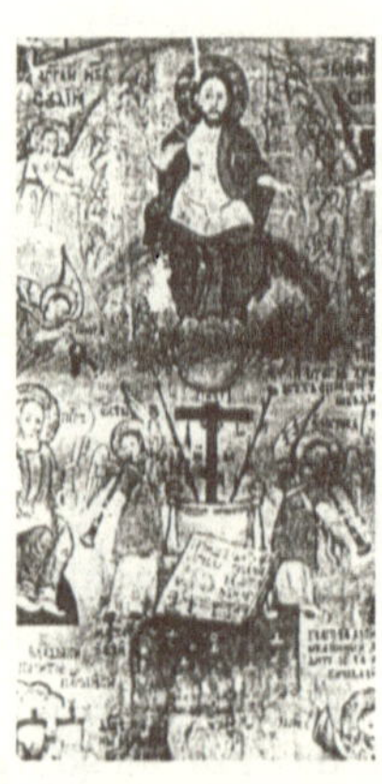

3.6 Son of Man in Mandorla, Świątkowa Mała. Photo: Romuald Biskupski.

case that the attribution to Rybotycze is also not justified. All three of these icons were in churches very close to one another, all quite far from Posada Rybotycka, and no other Last Judgments are as closely related to these three icons as they are to each other. It seems to me much more likely that the icons were commissioned from someone in the vicinity. Moreover, among these same villages is Świątkowa Mała, which has a Last Judgment about fifty years older than the others. It too bears a stylistic resemblance to the later icons of this microregion, and I consider it likely that the painter of the mid-eighteenth century icons learned his craft from the Yakov who painted in 1687 (fig. 3.6). There is a very local tradition here. We shall return to these closely related icons in the next chapter.

It is possible that other icons of the Last Judgment were in fact produced by the Rybotycze artists. Bernadett Puskás has written that Volosianka came, 'certainly, from the Rybotycze workshop.'[23] The Passion of Wola Wyżna has been definitively linked to Posada Rybotycka by a foundational inscription.[24] I am unable to determine whether the Last Judgment from this village was also by the same artist or from the same workshop, but this possibility cannot be excluded. On the whole, however, one must agree with Vasyl Otkovych that 'icons of the Last Judgment are rarely met in the Rybotycze school.'[25]

Another icon of the Last Judgment may also be linked with an identifiable artistic centre. Gronek considers the Passion of Lipie to be a product of the school of Sudova Vyshnia, a town halfway between Przemyśl and Lviv.[26] The painter of this Passion and the Lipie Last Judgment was the same person.

At this point I will attempt to generalize more about the icon painters of the sixteenth through eighteenth centuries, introducing some additional contextual evidence, but also, here and there, simply speculating. Although I have no indisputable evidence for it, I think that painters associated with monasteries and with large painting projects continued to work on icons throughout the sixteenth century. I would place Oleksii in that category. I think the continued participation of monks finds confirmation in the quality of work on icons such as Vovche and Stanylia from the second half of the sixteenth century (fig. 3.7). Even as late as the second half of the seventeenth century, an icon was signed by a certain 'Heorhii Pochaievsky,'[27] whose name suggests that he was from the famous monastery at Pochaiv, to the east of our region.

At the same time, however, there were less proficient painters engaged in the production of icons. Lukov-Venecia, the poor copy of Vanivka, was

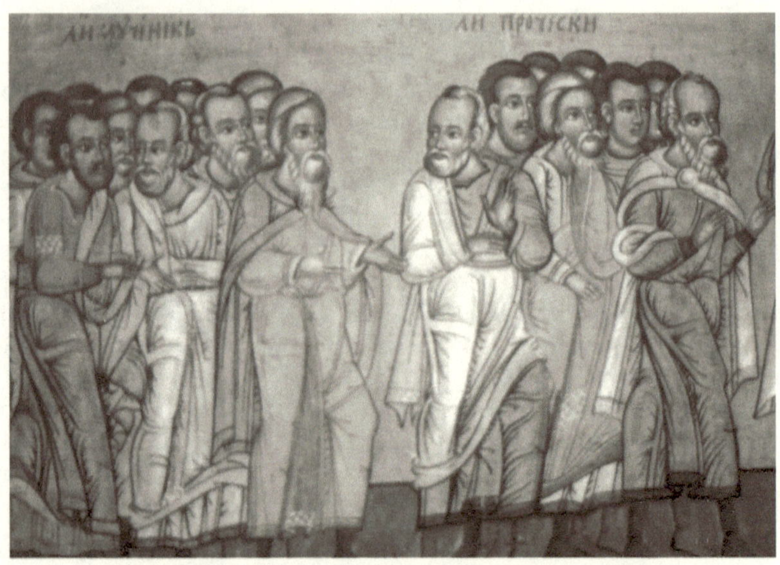

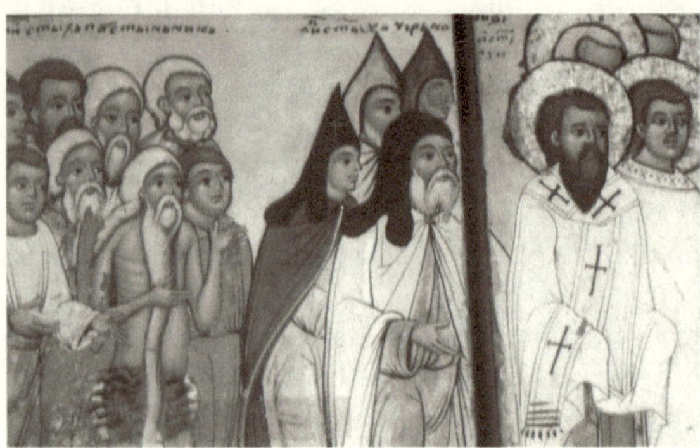

3.7 Martyrs and Prophets, Vovche, and Anchorites and Monks, Stanylia

painted in the first half of the sixteenth century. These less talented painters were secular, I imagine, and they predominated by the second half of the sixteenth century and increased thereafter. Some of these were probably painters from towns, not just Posada Rybotycka and Sudova Vyshnia, but also from elsewhere. An icon from 1579 was signed by Fedusko from Sambir[28] (the form of the name suggests a lay person); a family of icon and mural painters[29] who worked in the second half of the seventeenth century came from Medyka, a small town east of Przemyśl; an icon for a village was painted in 1725 in Nove Misto, northeast of

Dobromyl; an icon was painted in Rava Ruska in 1731;[30] and the iconostasis in a village in Maramureş was executed by 'Ilie, painter from Hust [Khust]' in 1737.[31] There were also important centres of icon painting in two larger towns, Przemyśl (until the mid-sixteenth century)[32] and Zhovkva (1660s–1760s),[33] but the small-town artists were much more active in Carpathian localities. Traditional icon painting on wood does not seem to have survived in the region's largest city, Lviv, although archival documents mention a number of Ukrainian painters there in the sixteenth century.[34] Perhaps the attraction of Polish renaissance and baroque culture in these larger centres deflected the local painters from producing for the rural communities with their established taste for large icons of the Last Judgment.

It is likely that in addition to small-town artisans who specialized in painting, other artisans also engaged in icon painting as a sideline. Carpenters and carvers worked on the village churches – indeed there were probably peasants in certain villages who specialized in this work,[35] and some of them perhaps also painted icons. When I visited the Transcarpathian village of Roztoka in July 2001, a crew of artisans was finishing up a new church; they performed basic construction, but also painted the iconostasis. A writer from Ostroh complained in 1588 that 'instead of excellent, pious painters of icons,' Orthodox sacral art was now executed by 'saddlers, bridlemakers, and other clowns,'[36] which I understand to mean simply artisans for whom the painting of icons was a sideline or for whom it was not their first profession. It might be recalled that Albrecht Dürer (1471–1528) started as a goldsmith and then switched to painting and printmaking.[37]

The case of Marko Domazhyrsky Shestakovych in the early eighteenth century demonstrates that some of the icon painters could have been villagers. As a member of the petty gentry, Shestakovych had some advantages over peasants that made it easier to become an icon painter – his mobility was not restricted as a serf's mobility was, and he had more free time to devote to a craft, since he was not expected to render labour rent to a landlord. But it is not likely that he lived any better than a peasant. From the tale that his icons suggest, he started his work as an icon painter in his own village and then moved south to paint a number of churches within a fifteen kilometre radius. I imagine this is typical. In the earlier period of the development of the Last Judgment icons in our regions, the icons were painted in monasteries or other centres and then conveyed to the churches where they were to be installed. Later on, though, the artists themselves were more willing to move. We shall be able to confirm this with the evidence to be adduced in the next chapter.

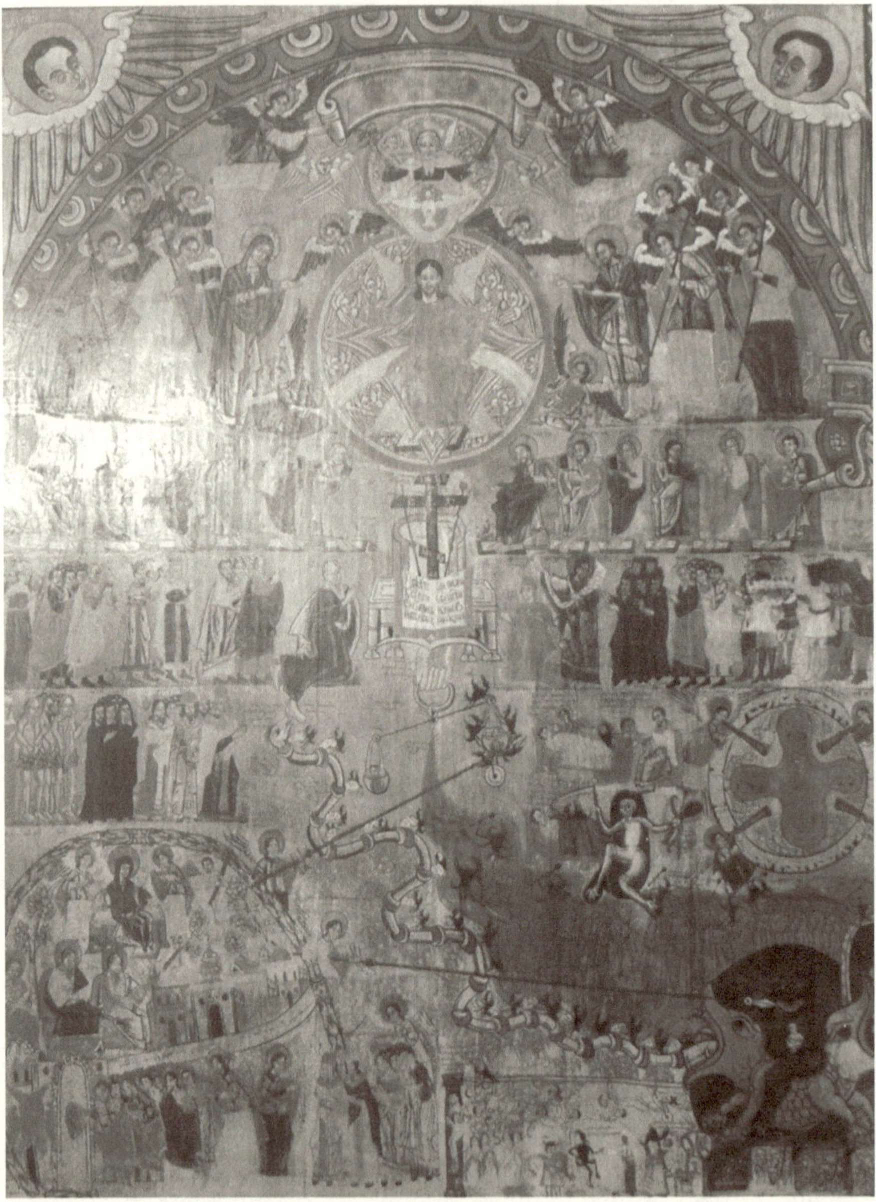

3.8 Jedlinka overview

Two Icons

Most of the rest of this chapter will be taken up with a study of how some of the older elements of the Last Judgment iconography were transformed and new elements added in the course of the sixteenth through eighteenth centuries. Since the emphasis there will fall on the iconography at the level of the individual elements, I want in this section to show how these icons worked as a whole. I will use Jedlinka as a typical example of the Carpathian Last Judgment as a collectively elaborated work of sacral art. I will then examine an icon, Krásny Brod, which has some very distinctive and interesting individual features. Other analyses of individual icons from this period can be found in the literature.[38]

Jedlinka

The icon which may be associated with the village of Jedlinka (fig. 3.8) is now held by the East Slovakian Museum in Košice. As was mentioned above, it was painted in the 1650s by Pavel of Muszyna. Where in the fifteenth-century icons heavenly Jerusalem and the fall of the rebel angels would have been painted, that is in the upper corners of the icon, in Jedlinka two angels appear. Neither looks much like a traditional Byzantine angel and instead both show the influence of Western sacral art. The angel in the upper right corner is labelled a cherub, the one in the upper left is a seraph. A decorative arch separates the angels from the rest of the icon. This particular treatment of the upper portion of the icon is peculiar to Jedlinka.

Moving down the centre, we see the angels rolling up the scrolls. Then within a sphere are the Ancient of Days, labelled as 'God the Father,' as well as the Holy Spirit in the form of a dove. Traditional Byzantine cherubim fly on either side of the sphere. The Son of man is sitting on a rainbow in a mandorla among the celestial powers, the mandorla borne by angels. He is flanked, as tradition dictates, by the Mother of God and John the Baptist. And behind them are, as the inscription tells us, 'angels of the Lord.' Beneath the mandorla is the throne with a crucifix and instruments of the Passion, also the book open to Matthew 25:34. Near the crucifix is an inscription: 'The cross of Christ as a mockery for the Jews' (krest khrystov zhydom na poruhaniie). There are six apostles on either side of the crucifix. Underneath the throne is the hand of God holding scales. From here a river of fire flows down and left into Gehenna. To the right of the throne is Adam in an attitude of worship. His heel is being bitten by a serpent with tollbooths whose tail is in the mouth of the two-headed beast in hell. An inscription near the serpent informs us: 'This is the serpent which for the devils led Adam and Eve in paradise into sin.' Behind Adam are choirs of various saints; another row of saints is underneath them. To the left of the throne is Eve, and behind her are Moses and the peoples. An inscription near Moses reads: 'Moses shows the Jews the true messiah, Christ.' His scroll is not entirely legible; it begins with the words, 'Come, wretched Jews, see ...' The peoples with Moses are Jews, Greeks and Rus', Poles and Germans, Moors and Tatars, and Turks. Below the saints on the right is paradise with all the traditional personages: the Mother of God with angels and the good thief, also the three patriarchs. Below them are the gates of paradise, into which the saints are entering. Below the peoples, on the left, is the resurrection of the dead. Four angels are trumpeting, as the inscriptions tell us, from north, east, west, and south. Another inscription says: 'The dead rise from the graves.'

In the centre of the icon at the bottom is the almsgiving fornicator, with his traditional inscription: 'This man gave alms, but did not give up his fornication. For his almsgiving he sees paradise, but for his fornication he suffers torment.' Continuing to the left on the bottom, we see the new hell (fig. 3.9). In the upper right corner of it is a drunk, and a devil is pouring drink into his mouth. Below him is a slanderer, hanging, as tradition suggests, by his tongue. Below him are two women whose breasts are being attacked by serpents. 'Childless women (*bezditkyni*),' the inscription tells us. To the left of them are two sorceresses, each with the vessel she used for mixing herbs resting on her head. Above the sorceresses hangs a murderer. Also hanging from the top, moving to the left, are a perjurer, false witness, robber, thief, miller (with a millstone around his neck), and someone who did not honour his father. Most of the lower centre and left of the new hell is taken up with an elaborate tavern scene. A bagpiper, fully clothed and even with a jaunty black hat, plays a tune while a devil dances another fully dressed woman into hell. Another devil we see whispering something to the tavernmaid. An inscription tells us that he is telling her to pour less than a full measure of beer. To their left a barrel of beer is filling up a jug. To the left of the new hell are the four traditional torments: '[outer darkness], gnashing of teeth, unsleeping worm, unheatable winter.' Above them are the beast of the apocalypse with Satan holding the soul of Judas. Satan is being pierced by a long lance held by an angel near paradise.

Except for some nuances, what I have described so far is mostly familiar from the fifteenth-century icons. But there are also some entirely new

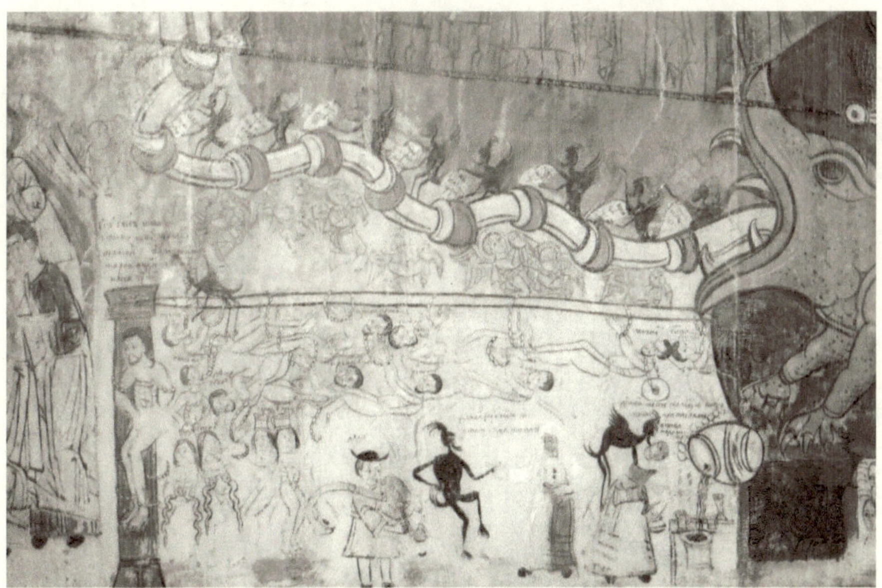

3.9 The New Hell, Jedlinka

elements, located in the space bounded by Moses and the peoples, the river of fire, and the resurrection and in the river of fire itself.

Just below Moses a man is lying in bed with an angel near him (fig. 3.10). The inscription reads: 'This righteous man has died. An angel has come and taken his soul. The death of the righteous man is with praises.' The latter sentence slightly reworks Proverbs 10:7: 'The memory of the righteous is with praises.'[39] Just below the righteous man is another man in bed, this time with a devil taking his soul. The inscription reads: 'This man is sleeping. He is not going to church. He is sleeping himself to sin. Satan leads him, and death stands behind at his heels. The death of sinners is evil.' A large figure of Death is indeed by the bed, carrying a scythe, a bow and arrow, a rake, and a broom. Above Death a man can be seen kneeling beside another man who is sitting. The inscription reads: 'This man came before a priest to confess his sin. A devil forbids him and has pressed his mouth shut.' A little devil is depicted holding the man's lips together. The priest is holding a book open to the penitent thief's words to Christ: 'Lord, remember me when thou comest [into thy kingdom]' (Lk 23:42). These motifs – the death of a sinner and a righteous man, the man sleeping through services, and the bad confession – were common

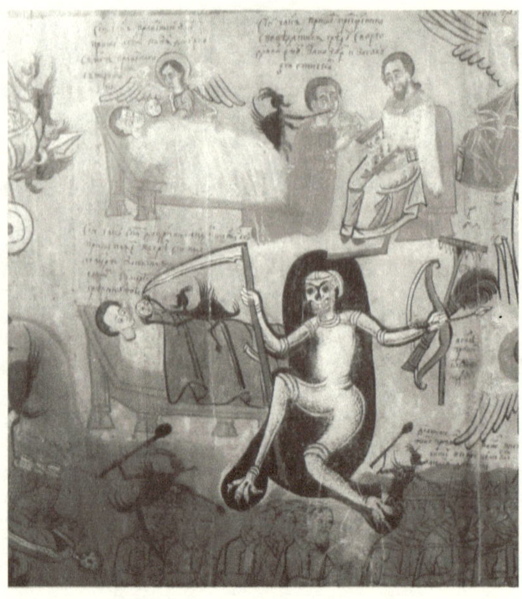

3.10 New Elements, Jedlinka

in the iconography after the fifteenth century, and we shall look more closely at each of them in turn later in the chapter.

In the river of fire there are also some new elements, but these are more particular to the Jedlinka icon. In the narrow part of the river, close to the scales, a devil can be seen pulling a woman into hell by her hair. An inscription informs us what is happening: 'A devil drags a childless woman to hell.' Below that scene a devil is shown pushing a hand cart with three women in it, each with a vessel on top of her head – 'A devil drives sorceresses in a hand cart to hell.' The hand cart was a familiar feature of the later iconography, but this is the only case in which it was filled with sorceresses. Further down the river several devils are mounted on the backs of a group of men and driving them forward with cudgels. The inscription tells us: 'Devils are driving kings, landlords, and impious, unjust people to hell.' Finally, further to the left, are men in chains – 'Devils lead apostates to hell.' This is similar to a scene on Trushevychi, an icon from the late sixteenth century, showing converts to the Polish faith, i.e., Catholicism, being dragged off to hell.[40]

As we see, the Last Judgment icon evolved from the fifteenth century by the elaboration of some of the older elements (here the new hell with some new inhabitants and an extended tavern scene) and by the accretion of new elements (Ancient of Days and Holy Spirit, deaths of a righteous man and sinner, sleeping through services, and bad confession). The Jedlinka icon is full of inscriptions explaining what is depicted. An explanation is even offered for the serpent – he is the one who led humanity into sin – and for the tavernmaid – she is cheating her customers. A few of the elements of the first Carpathian elaboration have been left out: the heavenly Jerusalem and the fall of the rebel angels, the prophet Daniel and his vision of the four beasts/evil kingdoms, and the monks flying into paradise. Although absent in this icon, they still appeared frequently in other icons until the middle of the seventeenth century.[41] Thereafter they were rather rare.[42]

The content choices made for Jedlinka suggest little concrete about its painter, Pavel Mushynsky. He was certainly concerned about confessional issues. He added an explanation of the crucifix that one does not find in other Last Judgments (that it stood there as a mockery to the Jews), he depicted a group of apostates being taken off to hell, and he grouped the peoples by religion – Jews, Eastern Orthodox, Roman Catholics, and Muslims. He also singled out women sinners more than most of the icons did. He depicted three childless women, two in hell with serpents on their breasts and another being dragged there by her hair, and three sorceresses. But what these emphases suggest is not clear.

Krásny Brod

Krásny Brod is a very different piece of work. It dates from the late sixteenth or early seventeenth century. The truly odd thing about the icon is that it is a copy of Lukov-Venecia, which itself, as we know, is a copy of Vanivka, our oldest icon (fig. 3.11). We can tell that it is copying Lukov-Venecia rather than Vanivka because the crucifix and Moses are missing, as in Lukov-Venecia (and not in Vanivka). Krásny Brod follows Lukov-Venecia closely for most of the icon, until the bottom, and since I went over in detail all the elements included in Lukov-Venecia when I discussed Vanivka in the first chapter, I shall concentrate here exclusively on the new additions.

That all of the additions occur in the lower part of the icon can be explained by two factors, one particular to Krásny Brod, the other of general relevance to the evolution of Last Judgment icons. The first factor is that Krásny Brod is simply a longer icon. Lukov-Venecia measured 171 cm x 130 cm, while Krásny Brod measured 218 cm by 132 cm.[43] The

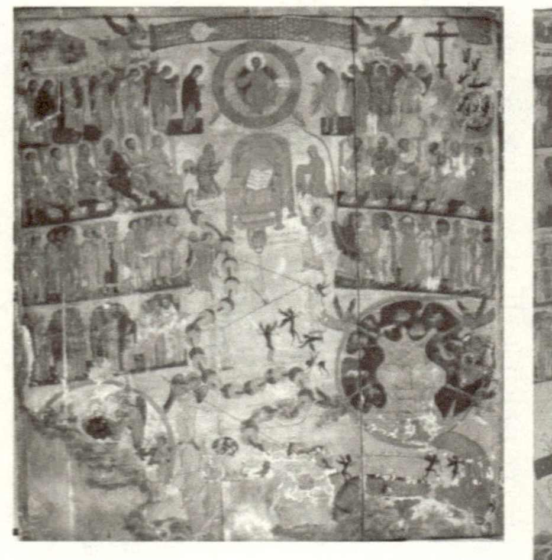
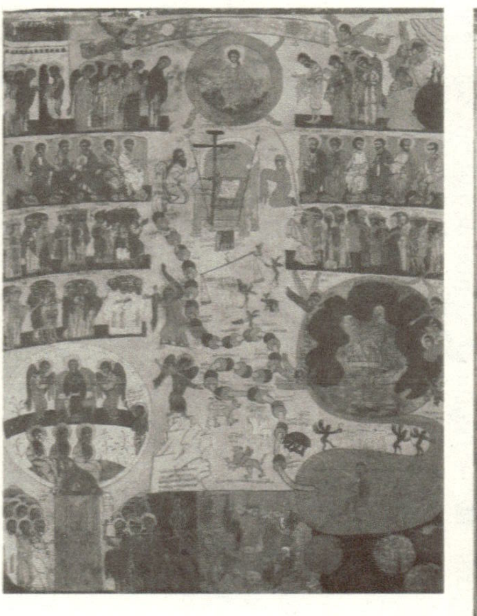
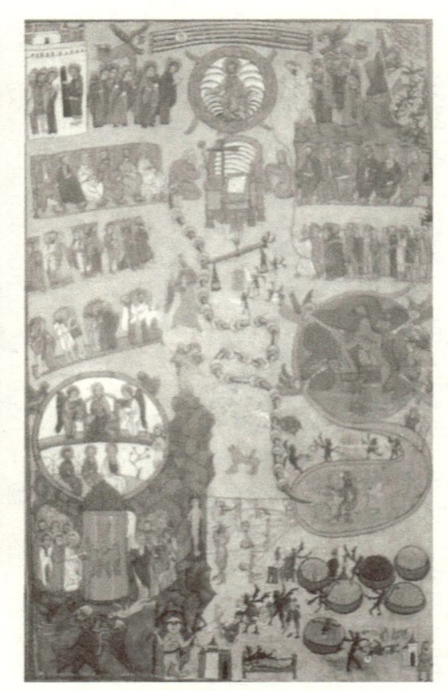

3.11 Vanivka, Lukov-Venecia, Krásny Brod. Source of Lukov-Venecia: Štefan Tkáč, *Ikony zo 16.–19. storočia na severovýchodnom Slovensku* (Bratislava: Tatran, 1982), 138, pl. 66.

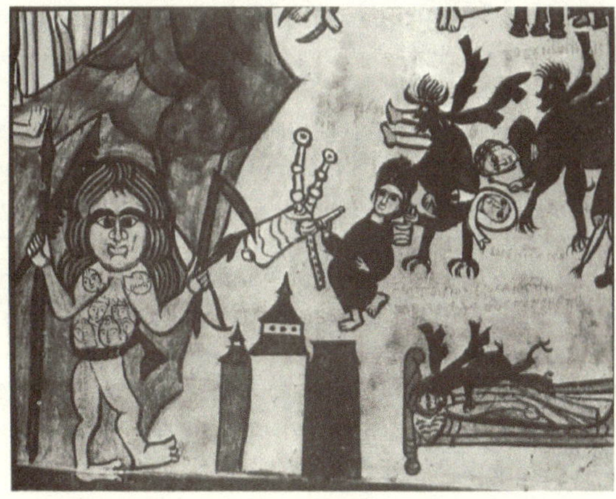

3.12 Death, Sleeper, and Musicians, Krásny Brod. Source: Štefan Tkáč, *Ikony zo 16.–19. storočia na severovýchodnom Slovensku* (Bratislava: Tatran, 1982), 152, pl. 72.

artist had more space to fill and did so with the products of his imagination. I think that the artist deliberately made this icon longer. The width of Krásny Brod is almost a perfect match to Lukov-Venecia, which shows he was carefully measuring when he cut his boards. He could have cut the boards off at 171 cm if he wished, but instead allowed nearly an additional half metre to express himself in. The second factor is that the bottom of the icon was the favoured portion for elaboration among the Carpathian icon painters. In Jedlinka, as we saw, the new additions were near the bottom of the icon. Even in the fifteenth century, those elements that were absent in the northern Rus' archetype of the Last Judgment were mostly added to the Carpathian icon in its lower portions (Death, the new hell, and the tavernmaid). Additions were made primarily with reference to death, sin, punishment, and hell, a tendency that, we shall see, grew in importance as the icons evolved.

The artist here added a figure of Death, a rather comical one from our perspective, a Sunday sleeper being kept warm by a devil, and musicians in the tavern (fig. 3.12). In the bottom left corner is a variation of the sleeper theme: 'A man was going to church, turned back, a devil leads him to hell.' Perhaps developing the theme from Lukov-Venecia, the artist puts two priests on the road to hell. One, shown with a devil on his back, 'took offerings, but did not perform the service; a devil rides him.' The inscription near the other priest is difficult to make out, but it may say that he performed the service incorrectly, so an angel is removing the sacrament from his mouth. A true innovation is the large bird in the bottom right corner under paradise. Again the inscription is difficult to decipher, and all I can read is '... is eating [sinful?] people.'

Is there anything we can say about the artist? He was obviously not satisfied with merely executing a copy and left room to express himself about matters that interested him. He was concerned about ritual and services. He may have been a monk, a member of the community in Krásny Brod. Yet his artistry, especially in the portions not copied directly from Lukov-Venecia, does not suggest someone trained in painting. His inscriptions too are difficult to ascribe to a monk, who would have been learned in Slavonic; the Krásny Brod inscriptions show the influence of the contemporary vernacular (the word for priest is twice spelled *pup* instead of *pop*, reflecting the pronunciation of the closed o in Rusyn/ Ukrainian dialects at that time).

Further Elaboration of the Carpathian Elements

Over time the depiction of all elements in the Last Judgment icon underwent modification, although the original Byzantine elements underwent less. The most radical modifications affected elements introduced during the first Carpathian elaboration, sometimes because the artists no longer understood why the original element was depicted as it was in the first place. In this section I will look at three transformations: the tollbooths, the peoples, and the inhabitants of the new hell, including the tavernmaid.

Tollbooths

The original tollbooths of the fifteenth century were situated on a serpent in the lower centre of the icon. This design remained on half of the icons produced in the sixteenth and first half of the seventeenth century (fig. 3.13).[44] In the second half of the seventeenth and the eighteenth century, it could be found on only about one eighth of the icons.[45]

Another design had emerged early in the sixteenth century, first appearing on the Vilshanytsia icon (fig. 3.14).[46] It represented the tollbooths as a series of booths stacked one upon another on the right border of the icon. We already encountered stacked booths in the previous chapter on the icon from Budeşti-Josani in Romanian Maramureş (fig. 2.28). The booths, as the rings on the serpent, showed a confrontation between a devil holding a scroll with the name of a sin and an angel holding a soul (fig. 3.15). Perhaps the purpose of painting booths on the

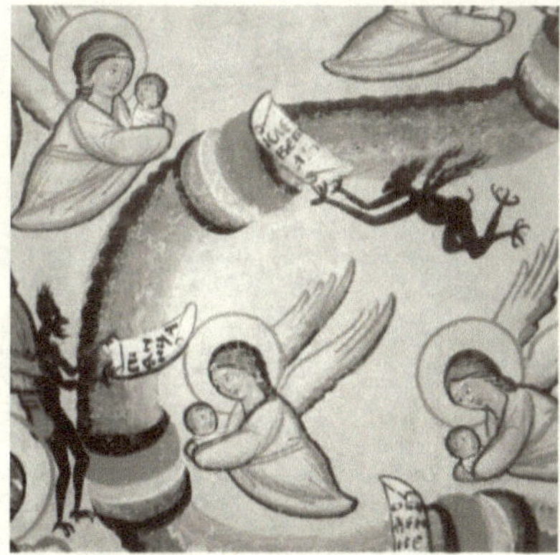

3.13 Tollbooths on Serpent, Paszowa

Table 3.1 Tollbooth Designs in Two Different Periods

	Serpent	Booths	Zigzag	No Tollbooths
sixteenth–first half of seventeenth centuries	8	7	1	0
second half of seventeenth–eighteenth centuries	3	9	4	8

side instead of on a serpent in the centre was to clear the centre of the lower portion of the icon and to allow for the depiction of additional elements. In the first period, these booths could be found on nearly half of the icons;[47] in the second period on about a third.[48]

The third design first appeared on Dolyna, an icon from the 1560s. It depicts a zigzag road with tollbooths at every turn in the road (fig. 3.16). Perhaps this was intended to depict tollbooths in a more literal fashion.[49] This design was only used once in the first period[50] and four times in the second (about one-sixth of the icons).[51]

Although all the icons in the first period had tollbooths of one design or another, a third of the icons in the second period had no tollbooths at all (fig. 3.17).[52] This omission perhaps reflects the influence of the West, which never displayed much interest in the idea of tollbooths and developed instead the concept of purgatory. Clearly, the original tollbooth was modified with the passage of time so that the serpent appeared less frequently, new designs appeared, and some tollbooths disappeared altogether. (See table 3.1.) Within our region there does not seem to be

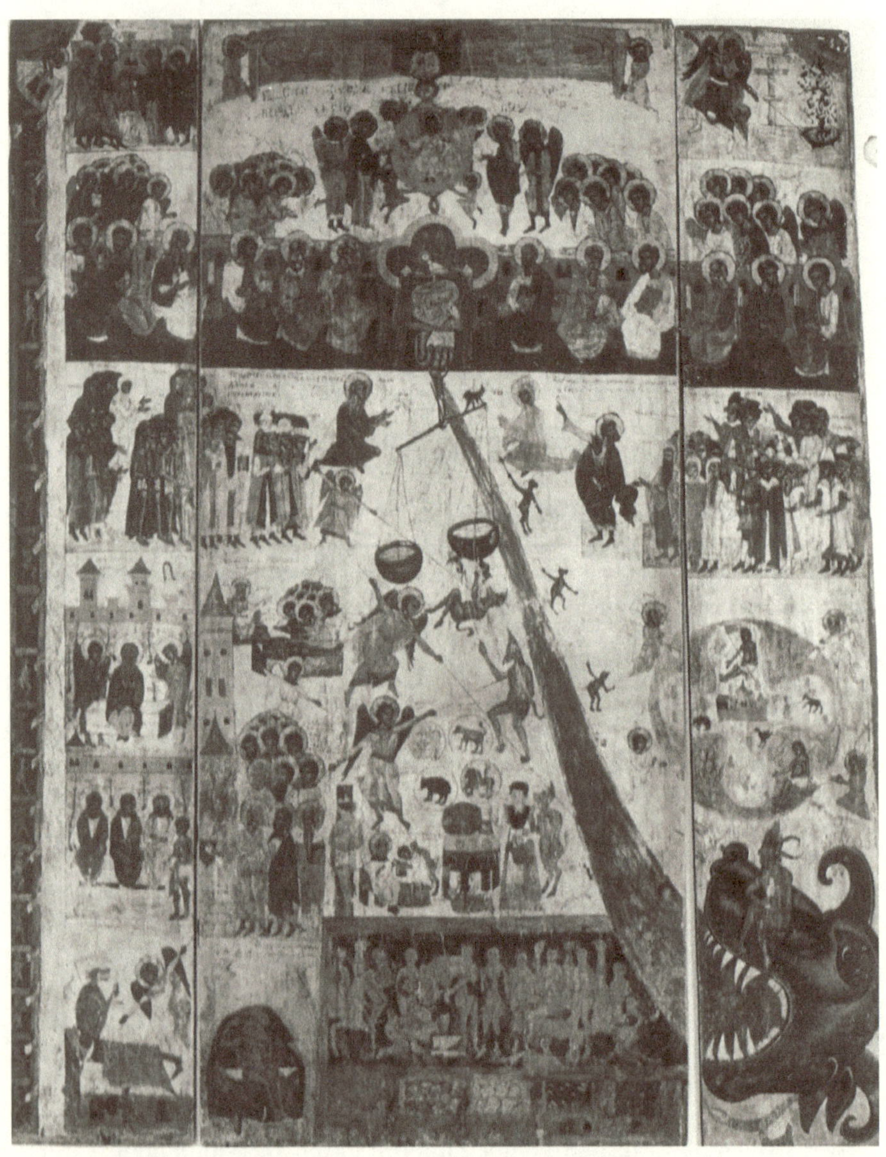

3.14 Vilshanytsia overview

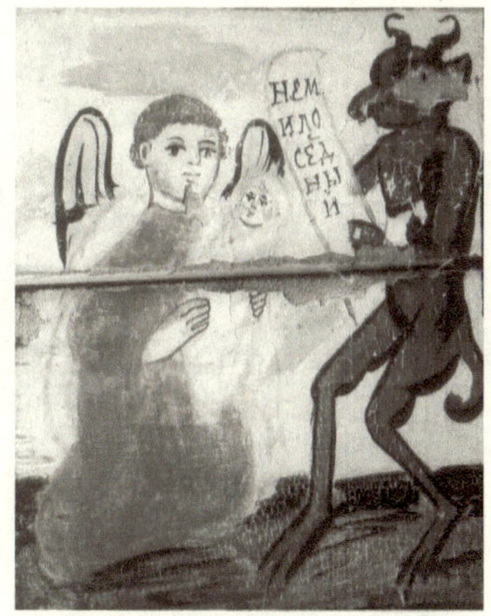

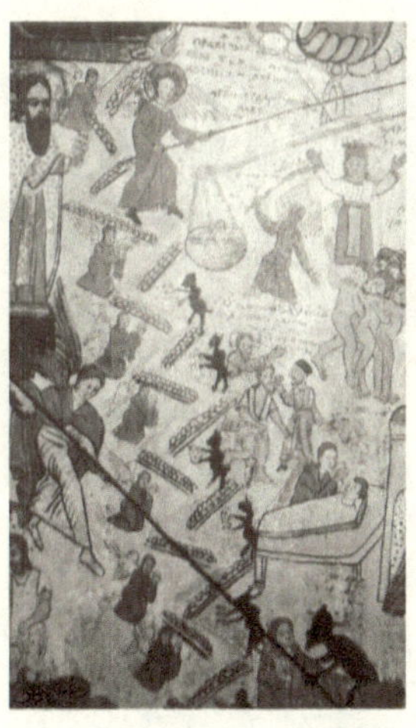

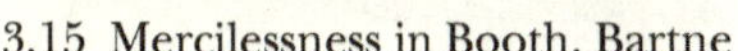
3.15 Mercilessness in Booth, Bartne

3.16 Zigzag Tollbooths, Tiushka

a geographical correlation at all for the different types of tollbooths. The serpent tollbooths were to be found also in Russia, the booths-style tollbooths only in the Carpathian region and Romanian Maramureş, and the zigzag tollbooths only in the Carpathian region.

Peoples

As I hope I adequately demonstrated in the previous chapter, the placement of Moses and the Jews next to the troupe of nations awaiting Judgment was a compositional innovation introduced first in northern Rus' in the fifteenth century. The fifteenth-century Carpathian icons took this element over without any difficulty. But later painters no longer understood why the peoples were positioned as they were. The current literature often refers to the peoples as 'the condemned peoples.' This is what seems to be indicated by a number of features of the iconography. They stand on the left side of the Son of man, with saints symmetrically opposite them on the right side. At the head of the peoples always stand the Jews, whom Moses explicitly condemns. Also present are Turks, Tatars, and other infidels. The river of fire often is depicted running through the peoples (fig. 3.18).[53] But if all these peoples were condemned, then what were Orthodox peoples, like the Greeks and Rus' doing in their midst? Unless one understood that this element combined

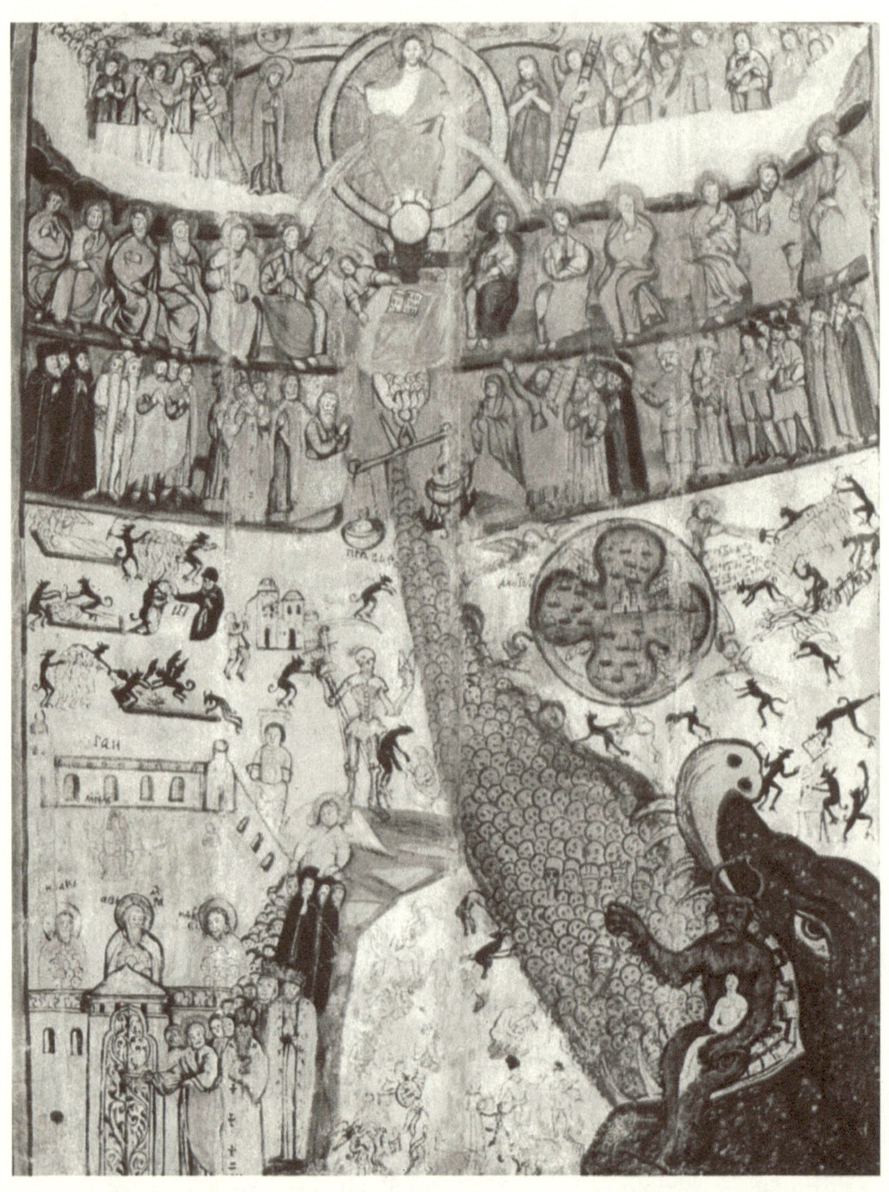

3.17 An Icon with No Tollbooths, Nová Sedlica. Source: Heinz Skrobucha, *Icons in Czechoslovakia* (London, New York, Sydney, Toronto: Hamlyn, 1971), pl. 44.

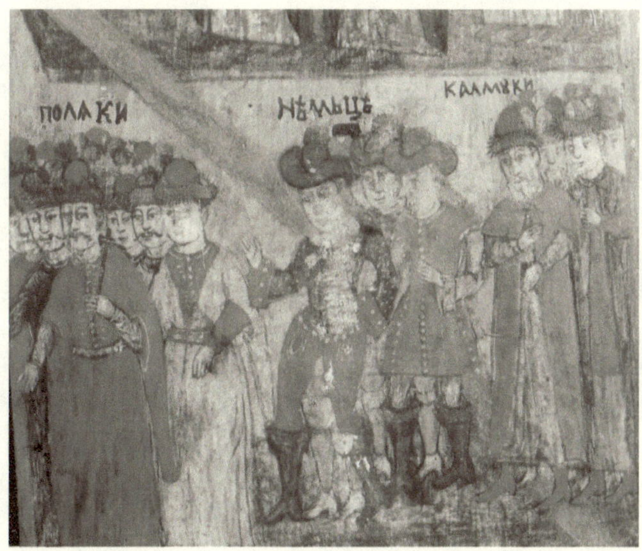

3.18 River of Fire Running through Poles, Germans, and Kalmyks, Moldavsko

two previously separate elements, one of which was indeed about a condemned people but the other of which displayed the universality of judgment, then the original depiction seemed contradictory.

A way to solve the problem, of course, was to omit the Orthodox from the depiction. The Moldavians eliminated the Orthodox when they first began to incorporate the peoples into Last Judgment iconography in the 1530s. The Orthodox were also excluded from a number of the Carpathian Rus' icons beginning in the second half of the sixteenth century,[54] probably in imitation of the Moldavians. This was a direct response to the iconographical contradiction that later artists discerned in the Moses and peoples element. Other elaborations of the peoples motif probably also resulted from the uncertainties that it posed.

Many artists reworked the motif to emphasise religion rather than nation. This is not surprising. A major difference between the context of the fifteenth century and that of later centuries is that the latter were permeated by confessional tensions. The sixteenth century opened with the Reformation. It ended with controversy throughout the Rus' lands in the Polish-Lithuanian commonwealth over the union of the Rus' Orthodox with the Catholic Church (the Union of Brest, 1596). Much of the seventeenth century, in the commonwealth as in the rest of Europe, was taken

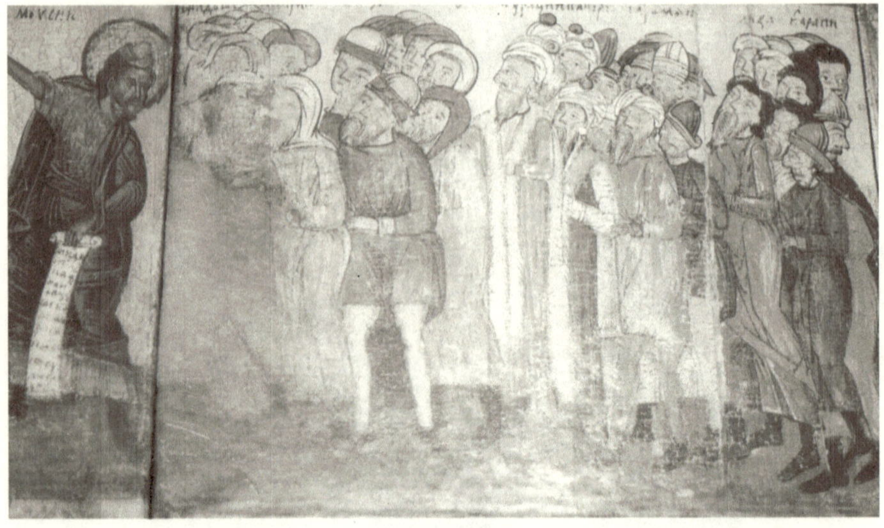

3.19 Moses, Jews and Karaites, Poles and Germans, Turks and Tatars and Armenians, unidentified and Arabs, Przemyśl Land Museum

up with wars that were partially wars of religion. The seventeenth and eighteenth centuries saw the entrance of our Carpathian territories into union with Rome, both in Hungary and Poland. This wrangling over religion, which we already noticed in the examination of the Jedlinka icon, was reflected in how and which peoples were portrayed in the icons.

There are eight icons, mainly from the sixteenth century, that present the peoples grouped by religion. As well as Jedlinka, which is from the mid-seventeenth century, they are Vilshanytsia, Bahnovate, Vovche, Stanylia, Paszowa, and Przemyśl Land Museum (fig. 3.19). Perhaps not accidentally, all these icons display the kind of better artistry that I would link with the monasteries; none of them can be considered folk or primitive. Wola Wyżna, from the second half of the seventeenth century, also has its peoples arranged in order of religion, but I am reluctant to place it at the same level of artistry as the icons just named.[55]

A related development was the inclusion of members of particular confessions alongside those defined by nation. All the surviving icons that do this come from the late seventeenth or eighteenth century, although there is evidence that the practice developed earlier.[56] Arians, i.e., Unitarians,[57] Calvinists,[58] heretics,[59] and Lutherans[60] all appeared in

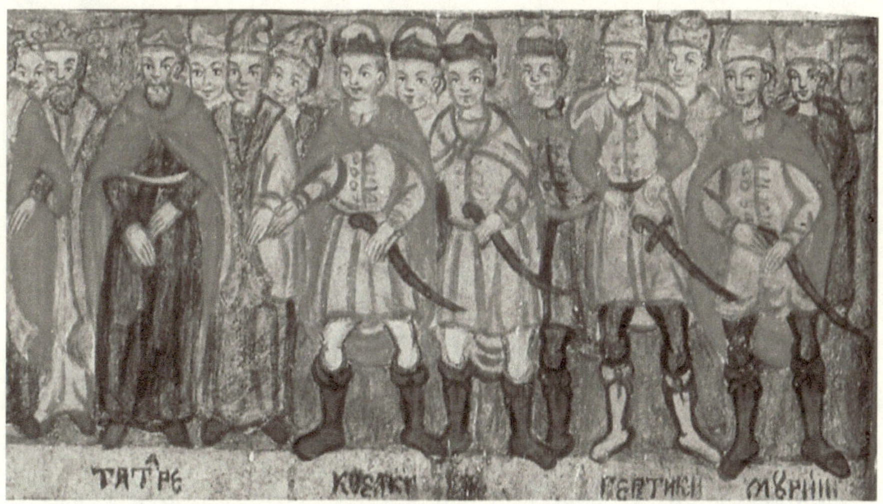

3.20 Tatars, Cossacks, Heretics, and Moors, Museum of the History of Religion

the icons alongside Jews, Tatars, Turks, and (usually) Rus' (fig. 3.20). In the eighteenth century, the Kalmyks began to appear on the icons, [61] probably because Peter I used Kalmyks during his campaigns in Poland – in 1708, in fact, Kalmyks appeared in Chełm, just north of our region.[62] The inclusion of the Kalmyks made particular sense because they were Buddhists and represented another religion (fig. 3.18).

The original icons of the fifteenth century knew only nine nations: Jews, Greeks, Rus', Poles, Germans, Turks, Tatars, Moors, and Armenians. Starting early in the sixteenth century the human geography of the icons was greatly expanded. The nations most frequently added were Arabs[63] and Hungarians[64] – more Muslims and Roman Catholic neighbours. The Karaites usually appeared in those icons in which the peoples were grouped by religion, since the Karaites also professed a form of Judaism.[65] Gypsies, who came to this region in the early fifteenth century, appeared in the icons from time to time,[66] as did other East European peoples – Albanians,[67] Czechs,[68] Romanians (as Muntenians[69] and Vlachs[70]), and Serbs.[71] One icon depicted 'Slavs,'[72] perhaps meaning Slovaks.

An icon from the later seventeenth century, most probably from Máramoros county, showed Cossacks among the nations.[73] Presumably they appear here because of Cossack incursions into Moldavia and alliances with Transylvania in the 1650s. One of the Cossacks in the icon is

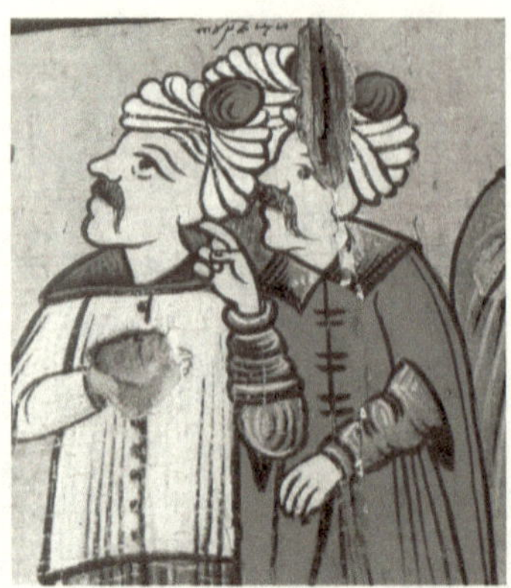

3.21 Disfigured Turks, Mala Horozhanka

shown extending his hand to a Tatar, a reference to the Cossack-Tatar alliances of the mid-seventeenth century (fig. 3.20). Other Europeans that appeared among the troupe of peoples were Spaniards,[74] Italians,[75] and Saxons.[76] A few exotic peoples also garnished the icons:[77] Egyptians and Ethiopians,[78] Ishmaelites, and Saracens.[79]

A few of the icons are particularly notable on account of their peoples element. Bartne does not actually depict any of the nations. Perhaps its bottom board is missing, an issue that we shall consider in the following chapter, but all that appears on the surviving icon is inscriptions. It is nonetheless the richest collection of peoples in the entire corpus of Last Judgments: Jews, Turks, Tatars, Germans, Moors, Poles, Serbs, Armenians, Galatians, Kalmyks, Franks, Magdeburgians, Hungarians, Calvinists, Lutherans, Vlachs, Gypsies, ‘and all pagans’ (*i vshytki pohanie*). (Since a few of these nationalities only appear here, I did not include them in the listing above.) Świątkowa Mała also had an original treatment of the peoples. It included Rus' among the peoples, but reflecting the confusion about why Rus'' was included among what appear to be condemned peoples, the artist also put ‘some Rus'' (*dekotra Rus'*) among the saved, along with Greeks. Among the ‘condemned peoples’ he put priests (*popy*), but balanced this condemnation by placing among the saved ‘God-loving and good-doing priests’ (*Boha liubiashchii i dobri chyniashche popy*). There is nothing particularly remarkable about the artist’s treatment of the peoples in Mala Horozhanka, but the reception is noteworthy: it appears that the Turks were shot with a musket and stabbed with a knife (fig. 3.21).

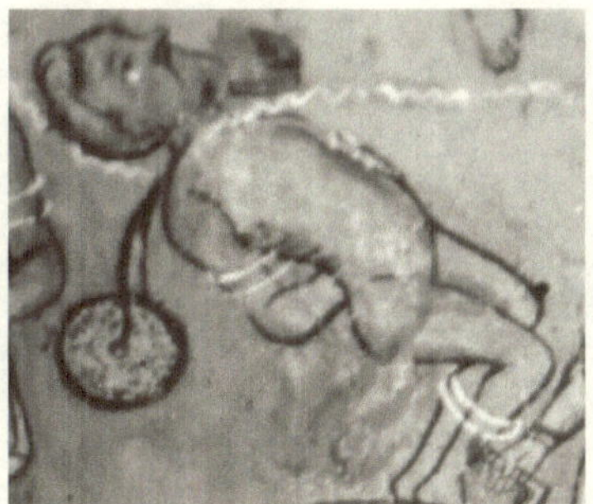

3.22 Miller, Hankowice

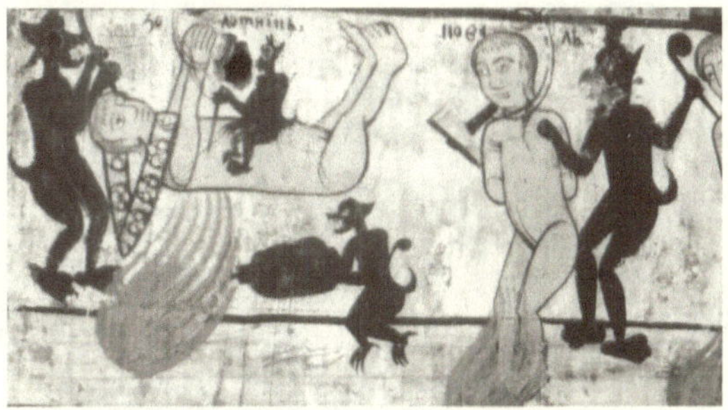

3.23 Goldsmith and Blacksmith, Dolyna

Diversification of the Inhabitants of Hell

Just as the element of Moses and the peoples did, the element of the new hell also underwent a population diversification from the sixteenth century on. Many of the new additions were craftsmen. The miller is the most common of them;[80] he is often seen in hell with a millstone around his neck, which makes him easy to recognize, even when the inscriptions are no longer legible (fig. 3.22). As Carlo Ginzburg observed, 'the age-old hostility between peasants and millers had solidified an image of the miller – shrewd, thieving, cheating, destined by definition for the fires of hell. It's a negative stereotype that is widely corroborated in popular traditions, legends, proverbs, fables, and stories.'[81] One of the icons even specifies that the tormented miller is 'an unjust miller.'[82] Other craftsmen in hell were blacksmiths,[83] coppersmiths,[84] goldsmiths,[85] tailors,[86] tanners,[87] and weavers.[88] They too were often accompanied by the tools of their trade (fig. 3.23).

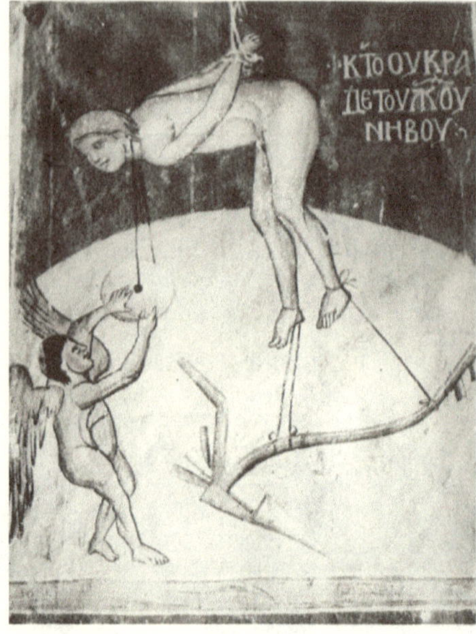

3.24 He Who Stole Someone Else's Land. Source: Pavle Mijović, *Dečani*, 3rd ed. (Belgrade: Jugoslavija, 1970), pl. 39.

Craftsmen were tormented in hell in Last Judgment images over much of the Orthodox world. A tailor with his shears appeared in a thirteenth-century Greek icon; a dishonest miller in a fourteenth-century Last Judgment in Cyprus; millers, tailors, and weavers in fourteenth- and fifteenth-century Cretan images; 'weavers who received at a good price and took extra of what was weaved by cheating on their promise and oath' in a Ukrainian icon from outside our region;[89] and a goldsmith in a mural in Lesnic, Transylvania.[90]

The idea that craftsmen will end up in hell was also confirmed in the reworking of 'The Journey of the Mother of God among the Torments' that we cited in the previous chapter. The Mother of God saw 'sinful millers' hanging upside down over fire with millstones around their necks. Archangel Michael explained: 'These men are artists and millers who dishonestly took others' seed and flour, who stole it, and therefore they are tormented so.' She also saw blacksmiths who stole others' iron when they were working it, weavers who stole thread and cloth, tailors, cobblers, and harness-makers.[91]

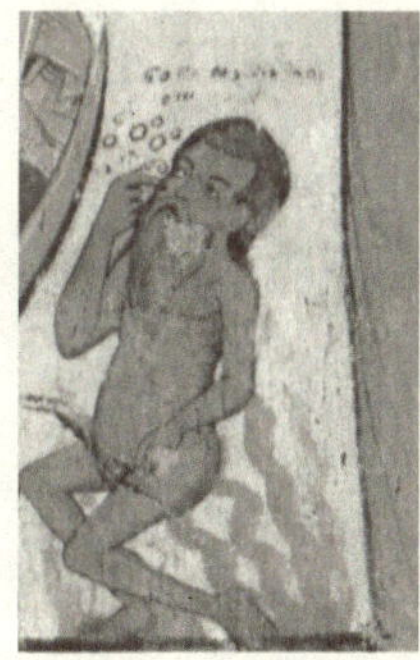

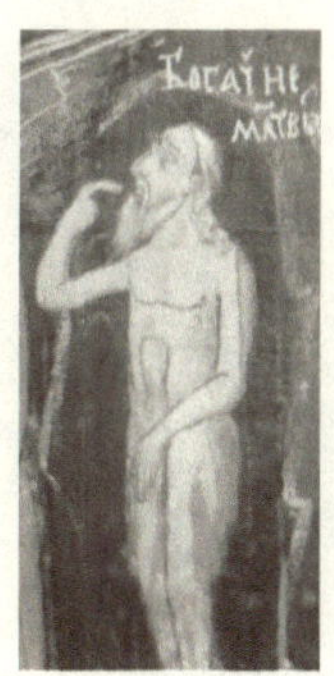

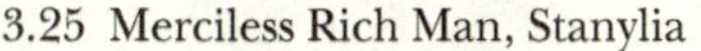

3.25 Merciless Rich Man, Stanylia

3.26 Merciless Rich Man, Lipie

It is the same story with someone who ploughed another's land. He can be found in a fourteenth-century fresco at Dečani in Serbia (see fig. 3.24) as well as in our Carpathian icons[92] and on a mural from 1793–4 in Romanian Maramureş.[93] The Mother of God also saw him on her journey through hell.[94]

In Dolyna a devil carries a merchant on his back, taking him to hell. A few of the icons have rich men in hell or right near it,[95] as did a Greek icon of the thirteenth century. These are descendents of the rich man from the Lazarus tale. The merciless rich men in both Stanylia and Lipie point to their mouths in the characteristic gesture from that parable (figs 3.25 and 3.26). Ukrainian sermons of the sixteenth and seventeenth centuries also condemned merciless rich men more generally. A Byzantine sermon that circulated widely in translation throughout Rus' lands in Poland-Lithuania explains the matter clearly: 'For whoever has much and does not perform mercy is a predator and usurer, even if he did no harm to anyone; because all that which the rich man possesses beyond his means and as surplus and he does not lend to the needy and poor, it is just as if he snatched it and took it away from those in want and poverty.'[96]

Two icons from the second half of the sixteenth century show judges or local officials, chained together by the neck, being led into hell.[97] Three eighteenth-century icons placed local officials in hell.[98] A 'blood-drinker' (*kryvopitsia* [*sic*]) appeared in one icon.[99] Rather than referring to vampirism, the blood-drinker probably denoted a sinner guilty of an injustice. The Mother of God's 'Journey' explains that 'merciless judges did not judge honestly, they drank others' blood.'[100] A sermon of Ephraim the Syrian said: 'Woe to him who cheats on the wage of his hired man, which is the same as drinking blood.'[101]

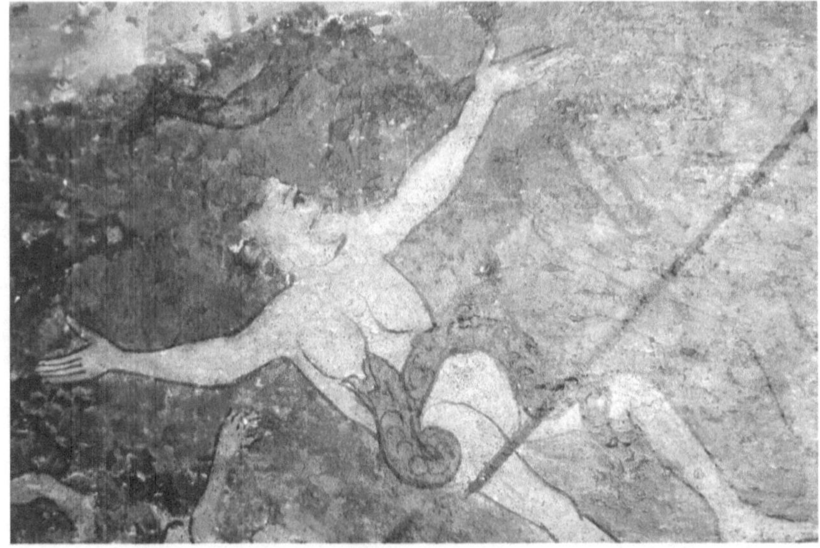

3.27 Woman Attacked by Serpents, no inscription, Tiushka

Although these infernal inhabitants were stock figures in the Balkans before they migrated to the Carpathians, they indicate that social issues were interesting the painters and presumably those who hired them. We shall see more evidence of this as we examine new elements that were incorporated into the icons. It is probably not a coincidence that the first half of the seventeenth century was a time of economic crisis in the Carpathian region.[102]

In the fifteenth century, as we have already seen, sorceresses and infanticides were painted with serpents attacking their breasts. So too were they depicted in the following centuries.[103] The motif was a popular one, and some icons portrayed two women with serpents. There was some extension too of the sins or conditions that precipitated this particular punishment (fig. 3.27). Childless women (*bezditkyni*) were now also afflicted with serpents,[104] presumably because their milk was going to waste. An icon from the second half of the seventeenth century shows a 'milk-destroyer' (*mlekohubtsa*) in hell. Although she has no serpents attached to her, her breasts are shown spurting milk that is thereby wasted (fig. 3.28).[105] Perhaps this lacteal theme explains why one icon shows a woman who stole butter attacked by serpents in the same way; I think it more likely, however, that the painter of this rather late icon, who no

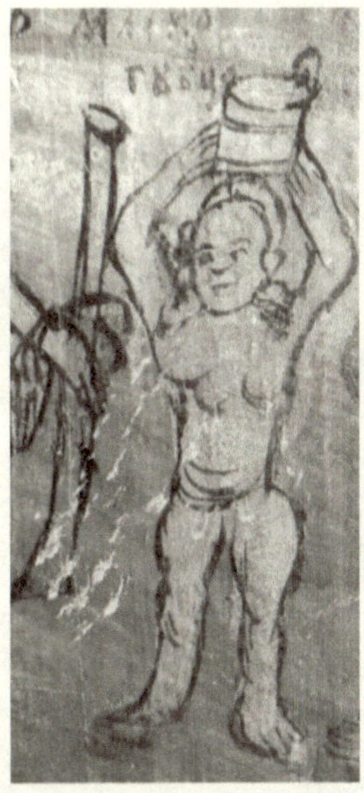

3.28 Milk-Destroyer, Dobroslava

longer understood the meaning of the almsgiving fornicator, also no longer understood the potion-mixing vessel on a woman's head and misinterpreted it as a pail for butter.[106] A late eighteenth-century icon from Transcarpathia has the most outrageous version of the serpents-on-the-breasts motif. A 'mouth-doer' (*ustedilitsa*), i.e., a woman who engaged in oral sex, is attacked by serpents, and the soul of a baby comes out of her mouth. Right next to her is a scene of a devil defecating into presumably the same woman's mouth, with an inscription saying 'all the devil's filth into her mouth' (fig. 3.29).[107] I cannot be sure that this scene was not repainted later and does not represent a later sensibility.

There are a few more sexual sinners in hell than there were before. Female fornicators[108] and adulterous couples[109] appear (fig. 3.30). A priest's wife is in Ruská Bystrá, but I have been unable to read the inscription fully; presumably she is there for a sexual transgression, as 'The Journey of the Mother of God among the Torments' recorded.[110] A godfather and godmother were in hell in Roztoka, probably because they were lovers and thus committed the sin of spiritual incest (fig. 3.31).[111] Others who found their way to hell in the sixteenth century and after were a desperate person,[112] a liar,[113] people who did not honour their

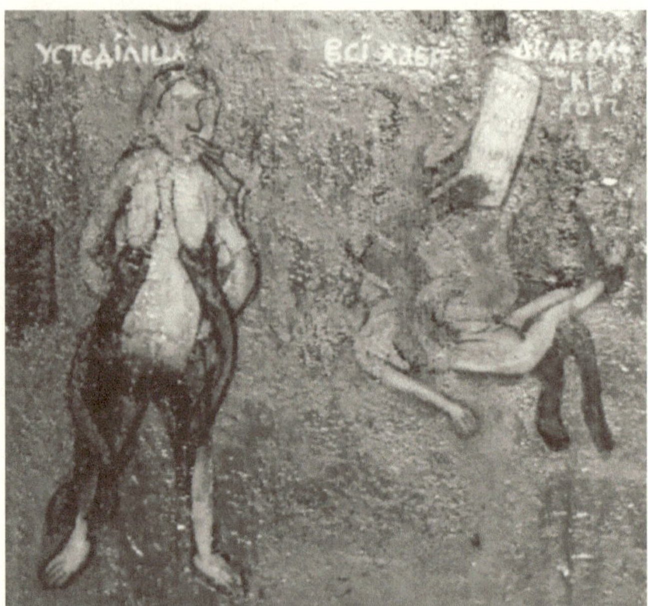

3.29 Mouth-Doer and Defecating Devil, Nehrovets

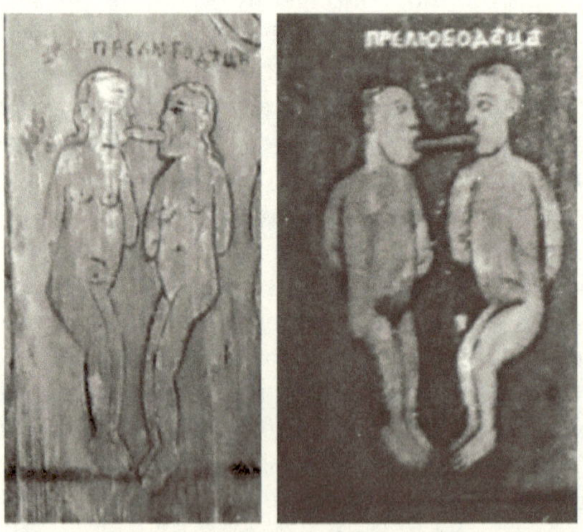

3.30 Adulterous Couples, Shelestovo and Nehrovets

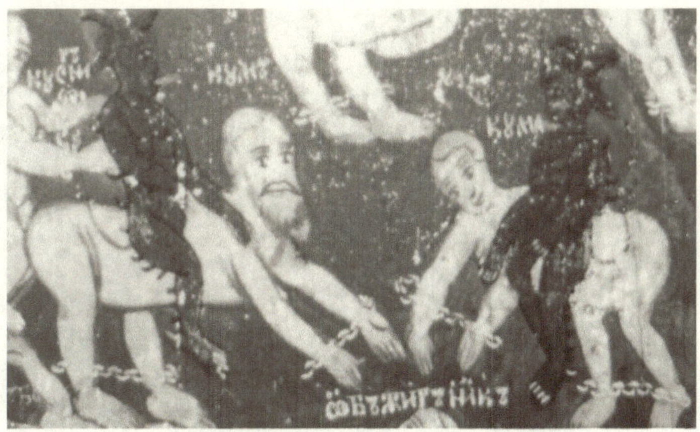

3.31 Godfather and Godmother, Roztoka

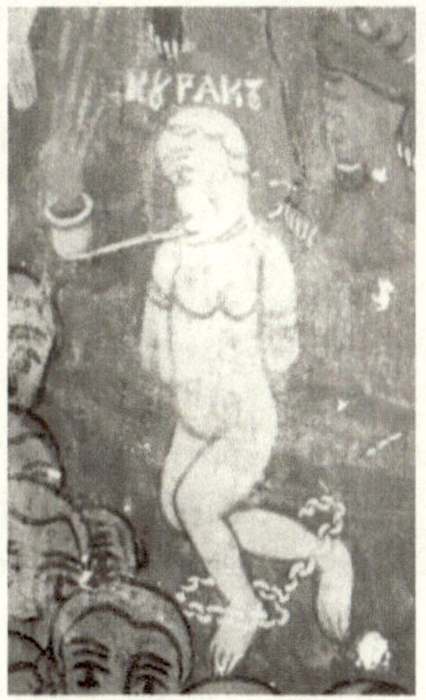

3.32 Smoker, Roztoka

parents,[114] people who changed their faith,[115] a quarrelsome man,[116] a smoker,[117] and a tobacco maid (fig. 3.32).[118]

The tavernmaid, as we saw in the previous chapter, had ended up in the new hell fully clothed, copied closely from a Gothic model. Painters after the fifteenth century certainly had no memory of this. They inherited a picture of a tavernmaid with a barrel and began to elaborate it, as they had elaborated much else in the icons. Perhaps the anomaly that the tavernmaid was the only figure with clothing on in hell suggested that the tavern was still on earth, but leading directly into hell. The painters

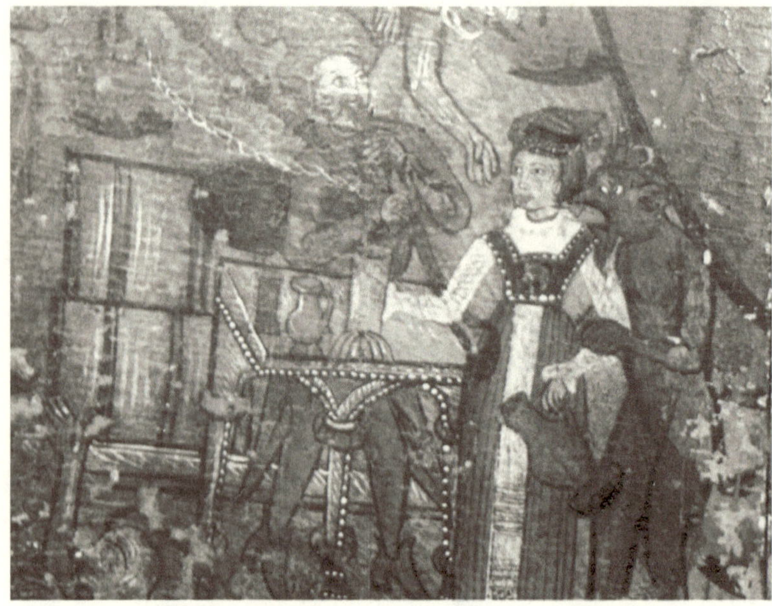

3.33 Piper and Tavernmaid, Kamianka Strumylova

added more clothed figures – customers, musicians, and dancers. Beginning in the mid-sixteenth century such elaborate tavern scenes often appeared in the bottom left corner of the new hell (figs. 3.33, 3.34, 3.35).[119] The musicians most frequently painted were bagpipers; the icons, after all, were painted for highland villages where sheep stomachs were plentiful. Moldavsko showed a dice-player along with the other stock figures. A few icons, none from earlier than the end of the sixteenth century, bear an inscription near the tavernmaid, saying that the devil is whispering to her not to pour a full measure.[120] I understand this to be a late interpolation made in the spirit of the cheating craftsmen in hell. It is likely that the formulation follows a Western model.[121]

New Elements

In addition to reworking the already existing elements, painters after the fifteenth century also incorporated new elements into the Last Judgment icon. For the most part, these innovations spread widely across the region and appeared in many icons.

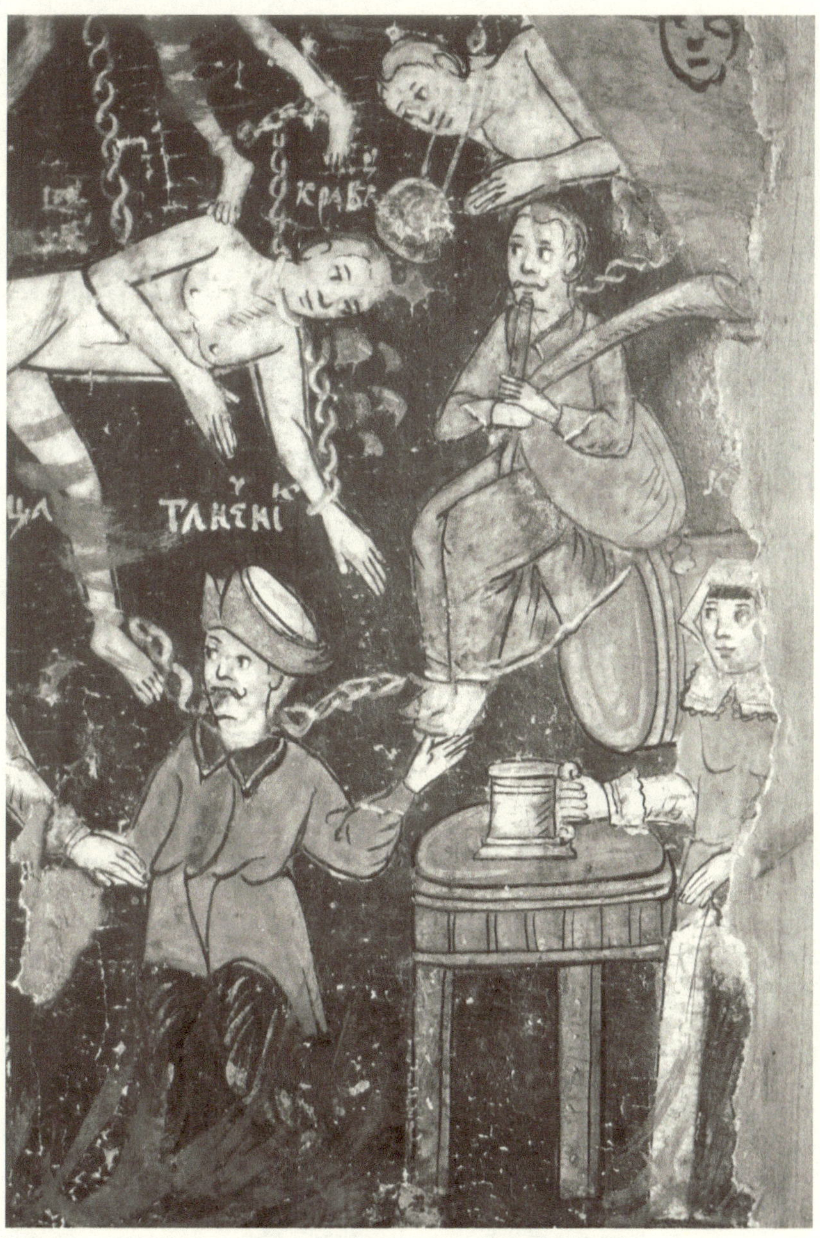

3.34 Piper, Tavernmaid, and Dancer, Lipie

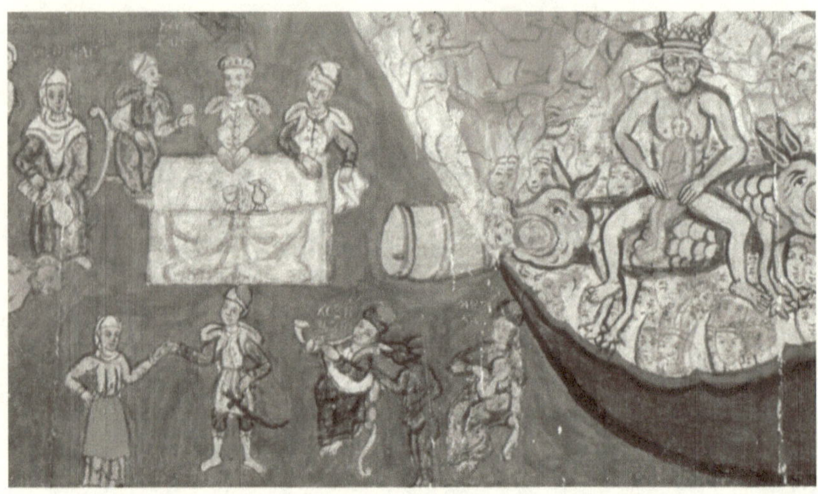

3.35 Tavern Scene, Museum of the History of Religion

The Ancient of Days and the Holy Spirit

A trinitarian motif entered the icon in the sixteenth century: in addition to the Son of man, the second person of the trinity, the first person, God the Father, was introduced in the form of 'the Ancient of Days' and the Holy Spirit in the form of a dove. The Ancient of Days and the Holy Spirit appeared frequently through the early seventeenth century, especially in icons of the monastic type; they are rarer thereafter.[122] The Ancient of days was positioned above the Son of man. Usually he was painted as an old man with white clothing and white beard, in order to match the description in Daniel 7:9: 'the Ancient of Days did sit, whose garment was white as snow, and the hair of his head like the pure wool.' The Holy Spirit was usually depicted as a white dove on the throne of judgment (fig. 3.36).

The Ancient of Days had been known in Serbian iconography since the 1250s, but not in connection with the Last Judgment. This figure first became associated with Last Judgment iconography in the frescoes of Snetogorsk Monastery in Pskov from 1313.[123] Novgorod-Tretiakov has the Ancient of Days directly above the Son of man, as in the Carpathian icons. The Ancient of Days remained a standard feature of Russian Last Judgment icons.[124] Northern Rus' iconography of the Last Judgment included the Holy Spirit less frequently. A fifteenth-century icon of the throne alone, ascribed to the school of Andrei Rublev, depicted the Holy

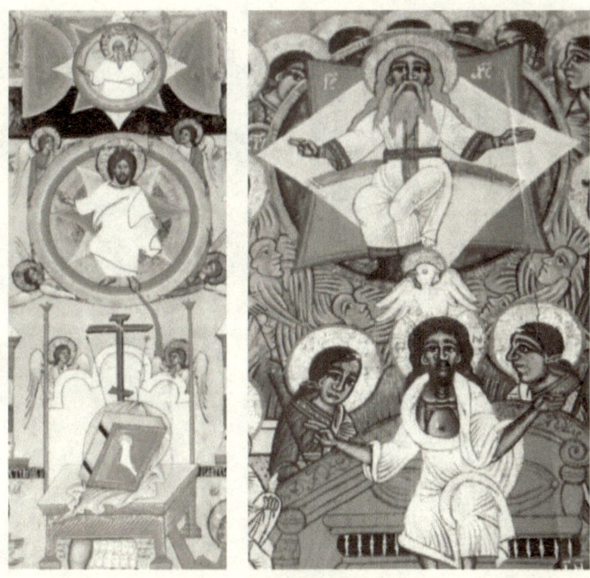

3.36 The Ancient of Days, Son of Man, and Holy Spirit, Stanylia and Mala Horozhanka

Spirit there as a white dove.[125] A sixteenth-century Last Judgment from Novgorod (Church of Ss Boris and Gleb-in-Plotniki) showed Christ, the Ancient of Days, and the Holy Spirit in a circle in the upper left corner of the icon.[126] Moldavian frescoes of the Last Judgment generally included the Holy Spirit, also situated on the throne, either alone or with the Ancient of Days.[127] The element seems to have appeared first in the Moldavian frescoes rather than in the Carpathian icons. It is perhaps not a coincidence that the combination of the Ancient of Days and the Holy Spirit began to fall out of Carpathian icons shortly after the last of the great Moldavian fresco projects was completed (Suceviţa).

Death Scenes

The depiction of death scenes also probably came to the Carpathian icons from Moldavia. A number of the Moldavian frescoes, beginning in the late fifteenth century and continuing through the sixteenth, show the death of a righteous man, usually accompanied by the death of a sinner.[128] An angel accepts the soul of the righteous man while David plays on a lute nearby, but a devil awaits the soul of a sinner and an angel of

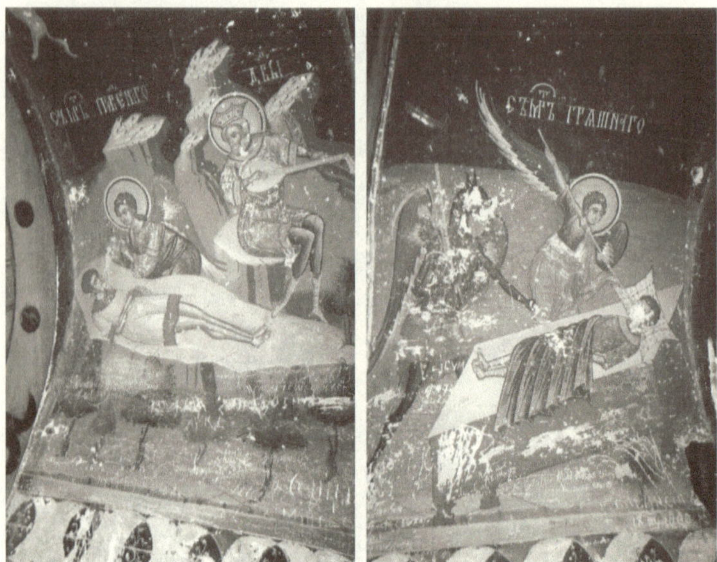

3.37 Deaths of Righteous Man and Sinner, Sucevița

death kills the sinner with a spear (fig. 3.37). The scene of the death of the righteous man has Byzantine roots that reach back to the early thirteenth century,[129] and a variant also appears in the Kyivan psalter of 1397,[130] but these were not connected with Last Judgment iconography. The scene is almost unknown on Russian icons of the Last Judgment.[131]

Death scenes of one sort or another appear on Carpathian icons from the sixteenth century onward,[132] with the frequency higher in the sixteenth and early seventeenth century than later (again, corresponding to the period of the Moldavian fresco projects). Many of them are very clearly the same pair of deaths as in the Moldavian frescoes, that is, of the righteous man and the sinner.[133] But others are instead clearly labelled as the deaths of poor Lazarus and the rich man.[134]

In the Carpathian icon, the personified Death, rather than an angel, was normally depicted in the act of slaying the sinner. Often this scene was accompanied by a verse from the psalms: 'The death of sinners is evil' (Ps 33:21).[135] Radelychi amends this verse to refer also to the rich man: 'The death of the rich sinner is evil.' Jedlinka, as we saw, modifies a verse from Proverbs to match the inscription for the righteous man: 'The death of the righteous man is with praises.' The 'with praises' also

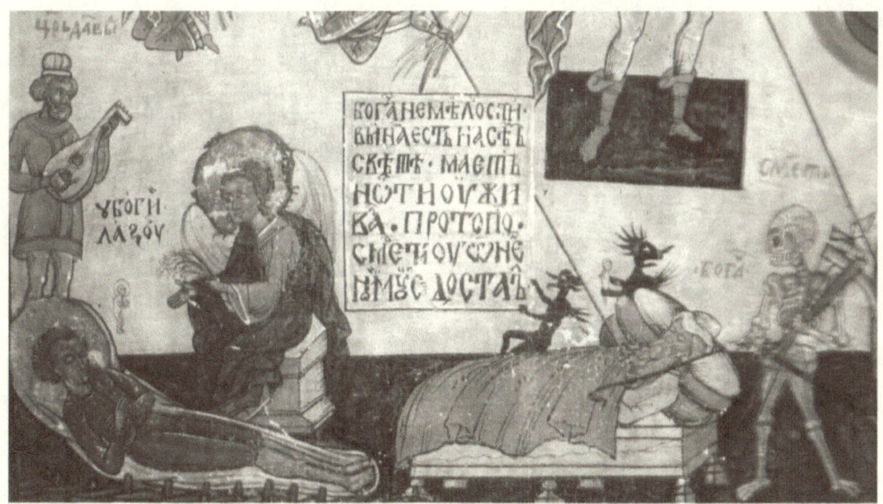

3.38 The Death of Poor Lazarus and the Rich Man, Bahnovate

appears above the death of the righteous man in Hankowice.[136] Bahnovate places the following inscription near the rich man: 'The rich man who is merciless to us is in this world, he uses his goods, but after death he will be tormented in the fire' (fig. 3.38).

The interest in the punishment of the rich man fits well with the social tendencies we have already observed in the expansion of the population of the new hell.

To Hell in a Hand Cart

Another element with social-conflict implications appeared in the icons at the end of the sixteenth century: devils driving sinners off to hell in a hand cart (fig. 3.39).[137] I have not been able to read many of the inscriptions. A late one just says that 'devils take sinful souls to hell.'[138] Jedlinka, as we saw above, put sorceresses in the hand cart. Three icons, however, identified the personages being wheeled off to hell as landlords. Lipie: 'A devil conveys on a cart lords and ladies to hell.' Plavie: 'A merciless landlord.' Świątkowa Mała: 'Devils lead a lord.' Another icon has the man in the hand cart dressed as a lord,[139] while another shows three men wearing crowns in the cart (fig. 3.40).[140] These depictions appear in the context of the complete enserfment of the peasantry on the Polish side of the border, which was completed by the first half of the sixteenth century,

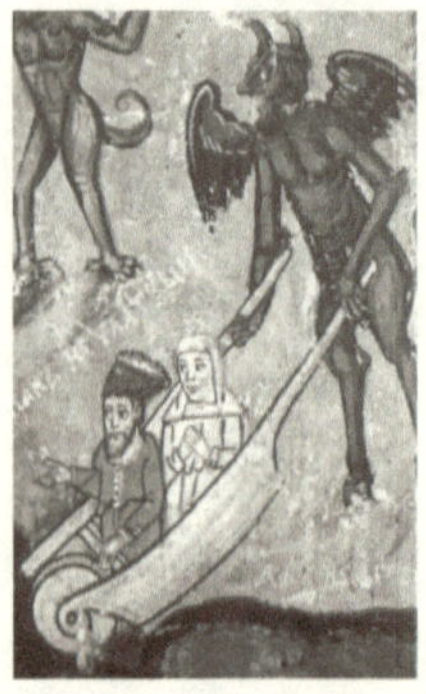

3.39 Merciless Landlord Being Carted off to Hell, Plavie

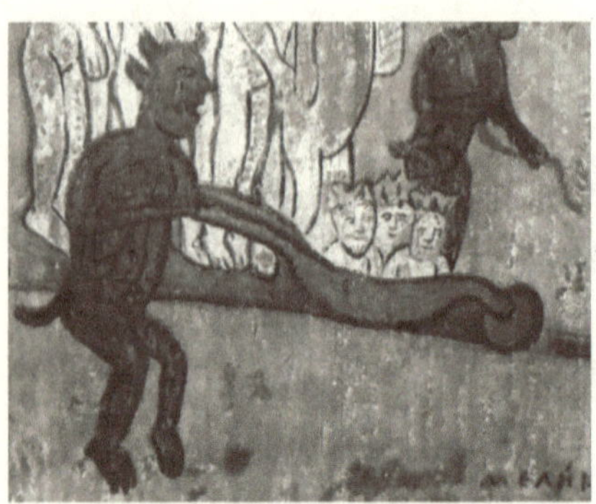

3.40 Men Wearing Crowns Carted off to Hell, Shelestovo

and of unusually high feudal rents.[141] As the 'Journey of the Mother of God among the Torments' explains, merciless princes and lords caused 'great destitution for poor people.'[142] The image of sinners in a hand cart, well known in the West, was generally absent in Orthodox Last Judgment iconography outside the Carpathians, but a Bulgarian icon from 1726 shows two peasants being carted off by a demon for working someone else's land.[143]

A related motif, also originating in the second half of the sixteenth century, is a devil carrying someone to hell on his back.[144] In some icons the figure appears twice. From the inscriptions I can make out, the sinners riding devilback are two tavernkeepers,[145] a lord,[146] a lady,[147] a merchant,[148] an official,[149] a dishonest priest,[150] and perhaps a vampire (*upir*) (fig. 3.41).[151]

Bad Confession and Sleeping through Services

We already encountered these two elements in the discussion of Jedlinka and Krásny Brod. In one, the devil persuades a sinner not to confess all his sins. In the other, a man is sleeping through services and has hell to pay for his choice of the bed over the church. The two motifs often appeared together in the same icon,[152] although they could also appear alone, especially the bad confession.[153] Uniquely, Lipie adds a third scene; the inscription is not fully legible, but it seems to depict a false witness at a trial (figs 3.42, 3.43, 3.44).

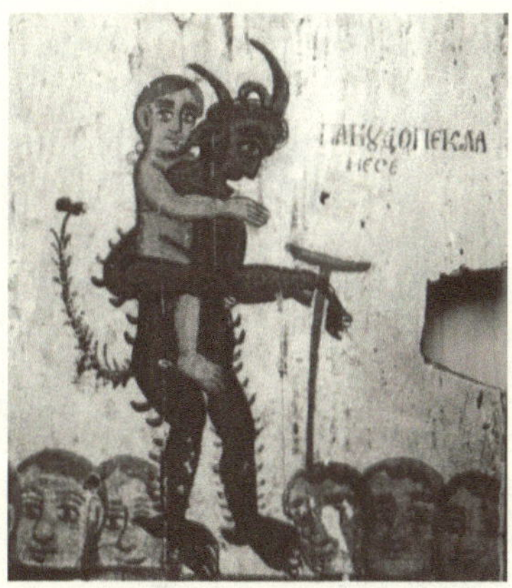

3.41 A Devil Carries a Lady to Hell, Roztoka

The bad confession has a textual source in Cyril the Philosopher's 'Sermon on the Exit of the Soul.' Here not only does the sinner withhold his sin, but the priest shares in the blame for not asking pointed questions about his sinful behaviour.[154] I think it likely, however, that the element became as popular as it did as a result of the religious controversies and reforms of the era. The element is known in Maramureş,[155] but not elsewhere.

The sleeper has an exact source: 'The Journey of the Mother of God among the Torments.' In this text, the Mother of God saw those who slept through services lying in fiery beds.[156] The element can be found in Last Judgment iconography in fourteenth- and fifteenth-century Crete[157] and in late eighteenth-century Maramureş.[158]

The Parable of the Unicorn

The parable of the unicorn is taken from 'Barlaam and Ioasaph,' a text erroneously ascribed to St John Damascene and well known in Rus' and throughout the Orthodox world.[159] The parable is meant to illustrate the vanity of the pleasures of this world. I will quote in full the relevant passage in G.R. Woodward and H. Mattingly's translation from Greek:

> These men that have foolishly alienated themselves from a good and kind master, to seek the service of so harsh and savage a lord [the world], that are

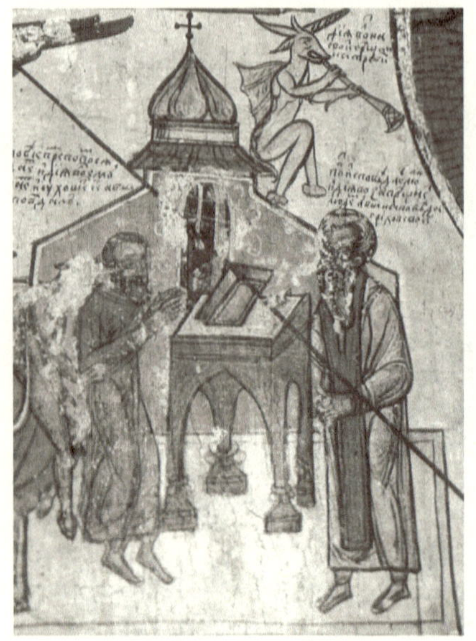

3.42 Bad Confession, Radelychi

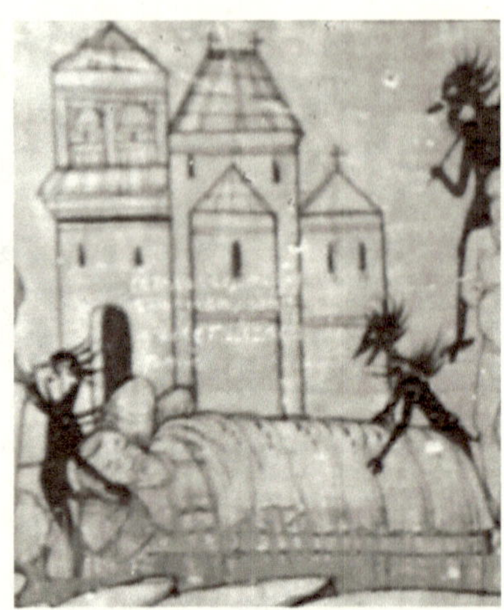

3.43 Sleeper, Bahnovate

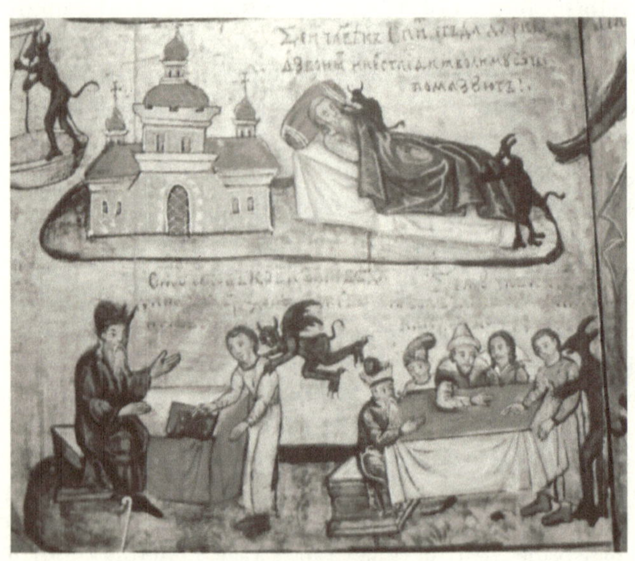

3.44 Scenes, Lipie

all agog for present joys and glued thereto, that take never a thought for the future, that always grasp after bodily enjoyments, but suffer their souls to waste with hunger, and to be worn with myriad ills, these I consider to be like a man flying before the face of a rampant unicorn, who, unable to endure the sound of the beast's cry, and its terrible bellowing, to avoid being devoured, ran away at full speed. But while he ran hastily, he fell into a great pit; and as he fell, he stretched forth his hands, and laid hold on a tree, to which he held tightly. There he established some sort of foot-hold and thought himself from that moment in peace and safety. But he looked and descried two mice, the one white, the other black, that never ceased to gnaw the root of the tree whereon he hung, and were all but on the point of severing it. Then he looked down to the bottom of the pit and espied below a dragon, breathing fire, fearful for eye to see, exceeding fierce and grim, with terrible wide jaws, all agape to swallow him. Again looking closely at the ledge whereon his feet rested, he discerned four heads of asps projecting from the wall whereon he was perched. Then he lift up his eyes and saw that from the branches of the tree there dropped a little honey. And thereat he ceased to think of the troubles whereby he was surrounded; how, outside, the unicorn was madly raging to devour him; how, below, the fierce dragon was yawning to swallow him; how the tree, which he had clutched, was all but severed; and how his feet rested on slippery, treacherous ground. Yea, he forgot, without care, all those sights of awe and terror, and his whole mind hung on the sweetness of that tiny drop of honey.

This is the likeness of those who cleave to the deceitfulness of this present life ...[160]

This scene first appeared in Dolyna, from the 1560s. It shows a man in the foliage of a tree. His eyes are turned upward towards the heavens. Honey drops are falling into his mouth. Two mice, one black and one ochre, are placed near the roots of the tree. There is an inscription near the figure, but it is illegible (fig. 3.45).[161] The only other appearance of this element on a Ukrainian-Carpathian icon is on the Last Judgment of Skole, from the eighteenth century. Here two devils have hooked the man in the tree around his neck and are dragging him down. There is no inscription (fig. 3.46).

The element does, however, appear twice in the Last Judgment iconography of Maramureş. In Budeşti-Josani, from the seventeenth century, a dragon is flying towards the tree with the man in it. At the trunk of the tree are two animals, presumably mice, one white and one black. The inscriptions near the animals are difficult to make out, but it seems that the white animal is labelled 'day' and the black animal 'night.' There is also an inscription near the man, but it is mostly illegible. All that can be made out are the first two words: 'This man ...' (fig. 3.47).

The fourth and final appearance of the man in the tree is on a late eighteenth-century mural in Cuhea. I have never seen it, nor a reproduction of it. The most I can do is repeat Heinz Skrobucha's description of it. A man emerges from a treetop with the same gesture of petition as in Dolyna. A devil is flying towards the tree. There is a partly legible inscription which says that this is a man who lived righteously, but was not free of sin and cannot decide whither – after which the inscription cannot be made out.[162] Unfortunately, Skrobucha's description is marred by his misunderstanding of what he was looking at.

Although this element had been correctly identified as the parable of the unicorn by the first serious investigator of the Carpathian icons, Ilarion Svientsitsky, Skrobucha rejected this identification. In Skrobucha's opinion, there are too many aspects of the story that are omitted in the icons and that a painter would have included if he had had this parable in mind. An obvious example is the unicorn, which appears on none of the Carpathian or Maramureş images. Nor would a painter, Skrobucha continued, invert the meaning of the tale by depicting a man coming out of a tree top instead of hanging from a branch. Moreover, the parable, and its interpretation by Barlaam, have nothing to do with the Last Judgment.[163]

The doubts advanced by Skrobucha sound reasonable, but they do not withstand confrontation with earlier iconography of the parable of the unicorn. There is a good example in the Serbian psalter from the fourteenth or early fifteenth century. The inscription clearly states 'A man is being chased by a fierce beast called a unicorn ...' It is the same figure who appears in Dolyna and the subsequent icons (fig. 3.48).

The Queen of the South, Joachim and Anna, Works of Mercy, and the Prophet and Bones

Here I have grouped four elements together because they are particular to only a few icons. These elements are rare in Carpathian iconography of the Last Judgment and unknown elsewhere in the Orthodox world. The queen appears in four icons. The earliest appearance is in Mala Horozhanka from the end of the sixteenth or beginning of the seventeenth century. This is the only case in which the queen is not accompanied by any other of the elements being examined here. Otherwise the queen appears in three icons from the seventeenth century: Museum of

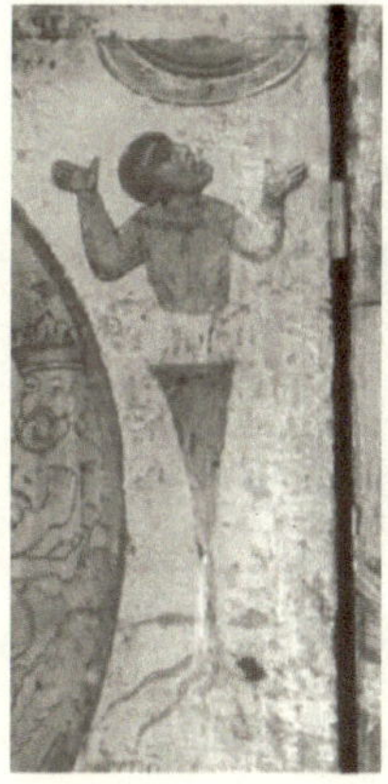

3.45 Parable of the Unicorn, Dolyna. Photo: Orest Krukovsky.

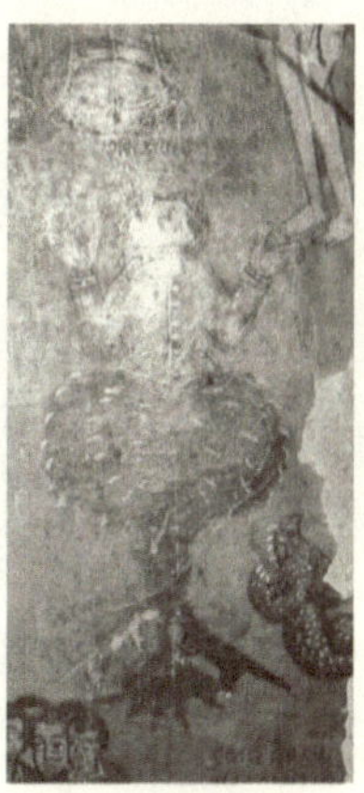

3.47 Parable of the Unicorn, Budeşti-Josani

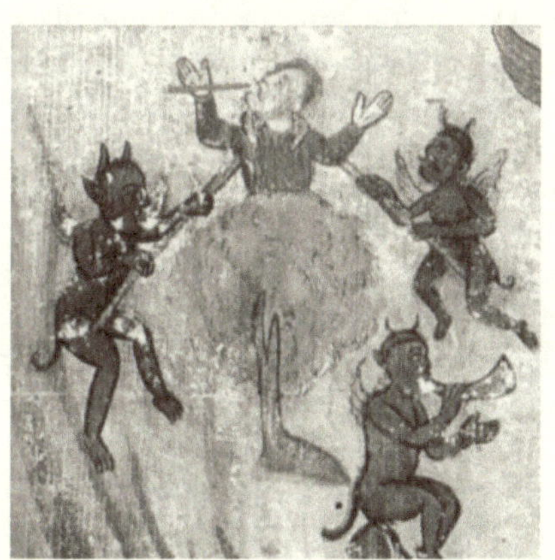

3.46 Parable of the Unicorn, Skole. Source: Oleh Sydor and Taras Lozynskyi, eds, *Ukrainian Icons 13th–18th Centuries from Private Collections* (Kyiv: Rodovid, 2003), 221, pl. 157.

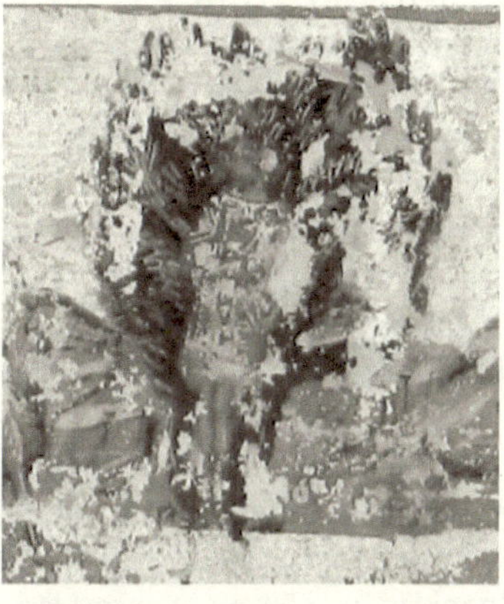

3.48 Parable of the Unicorn, Serbian Psalter. Source: *Der Serbische Psalter: Faksimile-Ausgabe des Cod. Slav. 4 der Bayerischen Staatsbibliothek München. Faksimile* (Wiesbaden: Ludwig Reichert Verlag, 1983), folio 2.

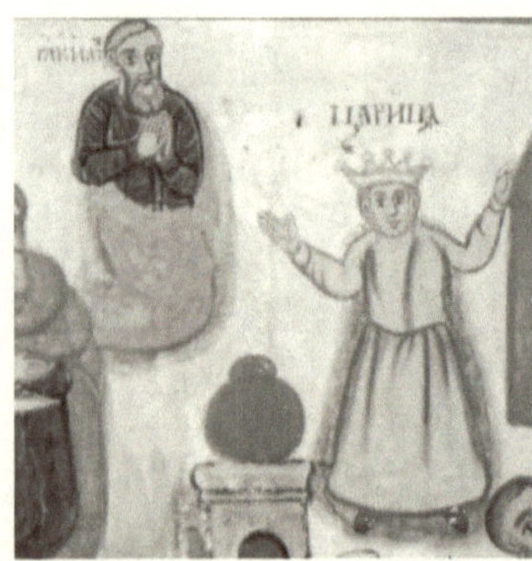

3.49 Joachim and the Queen, Roztoka

the History of Religion, Roztọka, and Tiushka (labelled 'queen of the earth'). Roztoka and Tiushka are located not far from each other in Transcarpathia, in the northern part of the old Máramaros county. The provenance of Museum of the History of Religion is not known (the museum has no record of its origin), but I suspect it comes from some place not too distant from these villages. The textual origin of the queen is clear: 'The queen of the south shall rise up in the judgment with the men of this generation, and condemn them' (Lk 11:31) (fig. 3.49).

Joachim and Anna appear only in Roztoka and Museum of the History of Religion. I know of no connection between the parents of the Mother of God and the Last Judgment. Certainly nothing in the Protoevangelium of James, the main source on these two saints, indicates a connection. The only explanation I have been able to think of, and I am aware of how weak it is, is that they are included because the church in Roztoka is under the invocation of the Presentation of the Mother of God, an event in which Joachim and Anna played a part. But I have never heard of this kind of inclusion in a Last Judgment icon. And even if this explains how Joachim and Anna entered Roztoka, it does not account for the presence of these same saints in the Museum of the History of Religion. To continue in the vein of tenuous explanations, one might speculate that the latter icon was modelled after Roztoka and simply incorporated the two saints without reflection. Joachim and Anna are absent in Tiushka.

Illustrations of the works of mercy appear in Roztoka, Tiushka, and the Museum of the History of Religion. In the latter icon, the works are only partly evident, because the right board is missing. These are the

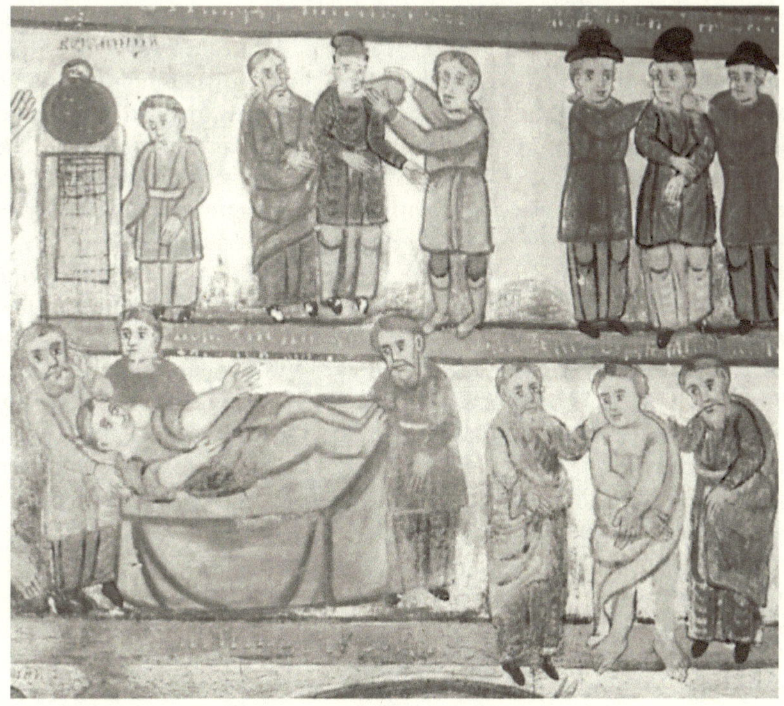

3.50 Works of Mercy, Roztoka

works of mercy mentioned in the Gospel of Meatfare Sunday: 'For I was an hungred, and ye gave me meat; I was thirsty, and ye gave me drink; I was a stranger, and ye took me in: Naked, and ye clothed me: I was sick, and ye visited me: I was in prison, and ye came unto me' (Mt 25:35–6). This is a natural addition to the icon of the Last Judgment. Perhaps its inclusion represents the influence of Western iconography,[164] but one need not posit this to explain the motif's presence in the icon (fig. 3.50).

In Roztoka, just to the left of the saints entering paradise, is a picture of a monk-like figure kneeling and weeping over bones strewn on the ground. The inscription near the scene quotes, with some corruption, from the funeral service: 'I remembered the prophet crying out: "I am ash and earth," and again I looked in the grave and saw bare bones.'[165] This is a reference to Genesis 18:27, which in the Septuagint version reads: 'And answering, Abraham said: Now I have begun to speak to my lord, though I am earth and ash.' A nearly identical image, but with a different text, has been preserved in the Serbian psalter on the same page as the parable of the unicorn,[166] while the same text with a different picture can be found in a seventeenth-century Russian *sinodik.*[167] The form in which the image appears on Roztoka is unique (fig. 3.51). Perhaps the element also appeared on the Museum of the History of Religion, but without the missing right board, one cannot say one way or another. In Tiushka this precise image is lacking, but in roughly the same position on the icon there is a picture of a man with arms outstretched in prayer, kneeling by what looks like the corpse of a child. The inscription is irremediably damaged. Near him are a woman and the figure of a child (fig. 3.52). It is not possible to say what is being depicted here, but it may also be the same motif as in Roztoka. The kinship among Roztoka, Tiushka, and the Museum of the History of Religion is further confirmed by the presence of a second figure of Death, who is riding a donkey, a feature they share with Budeşti-Josani.

Conclusions

The interest in the Last Judgment icons expanded after the fifteenth century, at first mainly to the east, and after the mid-seventeenth century also to the western ridges and southern slopes of the Carpathians. Still they remained in a fairly restricted area, in what is today eastern Slovakia, southeastern Poland, and the western oblasts of Ukraine, particularly Lviv and Transcarpathia.

Monks remained active as painters and incorporated ideas from the Moldavian fresco projects undertaken throughout the sixteenth century. But parallel to the work in the monasteries, painting was also moving out into other social strata. Already in the early sixteenth century, someone without the skill of the monastic masters made a copy of Vanivka (Lukov-Venecia), and later another individual with a rudimentary knowledge of painting made a copy of the copy (Krásny Brod). Small-town craftsmen, carvers and carpenters, and even talented villagers who had learned enough of the technique began to paint Last Judgment icons to satisfy the interest that had been awakened by these monumental works.

The aesthetic of multiple elements intensified. Old elements were elaborated and new ones added. The context in which this further elaboration unfolded was manifest in the numerous references to confessional and social issues, reflections of the religious controversies and

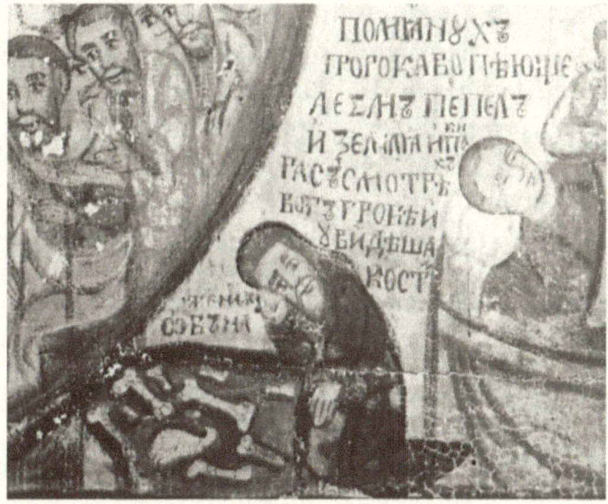

3.51 Prophet and Bones, Roztoka

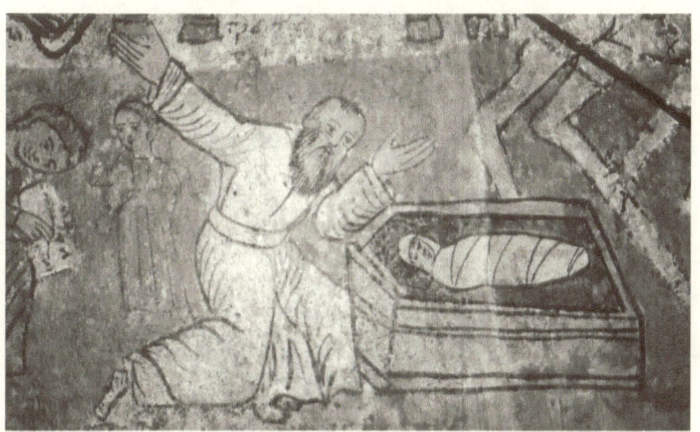

3.52 Figure Kneeling by Corpse, Tiushka

socio-economic transformations unsettling southwestern Rus' in the sixteenth through eighteenth centuries. Several other tendencies can be discerned: a heightened interest in sexual themes, a weaker comprehension of the original meaning of some of the elements, and the willingness to omit some traditional constituents altogether.

Agnieszka Gronek, in her study of the Passion icons, was able to demonstrate that in numerous cases the artists copied from Western, particularly Dutch and German, prints and from the engravings in liturgical books. Although I have spent many hours examining prints myself, I was unable to find a single instance in which a Last Judgment icon of the sixteenth to eighteenth centuries copied a motif from a printed Western source. Western influences on the Last Judgment iconography were not totally absent in this period, but it appears that the painters of the Last Judgment either found little that suited their purposes in the Western images or else did not bother to look to them for models. The Last Judgment icons of the Carpathians remained highly distinctive.

4 Disintegration

By the nineteenth century, Last Judgment iconography had largely disappeared in our region. If any Last Judgment images continued to be produced here, they were not the large works painted on linden boards with egg tempera. Materials and methods changed, as did tastes and interests. The eighteenth century saw the disintegration of what had been a vigorous tradition over the preceding several centuries. This is what we explore in this chapter.

Change of Materials

Linden boards remained the dominant material for Last Judgment icons through the first half of the seventeenth century, but after that they were rarely used. The collection of icons in the National Museum in Lviv has only three linden-board icons from after the early seventeenth century,[1] and one of them, from 1754, was painted with oils instead of tempera. By the mid-seventeenth century, the nobler deciduous trees were in decline in much of our region, and pine dominated the forests.[2] Occasionally earlier,[3] but particularly beginning in the second half of the seventeenth century, icons were painted on pine boards.[4] This change of wood did not result in iconographic differences. One pine-board icon was exceptionally large (Medynychi, 309 cm high), but most were about the same size as those painted on linden, i.e., about 175–265 cm high.

In the second half of the seventeenth century, icons also began to be painted on canvas, which had been woven in the region since at least the fifteenth century.[5] Perhaps the earliest Last Judgment icons on canvas that survive come from 1660–80, from western villages on the Hungarian side of the border (today eastern Slovakia). They still used tempera instead of oils. One of them, Vyšný Orlík, is quite conservative in its iconography. It is still a vertical rectangle with the almsgiving fornicator, the fall of the rebel angels, the tavernmaid, and tollbooths (in the booth form). It is also an icon that incorporates features of the further elaboration, such as the Ancient of days, the bad confession, the sleeper, tavern scenes, and hell in a hand cart (figs 4.1, 4.2). The other, Zboj/Uličské Krivé, is fairly traditional, judging by the top half of the icon, which is all that is still legible (fig. 4.3).

There are two other icons on canvas from the same region, also from the later seventeenth century: Topol'a (near Zboj/Uličské Krivé) and Tročany (near Vyšný Orlík). The more traditional of these two is Topol'a. It has the almsgiving fornicator, monks flying into paradise, the bad confession and sleeper, a merciless lord and lady riding a hand cart to hell, and many other traditional elements. It lacks the tollbooths, however, and is horizontal instead of vertical (figs 4.4, 4.5). Tročany, although vertical, is missing more elements, not only the tollbooths, but even such standard Byzantine features as Adam and Eve and the bosom of Abraham. It also contains innovations that are peculiar to it: to the left of paradise lie two beheaded corpses and above paradise is a Latin-style resurrected Christ (figs 4.6, 4.7).

Near the village of Tročany are Rakovčík and Kožany, both of which had Last Judgment icons painted on canvas. Rakovčík dates from 1789, Kožany from the 1790s; they are the work of the same artist. They look nothing like traditional icons of the Last Judgment. Both are horizontal. Neither bothers with tollbooths, the almsgiving fornicator, the bosom of Abraham, or the bad confession and Sunday sleeper. They are still recognizably descended from the same tradition, since we do see Moses and the peoples in both and, though differently positioned, the hand of God with scales in Kožany. Kožany shows gamblers playing cards in hell, probably derived from the elaborate tavern scenes. Both icons depict a serpent with an apple in its mouth. It looks different from the traditional tollbooth serpent, but perhaps that is its iconographic ancestor. Rakovčík for some reason displays a glove on the throne near the open book (figs 4.8, 4.9, 4.10, 4.11, 4.12, 4.13).

There appears to be an association between the use of canvas and the disintegration of the iconographic tradition. Perhaps crossing over to a new medium encouraged further experimentation. Or perhaps painters who used canvas were mixing more with their Roman Catholic counterparts. The latter is suggested by the pattern of diffusion. I am only aware of icons on canvas from those parts of our region that were included

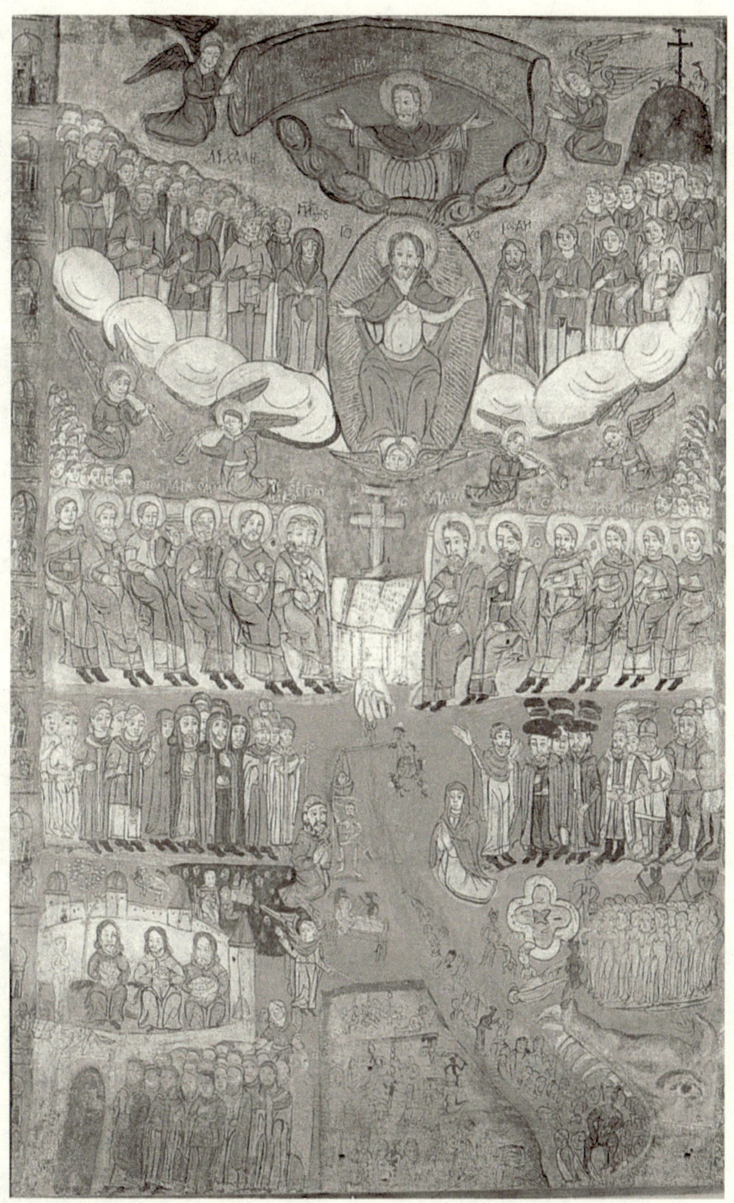

4.1 Vyšný Orlík overview. Source: Vladislav Grešlík, *Ikony Šarišského Múzea v Bardejove* (Bratislava: Ars Monument, 1994), pl. 37.

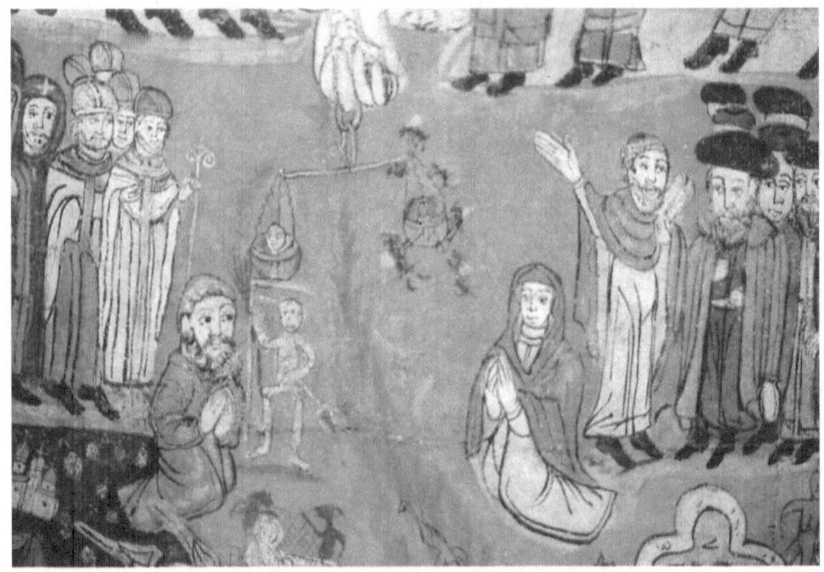

4.2 Vyšný Orlík, detail of lower central portion

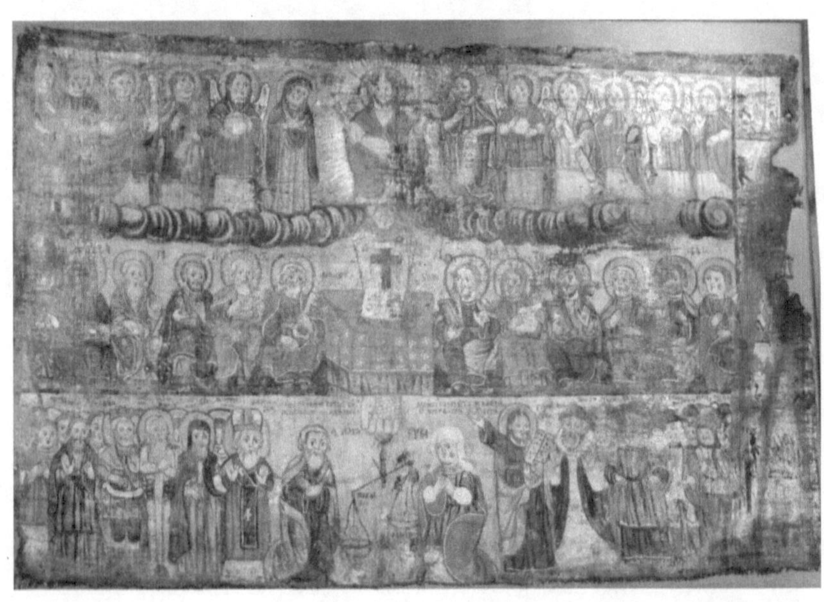

4.3 Zboj/Uličské Krivé, top half

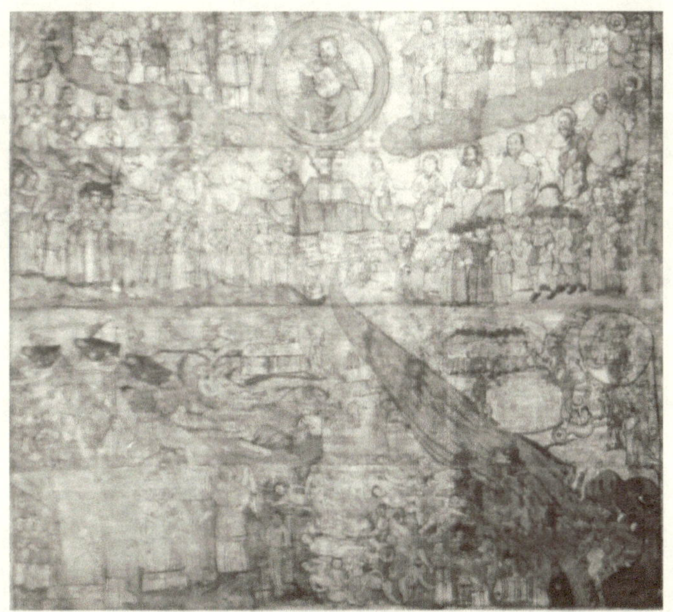

4.4 Topol'a overview

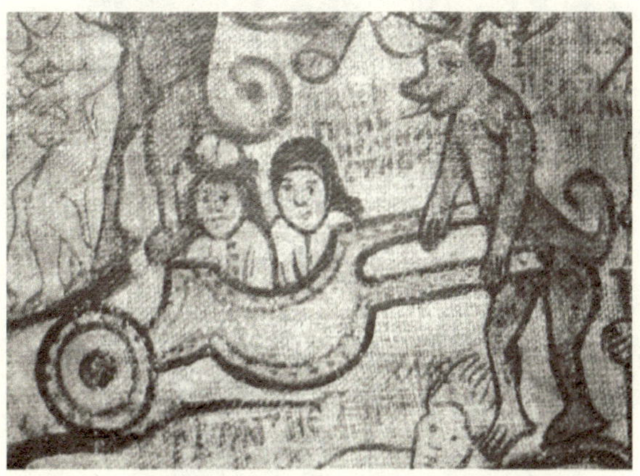

4.5 Merciless Lord and Lady, Topol'a

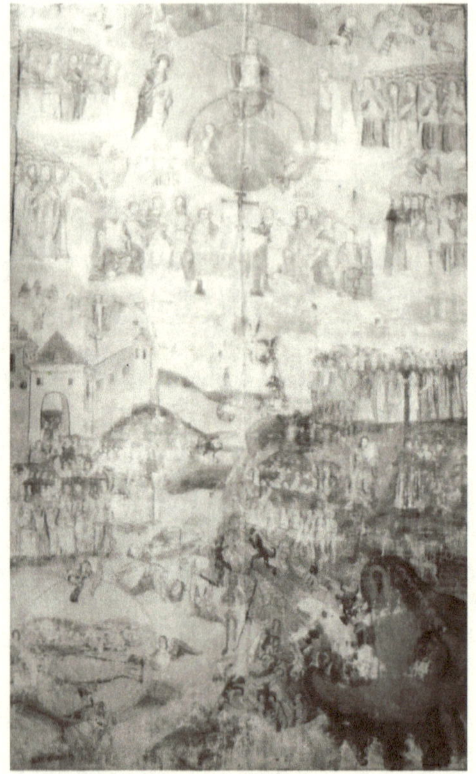

4.6 Tročany overview

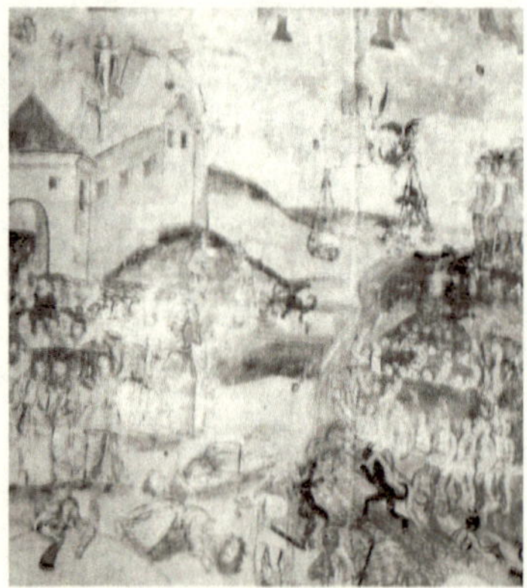

4.7 Scene near Paradise, Tročany

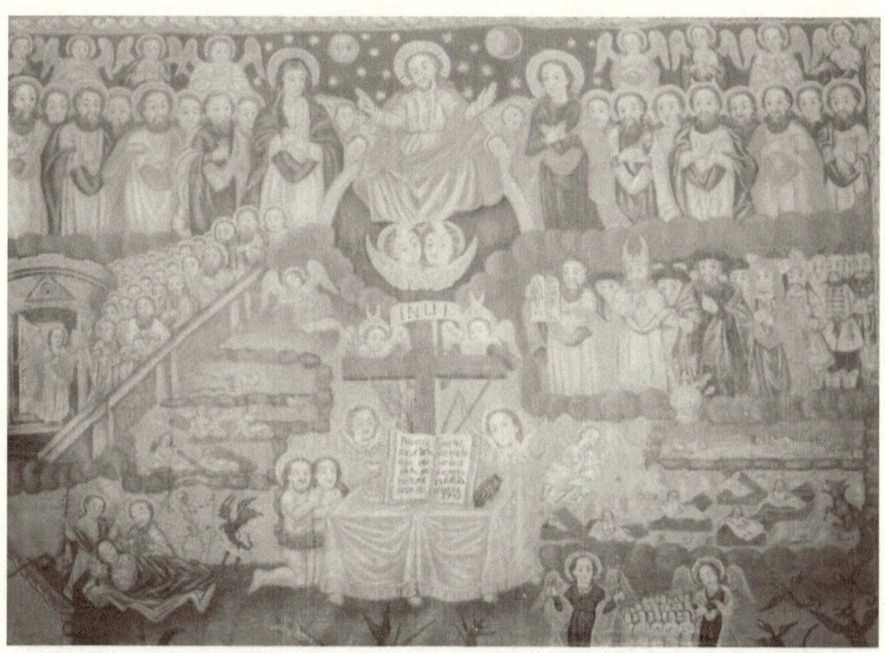

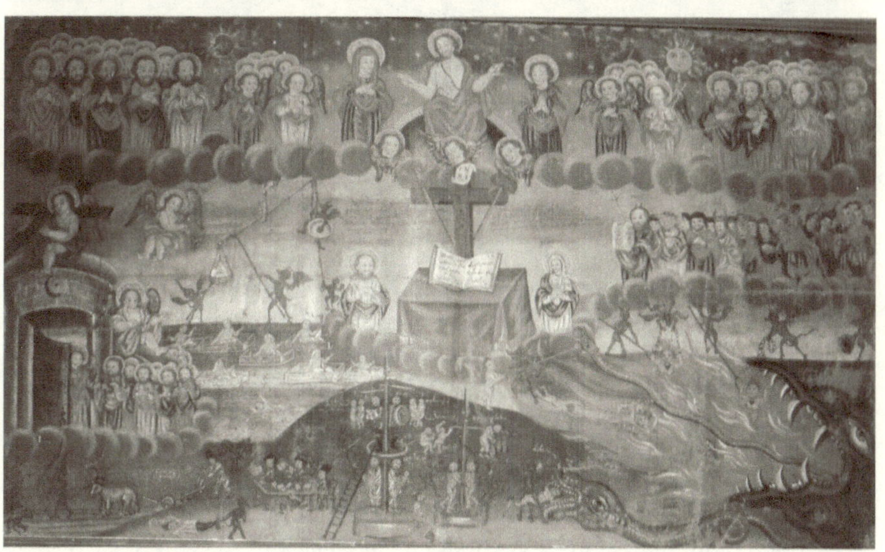

4.8 Rakovčík and Kožany overviews

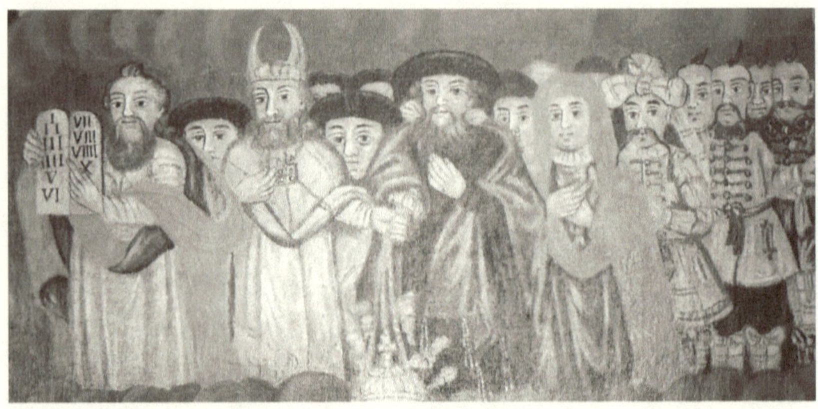

4.9 Moses and the Peoples, Rakovčík

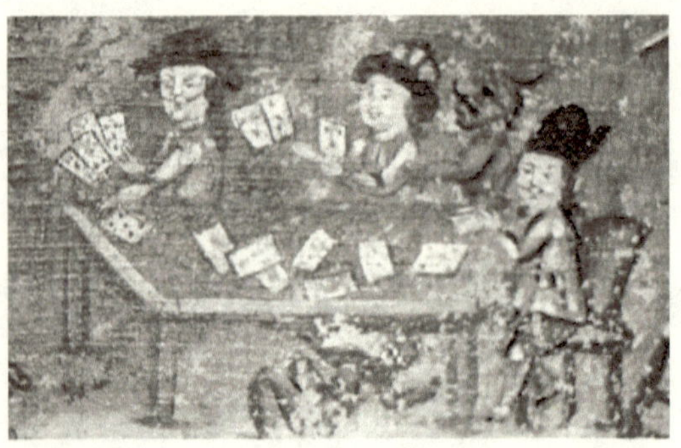

4.10 Gamblers, Kožany

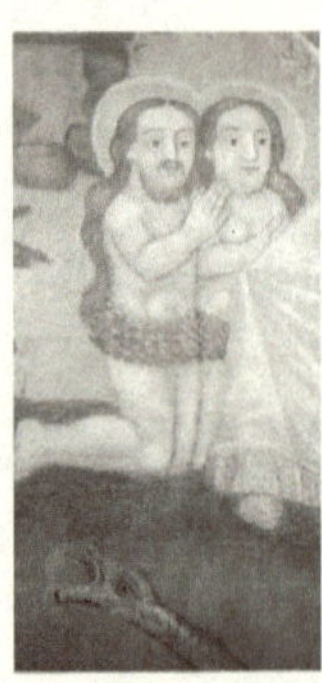

4.11 Adam and Eve and Head of Serpent, Rakovčík

within the borders of Catholic states – the Habsburg monarchy and Poland. I do not know of any from non-Catholic Transylvania. In fact, it may be the case that in our region canvas was used only when and where the church union had been introduced. (It is also possible, however, that painters did produce icons on canvas in northern Transylvania, but that they were not collected or are not very accessible.) Canvas was also used in Bukovina, which I shall discuss later in this chapter, but only after its annexation to Austria. Bukovina remained thereafter predominantly Orthodox, but many Greek Catholics from Galicia moved there early in the Austrian period and Greek Catholic parishes were established.

I have seen only the canvas Last Judgments of eastern Slovakia and of Bukovina, which I shall discuss later in this chapter, but Last Judgments

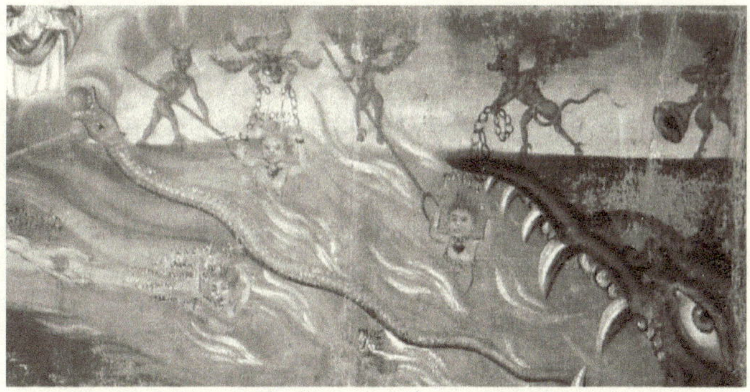

4.12 Serpent with Apple, Kožany

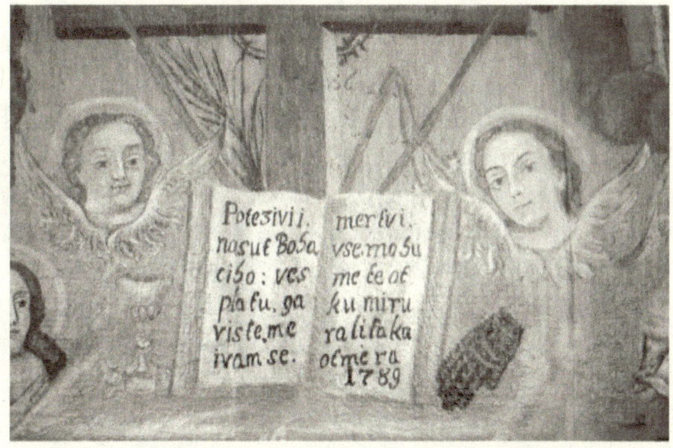

4.13 Throne with Book and Glove, Rakovčík

on canvas were widespread. The National Museum in Lviv has five that I have not seen.[6] One of these, Popeli, comes from near Drohobych; two come from Volytsia Derevlianska, which is southeast of Kamianka Strumylova; and one comes from Yezupil, far to the east of Dolyna. We know that there were many more. Visitations from the eighteenth century record many of them scattered over Przemyśl and Lviv eparchies (table 6.1) and also some in the Uniate parishes of Bratslav and Kyiv palatinates.[7] N.F. Sumtsov noted two icons on canvas in the collection of the Kyiv Theological Academy at the end of the nineteenth century. One was from the Cherkasy region and showed in hell, among others, a weaver with balls of thread, a usurer with a rope across his shoulders on which hung money purses, a drunk, and a witch. Another canvas, from the eighteenth century, showed a woman in bed under a red blanket with a demon standing at her feet and an inscription identifying her as too lazy to go to church, a judge riding to hell in a carriage drawn by two devils and attended by two more, a witch with her wood vessel for preparing herbs, a concubine (*nalozhnitsa*) with serpents on her face and breasts, a sorcerer with a serpent and glass, a sorceress picking some grain, a thief who stole sheaves of grain, a tailor with a measuring stick in his hand as well as scissors and some red material, a cobbler with a boot in his hands, a weaver with balls of thread, and a miller with his millstone. A bit below them were dancers, a fiddler, and two devils. An infanticide was pictured with a devil taking the dead child from her. There was also a tree with bees swarming about; while a devil encourages him, a thief takes honey from the hive. A godfather and godmother were partying on a hand cart, the godfather holding a flask and the godmother a glass; a devil was pushing them.[8]

An even more fundamental change in materials was the painting of the Last Judgment directly on the wooden walls of the church. This technique did not produce very durable results,[9] and so the murals have not come down to us in large numbers or in good shape. We know from visitations that there were more Last Judgment murals than have survived to our day (see table 6.1). Painters began to decorate the walls of churches in the general region at least from the first half of the seventeenth century (Potelcyh), but the first Last Judgment of this kind dates from about 1666. It is Drohobych-St George, painted on the southern wall by Stefan popovych Medytsky[10] – as the 'popovych' indicates, a priest's son. The space, of course, is not like an icon's. The artist had to work around two windows. In the top tier he placed Christ sitting on a rainbow. On either side of him were angels, holding a crucifix and the instruments of the Passion, including Veronica's veil. The Mother of God is to the right of them, and John the Baptist to their left. More angels stand behind these figures. The next tier down shows the seated apostles, divided into two groups by the throne with the open book. The hand of God with scales descends into the space between the two large windows. An angel in that same space spears a devil. To the right of the windows are both the saints and, one tier below them, Moses and the peoples. To the left of the windows is the mouth of hell, with Satan holding the soul of Judas and sinners entering the river of fire. Near the mouth of the beast is what looks to me like an adulterous couple, although the local Drohobych folklore has it that this is a homosexual couple.[11] The mural, as we see, has many of the traditional elements, but much is missing – Adam and Eve, the resurrection of the dead, the tavernmaid, the bosom of

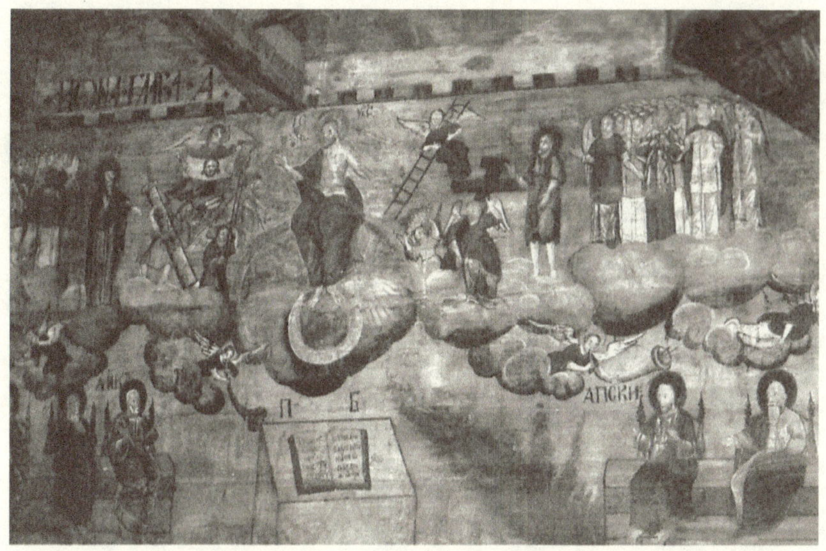

4.14 Drohobych-St George, upper centre

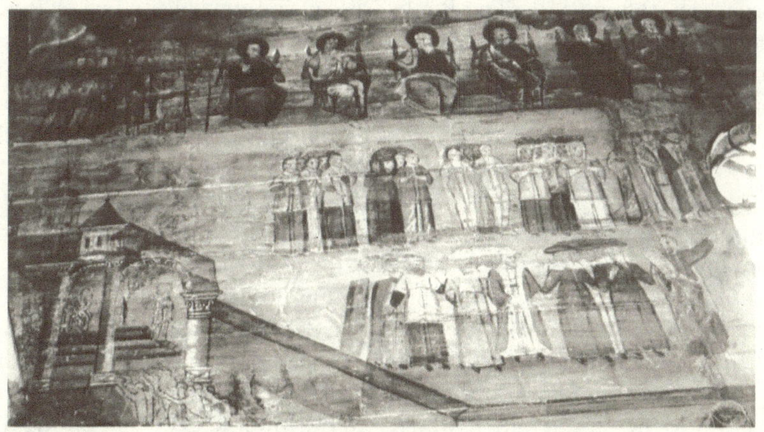

4.15 Drohobych-St George, lower right

Abraham, the bad confession and sleeper, even a distinct new hell. Elsewhere in the church, however, there are scenes that are usually associated with the Last Judgment: the figure of Death and the death of a righteous man (figs 4.14, 4.15, 4.16, 4.17).

The next mural was painted in 1676–9 on the northern wall of the Church of the Dormition in Novoselytsia, a village in the old Máramaros

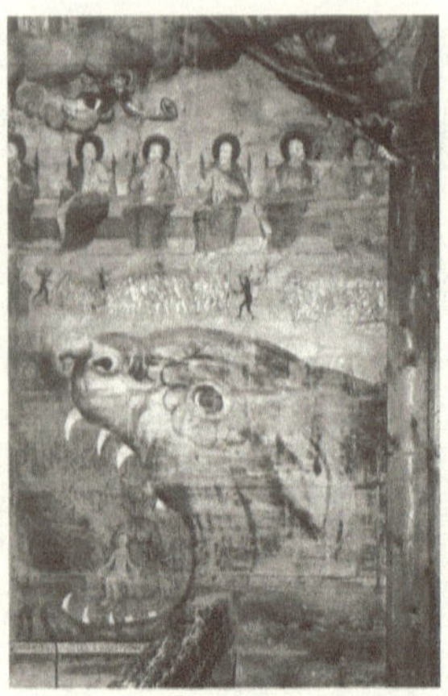

4.16 Drohobych-St George, lower left

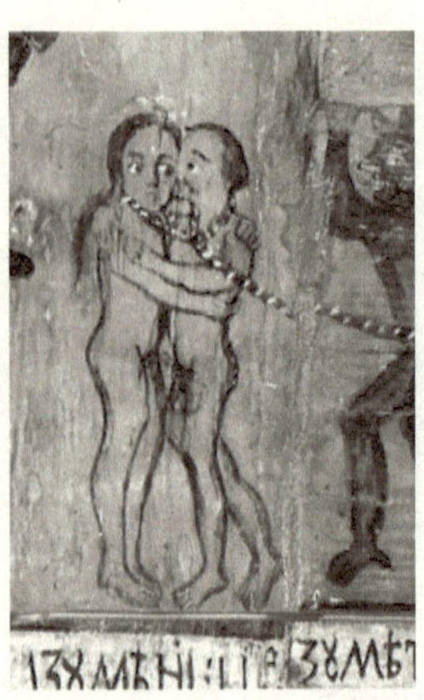

4.17 Adulterous or Homosexual Couple, Drohobych-St George. Source: Unknown (received from Myroslav Marynovych)

county, southwest of Nehrovets and not far from the Romanian linguistic border. There is a window on the left disrupting part of the mural; it was installed later, after the painter finished working on a large rectangular surface. Although this mural is missing some familiar elements as well, notably Adam and Eve and the almsgiving fornicator, it is still rather conservative. On the right and left sides of the mural are tollbooths in the form of stacked booths. The top tier is the deesis and angels, with Christ in the mandorla surmounted by the Holy Spirit where the Ancient of Days might normally be. The next tier is the apostles and throne, with the book open to the familiar passage of Matthew. Below them on the left are Moses and the peoples. On the lower right are the bosom of Abraham and the saints entering paradise. At the bottom centre is a sparsely inhabited new hell. The tavernmaid is there, dressed as usual, but being pushed in a hand cart towards Gehenna. Above the new hell and to the left are sinners on their way to the mouth of hell, which is in the lower left corner. Among the sinners is a smoker with a large pipe (figs 4.18, 4.19).

Little remains of the Last Judgment mural painted in 1683 on the northern wall of the Church of the Holy Trinity in Sykhiv. Sykhiv was a suburban village south of Lviv but has now been incorporated into the city. All that could be restored of the mural were the deesis, the apostles' heads, and the upper portion of the crucifix on the throne (fig. 4.20). There is an associated picture of death on the western wall (fig. 4.21).

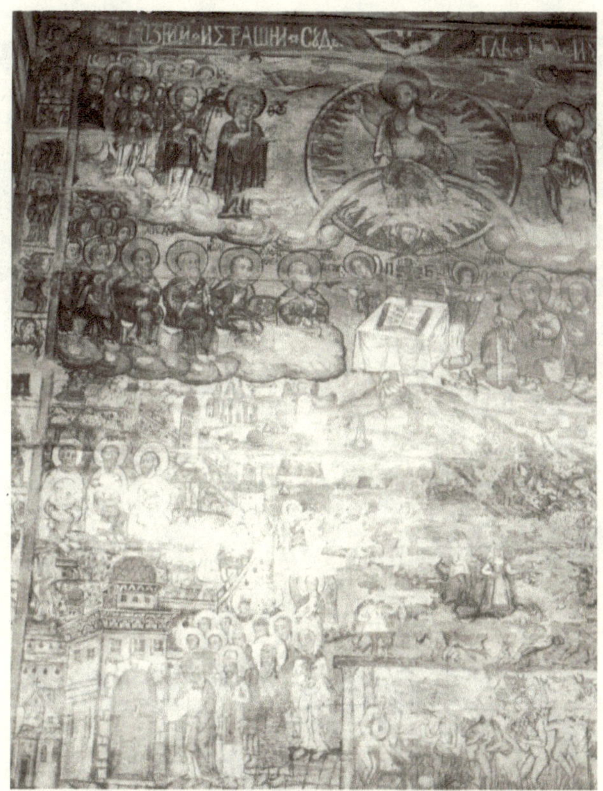

4.18 Novoselytsia, right side

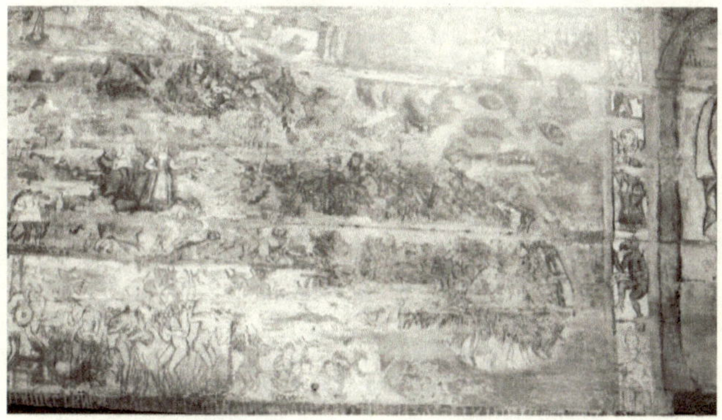

4.19 Novoselytsia, lower left

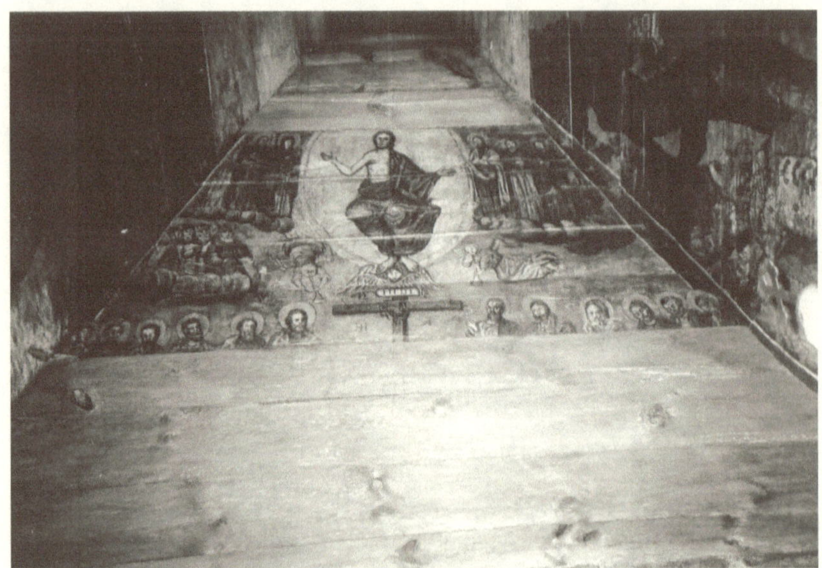

4.20 What's left, Sykhiv

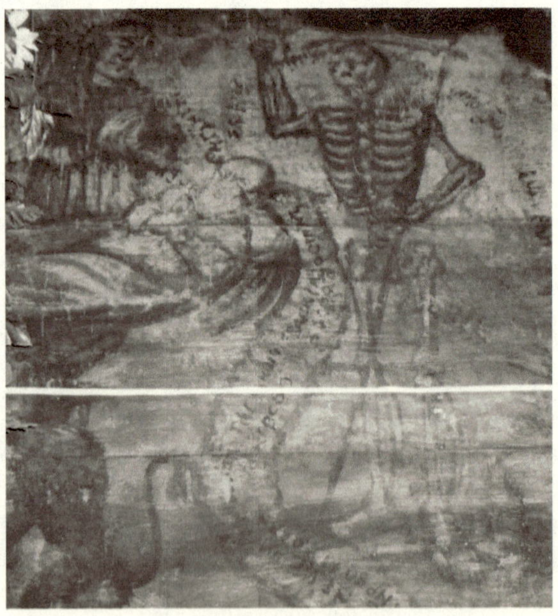

4.21 Death, Sykhiv

The situation is even worse with the mural on the southern wall of the Church of St Nicholas in Dmytrovychi, just south of Sudova Vyshnia. The mural was painted in 1698, probably by artists from the nearby town.[12] Today whatever is left of the mural is covered with plywood or particle board, which was painted with an archaizing Last Judgment in the 1990s. The current painting is not an attempt to reproduce the original mural.[13]

The mural in Chotyniec, northeast of Przemyśl, was preserved fairly well even before the recent restoration. It was painted in 1735 on the southern wall of the Church of the Nativity of the Mother of God. It differs considerably from the other Last Judgments we have examined. A great deal is missing, including the tollbooths, almsgiving fornicator, Adam and Eve, the hand of God, and Satan. There are some traditional elements as well, of course. At the top the heavens are being rolled up, and Christ is seated on a rainbow at the centre of a deesis. Moses and the peoples are included, but on the far right of the mural instead of on the left. The mural is more conservative when it comes to hell, however. There we find a miller wearing his millstone, a merciless landlord, and an infanticide with serpents on her breasts. These figures, though, are crudely drawn, in sharp contrast with the rest of the icon. This suggests to me that they were not part of the artist's original conception, but were added later by another hand (fig. 4.22).[14] Where the primary, professionally trained artist leaves tradition far behind is in the resurrection of the dead. Traditionally the resurrection was placed off to the left side and showed small bodies emerging from graves. For the Chotyniec artist, however, the rising of bodies from the graves occupies almost the whole bottom of the wall (fig. 4.23). The artist used the opportunity to paint some very naturalistic images. Jarosław Giemza has suggested that the mural in Chotyniec has a common source with a copper engraving executed by Averkii Kozachkovsky and published in the Caves Monastery in Kyiv in 1754 (fig. 4.24).[15]

It is not clear whether one should count the mural in Piilo, a village east of Dolyna, as a Last Judgment or not. Pavlo Zholtovsky described it as follows: 'There are two scenes of hell on the southern and northern walls [of the narthex (*babynets'*)], and these are what the traditional composition of "The Terrible Judgment" have been reduced to.'[16] The murals were painted sometime between 1778 and 1794. They no longer exist, since the wooden church that housed them was burned down, probably by political arsonists, in 1965. There are an artist's drawings of fragments of the mural; we shall consider them later on in this chapter, in the section on the titillating and grotesque.

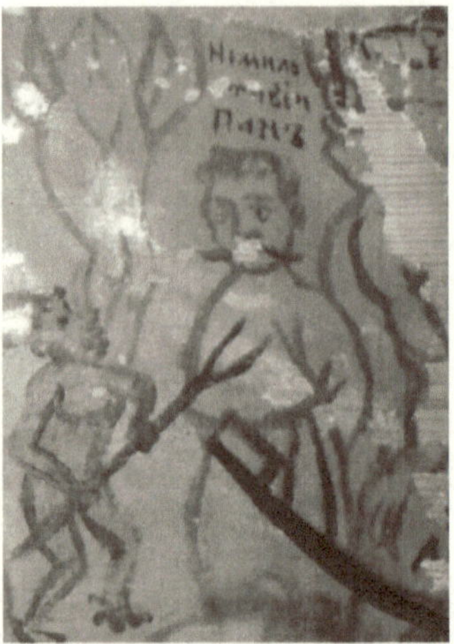

4.22 Merciless Landlord, Chotyniec

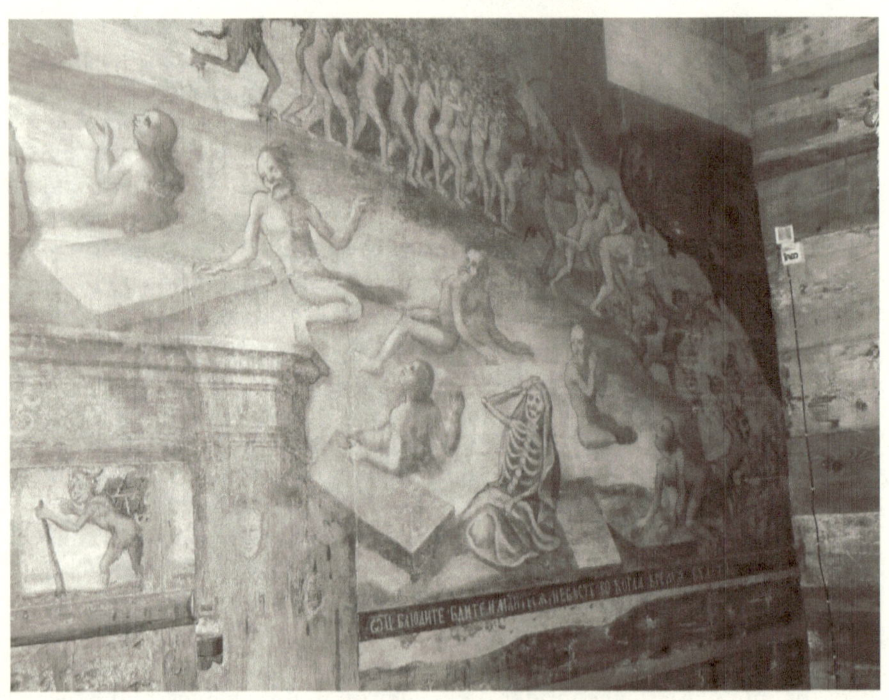

4.23 Chotyniec. Photo: Jarosław Giemza.

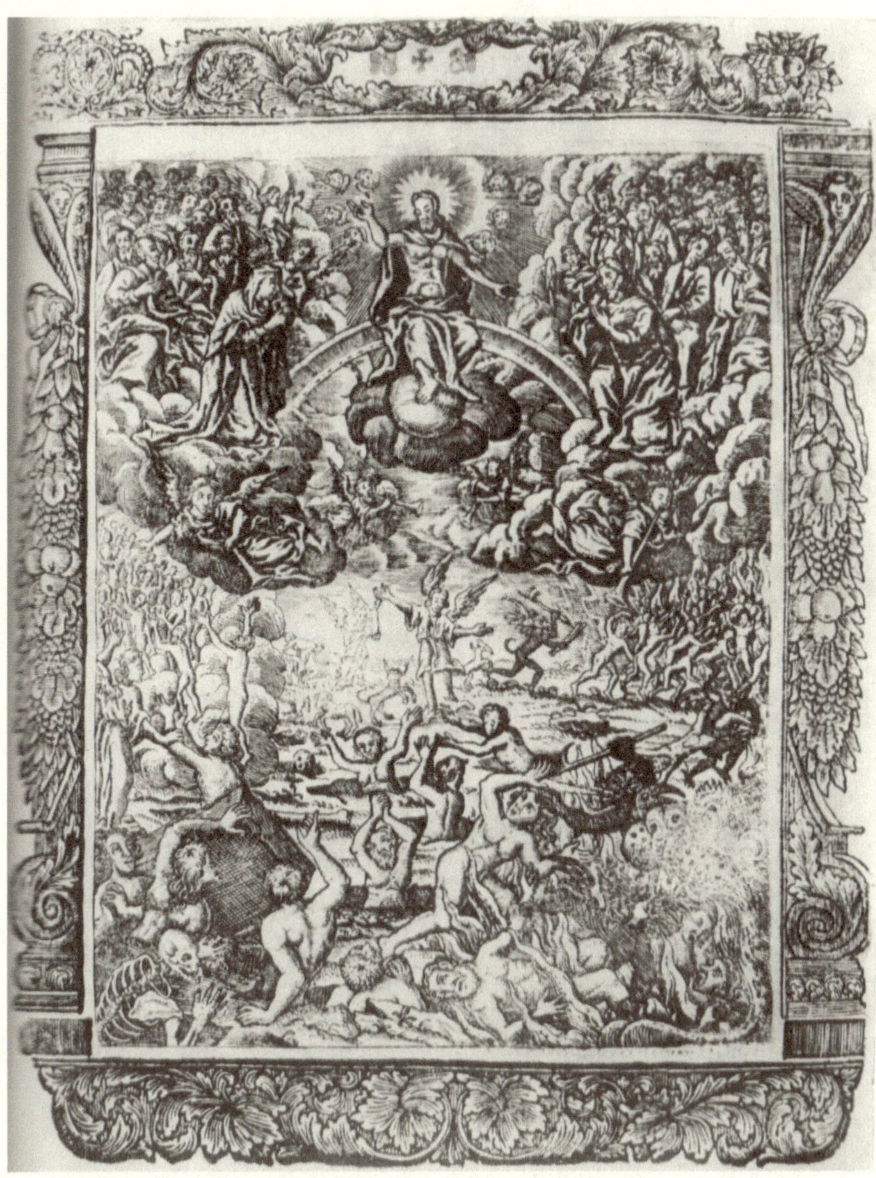

4.24 Averkii Kozachkovsky, Last Judgment. Source: H.N. Lohvyn, *Z hlybyn. Hraviury ukrains'kykh starodrukiv XVI–XVIII st.* (Kyiv: Dnipro, 1990), pl. 428.

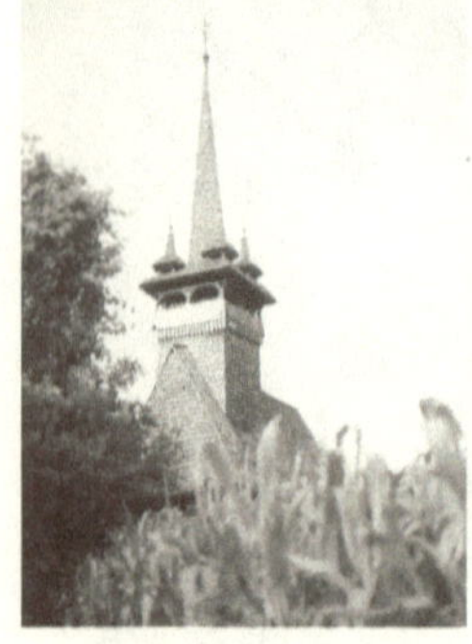

4.25 Church in Oleksandrivka

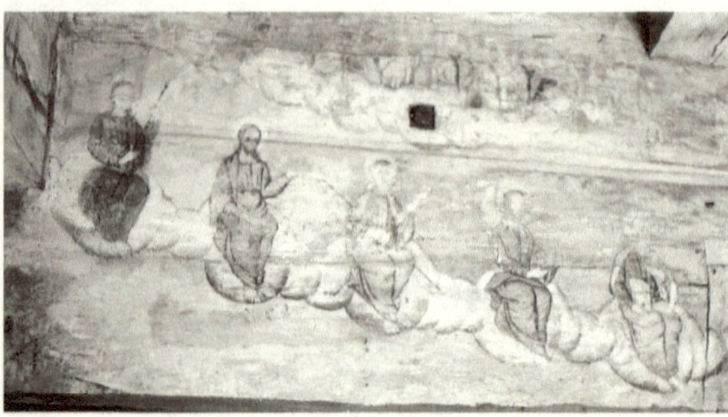

4.26 Surviving fragments, Oleksandrivka

Oleksandrivka is a village in central Máramaros, west of Novoselytsia. A mural of the Last Judgment was painted here in the Church of St Paraskeva in 1779, on the east wall, which once divided the nave and the *babynets'*. Only a few fragments have survived (figs 4.25, 4.26).

There are two very closely related murals in two nearby villages south of the Hungarian border: Kožuchovce from 1785 and Bodružal from the 1790s. Both are probably by the same artist. The mural on the northern wall in Kožuchovce was accidentally destroyed after the church was moved to an open-air museum, but there are photographs of it. The mural in Bodružal is still on the northern wall in the Church of St Basil in the village. The mural in Kožuchovce has a feature in common with the canvas icons from Rakovčík and Kožany, which are not far away to the southwest: the serpent with the apple in his mouth. Bodružal has a serpent as well, but it has rings like a tollbooth serpent and the head is not visible. Both murals are truncated versions of the traditional Last Judgments. The lower right portion of Bodružal has been destroyed, deliberately, as we shall see (figs 4.27, 4.28, 4.29).

The murals were scattered over the same territory as the traditional icons. There are only two cases of clustering: in central Máramaros (Novoselytsia and Oleksandrivka) and in north central Hungary, today eastern Slovakia (Kožuchovce and Bodružal). Both cases are interesting. Novoselytsia and Oleksandrivka are situated near Romanian Maramureş, where, as we shall soon see, Last Judgment murals were also very popular. While researching this book I have at various times classifed Novoselytsia and Oleksandrivka as Romanian and, in the same general

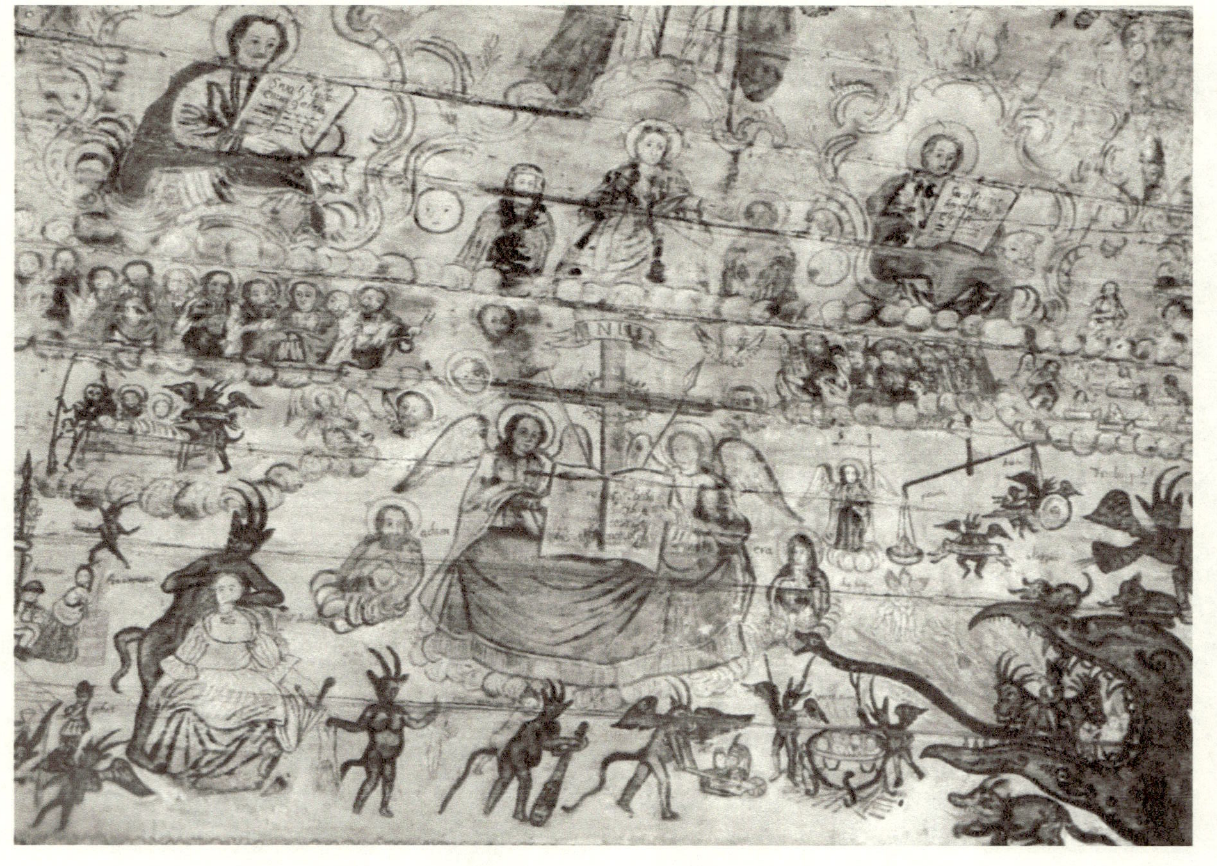

4.27 Kožuchovce overview. Source: Vladimír Hyhlík, *Košice*, intro. Ladislav Cselényi (Martin: Osveta, 1959), pl. 102.

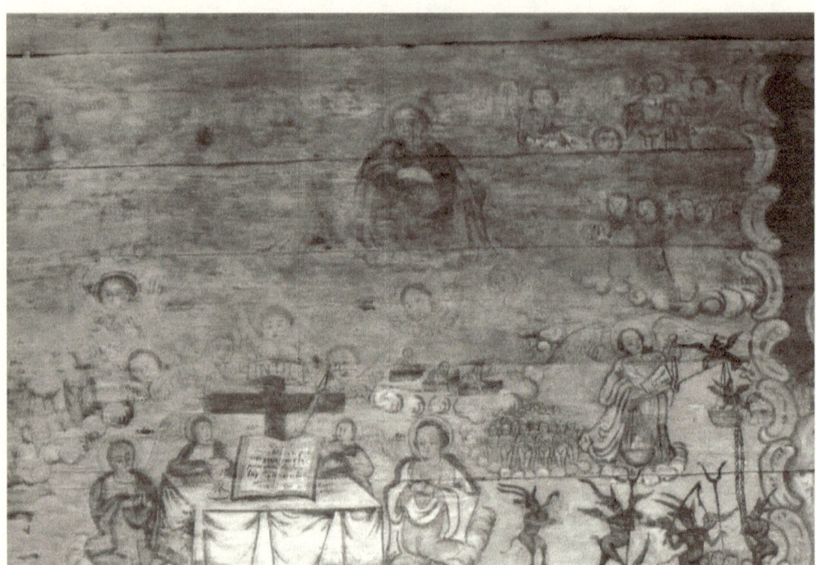

4.28 Bodružal, upper portion

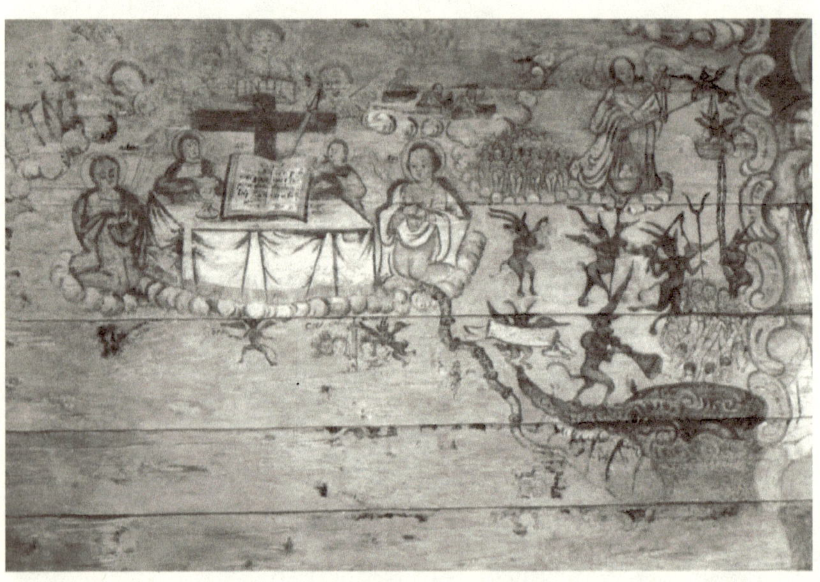

4.29 Bodružal, lower portion

area, Serednie Vodiane as Rusyn/Ukrainian. In the end, I decided that the ascriptions were the other way around, but there is probably a continuum here rather than a neat classification. Kožuchovce and Bodružal are interesting because of their connection with two nearby villages where canvas icons were painted in the same period (Rakovčík and Kožany). This bespeaks the same kind of very local tradition we encountered in the microregion formed by Bartne, Nieznajowa/Rozstajne, Świątkowa Mała, and Świątkowa Wielka.

We do not know much directly about the painters of the murals, except that one was a priest's son from the town of Medyka. Indirectly we know, however, that they had to be mobile and willing to work for an extended period of time outside their own community. They certainly could not have been serfs, and it is at least unlikely that they would have been monks.

There were further changes of material in the nineteenth century. In what is today Ivano-Frankivsk oblast, Last Judgments were occasionally painted on glass (fig. 4.30).[17] Last Judgments on glass seem to have been more common in Transylvania,[18] but it may just be that Transylvania's icons on glass have been better studied than Western Ukraine's. Surely such icons were more widespread across the Carpathians, appearing, I imagine, also in Bukovina and Maramureş, although I have no direct evidence. Icons on glass were made by villagers and sold at markets. They hung in peasant homes, not in churches.[19] In the Pokuttia region (also Ivano-Frankivsk oblast) scenes of the Last Judgment appeared on ceramic tiles for stoves (fig. 4.31).[20]

Bukovina and Maramureş

In attempting to delineate the borders of the phenomenon I was investigating, I made some initial explorations of Bukovina. By Bukovina here I mean the northern part of what was once the Austrian crown land of Bukovina, but earlier had been northern Moldavia and now is most of Chernivtsi oblast in Ukraine. The region interested me because it is the territory lying between the southeasternmost extensions of our Carpathian Last Judgments[21] and the Moldavian frescoes and monasteries, which in fact are located in the southern part of Austrian Bukovina. Very little has been noted in the literature about Last Judgments in Bukovina, and I was reduced to just hiring a car for a few days and visiting as many older-looking churches as I could to see what was inside. My findings therefore are very fragmentary. A complete list of the Bukovinian images that I did find is

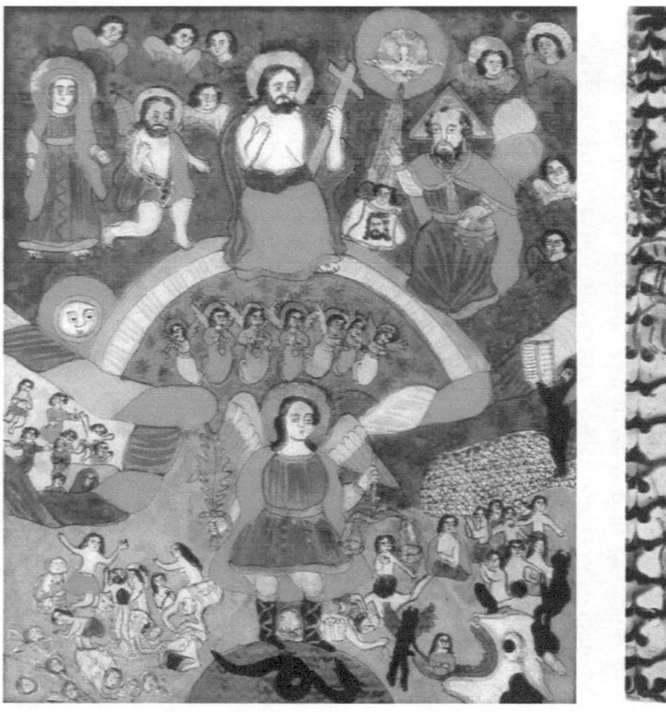

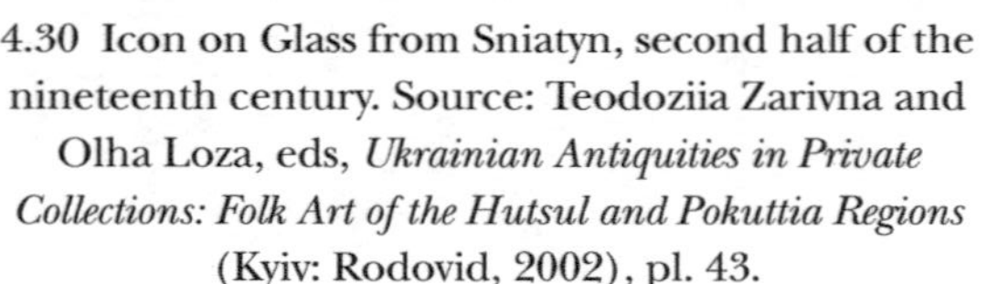

4.30 Icon on Glass from Sniatyn, second half of the nineteenth century. Source: Teodoziia Zarivna and Olha Loza, eds, *Ukrainian Antiquities in Private Collections: Folk Art of the Hutsul and Pokuttia Regions* (Kyiv: Rodovid, 2002), pl. 43.

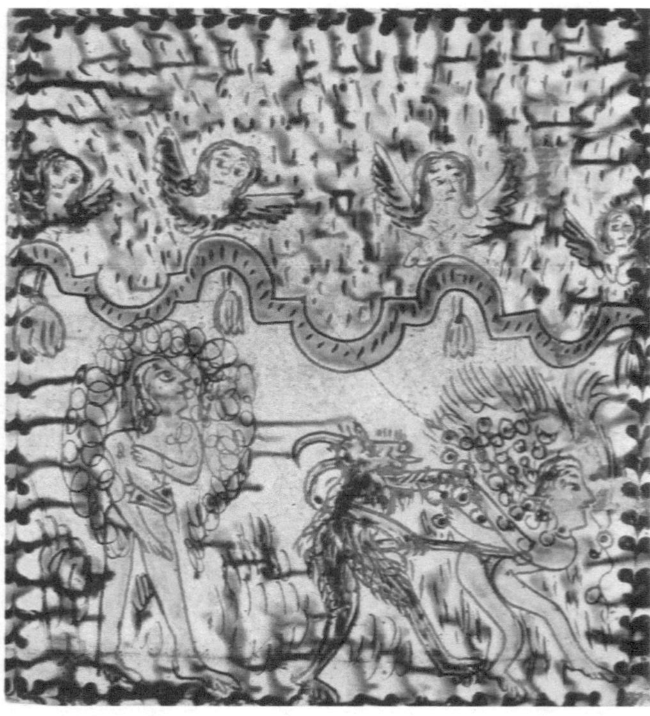

4.31 Ceramic Tile from Ispas by Oleksa Bakhmatiuk, 1860s. Source: Teodoziia Zarivna and Olha Loza, eds, *Ukrainian Antiquities in Private Collections: Folk Art of the Hutsul and Pokuttia Regions* (Kyiv: Rodovid, 2002), pl. 290.

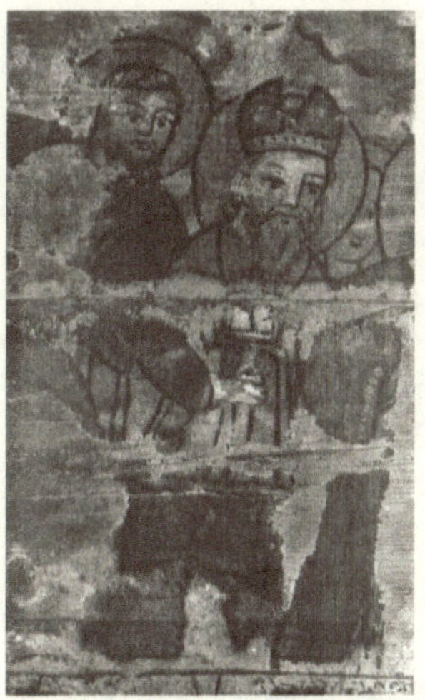

4.32 Fragment, Berehomet. Source: *Istoriia ukrains'koho mystetstva v shesty tomakh*, vol. 3, *Mystetstvo druhoi polovyny XVII–XVIII stolittia* (Kyiv: Akademiia Nauk Ukrains'koi Radians'koi Sotsialistychnoi Respubliky, Holovna redaktsiia Ukrains'koi Radians'koi Entsyklopedii, 1968), 166.

presented in the catalogue near the end of this volume. I am including my notes on Bukovina here, because the images consisted overwhelmingly of icons painted with oils on canvas; in addition there were two frescoes and one mural. I found here no icon painted on wooden boards. The vast majority of images were from the nineteenth century and after.

The earliest surviving image from Bukovina is a mural painted in the second half of the seventeenth century on the north wall of the Church of the Transfer of the Relics of St Nicholas in Berehomet, Kitsman raion. An old man from the village told me when I visited on 7 June 2005 that the church had been floated down the Prut River to its present location some three hundred years ago. The mural is now covered with plywood and wallpaper. Parishioners told me that restorers had come down from Lviv to examine it and said that nothing could be done to save it. A small fragment of the mural has been published (fig. 4.32).

Perhaps the next oldest is a neoclassical fresco in Horecha Monastery, on the outskirts of Chernivtsi, from 1767. It is a simplified version of the Last Judgment with no evident relation to the Carpathian elaboration. It shows Christ, reminiscent of the risen Christ of Latin iconography,

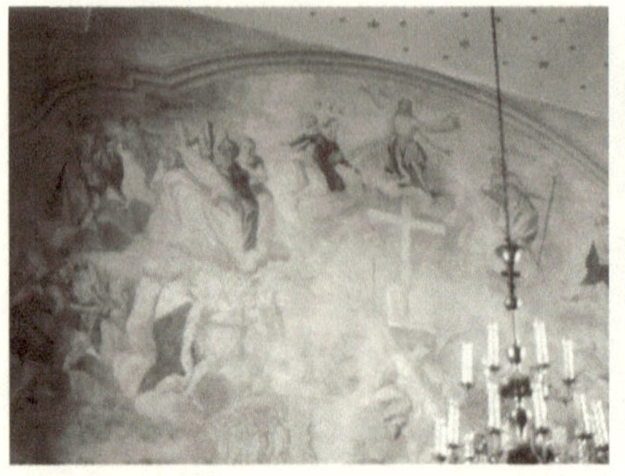

4.33 Horecha, upper right

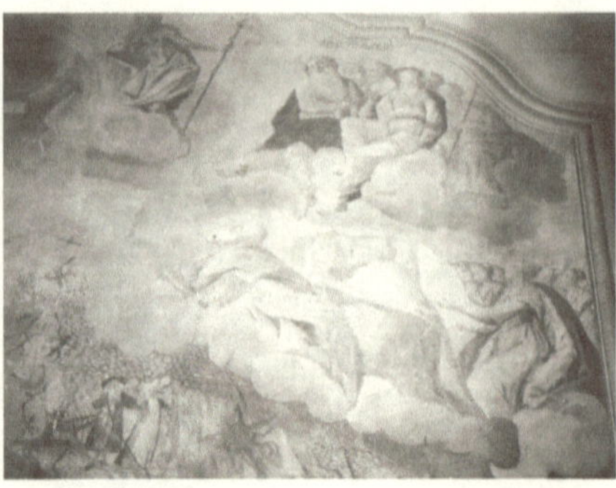

4.34 Horecha, upper left

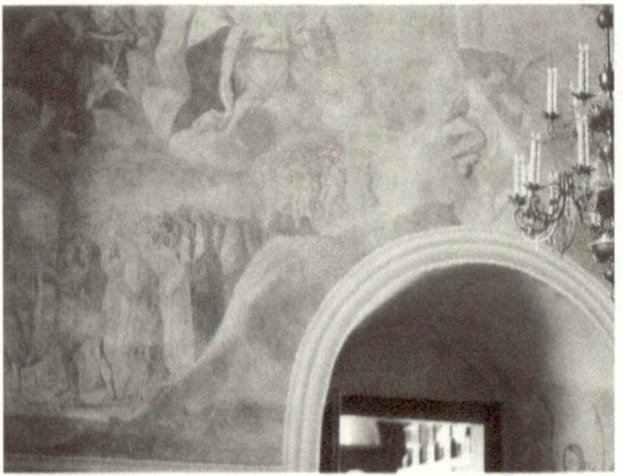

4.35 Horecha, bottom right

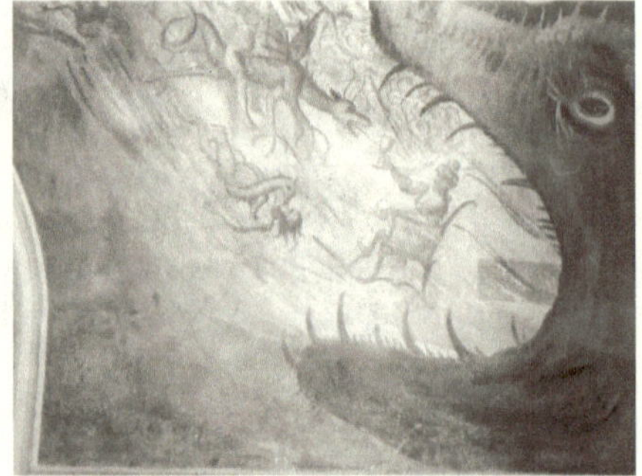

4.36 Horecha, bottom left

standing in front of a rainbow. To his right and left are the Mother of God and John the Baptist. Below him are the cross and book, which stand in for the throne. In the upper right are the choirs of saints, and David can be spotted among them playing a harp. In the upper left are the apostles. Below them seem to be saintly figures from the Old Testament led by Abraham holding the sacrificial knife. In the bottom right are saints entering paradise, on the bottom left sinners entering hell. Among the hell-bound are a Jewish couple dressed in contemporary costume, a naked woman riding a monster, and another woman being attacked by snakes (figs 4.33, 4.34, 4.35, 4.36).

Also from the eighteenth century is a large horizontal icon on canvas originally from Pohorilivka, Zastavna raion (fig. 4.37). Unusually, the right half of the icon is devoted to hell and punishments. In the upper portion are rows of individual pictures of various sinners and craftsmen subjected to individualized tortures. Below them the mouth of hell opens

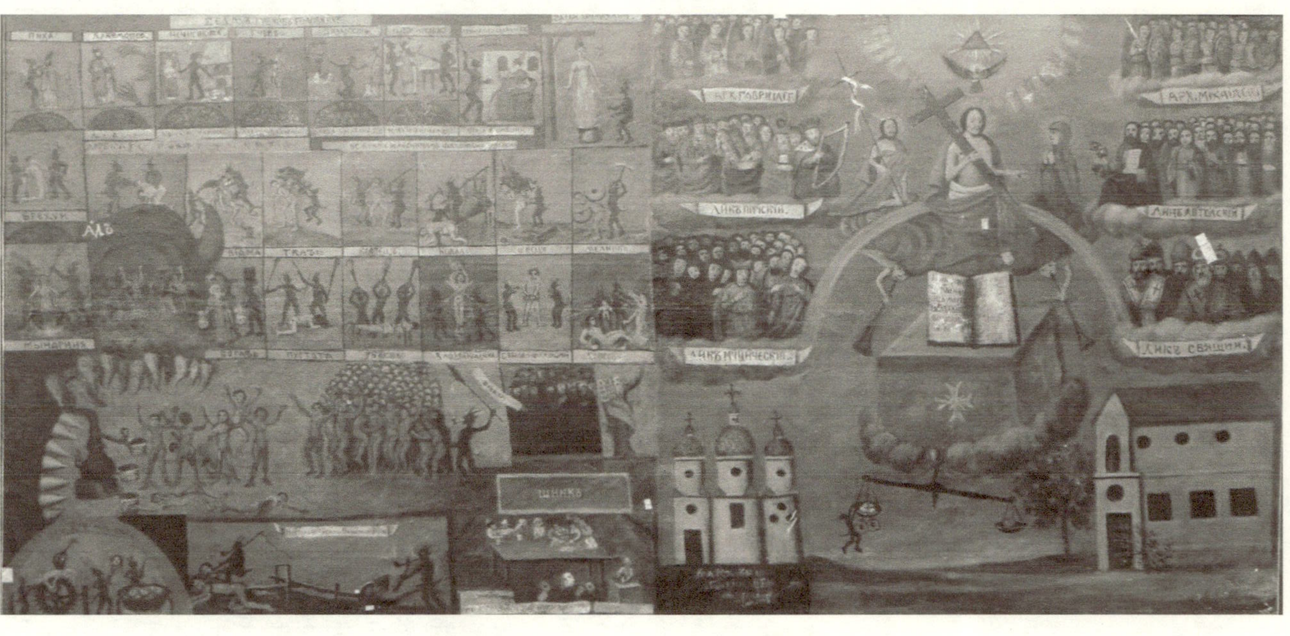

4.37 Pohorilivka overview. Photo: Valerii Helchuk.

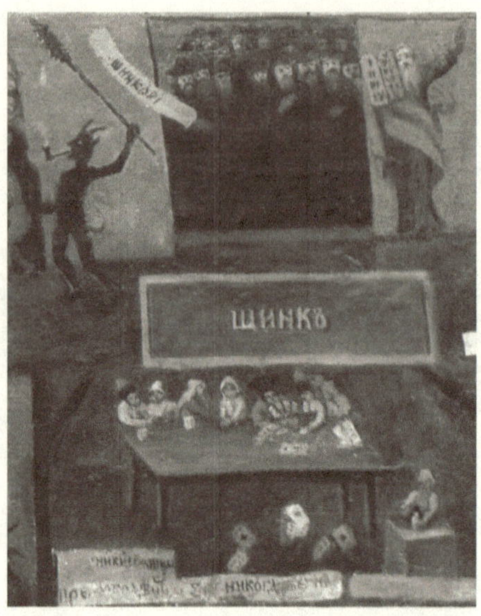

4.38 Tavernkeepers and Gamblers, Pohorilivka. Photo: Valerii Helchuk.

over a larger torture chamber. In the bottom right corner devils torture one man over a rack and boil heads in a kettle. To the left devils are smoking pipes and ploughing with unjust lords in harness. Towards the centre, Moses is leading a group of Jewish men identified as tavernkeepers. Below them a sign says 'Tavern,' and gamblers play cards while a tavernmaid fills a glass (fig. 4.38). The left side of the icon is devoted to heaven. The Son of man sits on a rainbow, holding a crucifix. To his right is John the Baptist and to his left the Mother of God, the opposite of their traditional positions. Choirs of saints flank them, and below Christ is the book and throne, from which scales are suspended. To the right of the scales is a church, perhaps meant to be the old church in Pohorilivka. To the left is a building with a fruit tree in front of it, perhaps paradise. The icon differs markedly from the traditional Carpathian icons, but it shares some features with them as well, such as the tavernmaid and tavern scenes and the unjust landlords. It also shares some features with the murals of Romanian Maramureş, as we shall see later on.

The nineteenth- and twentieth-century icons on oil are quite diverse. Only one of them that I saw is basically similar to the Carpathian model – Roztoky (fig. 4.39). Most of them are primarily inspired by Western models, such as the twentieth-century Pohorilivka and Hlynytsia (figs 4.40, 4.41).

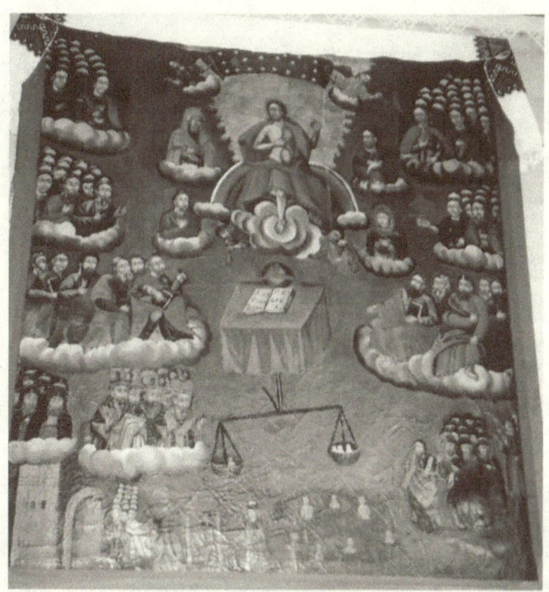

4.39 Roztoky overview

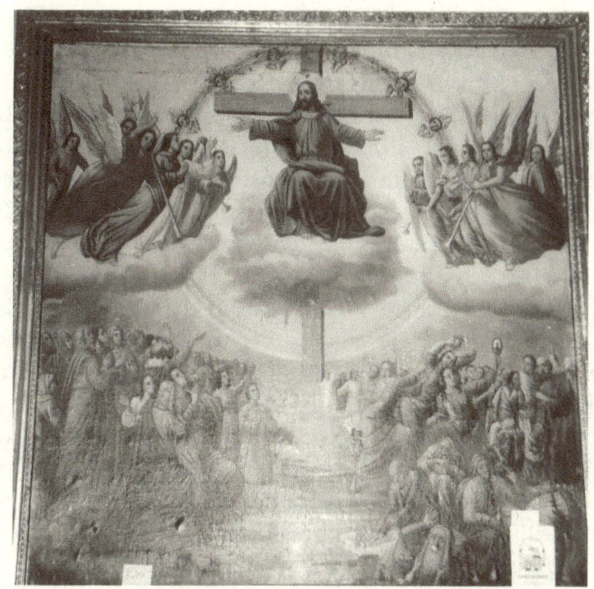

4.40 Pohorilivka (twentieth-century) overview

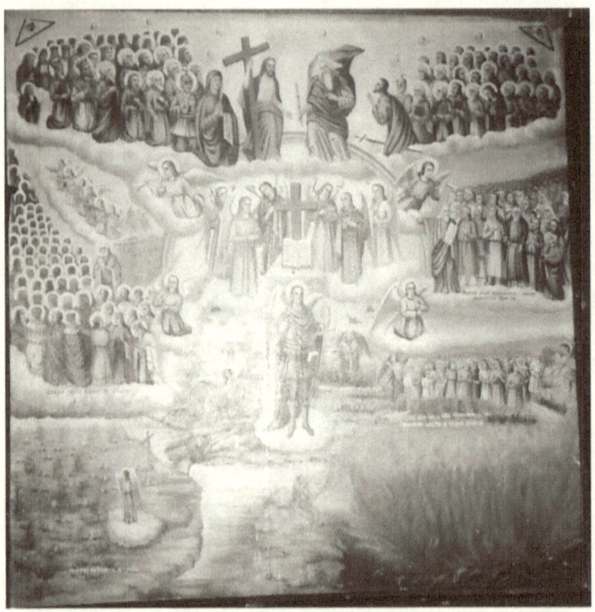

4.41 Hlynytsia overview

The icon of Vyviz was painted in the 1990s or early 2000s. It used as a model a lithograph from a century earlier, with 'Last Judgment' written at the bottom in German, French, Spanish, English, and Italian. I encountered a copy of the lithograph in the open-air museum at the Museum of Folk Architecture in Sanok,[22] which probably acquired it from a peasant cottage in the Lemko region. The dependence of the Vyviz icon on the lithograph is particularly evident in the figures of the angels in the centre: both images show an angel dressed in green in the same pose and holding a book overhead in the centre, and both have almost identical angels flanking the central angel. The poses of the Christ figure are the same in the two icons as well (fig. 4.42). Evidently, the same lithograph was circulating in Bukovina. The most significant and characteristic departure of Vyviz from the lithograph is an expanded and more graphic hell, which features a few buxom, naked sinners.

Along the same lines, a few icons continue where the eighteenth-century Pohorilivka left off and devote considerable space to imaginative punishments for a variety of sinners, for example, Kamianna and Kitsman (fig. 4.43). We shall take a closer look at this particular strain of

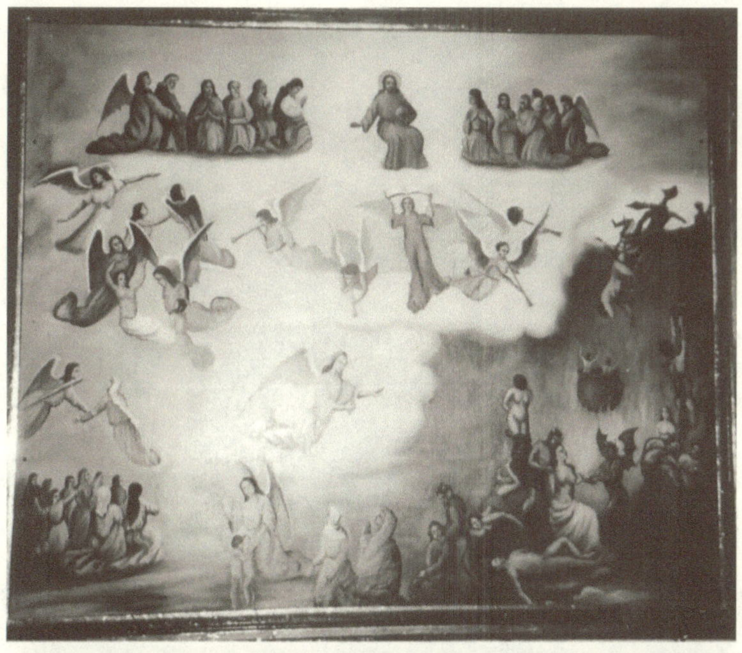

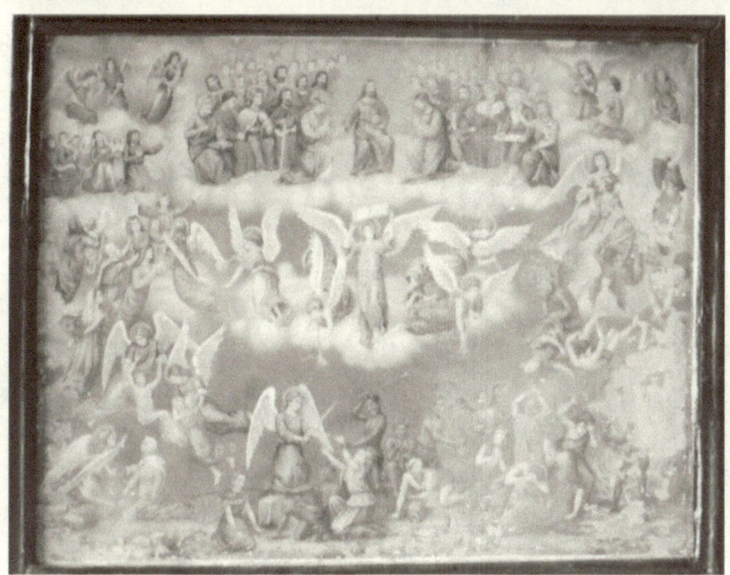

4.42 Vyviz overview and Last Judgment Lithograph

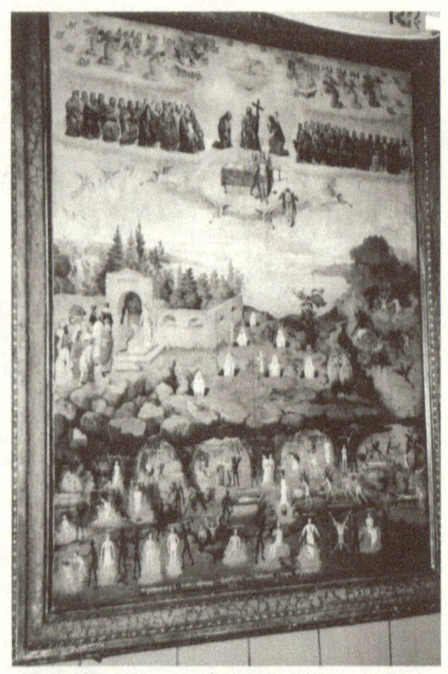

4.43 Kamianna overview

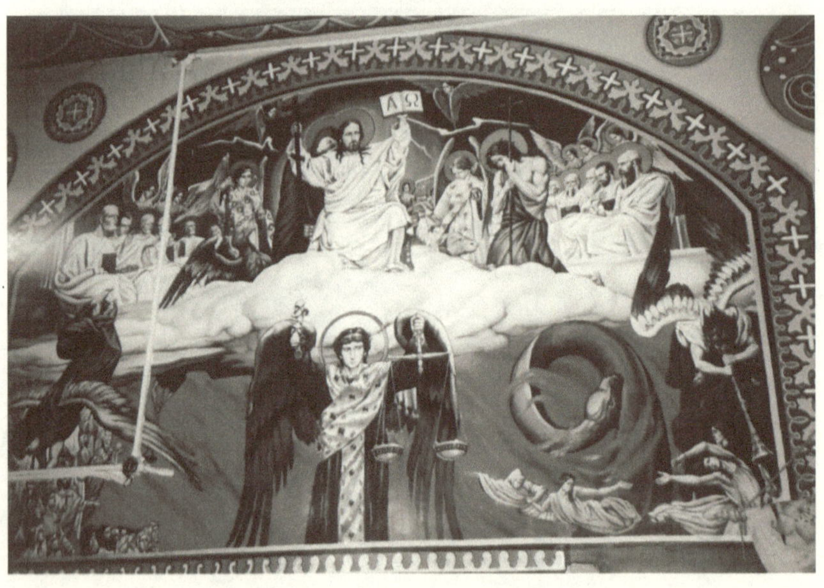

4.44 Dubivtsi overview

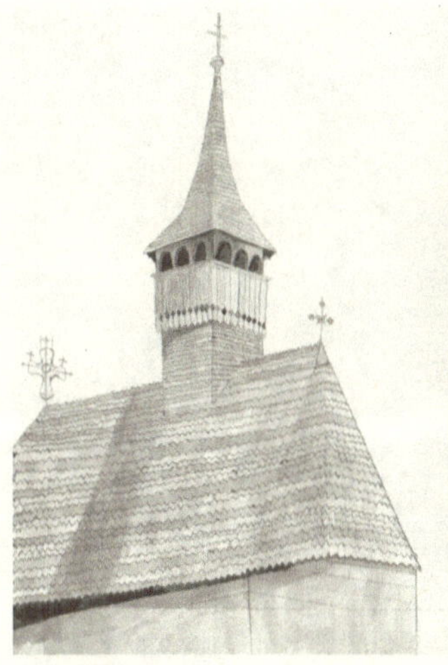

4.45 Typical wooden church of Maramureş. Drawing: Mykhailo Himka.

Bukovinian iconography later in this chapter. The village of Dubivtsi has a beautiful fresco in the modern style, probably executed in the interwar period (fig. 4.44).

The taste for the Last Judgment came late to Bukovina. The taste expanded outside our classical Carpathian region into another Carpathian region, but it was not a taste for the old tradition. The taste arrived at a time when the Last Judgments were being painted on canvas. The painting was much more naturalistic, and the compositions much freer, more sensual, and less thoughtful. The images were easier to purchase as well, since oil or tempera on canvas was a relatively inexpensive medium. The canvases were smaller than the old Last Judgments on wood. Kitsman, for example, measures 163 cm x 117 cm, and many are smaller than that. Even cheaper were coloured lithographs. I did not see it, but I was told by the pastor that there is a lithograph of the Last Judgment in the Church of St John the Baptist in Putyla, Putyla raion.

I also followed the southern boundaries of our icons into Romanian Maramureş (fig. 4.45). I was unable to visit all the localities with a surviving Last Judgment; the catalogue contains a longer list of localities with a Last Judgment image of one sort or another, but I doubt that it is comprehensive. Literature on the Maramureş Last Judgments exists, but it is not large.

There is one of our traditional icons on wood in Maramureş, Budeşti-Josani. I have already mentioned it several times. It seems to date from

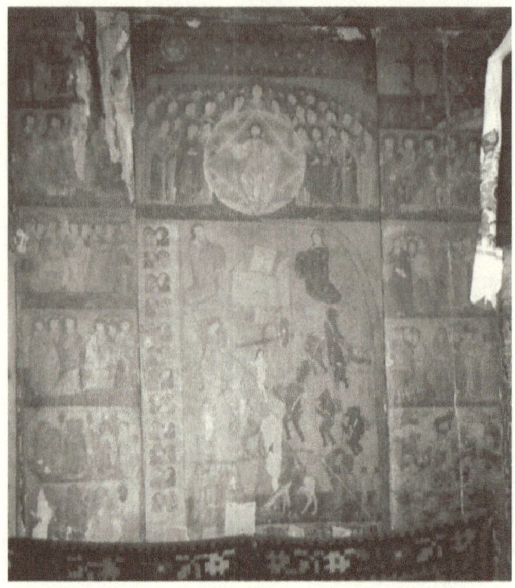

4.46 Budeşti-Josani overview

the seventeenth century and to be the oldest Last Judgment image in the region (fig. 4.46). The Tatars burned most of the wooden churches here in 1717, so there is little left from before that time. Budeşti-Josani refers to the church in the lower part of the village of Budeşti. In the upper part, Budeşti-Susani, is the latest Last Judgment image that I found in Maramureş – a lithograph from the late nineteenth or early twentieth century. Otherwise all the images are murals, the earliest of which (Serednie Vodiane) may date to the seventeenth century or, at the latest, to the early eighteenth and the latest of which were painted in the 1820s (Rozavlea and Şieu). Evidently, the taste for the Last Judgment appeared earlier in Maramureş than in Bukovina, and the favoured material was different. The Maramureş murals are much more conservative than the Bukovinian icons on canvas. Many of the familiar scenes appear, the depictions are not naturalistic, and the technique does not seem much different from that used in Carpathian murals. The interrelationship of the iconography of Romanian Maramureş and the Ukrainian-inhabited Carpathians would repay closer investigation. Here I can just signal that their iconographies of the Last Judgment are closely related and that the interest in this theme in Maramureş seems to have appeared later (figs 4.47, 4.48, 4.49, 4.50, 4.51, 4.52, 4.53).

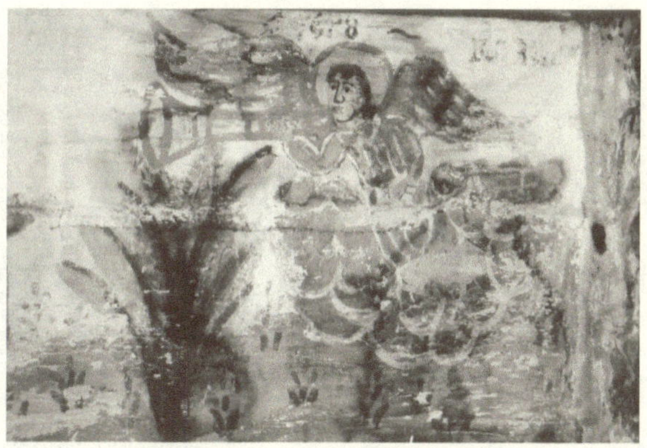

4.47 Trumpeting Angel, Rogoz

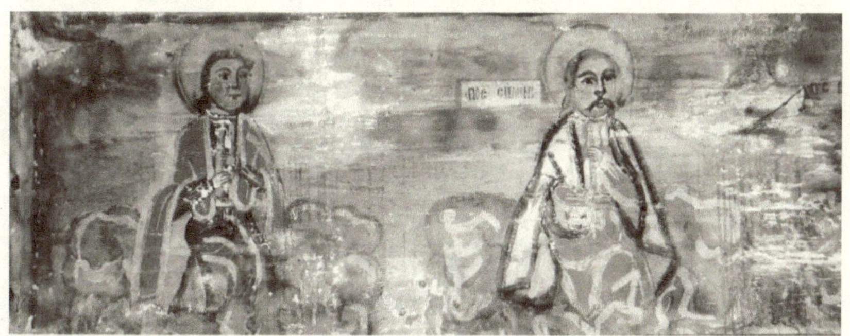

4.48 Apostles, Rogoz

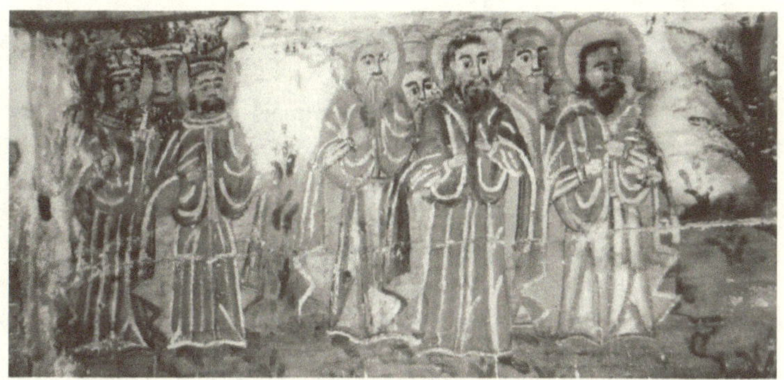

4.49 Choirs of Saints, Rogoz

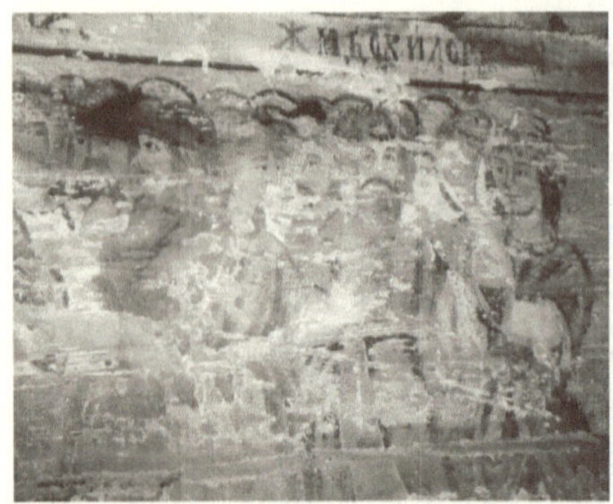

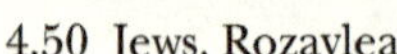

4.50 Jews, Rozavlea

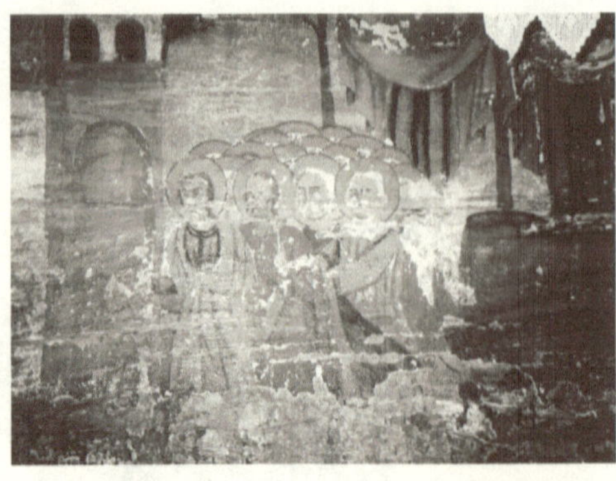

4.51 Saints Entering Paradise, Şieu

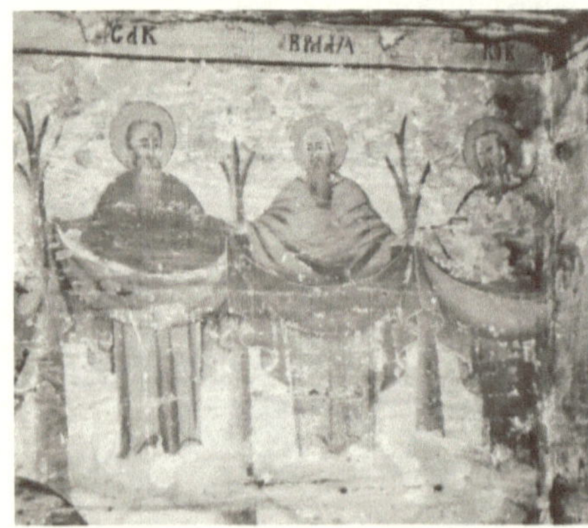

4.52 Bosom of Abraham, Rozavlea

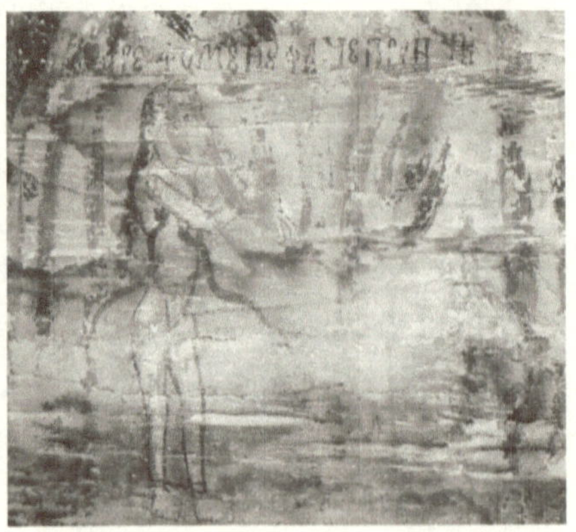

4.53 Childless Woman, Rogoz

The Disintegration of Cultural Traditions

In the later Last Judgment icons and murals we can observe the old cultural traditions breaking down. We have already seen the abandonment of many of the elements that had traditionally been part of the composition. We have also seen a change in painting style, particularly in the icons on canvas, but also in some of the murals.

Occasionally it is possible to discern that the painters were losing their grasp of the iconographic traditions. The resurrection in Vyšný Orlík, for example, suggests the traditional resurrection scene to those who know it, but the vague form that is actually painted there leaves some doubt about whether the painter knew what he was representing (fig. 4.54). An unambiguous case is the treatment of the almsgiving fornicator in Roztoka. To begin with, he is not facing paradise, which is essential to the story – he sees paradise, but feels the torments of hell. Moreover, his inscription is broken up. Near him in Roztoka there is an inscription that reads: 'The man gave alms, but he did not confess his sins; he feels torments.' But in an altogether different part of hell, over another figure not tied to a post, are words that belonged in the middle of the inscription just cited: 'and he persisted in his fornication.' To my mind the most glaring testimony to the loss of meaning occurs in the Hlynytsia icon from Bukovina. It is Moses before a group of people, pointing in the general direction of the Son of man, who is holding his cross. It looks much like Moses and the Jews and the peoples, except that the distinctive national costumes have been replaced by generic antique clothing. The inscription reads: 'Moses leads the righteous and points out the crucified Christ' (fig. 4.55). Various borrowings from Roman Catholic traditions can also be found. The eighteenth-century Pohorilivka icon, for example, depicts the seven deadly sins.

A further sign of the decline of the old culture was the switch from Cyrillic to Latin in the Kožuchovce-Bodružal-Rakovčík-Kožany microregion at the end of the eighteenth century. The Rakovčík icon has a single Cyrillic inscription: the initials for 'Jesus of Nazareth King of the Jews' above the cross on the altar. But the open book has its text in the Rusyn/Ukrainian language written in Latin characters. In Library of Congress transcription it reads:[23]

Po[d']te zhyvi i mertvi,
na su[d] Boha vsemohu-
chiho: vezmete ot-
platu, iaku miru
vyste meraly taka
i vam se otmera.

That is: Come you living and dead to the Judgment of almighty God: take your repayment, by whatever measure you measured, by such you will be measured (cf. Mt 7:2, Mk 4:24, Lk 6:39). (Of course, the text traditionally on the throne book was Mt 25:34 [fig. 4.56].)

The Bodružal mural seems to employ the same practice: the cross inscription is in Cyrillic,[24] but the text in the book is in Latin characters. The text here is hard to make out, but it seems similar to the one in the Rakovčík icon. A few words are legible in what vestiges of hell remain: *cerkownice* (women who kept up the church) and *bohac* (rich man).

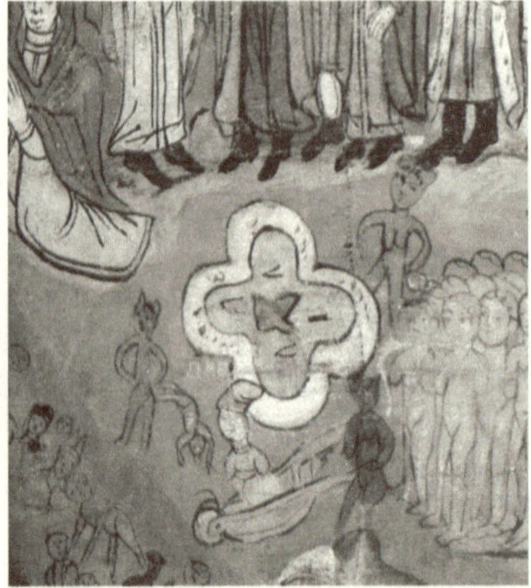

4.54 Resurrection, Vyšný Orlík

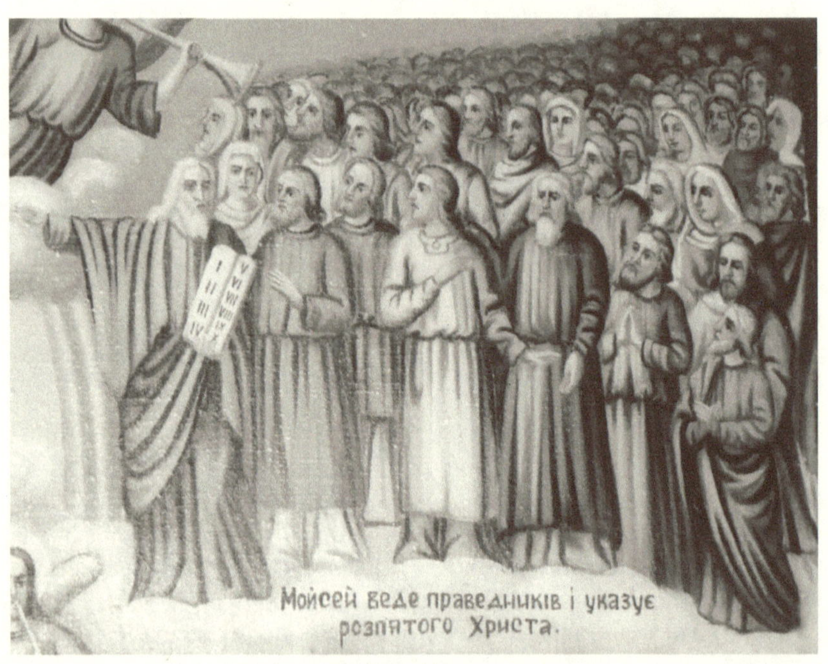

4.55 Moses and People, Hlynytsia

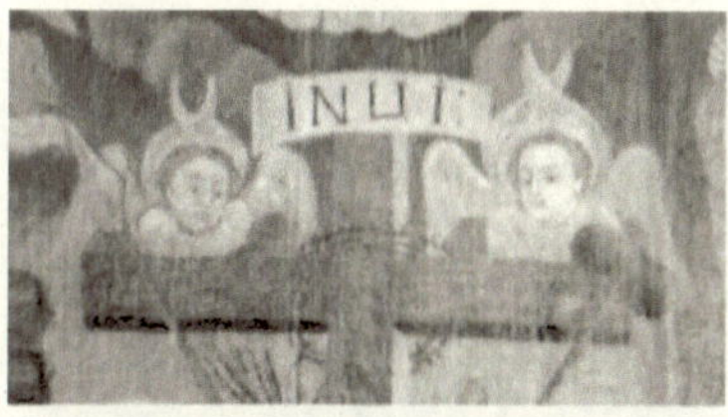

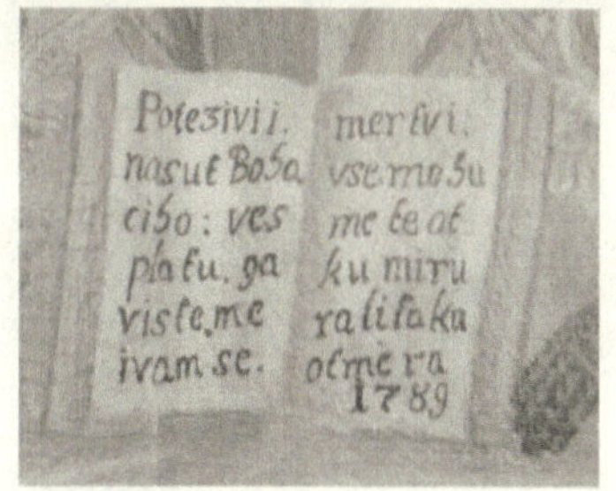

4.56 Inscriptions, Rakovčík

The most notable case is the Kožany icon on canvas. The older, wooden icons in the Kožany church all have Church Slavonic inscriptions in Cyrillic. On the iconostasis in this church there is even an icon of Ss Anthony and Theodosius of the Kyiv Caves Monastery. Yet all the texts on the canvas Last Judgment, even including the inscription over the cross, are in Latin characters, and the language, except for the Latin-language abbreviation over the crucifix, seems to be a form of Slovak (e.g., the inscriptions use *križ* for cross and *mlynar* for miller).

The Effacement of Hell

An important symptom of the disintegration of the traditional Last Judgment iconography is the removal of hell from the icons and murals. If you compare the murals of Kožuchovce and Bodružal above (figs 4.27, 4.29), it is readily evident that hell has been effaced from Bodružal. The icon on canvas Rakovčík comes from the same microregion. It too has hell, in fact the whole bottom part of the canvas, removed. The icon has a painted border around it, but the border is absent at the bottom, and some figures are cut off (fig. 4.57). In both Rakovčík and Kožany are serpents with red apples in their mouths. From the Kožany icon we know that the serpent with the apple should be long, and issuing forth from the jaws of hell. In the Rakovčík icon only a small part of the serpent is left in the picture, additional proof that hell has been deliberately obliterated here (fig. 4.58).

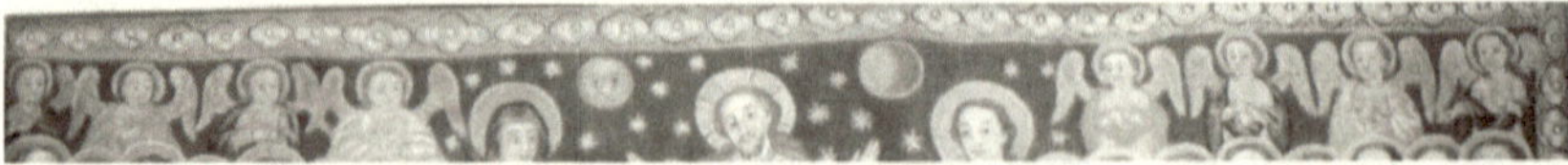

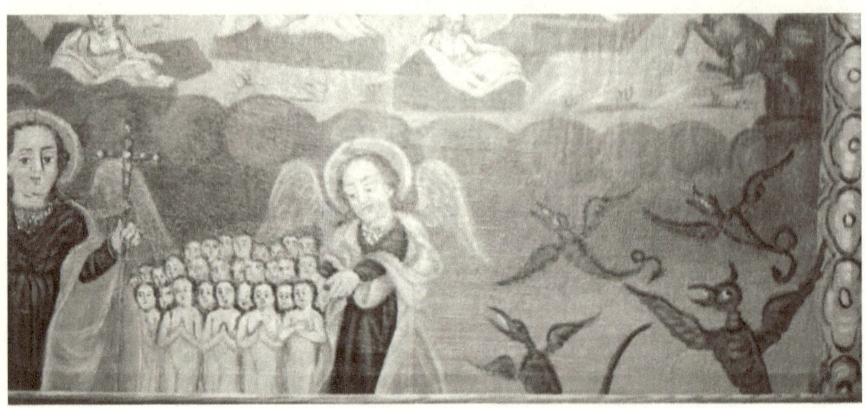

4.57 Edges, Rakovčík

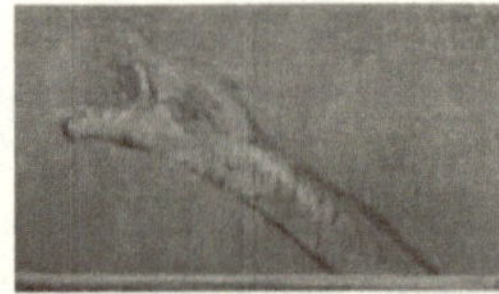

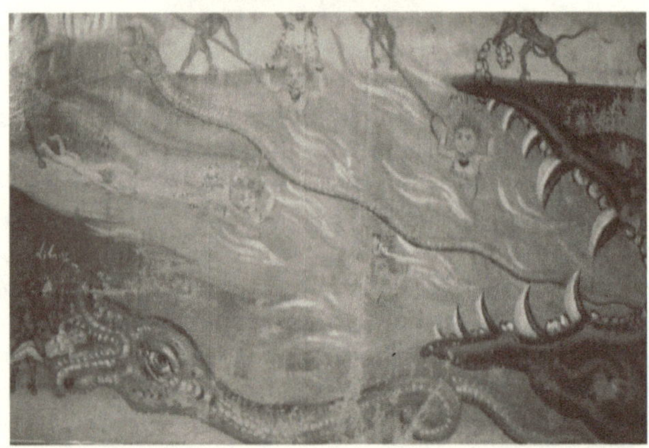

4.58 Serpents, Rakovčík and Kožany

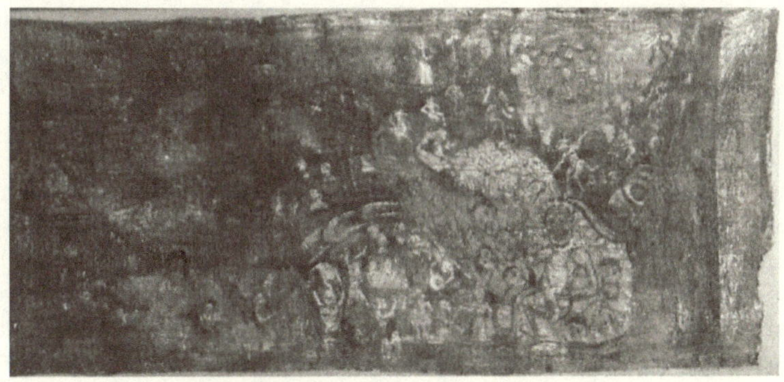

4.59 Zboj/Uličské Krivé, bottom half

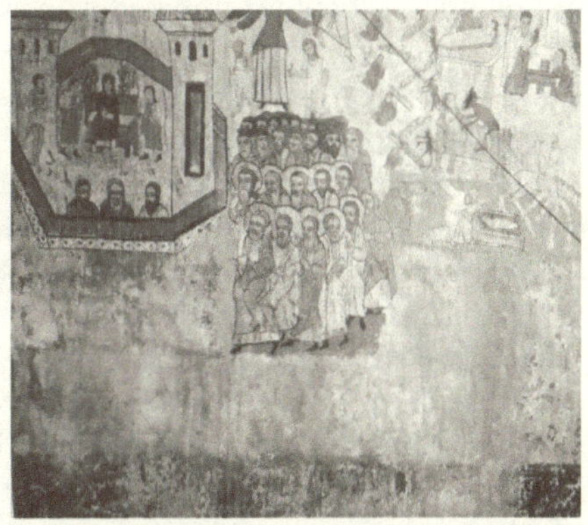

4.60 Effacement of Hell, Tiushka

The top half of Zboj/Uličské Krivé, as we saw (4.3), is fairly well preserved, but the bottom half is so damaged that it is almost illegible (4.59). I have concluded that what once was a single canvas was cut in half horizontally: the well-preserved top half was kept in church and venerated, while the bottom half was kept separately and exposed to damage. This is another case in which the depiction of hell was deliberately removed from the icon. Tiushka shows a very careful effacement of hell and other lower parts of the icon. The bosom of Abraham and saints entering paradise are preserved on the icon, but hell and even the gates of paradise have been removed (fig. 4.60). Hell has been sawn off Galicia-City Museum 1, and Izky has been repainted so that most of hell is missing.

In the previous chapter we looked at four related icons from the microregion of Bartne, Nieznajowa/Rozstajne, Świątkowa Mała, and Świątkowa

Wielka. Świątkowa Mała was painted in 1687, the others in the first half of the eighteenth century. The difference between the icon from 1687 and those from the early eighteenth century is striking (fig. 4.61). The 1687 icon is painted on the traditional three vertical boards. All three of the others are painted on one horizontal board. More than a third of the 1687 icon depicts paradise and hell of the type usual in the traditional Carpathian elaboration. None of the three eighteenth-century icons depict either paradise or hell. All are truncated in this respect. It is probable that hell was omitted deliberately (and also paradise for compositional reasons). I also encountered some removal of hell in Maramureş. Part of hell in Rogoz was painted over, and what was left was covered up with a large cupboard. In Budeşti-Josani, the lower part of the icon is hidden by embroidered cloth (see above, fig. 4.46).

The effacement of hell was probably connected with parish visitations. These were initiated in our region by the Uniate Synod of Zamość of 1720.[25] Either the bishop himself or specially appointed visitors would visit each parish, reporting on its material and spiritual conditions. The visitation records routinely described the artistic furnishings of the church, including noteworthy icons and murals. Sometimes the visitors would make comments on the quality of the artistic works. They also paid some attention to content. Vasyl Otkovych has found notes in the visitations referring to murals of the Last Judgment that said 'to '"erase," to "whitewash" these "various horrors (*strashydla*)."'[26] A Uniate eparchial decree from 1766 ordered priests to warn their parishioners against buying inferior and inappropriate icons, such as those produced in Posada Rybotycka; such icons were unacceptable in churches.[27] A concern with the content of icons was also noticeable in eighteenth-century Russia. Tsar Peter I in 1722 commanded that icons 'are to be painted in accordance with ecclesiastical customs and the Acts of the Council [of 1667]'; he also appointed a superintendent of icon painters.[28] The Orthodox metropolitan of Kyiv, Havryil (Kremianetsky), concerned about the social criticism in Last Judgment iconography, issued an order in 1774 to rid the fresco of the Apocalypse in the Cathedral of St Sophia of 'various inappropriate (*nepristoinye*) things and people in crowns and various clothing ... to erase them, and make only darkness and fire and to leave the people in it naked.'[29]

The Titillating and the Grotesque

The concerns of the visitors in our region may well have been provoked by the unedifying scenes that were finding their way into the Last Judgment icons, particularly into their infernal regions. In the previous

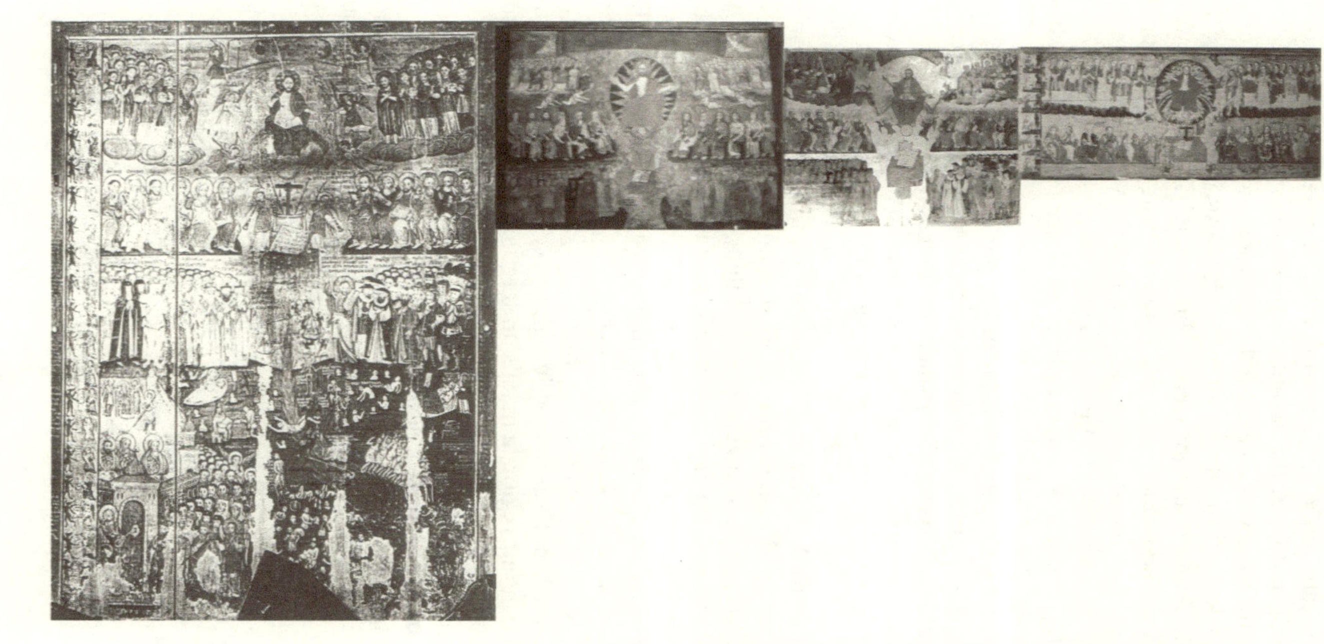

4.61 Świątkowa Mała, Nieznajowa/Rozstajne, Świątkowa Wielka, and Bartne. Photos of Świątkowa Mała and Świątkowa Wielka: Romuald Biskupski.

chapter we already noted an increasing interest in sexual sin in icons on wood after the middle of the seventeenth century; this even led to the depiction of the woman who engaged in oral sex and then paid for it by receiving the devil's filth into her mouth (see above, fig. 3.29). The interest in sexual themes is also evinced in the murals. Chotyniec shows naturalistically painted women with full, round breasts emerging from the tombs (fig. 4.62). A comely mermaid, naked to the waist, decorated one of the walls in Piilo, although she is probably not connected with the Last Judgment (fig. 4.63). In Rogoz the artist introduced a group of 'whores' (*kurve*) into hell (fig. 4.64).

There was also more interest in the grotesque. Prominent in the resurrection scene in Chotyniec is a naturalistic skeleton (fig. 4.65). The mural at Piilo graphically depicted the torment of sinners (fig. 4.66).

In Bukovina painters and, one assumes, viewers seem to have developed a special delight in tortures, beginning with the eighteenth-century Pohorilivka canvas (fig. 4.67). Nineteenth-century icons like Kitsman and Kamianna displayed a large assortment of punishments: a disobedient child is attacked by a dragon while standing in fire, a woman who believed a fortune teller kneels in fire while a devil reads her cards, a proud man has a spike pounded into his head by a devil, a false witness is skewered on a devil's pitchfork, and so on. For the most part these are additions limited to Bukovina, but there are also exceptions. Both Kamianna and Kitsman show a man being hung upside down for desiring someone else's wife, and in the Kamianna icon a devil is sawing the man's groin; on Topol'a as well, although two centuries earlier and from the other side of our region, a man is undergoing the same punishment (figs 4.68, 4.69, 4.70).

Two eighteenth-century images, Pohorilivka from Bukovina and Poenile Izei from Maramureş, show a devil punishing a blacksmith by inserting a bellows into his anus and another devil punishing a cobbler by pounding a spike into the same place (figs 4.71, 4.72). These must have been popular scenes, perhaps circulating as prints. Clearly, taste was running 'beyond the bounds of beauty,' as Dmytro Chyzhevsky put it. In this grotesque iconography we see 'the baroque love of images of horrors, cruelty, corpses, death, and the like.'[30]

Conclusions

The tradition of Last Judgment icon painting that flourished in the Carpathians in the fifteenth, sixteenth, and seventeenth centuries had

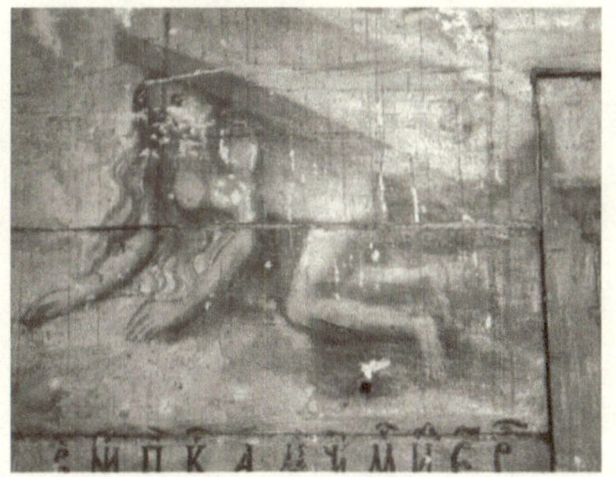

4.62 Woman Rising from a Grave, Chotyniec

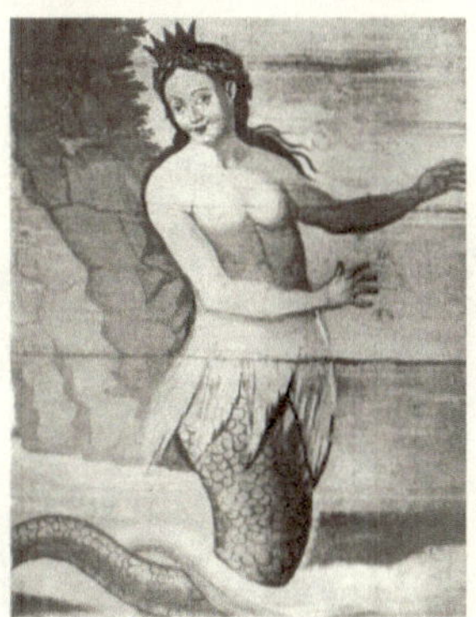

4.63 Mermaid, Piilo. Source: P.M. Zholtovs'kyi, *Monumental'nyi zhyvopys na Ukraini XVII–XVIII st.* (Kyiv: Naukova dumka, 1988), 118.

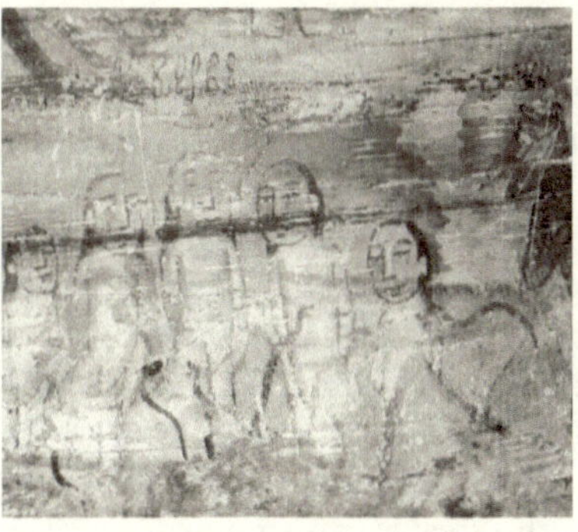

4.64 Whores, Rogoz

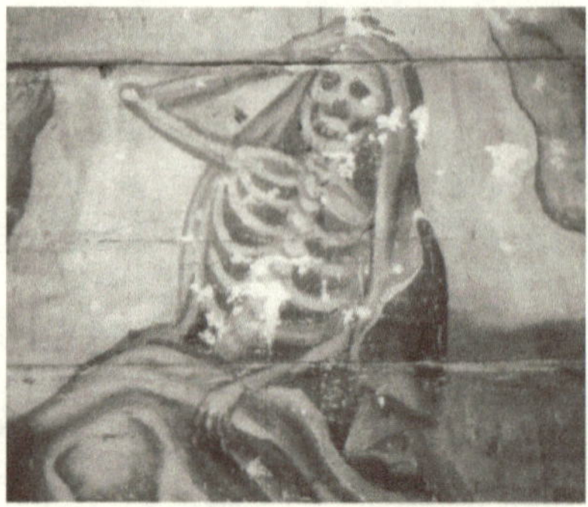

4.65 Skeleton, Chotyniec

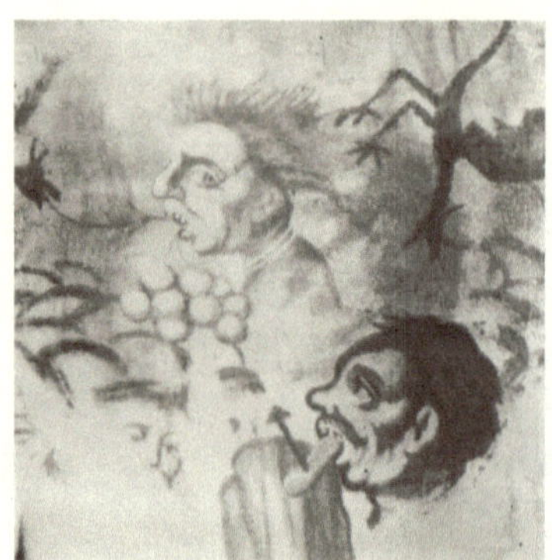

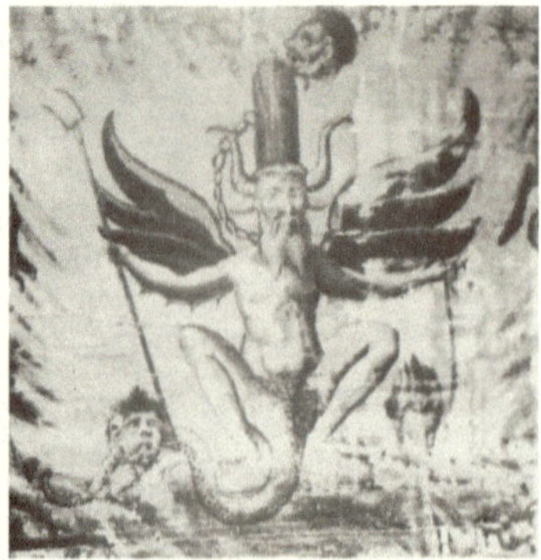

4.66 Tortures, Piilo. Source: P.M. Zholtovs'kyi, *Monumental'nyi zhyvopys na Ukraini XVII–XVIII st.* (Kyiv: Naukova dumka, 1988), 118.

disappeared by the nineteenth. There were certainly still echoes of it, but the original phenomenon had disintegrated. Forests with linden trees were much reduced, and the traditional linden boards gave way to new surfaces: pine, canvas, and log walls. With the use of canvas, oil frequently replaced tempera as the painting medium. Working with oil on canvas probably created more common ground with other artists who were not painting in the traditional Orthodox way. Working on the walls of churches freed the iconography from its previously restrained vertical form. Canvases and even icons on board also reflected the new possibilities and were painted in horizontal form. The iconography spread from the old heartland in the new forms to new territories. The taste for Last Judgment icons had been expanding to the south from the heartland,

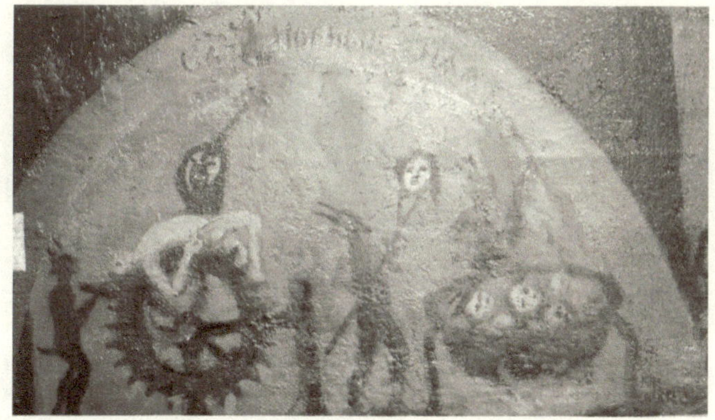

4.67 Torture Chamber, Pohorilivka

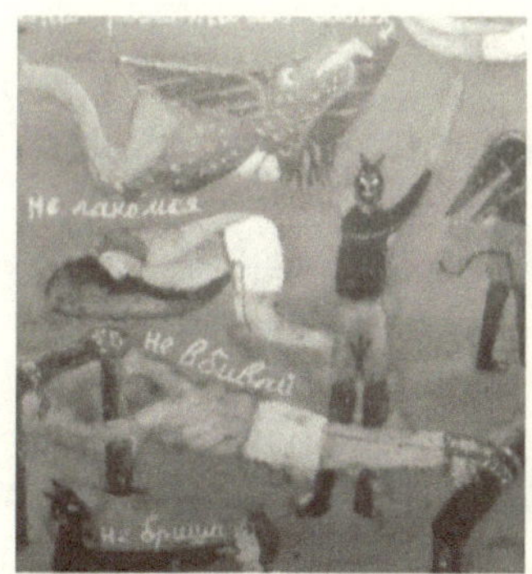

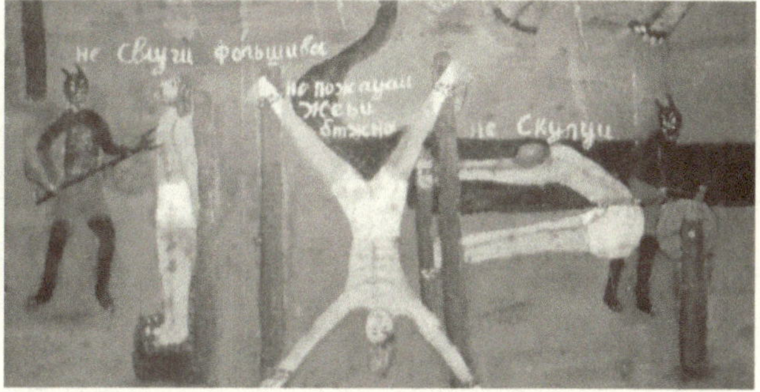

4.68 Torments, Kitsman

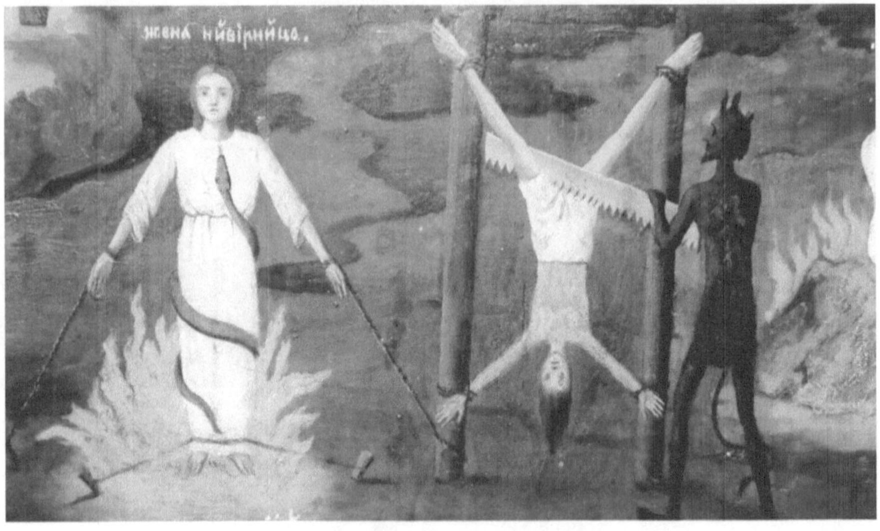

4.69 Torments, Kamianna

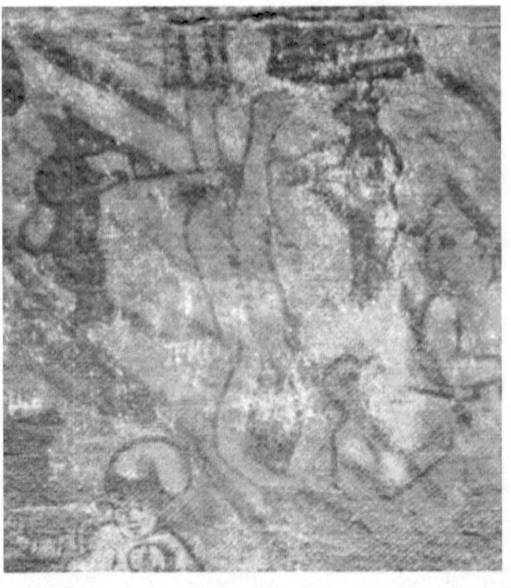

4.70 Man Being Sawn, Topol'a

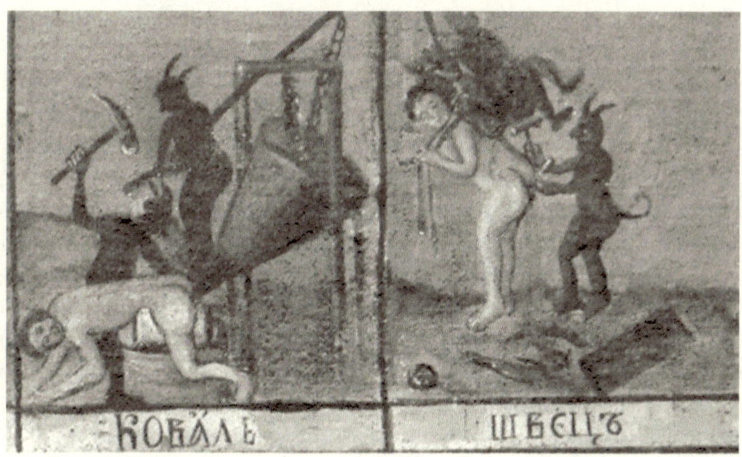

4.71 Blacksmith and Cobbler, Pohorilivka. Photo: Valerii Helchuk.

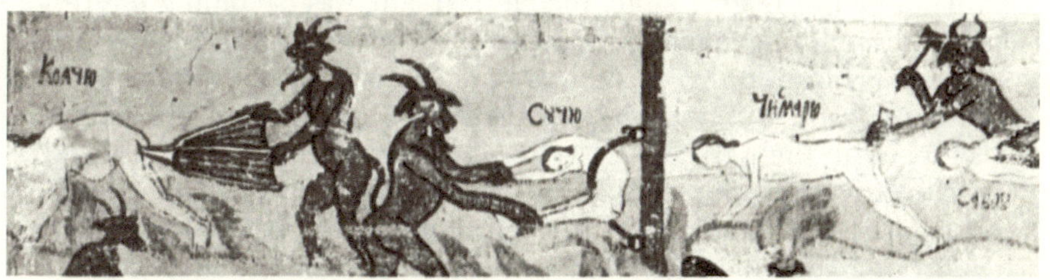

4.72 Punishment of Craftsmen, Poienile Izei. Source: Anca Pop-Bratu, *Pictura murală maramureşeană: Meşteri zugravi şi interferenţe stilistice* (Bucharest: Editura Meridiane, 1982), pl. 85.

and in the seventeenth century it reached Romanian Maramureş. Some icons were painted for churches there, but the real flourishing of Last Judgment iconography in this region took the form of murals on church walls. Somewhat later the iconography spread to Bukovina as well, mainly in the form of icons on canvas. In both of these new territories, the iconography developed a more explicit interest in sexual sin and punishment, tendencies that had already been developing in the traditional icons since the middle of the seventeenth century.

The artists were changing as well. We do not know if any monks painted icons on canvas. I doubt that they painted the walls of churches. That task required someone who was willing to spend a long time in another locality. Itinerant craftsmen, specialized village craftsmen, and priests' sons who were not going to follow their father's calling were the kind of people who would be interested in such work, not monks. The level of learning that went into the formation of a Last Judgment painter was sinking. The artists seemed to be more interested in satisfying the tastes of those who commissioned them than in instructing them. They painted things that aroused the peasants' curiosity. Some of them clearly had professional training and painted in a naturalistic style. While in the traditional depictions of hell the formulaic nakedness of the sinners suggested nothing sexual, the new depictions certainly did. In Bukovina, the artist (artists?) who painted the many tortures of Kamianna and Kitsman clothed the victims; obviously, he was ashamed of nakedness in a way that the old icon painters were not. Also in Bukovina, the artist who painted Vyviz had the same prurient feelings about nakedness, but revelled in it. These are but two sides of the same coin.

While the popular taste was growing ever more interested in the titillating and the grotesque, the clerical elite was becoming interested in disciplining. This was the era of the Counter-Reformation, of confessionalization projects undertaken to raise the cultural level of the clergy[31] and to reform the spiritual life of the masses. Bishops sent visitors to all the parishes in their eparchies. They were there to inspect. Were the people receiving the sacraments? Was the priest setting a good example? Was the church being cared for? What were the icons like? When the reformers, whether visitors or individual pastors, found things they did not like in the Last Judgment icons, they had them effaced or cut off. An eighteenth-century icon painter in the Bartne region preemptively omitted the traditional lower portions from his icons. It is reasonable to suppose that the reformers began to discourage the practice of placing Last Judgments in the churches. Indeed, outside Bukovina, where the canvas tradition still flourished, such Last Judgments as were still produced in our region in the nineteenth century were for use in the home. Small Last Judgment icons, painted on glass by peasants and sold in the markets, were taken home, blessed by the priest, and placed on a shelf with other icons. More rarely, scenes of the Last Judgment appeared on stove tiles.

Perhaps another factor leading to the disintegration of the tradition was that the common people's ideas about the Last Judgment were changing in the eighteenth and particularly in the nineteenth century. Sermons were changing, for instance, including sermons on the Last Judgment. In 1794 there appeared in print a sermon collection from Pochaiv Monastery, which was then Uniate. The sermons were written in the Ukrainian vernacular or, as the foreword put it, in 'the simple and ordinary Rus' language' (prostyi i zvychainyi ruskii iazyk). Judging from the number of copies I have run across, without particularly searching for it, it must have enjoyed considerable popularity among the clergy. It was not, however, a work in the Eastern Christian tradition. In fact, the collection had started life in Italian and was later translated into Polish before it was published in Ukrainian. The one sermon on the Last Judgment opened by exhorting the faithful to abstain from excess, especially drunkenness, which is the source of other sins; it returned to the theme of moderation at the close of the sermon as well. The main content, however, was a summary of the day's Gospel in simple words. There was no mention of the river of fire or throne or other characteristic motifs of the Byzantine tradition, and specifically Western formulations were present, such as 'mortal sin' and Christ referred to as 'the Son of the Virgin Mary.'[32] This is, of course, not the same thing as the switch from Cyrillic to Latin writing in Kožany, but it is part of the same process of the replacement of the traditional Byzantine and post-Byzantine spiritual culture with that of the Catholic Counter-Reformation.

5 Conclusions

I am dividing these conclusions into two parts. The first, shorter part recapitulates, in point form, the major conclusions that flow from the evidence and argument of this book. Some of these conclusions are firmly established by the evidence; others are rather suggestions. The second part of the chapter consists of methodological reflections.

Research Results

- The Carpathian icons of the Last Judgment originated, probably in the fifteenth century, in the region around Staryi Sambir (Poliana, Mshanets', Lavriv, Spas), which remained the heartland of this set of sacred images. In the sixteenth century the icons spread in a scattered way to localities in the plains to the northeast, but in a more concentrated way in the mountainous terrain to the south, both directly south and to the south and then east (in the direction of Drohobych). The icons also began to move to the west in the sixteenth century, but did so more intensively in the seventeenth and eighteenth centuries. In the west, the icons spread primarily along the crest of the mountains, along the old Polish-Hungarian border. When the icons on wood were supplemented by icons on canvas and murals beginning in the second half of the sixteenth century, these new images could be found throughout the range of the icons on wood, but also extended much further. The murals extended further south from the heartland into Romanian Maramureş and, to a lesser extent, into Bukovina. The canvasses extended into Bukovina and into Right-Bank Ukraine.

- The icons of the Last Judgment in the Carpathian churches originated as a substitute for the frescoes of the Last Judgment that had been widespread in the Rus' tradition and were also being painted in Moldavia and the Balkans. Destined for rural communities and wooden churches, these large icons on linden boards were a convenient and affordable way to include the Last Judgment within the church's program of visual art. The icons could be painted elsewhere, then disassembled into their three or four boards, loaded on a cart and transported to the village, and reassembled in the church.
- The original icons of the fifteenth century were primarily based on a prototype developed in northern Rus', of which the Novgorod icon held by the Tretiakov Gallery in Moscow is the extant example closest to the Carpathian icons. The northern Rus' model was supplemented by visual borrowings from local Gothic depictions of the Last Judgment. In the origins of the Carpathian Last Judgment icon, Moldavian influences or a hidden Kyiv-Halych tradition played no part at all.
- The knowledge of the northern Rus' prototype was probably brought to the Carpathians by monks from northern Rus' who stayed in Carpathian Rus' monasteries either on their way to the south (Constantinople, Athos, the Holy Land) or while engaged in painting projects in Poland.
- The work of inventing visual elements to correspond to certain texts was primarily accomplished in Byzantium and northern Rus', not in the Carpathian monasteries. An exception were certain additions made in the sixteenth and seventeenth centuries based primarily on 'The Journey of the Mother of God among the Torments.'
- Moldavian iconography influenced Carpathian icon painting only in the sixteenth century, at the time when the Moldavian princes and boyars commissioned many fresco projects for monasteries.
- The original painters of the icons were monks, although perhaps they were professional iconographers associated with or resident in monasteries. Over time their participation diminished until, in the end, small-town craftsmen and painters of mixed origin dominated the production of the images. Roughly estimated, the balance changed in the seventeenth century. The earlier images can be considered products of a more elite and universal religious culture – painted by monks, probably at first encouraged by them and by such Rus' gentry as were in the area, and acting in conformity with the larger Orthodox

tradition at the time. The later images were more plebeian and particular – painted by craftsmen and even villagers, with themes appealing to the peasants' tastes and interests, and continuing what had become a local, sometimes even microregional, tradition. By the eighteenth century the elite of the church became suspicious of the images and began to efface the depiction of hell.

- Over time new elements entered the icons. The additions were primarily to the lower part of the icon and concerned sin and punishment. They often had social dimensions, and some, especially in the eighteenth century, were titillating and/or grotesque.
- The original icons of the fifteenth century were almost identical to one another, containing, with a few exceptions, the same elements in the same placement. In later centuries, and increasingly so over time, the icons became more diverse as new elements were added and old ones disappeared from them. By the eighteenth century the images of the Last Judgment were very different one from another. There were microregions with their own new traditions. Even the materials varied widely, including now canvas and the walls of churches; the images on the latter materials never shared the kind of relative uniformity that characterized the icons on boards.
- In the eighteenth century the influence of Roman Catholicism is noticeable on some of the icons.
- This investigation concerned specifically images of the Last Judgment. Although much that has been said here probably helps illuminate the history of other icons and murals in the Carpathians, it must be kept in mind that the Last Judgment image had its specificities: it was a complicated icon, meant to substitute for an entire wall of a masonry church, and the simplest craftsmen (the Rybotycze school, for example) did not often attempt it.

Methodological Reflections

In the course of researching and writing this book, I had to discard many of the assumptions and hypotheses I started out with. I had undertaken this project because of a dissatisfaction with the way the Ukrainian historical paradigm dealt with the prenational cultural past. I saw that the national narrative seemed able to accommodate only those cultural phenomena that fed into the historical result of the production of a Ukrainian nation. Its account of early modern culture emphasized the religious polemics of the late sixteenth and seventeenth centuries, which were understood as part of the self-definition of a Ukrainian nation against the Catholic, Polish other. I wagered that I would get deeper into the internal workings of the old culture if I concentrated on some large site of cultural production that was not connected with the national movement, in fact, that represented some thread that was broken before the crystallization of the Ukrainian idea in the early nineteenth century. This led me to the Last Judgment, which had been the subject of translated scriptural, patristic, and liturgical texts, of sermons and songs, and of frescoes, icons, murals, and engravings, but which did not survive, and could not survive, in the self-conscious nation. Much of this was right. I had caught scent of some important possibilities. But I imagined in the original formulation of my project that I would be uncovering some holistic 'traditional Ukrainian culture' that was being hidden by a modernized, secularized, and nationalized version of the true Ukrainian cultural history.[1]

One thing that was fundamentally wrong here was the positing of a prenational culture that was the mirror image of how the national culture projects itself: as unified, or at least as the prime conceptual unit of 'a culture,' as the relevant space in which internal cultural communication takes place. Andriy Zayarnyuk, when he was my doctoral student, immediately saw from the text of my project formulation that there was a problem here, which he identified as 'essentialism.' Although his warning to me was very helpful, I was unable to internalize it enough to abandon the habit of working for years within the normal paradigm of my discipline, the national paradigm. Even as I was mounting a critical assault on that paradigm, I was so immersed in it that I could only imagine I would find a different version of it on the other side. Only in the painstaking collection and comparison of evidence and in the sheer time spent thinking about the material and its problems was I able to free myself from the assumptions that derived from the simple inversion of a national paradigm and that prevented me from solving the puzzles that my sources posed to me.

One example of this is that I began this work imagining that I would be able to trace the evolution of Ukrainian Last Judgment iconography primarily through proto-Ukrainian sources. I thought I would start with the *Primary Chronicle*, because there is a passage there, under the year 986, that describes how a Byzantine missionary used a Last Judgment icon to persuade Prince Volodymyr to accept Christianity.[2] From there, I thought, I would move to the twelfth-century frescoes in St Cyril's in Kyiv, painted by Byzantine masters with the help of local Slavs. The next move was clear: to the Kyivan psalter of 1397.[3] Then, to our fifteenth-century icons in the Carpathians. I would delineate the evolution, the accumulation of a particular heritage. There might be a few missing links, of course, but I should be able to discern the general line of development. This plan did not work because it could not work. The icons of the Carpathians were too different from the other surviving Last Judgment images. The latter exhibited the features of the standard Byzantine iconography of the Last Judgment and nothing more, while the former contained many new elements that were known only in them and in icons from northern Rus'.

Perhaps the rupture between the Carpathian icons and the frescoes and manuscript illuminations of Kyivan Rus' would not have been so evident had I concentrated on a less complex iconography than the Last Judgment. But the Last Judgment had this peculiarity from the very inception of its iconographic tradition, that it was composed by the accretion of many discrete elements and that it testified to its evolution by the addition, subtraction, and modification of those elements. This iconography was an exceptionally sensitive indicator of its chronological and intercultural relationships. Concentrating on these particular icons led me to doubt my original assumption, which is also the assumption of the highly nationalized Ukrainian art history, that these icons can trace their origin to Byzantium via Halych and Kyiv. This would be the view that Byzantine masters taught the Rus' in Kyiv how to paint Orthodox sacral art; that with the devolution of political, ecclesiastical, and cultural authority in old Rus', the cities of the Galician-Volhynian principality – Halych, Lviv, and Przemyśl – became important artistic centres that developed the artistic traditions of Kyiv; and that the icons that are to be found in the nearby Carpathian mountains are just survivals of that brilliant tradition. This smooth narrative, however, did not fit the evidence.

Many Polish scholars have had misgivings about this narrative, in a few cases perhaps motivated by an agenda to minimize the East Slavic character of and in particular Ukrainian claims to the Lemko region.[4] They have instead called attention to the simultaneity of the appearance of the icons in the mountains and the settlement of the mountains by Vlachs, that is, what today we would call ethnic Romanians. Studying icons other than the Last Judgment, they have suggested that the Carpathian icons had Moldavian, i.e., also Romanian, origins, the idea being that the Vlachs brought with them or hired painters from Moldavia to decorate their churches. This theory, which is likewise based on an assumption of national commonality, also has serious problems. One, never clearly engaged in the literature, is that the migrating Vlachs bypassed Moldavia to reach the northern slopes of the Carpathians. There was no major movement of migration from Moldavia north into Poland. But for me the most convincing argument is chronological: all the characteristics that are held in common by Moldavian and Carpathian images of the Last Judgment and are not part of the general Byzantine synthesis appeared first in the Carpathian and only later in the Moldavian Last Judgments. Moreover, the Moldavian images were frescoes, and the Carpathian images were icons on linden board. There were no Moldavian icons on boards that predated the Carpathian icons on boards. In fact, I have never seen a Moldavian Last Judgment icon on boards from any period. As my work on Last Judgment images progressed, and as I encountered them in different forms – frescoes, icons on wood, icons on canvas, and murals on wood walls – I understood that the jump of an iconography from form to form was not merely technical, but that it involved a modification of the iconography itself. It seemed to me that I should concentrate on linden boards to explain linden boards.

The connection between the icons of the Last Judgment in northern and Carpathian Rus' had certainly been discerned by other scholars before me,[5] but for me it developed into a larger and more significant issue. The objections I had to the Kyiv-Halych and Moldavian hypotheses did not apply to the northern Rus' connection. There were iconographic elements shared exclusively or almost exclusively by the Carpathian and northern Rus' traditions; there was no chronological conflict, since these elements appeared in both iconographies around the same time, in the fifteenth century; and both traditions used the linden-board icons. The 'only' problem was how to explain the origin of the connection. The Kyiv-Halych connection was explained by proximity – Lviv, Halych, and Przemyśl are not far from the mountains. The same holds true for the Moldavian connection. But northern Rus' is about a thousand kilometres away from the Carpathians, and in the fifteenth century Poland shared no border with the northern Rus' principalities.

Perhaps Lithuania, at that time saturated in Rus' high culture, served as a mediator between Carpathian and northern Rus'. If so, Volhynia would have played the strategic role. Or perhaps the painters who were going from Pskov to Kraków to paint the Last Judgment and other murals in Holy Cross Chapel brought the idea of Last Judgment icons to the Carpathian region. Or perhaps their predecessors, from Tver, were the ones. Or perhaps it is as I have interpreted it at the end of my reflections on the problem: that a universal Orthodox high culture was accessible in monasteries even in the Carpathians, even in those modest brotherhoods, without large libraries and scriptoria, but capable of, and likely to be, hosting monks from throughout the Orthodox world. Indeed, even if we find evidence that leads us to look more closely at Lithuania and Volhynia or at the teams of painters who worked on the Orthodox frescoes in Poland, we would still need the monasteries to instil the practice of this kind of icon painting locally.

We can see that the work of creating elements on the basis of texts was done outside the Carpathians, in Byzantium and northern Rus'. What was added locally was assimilated visually – bits of Gothic art that appealed to a developing local sensibility. I think an analogy may be helpful here, even if it is terribly anachronistic. In small community colleges throughout North America one can find the same culture that is produced by Nobel prize winners and other leading scholars on the east and west coast – the community colleges share in a culture that others produce. This analogy may be helpful in thinking about the Carpathian monasteries and what they borrowed to create what after all ended up being a very local icon.

When I started this project I was not sure why almost all the old icons came from the Carpathian region. Was this where most of them were produced or just where more of them survived? The Ukrainian art historians and museum workers with whom I spoke encouraged the latter hypothesis, which I was leaning to anyway, since it fit with my working hypothesis of a holistic 'traditional Ukrainian culture.' The story that I was being told and that I explored first was that at one time Last Judgment icons could be found throughout Ukraine, but only Galician examples survived to the present. This region was far from the Tatar khanate and therefore less frequently raided; this explains why its artwork was better preserved.[6] Mountain communities would be even better protected from the horseback Tatars. (I was not aware at the time that Maramureş, which had these same features of distance from the khanate and mountainous terrain, suffered terrible destruction from a Tatar attack as late as 1717.) Then I was told that many Ukrainian icons were destroyed after 1722 when Tsar Peter I issued his decree regulating icon painting.[7] According to the nationalist art historian Dmytro Stepovyk, the dearth of Ukrainian icons outside the Carpathian region is to be blamed on 'the tsardom of Muscovy together with the patriarch of Moscow – the eternal enemies of the independence of Ukraine and the Ukrainian church'; many icons were destroyed in the nineteenth century 'by those who hated the Ukrainian style of icons – the representatives, bishops and priests of the Russian Orthodox church.'[8] The Carpathian region, of course, was outside the borders of the Russian empire, and so was spared this devastating iconoclasm. In the twentieth century the Bolsheviks destroyed numerous Ukrainian icons as well.[9] Their worst work was done in the 1920s and 1930s, before Western Ukraine was annexed to the Soviet Union; and Ukrainian-inhabited territories in Czechoslovakia and Poland never fell under direct Soviet rule and did not experience the same intensity of religious persecution as other Ukrainian ethnic territories did. In short, the national narrative held that there once was a universal Ukrainian iconographic culture, but most of it was destroyed by the Tatars, Russians, and Communists; only in the inaccessible westernmost reaches did the old icons, representative of the tradition, survive.

Let me sort out what I consider to be true in this account. The Carpathian region was by no means free of Tatar raids, but the raids were not so frequent and depopulating as those in the central Ukrainian lands. That is one of the reasons why these mountain communities flourished in the fifteenth century and could afford to adorn their churches with monumental art. And indeed, the depopulation of the central lands and the destruction of the cities by the Tatars mean that we can only guess about what sort of sacral art existed there. In fact, we have no icons at all from the Kyiv region dating from the fourteenth through sixteenth centuries.[10] As to Peter I's decree of 1722, I am not familiar with any evidence, as distinct from suppositions,[11] that indicates it was directed against the specificity of Ukrainian icons. The Soviet destruction of icons and other sacral art was indeed furious and does partly account for the poverty of icon collections on the territory of pre-1939 Soviet Ukraine. However, this does not explain enough. The icon collection in the National Museum in Kyiv survived the worst periods of Stalinist and Khrushchevian antireligious campaigns; nonetheless, the bulk of this collection, and almost all the earlier and significant pieces, came from our Carpathian region.

The view that I started with, that icons survived better in the Carpathians than elsewhere in Ukraine, was correct. The idea, however, that there was one single iconographic tradition, of which the Carpathian icons were just surviving examples, was wrong. Certainly in the case of the Last Judgment icons, this was a local tradition. We can see it in the unique composition of the three fifteenth-century icons, which drew on Byzantine, northern Rus', and Gothic elements. We can also see it in the paths that the diffusion of these icons took. There was not a specifically Ukrainian Last Judgment icon. The culture was too fragmented for that. The tradition was regional, and the region expanded greatly before the tradition petered out.

As the tradition developed, it changed. We cannot even speak of a single, unified tradition. It changed over time, with different emphases in different periods and even different materials. Again, the culture was much more fragmented and much more dynamic than I had imagined it; it turned out to be a peripatetic shape-shifter of a tradition.

Also not realizing this, one of the formulators of the national art-history narrative, Pavlo Zholtovsky, tried to figure out the one Last Judgment on wood, in fact on linden boards, that survives from early modern Kyiv, a seventeenth-century icon that once hung in the hospice of St Michael's Golden-Domed Monastery (fig. 5.1).[12] Because it looked different from the Carpathian icons, which he felt interpreted the Last Judgment freely, because it had some motifs that he considered to be 'traditional-canonical,' he ascribed parts of the icon to a completely hypothetical Russian artist.[13] This speculative conclusion derived from the assumption that all Ukrainian icons must have possessed some common essence.[14]

Another assumption I had to abandon from my original vision of this project was that I could bring together into one coherent study the entire set of artefacts produced around the Last Judgment within what I was imagining as Ukrainian culture. I was interested in texts of all sorts, whether original, such as sermons composed in the seventeenth century, or (actually better for my envisioned purposes) texts that were translated elsewhere and only copied or printed in Ukraine, such as Lenten triodia with Roman the Melodist's sticheria for Meatfare Sunday. I was interested in scripture, apocrypha, sermons of the church fathers and seventeenth-century humanist clerics (see Appendix 4), hymns, and even folk customs, as long as they concerned the Last Judgment. I had imagined that they would all fit together like the pieces of a jigsaw puzzle to reveal a harmoniously composed picture. Again, I was lumping when the correct procedure was disaggregating, analysing. I certainly learned things from my work with these other artefacts, but very little of it was directly applicable to the icons. Most of what I came to understand about the icons came not from texts, but from the careful comparison of one image with another.

The visual culture of the Last Judgment was rooted in textual sources, to be sure, but most of that rooting had occurred outside the Carpathians, in large Orthodox realms with the means to support that kind of learned activity. More than the prosperity of shepherds was required to maintain that level of intellectual infrastructure. That the Orthodox culture in the Carpathian region was as vital as it was owes something to the presence of the Moldavian monasteries in the vicinity.

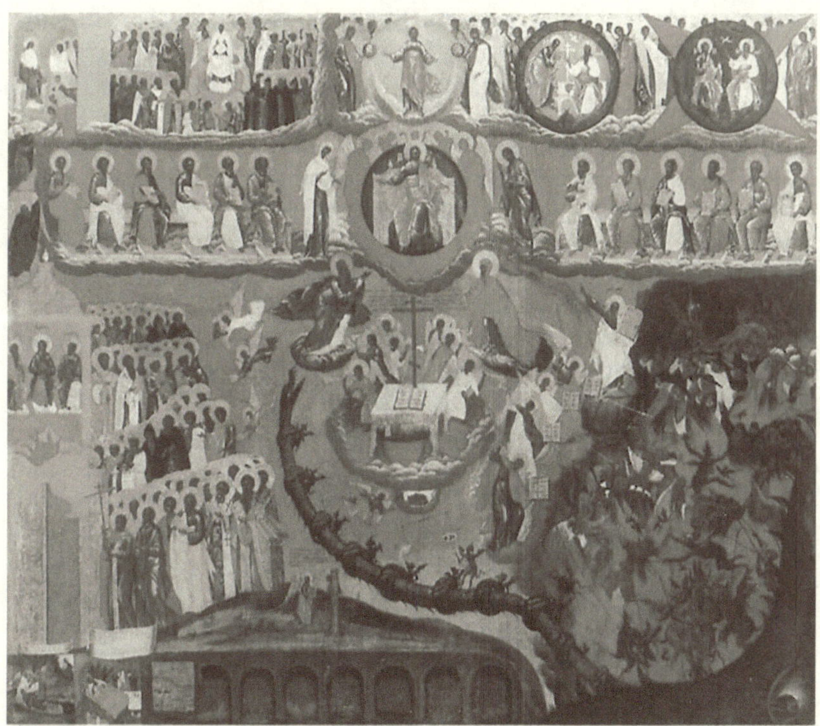

5.1 Last Judgment of St Michael's Golden-Domed Monastery in Kyiv. Source: Larysa Chlenova et al., *Shedevry ukrains'koho ikonopysu XII–XIX st.* (Kyiv: Mystetstvo, 1999), pl. 30.

This disconnect between the visual and the textual has something to do with the sociology of our icons. They started out closer to the high-culture end of the spectrum. They were for the most part a distillation of an iconography worked out in learned monastic spheres. They were skilfully painted by monks using a well developed technique of icon painting. They were painted to exalt the wooden churches in the mountains, giving them a monumental depiction of the Last Judgment reminiscent of the frescoes of the great churches of Orthodoxy. They were also painted as objects with which to worship, with which to express a connection with the divine. They spoke about the great questions: how should one live? what is the meaning of death? But right from the start, there were small touches that pointed to the lower end of the cultural spectrum. I think particularly of the tavernmaid. She appears in none of the frescoes anywhere in the Orthodox world. She is a sign that these Last Judgment icons were painted not for princes and monks, but for shepherds and farmers. She is a didactic inclusion.

Later the tavernmaid was joined by some drunks, dancers, and musicians. This element was elaborated with enthusiasm in a way that the rolling-up of the heavens or the deesis never was. The more abstruse elements, those linked with Daniel's vision, for example, began to disappear from the icon. The painters were no longer just monks, and by the end there were no monks at all involved in the painting. The icons began to reflect more and more the interests and cultural level of the peasants who commissioned them. They still served their purpose as holy images for the church, and commissioning one was still a great act of piety, but the icon also more frequently addressed popular concerns. It is worth recalling that these icons were painted in an age and in circumstances that saw relatively little reproduction and circulation of images. They were therefore that much more notable and that much more powerful. When the painter put a priest or a landlord in hell, it was a potent message. When he depicted lewdness lewdly or dwelled on tortures, he appealed to an unrefined sensuality. In time, I am saying, the lower end of the spectrum grew in significance. The Last Judgments became more and more popular works, aimed at the illiterate or semi-literate highland villagers, expressing their concerns, amusing and arousing them, until there was a disciplining reaction on the part of the educated clerical elite.

One of the reasons I undertook this work with the icons was to explore the mentalities of a society that left few written records. Nine years ago, at the conception of this project, I wrote: 'We must reread our sources, expand our conception of what constitutes the sources and find new sources.'[15] I think I have succeeded in using the Last Judgment icons as just such untraditional historical sources and thus opening to view a vanished cultural world. The view is microhistorical and fragmentary, perhaps resistant to translation into firm propositions, but in the end, I am convinced, this is a reflection of the way the history of culture actually unfolds.

Appendix 1 Place Names in Different Languages

G = German
H = Hungarian
P = Polish
Ro = Romanian
Ru = Rusyn
S = Slovak
U = Ukrainian

Bahnovate (U), Bahnowate (P)
Bârsana (Ro), Barczánfalva (H)
Bartne (P, Ru), Bortne (Ru, U)
Berehomet (U), Berhometh am Pruth (G)
Bodružal (Ru, S), Bodruzhal (U)
Bogliarka (S), Boglárka (H, Ru), Bohliarka (U)
Borşa (Ro), Borsa (H)
Borshchovychi (U), Borszczowice (P)
Brzegi (P), Berehy (U)
Budeşti (Ro), Budfalva (H)

Călineşti-Căieni (Ro), Felső Kálinfalva (H)
Chernivtsi (U), Czernowitz (G), Cernăuţi (Ro)
Chotyniec (P), Khotynets (U)
Corneşti (Ro), Sinfalva (H)
Cuhea (Ro), Izakonyha, Konyha (H), Bogdan Voda (Ro, current)

Deseşti (Ro), Desze (H)
Dmytriie (U), Dmytrze (P)
Dmytrovychi (U), Dmytrowice (P)

Dobromyl (U), Dobromil (P)
Dobroslava (Ru, S, U), Dobroszló (H)
Dolyna (U), Dolina (P)
Dragomireşti (Ro), Dragomérfalva (H)
Drohobych (U), Drohobycz (P)
Dubivtsi (U), Duboutz (G)
Dubrovytsia (U), Dąbrowica (P)

Fereşti (Ro), Fejérfalva (H)

Giuleşti-Mănăstirea (Ro), Máragyulafalva (H)
Gorlice (P), Gorlyckŷ (Ru)

Hankovychi (U), Hankowice (P)
Hankowice. See Hankovychi.
Hlynytsia (U), Hlinitza (G)
Horodok (U), Gródek (P)
Hrushovo (U), Körtvélyes, Szentmihalykörtvélyes (H), Peri (Ro), Hrušovo (Ru), Hrushove (U)

Ieud-Deal (Ro), Jód (H)
Izky (Ru, U), Iszka (H)

Jasło (P), Yaslo (Ru)
Jedlinka (S), Borókás (H), Jalynkŷŷ (Ru), Yalynky (U)

Kamianka Strumylova (U), Kamionka Strumiłowa (P), Kaminka Buzka (U, current)
Kamianna (U), Kamena (G)
Khust (U), Huszt (H), Chust (Ru)
Kitsman (U), Kotzman (G)
Klitsko (U), Klicko (P)
Košice (S), Kassa (H)
Kožany (S, Ru), Kozsány (H), Kozhany (U)
Kožuchovce (S), Körmös, Kozsuhòcz (H), Kožuchivci (Ru), Kozhukhivtsi (U)
Krásny Brod (S), Laborczrév (H), Krasnŷj Brid (Ru), Krasnyi Brid (U)

Lavriv (U), Ławrów (P)
Lipie (P), Lypie (U)

Lukivtsi (U), Lukawetz am Sereth (G)
Lukov-Venecia (S), Lukó (H), Lukiv (Ru, U), Venécze (H), Venetsiia (U)
Luzhany (U), Luzan (G), Lujeni (Ro)
Lviv (U), Lemberg (G), Lwów (P)

Mala Horozhanka (U), Horożanna Mała (P)
Medynychi (U), Medynice (P)
Moldavsko (U), Mołdawsko (P)
Mshanets (U), Mszaniec (P)
Mukachevo (U), Munkács (H), Mukačevo (Ru), Mukacheve (U)

Nehrovets (U), Felsőkalocsa (H), Negrovec' (Ru)
Nieznajowa (P), Neznajova (Ru), Neznaieva (U)
Nová Sedlica (S), Novoszedlicza, Újszék (H), Novoselyca (Ru), Novoselytsia (U)
Novoselytsia (U), Sósfalu (H)
Nowy Sącz (P), Novyi Sanch (Ru)

Oleksandrivka (U), Ósándorfalva, Sándorfalva (H), Šandrovo (Ru)
Onceşti (Ro), Váncsfalva (H)

Paszowa (P), Pashowa (U)
Piilo (U), Pojło (P)
Plavie (U), Pławie (P)
Pohorilivka (U), Pohorloutz (G)
Poienile Izei (Ro), Sajó-Polyána, Sajómezö (H)
Polana. See Poliana.
Poliana (U), Polana (P)
Popeli (U), Popiele (P)
Powroźnik (P), Povoroznik (Ru), Povoroznyk (U)
Prešov (S), Eperjes (H), Priashiv (U)
Przemyśl (P), Peremyshl (U)
Putyla (U), Storonetz-Putilla (G)

Rădăuţi (Ro), Radivtsi (U)
Radelychi (U), Radelycz (P)
Rakovčík (S), Felső Rákócz (H), Rakivčík (Ru), Rakivchyk (U)
Rogoz (H, Ro)
Rozavlea (Ro), Rozália (H)
Rozstajne (P), Rostajne (Ru, U)

Roztoka (Ru, U), Rosztoka (H)
Roztoky (U), Rostoki (G)
Ruská Bystrá (S), Oroszbisztra, Oroszebes (H), Rus'ka Bŷstra (Ru), Ruska Bystra (U)
Rybotycze (P), Rybotychi (U)

Sat Şugătag (Ro), Sugatag, Falu Sugatag (H)
Serednie Vodiane (U), Közep-Apsa (H), Apşa de Mijloc (Ro)
Shelestovo (U), Szélestó (H), Šelestovo (Ru), Shelestove (U)
Şieu (Ro), Sajó (H)
Sighet (Ro), Máramaros Sziget (H)
Skole (P, U)
Skoryky (U), Skoryki (P)
Smilna (U), Smólna (P)
Spas (P, U)
Stanylia (U), Stanila (P)
Stanyslaviv (U), Stanisławów (P), Ivano-Frankivsk (U, current)
Staryi Sambir (U), Stare Miasto, Stary Sambor (P)
Suceava (Ro), Suchava (U)
Sudova Vyshnia (U), Sądowa Wisznia (P)
Sukhyi Potik (U), Suchy Potok (P)
Şurdeşti (Ro), Dióshalom (H)
Świątkowa Mała (P), Svjatkivka (Ru), Sviatkova Mala (U)
Świątkowa Wielka (P), Svjatkova (Ru), Sviatkova Velyka (U)
Sykhiv (U), Sichów (P)

Tiushka (U), Csuszka (H), Tjuška (Ru)
Topol'a (S), Kistopolya (H), Topolia (U)
Torky (U), Torki (P)
Tročany (S), Trocsány (H), Trochany (U)
Trostianets (U), Trościaniec (P)
Trushevychi (U), Truszowice (P)

Uličské Krivé (S), Görbeszeg, Ulicskriva (H), Kryvŷj (Ru), Ulychske Kryve (U)
Ust-Putyla (U), Uscie Putilla (G)
Uzhhorod (U), Ungvár (H), Užhorod (Ru)

Vanivka. See Węglówka.
Velyke (U), Wełykie (P)

Vilshanytsia (U), Olszanica (P)
Volosianka (U), Hajasd (H), Volosjanka (Ru)
Volytsia Derevlianska (U), Wolica Derewlańska (P)
Vovche (U), Wołcze (P)
Vyšný Orlík (S), Felső Odor, Felső Orlich (H), Vŷšnij Verlych (Ru), Vyshnii Orlyk (U)

Węglówka (P), Vanivka (U)
Wola Wyżna (P), Vola Vyšnja (Ru), Volia Vyzhnia (U)

Yasinka Masova (U), Jasionka Masiowa (P)
Yezupil (U), Jezupol (P), Zhovten (U, current name)

Zavadka (U), Zawadka (P)
Zboj (S), Harczos (H), Zbuj (Ru), Zbii (U)
Zhovkva (U), Żółkiew (P)

Appendix 2 Ephraim the Syrian's *Sermon on the Second Coming of Our Lord Jesus Christ*: Summary

My Christ-loving brothers, hear about the second and terrible coming of our Lord Jesus Christ. When I mentioned that hour I trembled from great fear. Who can describe it? When I think of it my eyes gush with tears, my voice disappears. Such great and terrible miracles have never occurred before.

How fearful that day is. How frightened we get by thunder and lightning – wait till we hear the trumpets blow!

Then the bones will rise in Hades and seek their parts. Men will come from the four corners for judgment. The earth and sea will give up their dead. A river of fire will devour the whole earth and everything in it. The heavens will roll up like a scroll. Then we will see a new heaven and new earth. How will we feel when we see the judgment throne and the true cross?

The merciful and repentant will rejoice. The poor who have been helped will intercede for their benefactors.

All will be filled with dread at the arrival of the great king and judge, accompanied by the heavenly powers. He will come on clouds. There will be no place to run. The vision in Daniel 7 will be enacted. All our deeds will be recorded in the books mentioned there. Everyone will need a confession of the true faith free from any heresy, baptism, and a clean garment. At baptism we renounced all Satan's works, including fornication, adultery, falsehood, theft, envy, sorcery, anger, blasphemy, drunkenness, pride, idleness, and so on. Whoever has committed sin has fallen from grace. We will be held accountable for our baptismal promise.

Bishops will have to account for the way they supervised their flock. All believers will have to account for how they behaved in the household (wife, children, male and female slaves). Kings will be questioned about their actions.

The monks ask: What then? Ephraim says: My heart aches to speak of it; let us stop this conversation. But the monks press him further.

Then God will separate the sheep from the goats. The righteous (who did good deeds, loved the poor and orphans, forgave their brothers) will shine like the sun. They will be placed on the right hand. The others will be on the left: those who had no fruits, angered the good shepherd, were given to gluttony, drunkenness, and hard-heartedness, like the rich man who showed no mercy to poor Lazarus. Those on the right will be sent to the kingdom; those on the left, to eternal fire (Mt 25:34).

The sinners will be told that since they were without mercy, they will receive no mercy. They served another lord, i.e., the devil.

The monks ask: Will they all go to the same torment, or are there different torments? Answer: the torments are varied, as the Gospel teaches us. There is the outer darkness, implicitly also a deeper darkness, the gnashing of teeth, the worm that does not die, the lake of Gehenna, Tartarus, the fire that cannot be quenched, things under the earth (Phil 2:10), destruction (Mt 7:13), the lower parts of the earth (Eph 4:9), Hades, and the bottom of Hades (the place of the most torment). Sinners will be allotted to these various places depending on their sins.

People who lay about and sleep, who live in luxury and laugh, will be in trouble. It is necessary to weep and repent. Woe to the adulterer! Woe to the drunkard! Woe to those who have 'the harp, and the viol, the tabret, and pipe, and wine ... in their feasts; but they regard not the work of the Lord' (Is 4:12). Woe to those who reject sacred scripture, who incline towards demonic teachings, who write untruth, who are given to sorcery and related works. Woe to him who cheats on the wage of his hired man, which is the same as drinking blood. Woe to those who judge falsely, who defile the faith with heresies, who are sick with envy and hatred. Woe to all those whose lot it is on that terrible day to stand on the left! They will receive sentences appropriate to their sins. Just as there are many ways to salvation, so there are many kinds of torment.

Whoever has tears and compunction, weep with me. I cannot bear the thought of the separations that will occur at that time as bishops are separated from their fellow bishops, priests from priests, and deacons from deacons. Rulers will also be separated. There will be no help for them: no wealth, no flattering attendants. Those who had no mercy will be shown none. Parents will be separated from children, friends from friends. It will be sad when spouses are separated, spouses who did not preserve their bed undefiled. Separated out will be those who were virgins in body, but who were merciless and cruel.

But I will pass over much in silence, since fear and trembling overcome me. I will just briefly note that as they are taken by the merciless angels to their place of torments they will pass by and see paradise and their righteous friends. They will move further and further away until they are completely cut off from them and from God. They will see they are without hope. They will regret that they did not attend to the Gospel. They will ask: Where are the parents who bore us? our children? our friends? our wealth? our property? our banquets? our kings and rulers? Why can none help us? It is too late for repentance. We are unworthy of mercy – God's judgment is just. Save us, o apostles, o prophets and martyrs, o patriarchs, o monks, o honourable and life-giving cross, o kingdom of heaven, o heavenly Jerusalem, o Mother of God. We cannot see any of you!

Then each will go to his place of torment, 'where their worm dieth not, and the fire is not quenched' (Mark 9:46).

Now I have told you what you asked about: what the lazy and unrepentant will experience, how those who ridiculed the Lord's commandments will themselves be ridiculed. My blessed beloved! Let no one be fooled into thinking that what I have told you is empty words. We will instead all believe in the resurrection of the dead and judgment. Being suspicious of all that is temporal and casting it aside, let us concern ourselves with what answer we will give before the terrible judgment seat at that tremulous and terrible hour, which is full of tears and pain and affliction. Be attentive, brothers, be sober, pray, have mercy, be ready, 'for ye know neither the day nor the hour wherein the Son of man cometh' (Mt 25:13). The prophets – Isaiah, Malachi, Habakkuk, and others – have warned us that this day is coming. So have Saints Paul and Peter. Our Lord himself says: 'And take heed to yourselves, lest at any time your hearts be overcharged with surfeiting, and drunkenness, and cares of this life, and so that day come upon you unawares. For as a snare shall it come on all them that dwell on the face of the whole earth' (Lk 22:34–5).

We will go along this path, my brothers, in order to inherit eternal life, along the path trod by all who have loved Christ. It is difficult, but there is rest at the end. Going along the path entails repentance, fasting, prayer, vigilance, modesty, spiritual poverty, neglect of the flesh, sleeping on the bare earth, hunger, thirst, nakedness, alms, tears, weeping, sighing, kneeling, dishonour, persecution, poverty. It means to suffer and be hated, to forgive your debtors and lay down your life for your friends and ultimately to shed your blood for Christ if circumstances call for it. Who goes through these strait gates and narrow path will receive a heavenly reward. The wide gates and large path lead to destruction – this is making jokes, dancing, music, fancy clothes, expensive evenings, carefree singing, soft beds, gluttony, hatred for one's brother, and, worst of all, a failure to repent and remember the exit from this life. At the end of this path they will find not drinking but thirst, not laughter but lamentation, not music but wailing, not plump flesh but worms, not dancing but the company of demons.

Let us not follow this path. The martyrs remembered this day and did not spare their bodies, but suffered torments in the hope of a crown. And others in the deserts and mountains have laboured with fasting and virginity. Not only men, but women – the weaker sex – have achieved the heavenly kingdom. Who will be able to bear the shame when women on that day will be crowned, but many men disgraced? And not just in the deserts and mountains, but even more in the cities, on islands, and in the churches there is a multitude of people working towards salvation.

David prayed to God every night with tears: 'And enter not into judgment with thy servant' (Ps 143:2). If blessed David is afraid, then prepare yourselves, brothers, with confession, repentance, prayer, fasting, tears, hospitality. Let us not cease – all together: men and women, rich and poor, slaves and freemen, old and young.

Let no one say he has sinned too much for forgiveness. God is the God of the repentant.

Let no one dare to say he has not sinned at all. Whoever says this is blind. He fools himself and does not know how Satan steals into his words and deeds, through his hearing, his eyes, his consciousness, his thoughts. Who can boast that his heart is innocent and all his feelings pure? No one is without sin, only God.

Have we sinned? Let us repent. Have we sinned a thousand times? Let us repent a thousand times. God rejoices in our repentance; he will give us rest. Approach the choirs of the righteous. There is the bosom of Abraham, the heavenly Jerusalem.

There there will be no devil, no death, no fasting, no sorrow, no quarrelling, but joy and peace, peace of mind and ecstacy, unceasing joy, eternal merriment, light without evening, sun without setting. There will be myriads of angels, thrones of the apostles, sceptres of the patriarchs, crowns of the martyrs, praises of the righteous.

This is the place I [the Lord] have prepared for those who weep in repentance, for the peacemakers, for those persecuted for my sake. Whoever came to me shed his bad ways. Magicians coming to me cast off their magic and studied theology; publicans left their tollbooths and made churches; persecutors stopped persecuting and wished to be persecuted. Fornicators started to love virginity. The robber became an inhabitant of paradise.

Beloved, you have heard the voice of the Saviour. Glory to his love of humanity, glory to his patience, glory to his goodness, glory to his condescension. Remember: he is the God of the repentant. Amen.

Based on Ephraim Syrus, *Tvoreniia*, 216–35.

Appendix 3 *The Life of St Basil the New*: Summary

The life is written by his disciple Gregory. Basil was a miracle worker. In particular, he was clairvoyant: he could tell the future and he knew secrets. In one instance, he appeared to Gregory in a dream.

Basil had a widow who took care of him, Theodora. But she died, having first taken monastic vows. Gregory was concerned about what happened to her after death, what her lot was. He asked Basil if it was possible to find out. Basil said he would let him know.

Gregory had a dream. He saw Theodora, who said that she would have met a frightful death because of her sins if it were not for the prayers of St Basil the New. The pain of death is great, she said, like jumping into a fire naked. The parting of the soul from the body is painful, especially for sinners like her. She suddenly saw a multitude of evil spirits who looked like Ethiopians standing around her death bed. They brought books where her sins were recorded. But two angels, in the form of youths, appeared to her and angrily said to the evil spirits: 'You dark enemies of the human race, why are you disturbing and tormenting the soul of this dying woman? Rejoice not, because nothing here belongs to you.' At this the shameless spirits began to read sins from the books of sins. Then Death came, gave her a cup to drink from, and cut off her head. The angels then took her by the hand and led her off. She saw her lifeless body lying on the bed like clothes she had taken off. As the evil spirits recounted her sins, the angels countered with lists of her good deeds, such as giving a poor man bread or buying incense for the church. The good deeds would redeem her sins. St Basil appeared and gave the angels a small chest which they could also use for his servant at the toll-booths. This upset the evil spirits very much. Basil returned also with jars of aromatic ointments which the angels poured on Theodora until her soul shone brightly.

They went through tollbooths in the air. Some of the sins that the evil spirits read to her she had completely forgotten, they had happened so long ago. The angels from time to time gave something to the evil spirits from the chest given by Basil.

The tollbooths she went through were these:

1 Slander
2 Insult
3 Envy
4 Lying
5 Anger and rage
6 Pride and arrogance
7 Idle and obscene talk
8 Usury and deceit
9 Falsehood and vainglory
10 Greed
11 Drunkenness
12 Grudge-bearing
13 Sorcery
14 Gluttony and epicurism
15 Idolatry
16 Sodomy and pedophilia
17 Adultery
18 Robbery [this term includes assault of all kinds]
19 Theft
20 Fornication
21 Mercilessness and cruelheartedness
[Some variants include judgment of others, sloth, stinginess, murder, heresy.]

One of the angels told Theodora that the recorded sins can prevent entrance into paradise and take the soul directly to the abyss in which the evil spirits themselves live. And there the soul will remain until the second coming of Christ.

Theodora asked the angels if every sin will be remembered at the posthumous tollbooths and was there nothing one could do in one's lifetime to mitigate the sins. The angels said that not all are so tested, only those like her who had not made a confession with a pure heart before death. If she had confessed without shame and fear every sin to her spiritual father, if she had made up for many sins with good works, and if she had received forgiveness from her spiritual father, then she would not have been examined with reference to a single sin.

The evil spirits at the tollbooths frequently add false sins to the list.

When Theodora finished with the booths, she saw the white throne of God.

She took Gregory on a tour of paradise. He saw the saints with various beautiful chambers for the apostles, prophets, martyrs, and others. He visited the dwelling of Abraham, which was filled with flowers, myrrh, and aromatics. Then he toured the lower depths and saw the terrible torment of the sinners. Back in paradise he saw a large banquet table with gold vessels filled with wonderful-smelling fruits. People here did not have terrestrial bodies, but luminous human forms. Then Gregory went home. At the same time, he woke up.

He went to Basil to find out if this was just a dream or if he did visit the heavenly kingdom. Basil said that his body slept, but that he did go there. Gregory realized that he had had a vision sent by God.

Various miracles of St Basil are recounted. Later the narrative is told in Gregory's voice.

One day, sitting in my cell, remembering and repenting over my sins, a thought came into my head: how great was the faith of the Jews! I thought of Abraham, Isaac, and Moses – great figures. Reflecting on the Old Testament, I thought: what a fortunate and God-pleasing nation. I reread the Old Testament and became even more convinced of this. Then I thought to consult my teacher Basil.

Basil immediately knew what I had been thinking and was angry at the train of my thought (also that I stopped in at the race track on my way to see him). Basil reminded me: the Jews denied the Son of God and frequently fell into idol worship; the New Testament rejects the Jews; and they have been punished by being despised and scattered over the earth. Formerly the Jews did observe the law, but not since the time of Christ; now they only observe the externals, such as circumcision. They now form the council of Satan; they are the sons of the devil and the portion of the Antichrist. Satan is pleased that they rejected Christ and by oath took his blood upon themselves and their children. Now there is a new Israel: the Christian people. Whoever rejects the Son of God and the Trinity is damned to torments in this life and the next.

I expressed gratitude to Basil for his profitable words and asked him for some sign to confirm that all which he said was true.

That night as I lay in bed, I suddenly saw myself on a fertile field adorned with all possible beautiful flowers. There was a gentle, cooling breeze which wafted a luminous, aromatic smoke. A luminous young man in white approached and explained that I had arrived here thanks to Basil that I might learn about the various nations. He led me eastward. We rode on a cloud, first to a beautiful place, then to a terrible place. We saw the Jerusalem which is above, that is, the Sion not created by human hands. The guide explained that in this New Sion only those reside who believe in the teachings of the church; nonbelievers dwell in eternal fire.

Then four youths announced to all that the judgment and the resurrection of the dead were about to take place. A column of fire appeared, and from it issued a loud voice which ordered all bones and body parts to reconstitute themselves. A youth with a fiery scroll was dispatched to Satan saying that his three years of rule on earth were at an end. The regiments of the celestial powers rode through the air on horses of fire. From their ranks emerged trumpeters whose trumpeting shook the whole earth. Bodies began to form, all were the same age, each man stood with his wife, and each nation was united. I saw that some had faces as bright as heaven, others' faces were not as bright. Each held a book and had an inscription on the forehead or above the head. Some inscriptions read 'Prophet of the Lord' or 'Evangelist' or 'Pure of Heart' or 'Peacemaker,' and these people shone. Those who had inscriptions like 'Malice' or 'Impurity' had dark faces; some had faces full of worms, some were covered from head to toe in stinking manure. These sinners lamented the impending judgment.

Some asked who is God? who is Christ? We do not know them, for we had many gods. We served them and now they should help us.

Others said: If it is the God of Moses who resurrects us, then we will receive much, for we have been scattered over the entire cosmos. But woe to us if the Son of man comes to judge us, for we hated him, insulted him, did him much evil, and handed him over to death; we then killed his disciples. He will be judged for claiming to be the Son of God. It would be good if we could see him here among those to be judged, to be held accountable for his lie. As the Jews discussed these things they passed the word around among them to look out for Christ, apprehend him, and turn him over to the judge.

Red inscriptions appeared on some people: 'Murderer,' 'Thief,' 'Fornicator,' 'Idolator,' 'Child-killer,' 'Heretic.' All the unbaptized and unshriven lamented.

Angels brought a bright cross and placed it in view of all on the throne. The Jews trembled with fear, shame showed on their faces; the cross was a bad sign, the sign of the Crucified One. O woe is us! they said. Jesus

Christ, whom the Christians praise, wants to judge all. When they heard the angels singing Jesus's praises along with God the Father's, they began to lament that they did not expect him.

The trumpets blared, announcing that the judgment was to begin. Jesus came on a cloud with a multitude of incorporeal servants. He sat on the throne. The angels said to him: You are Christ the Son of the Living God whom the Jews crucified. Hearing this, Annas, Caiaphas, Arius, Mohammed, and all the Jews trembled.

The Lord looked at the heavens, and they retreated. He looked at the earth, and it too withdrew. Then a new heaven and a new earth appeared in their place. The Lord looked at the sea and it turned to flame, engulfing sinners and unbelievers. Some Jews were saved from the flame: those who believed in divine providence and did not worship idols.

Wailing came from the fiery sea. Those who were untouched rejoiced that they had kept God's law.

The Lord separated them into left and right, as described in Matthew 25. There was a great number of sinners, but few righteous, because only one of three or four Christians was saved, of Old Testament people barely one in a thousand or even ten thousand was saved, of those who lived from Adam to Abraham only one of thirty or forty thousand was saved.

On the right, in the following order, there approached the throne the Mother of God, John the Baptist, the twelve apostles, the seventy disciples of Christ, martyrs, confessors, and so forth. Those on the left wept bitterly. The Jews sought Moses, but could not find him, because he was with Abraham, Isaac, and Jacob on the right.

When the just women entered, I asked an angel if wives could have their husbands and vice versa. The angel said that all corporeal desires are gone here – they will all live as angels.

The Lord divided up all sinners by nationality and religion. Angels began to pitch the sinners into the fiery sea. They started with those Christians who rejected Christ during times of persecution, then robbers and murderers, thieves, and so forth. The adulterers tried to plead that they had never rejected God, but the Lord responded to them with anger. Many sinful monks were pitched into the fire. Arius and Nestorius and their followers met the same fate.

When it came time for the Jews, they summoned Moses as their witness. Moses did appear, in glory, but he condemned them. Off they went to hell.

Based on Antonii, *Sud za grobom*, and Vilinskii, *Zhitie sv. Vasiliia Novago.*

Appendix 4 Early Modern Ukrainian Sermons on the Last Judgment

Dozens of different sermons on the Last Judgment circulated in Ukrainian lands in the seventeenth and eighteenth centuries. Here I briefly review a selection of them in order to both indicate the variety and evolution of these sermons and to present a sampling of their contents.

Pseudo-Callistus, Teaching Gospel, 1569–1637

Although some sermons are preserved from an earlier period, the compilation of sermon collections in Polish-Lithuanian Rus' dates to the latter sixteenth century and originates as a response to the emphasis placed on preaching by both the Reformation and the Counter-Reformation.[1] The groundbreaking work was the teaching Gospel (*Ievanheliie uchytel'noie*) published by Ivan Fedorov in Zabłudów (northern Podlachia in the Duchy of Lithuania) in 1569.[2] This work was reprinted in Vilnius in 1580 and 1595 and in Krylos in Galicia in 1606. The collection was based on an eleventh-century Greek homiliary that was translated into Slavonic in Bulgaria in the late fourteenth century. (In seventeenth-century editions of this work it was mistakenly ascribed to the mid-fourteenth-century patriarch of Constantinople, Callistus.) The Fedorov publication was in Church Slavonic.

The Orthodox churchman and scholar Meletii Smotrytsky reworked the text of pseudo-Callistus's sermon collection by translating it all into the Ukrainian vernacular. The Gospel passages themselves were translated from a Polish translation of the New Testament and the sermons from the Church Slavonic. The Vilnius Brotherhood published Smotrytsky's edition of the teaching Gospel in Vievis in Lithuania in 1616.[3] Smotrytsky's teaching Gospel was immensely popular and was reprinted by Petr Mohyla in 1637 in a somewhat more Slavonicized version.

The teaching Gospel of pseudo-Callistus contained one sermon on the Last Judgment, which can also be found copied in manuscripts.[4]

The content of the sermon shows the influence of the Greek St Ephraim the Syrian, informing the faithful about the new earth and new heaven, the traditional torments of the damned (i.e., the gnashing of teeth, unsleeping worm, eternal fire), the universality of the judgment encompassing 'pagans and Jews, Christians and heretics' (21) as well as 'rich and poor, small and great, superiors and subjects, male and female sex, young and old, famous and unknown' (22v), the revelation of all sins, the inability of relatives and protectors or bribes to influence this just judgment, the great fear that will encompass sinners, the preparation of the throne of judgment and the river of fire, the separation of the sheep and the goats, and the appearance of the Lord's sign in the heavens (i.e., the cross).

In line with the Gospel for Meatfare Sunday, the sermon pays particular attention to mercy shown towards those in need. 'For every person who is poor, orthodox, humble and grateful is Christ's brother, also because Christ himself lived in poverty and need' (26). 'Woe to sinners, but even greater woe to the merciless.' The merciful preserved 'love, which is the root of all virtues,' while the merciless 'were in love with hate, which is the origin of all evils and the main enemy of love.' 'People of mercy and brotherly love are like the merciful and mankind-loving God, while people without mercy, who hate their brothers are like the merciless, mankind-hating devil' (26v).

Kyryll Trankvylion Stavrovetsky, *Ievanheliie uchytel'noie*, 1619

In 1619 the then still Orthodox churchman Kyryl Trankvylion Stavrovetsky published in Rokhmaniv, at his own press, a teaching Gospel bearing the plain title *Ievanheliie uchytel'noie.* The sermons included in it bore some relationship to sermons of Patriarch Philotheus of Constantinople, but seem mainly to have been his own original compositions.

The reaction of the hierarchy was negative. They distrusted the innovation of original sermons as well as Trankvylion's leanings towards Catholic theology. In the early 1620s a council of Ukrainian bishops convoked by Metropolitan Iov Boretsky of Kyiv condemned this teaching Gospel; anyone who had one was to be anathematized. Rejected by the Orthodox prelates, Trankvylion became a Uniate in 1626. In the following year the Moscow patriarchate ordered that the many copies of his teaching Gospel that had been imported into Moscow be burned.[5] Nevertheless, a number of copies have survived.[6] His teaching Gospel has two Last-Judgment sermons for Meatfare Sunday, each in two parts. Part 1 of the first sermon concerns the end of the world and the second coming of Christ, and part 2 describes the judgment itself. The second sermon describes the punishments of hell and rewards of paradise respectively in parts 1 and 2. The language of the sermons is a compromise between Church Slavonic and the vernacular.

In depicting how the world will end, Trankvylion ascribes a negative role to the Jews. They will be sent a false messiah, the Antichrist who will precede Christ's second coming (15v). When Christ himself comes, the cross and the instruments of his Passion will appear in the sky 'as an accusation against the unfaithful Jewish people' (17). No other people or religious grouping is singled out in his sermon.

As do many other sermons on the theme of the Last Judgment, Trankvylion's emphasize the importance of acts of mercy. 'Because you did not perform acts of mercy for the poor, he sends you to Gehenna. Even if you were not a fornicator or robber, nonetheless just for the lack of mercy the Lord sends him to torments ... For he did not say to them "You have killed, committed adultery," but instead that you did not perform acts of mercy for those in need, for my lesser brother' (18v–19). Among those specifically damned are merciless rich people (*nemylostyvykh bohatyrev*) (20v, also 21).

Tranvylion's hell is truly frightening. In it is the 'fire-born Leviathan, the large fish of the fiery sea, the soul-disintegrating whale, who is as large as the greatest mountain or as a thousand unscaleable mountains; his size is very terrible. From his mouth issues thunder, a flame of fire that can be seen from afar as cannon fire; when he so laughs a malodorous smoke issues from his ears as if from a great oven and it covers the entire land of Gehenna; from his nostrils issues a puffing like storm winds which heats up the fire of Gehenna to the torment of sinners' (24).

There are individual punishments to fit particular sins. Gluttons will endure great hunger, and the lazy will have to work without respite (24v). In paradise, on the other hand, those who love to work will become even more industrious (27v). But also in paradise there will be 'beds of eternal rest, covered with light' (28v).

In hell, the senses and parts of the body that aided in sin will be tormented. Adulterous eyes will ceaselessly shed tears of blood and see only torments and darkness. Ears which 'have paid careful heed and listened to the songs of fornicating women and various musicians' will now hear 'the voice of disgusting demons' and the wailing of sinners (24v). Legs that hurried to shed blood or engage in sexual sin will be bound with fetters of fire and never enter a cool place. Nostrils, which 'because of a good smell inclined to fornication,' will now be exposed to 'an eternal stink' from the 'damned stinking goats,' i.e., sinners, from demons who smell like rotten dogs, and from the pool of Gehenna (25). In paradise, of course, the resurrected bodies of the righteous will exude 'the aroma of the most sweet smells' (28v).

Antonii Radyvylovsky, *Vinets' Khrystov z propovidii nedelnykh*, 1688

Kyivan churchman Antonii Radyvlovsky published two sermon collections, neither of which claimed to be a teaching Gospel or to be anything other than original compositions. His *Ohorodok Marii Bohorodytsi* (The Garden of Mary the Mother of God) from 1676 was a collection of sermons for feast days, while his *Vinets' Khrystov z propovidii nedelnykh* (A Garland for Christ from Sunday Sermons) from 1688 contained sermons for Sundays, including two for Meatfare Sunday that concerned the Last Judgment.[7] The language of the sermons is a compromise between Church Slavonic and the vernacular.

Stylistically these sermons moved beyond traditional forms. One of the sermons, for example, is an extended baroque conceit on how the Last Judgment is analogous to lightning (417–21). Also, as was typical of Ukrainian homiletics in the baroque era, the sermons draw not only on scripture and the fathers, but also on secular literature; the sermons contain references to historical figures like Alexander the Great, Darius, and Caligula. The sermons also demonstrate the influence of Latin theology in Kyiv: St Augustine is quoted (419) and mortal sins mentioned (419v).

As to content, the sermons are notable for their emphasis on the severity of the Last Judgment. According to Radyvylovksy, even the Mother of God will at that moment turn away from sinners seeking her intercession and instead will ask her Son 'for the execution of divine justice on sinners' (414). Even the smallest sins, such as joking, will be punished (415).

In chapter 4 I discussed a sermon collection in the vernacular published by the Uniate Basilians at the end of the eighteenth century, *Nauky parokhialnyia*,[8] that was basically Roman Catholic in origin and theology.

The Last Judgment sermons comprised both original works and translations and adaptations from both Eastern and Western sources. The earlier works adhered more to the Greek tradition, while later sermons were original compositions influenced by rhetorical strategies learned from the West; at the very end, there were sermons that hardly differed from the Roman Catholic usage. The pattern here – older sermons closer to the Byzantine tradition, but the connection loosening with the passage of time – is similar to what we find in the development of Last Judgment iconography. However, I have not been able to ascertain any influence of Ukrainian sermons on the Last Judgment iconography of the Carpathians, nor have I found any allusion in the sermons to this iconography.

Catalogue of Images of the Last Judgment

Carpathian Icons and Murals, Fifteenth-Eighteenth Centuries, Used for This Study

The information for each icon is provided, as available, in the following order: dating, location, inventory number, material/type of image, other information, select bibliography.

Bahnovate

Sixteenth century. National Museum in Lviv, 36454/I-2122. Tempera on linden. Hordyns'kyi, *Ukrains'ka ikona*, pl. 142–3. Lohvyn et al., *Ukrains'kyi seredn'ovichnyi zhyvopys*, pl. LXXXIII. Helytovych, *Bohorodytsia z Dytiam i pokhvaloiu*, 43.

Bartne

Mid-eighteenth century. Castle Museum in Łańcut, 582. Tempera on wood.

Bodružal

1790s. In situ in Church of St Basil (originally St Nicholas). Mural. Brázdilová, 'Kostol svätého Michala archanjela w Bodružali' (but this article has the name of the church wrong and the accompanying illustration shows Kožany, not Bodružal).

Bogliarka

1660s (1661?). Slovak National Gallery in Bratislava, NL 24/2, but in storage in Zvolyn. Tempera on wood. Chmelinová et al. *Monogramista C.Z.* Škoviera, 'Ikona Strašného súdu a jej text(y),' 139, 143.

Borshchovychi

Beginning of seventeenth century. National Museum in Lviv, 4341/I-1376. Tempera on linden. Only the upper half of the central part of the icon remains. No image was available to me. Sydor, 'Reiestr ikon Strashnoho Sudu v kolektsii NML,' no. 21.

Brzegi

First half of eighteenth century. Hanging in the Grąziowa church in the open-air portion of the Museum of Folk Architecture in Sanok, 3388. Tempera on wood. This is a small two-sided icon, with a Protection on the other side. It was probably placed on the tetrapod for veneration on Meatfare Sunday and is not part of the set of large Last Judgment icons painted for church walls.

Chotyniec

1735. In situ in Church of the Nativity of the Mother of God. Mural. Restored in the mid-2000s.

Dmytriie

Eighteenth century. National Museum in Lviv, 50237/I-3920. Oil on pine. No image was available to me. Sydor, 'Reiestr ikon Strashnoho Sudu v kolektsii NML,' no. 31.

Dmytrovychi

1698. In situ in Church of St Nicholas. Mural. The original mural is covered with a new mural on plywood. No image of the original was available to me. Otkovych, 'Wyposażenie cerkwi p.w. świętego Mikołaja w Dmytrowicach,' 499.

Dobroslava

Second half of seventeenth century. In situ in Church of St Paraskeva. Tempera on wood. Central board missing. Tkáč, *Ikony*, pl. 132 (mirror image). Ševčiková, 'Ikony z drevených kostolíkov a ich reštaurovanie,' 47.

Dolyna

1560s. National Museum in Lviv, 12381/I-1451. Tempera on three pine boards. Attributed to Master Dymytrii. Svientsits'ka and Sydor, *Spadshchyna vikiv*, 16–17, pl. 41–4. Sydor, 'Ikony maistriv Oleksiia i Dymytriia,' 144–8. Skrobucha, 'Zur Ikonographie des "Jüngsten Gerichts,"' 62, 69.

Dolyna-Dymytrii Circle

Second half of sixteenth century. National Museum in Lviv, 2424/I-20. Tempera on linden. Only a fragment of the lower centre remains. The icon is attributed to the circle of Master Dymytrii. No image was available to me. Sydor, 'Reiestr ikon Strashnoho Sudu v kolektsii NML,' no. 7.

Drohobych-Elevation

Mid-sixteenth century. Church of the Elevation of the Holy Cross, a branch of the Drohobychchyna Museum. Tempera on wood. Only the right board of three has survived.

Drohobych-National Museum

1685. National Museum in Lviv, 2512/I-1978. Tempera on pine. Only a small reproduction was available to me. Sydor, 'Reiestr ikon Strashnoho Sudu v kolektsii NML,' no. 26.

Drohobych-St George

Circa 1666. In situ in Church of St George, a branch of the Drohobychchyna Museum. Mural. The mural has been restored by Lev Skop. Svientsitskyi, *Tematychnyi uklad* (the plate is missing in the 1998 reprint). *Istoriia ukrains'koho mystetstva*, 3:158, 162. Zholtovs'kyi, *Monumental'nyi zhyvopys*, 80–1, 86.

Dubrovytsia

Beginning of the seventeenth century. National Museum in Lviv, 4296/I-1283. Tempera on linden. Fragment of the top half of the central portion. No image was available to me. Sydor, 'Reiestr ikon Strashnoho Sudu v kolektsii NML,' no. 20.

Galicia-City Museum 1

Eighteenth century. City Museum: Spiritual Treasures of Ukraine, Kyiv. Tempera on board. Provenance uncertain. The dating is mine. The museum dated it to the end of the seventeenth century, but there was a general tendency in this museum to date items too early, and many datings were in the process of being corrected when I visited in 2005.

Galicia-City Museum 2

Eighteenth century. City Museum: Spiritual Treasures of Ukraine, Kyiv. Tempera on board. Provenance uncertain. The Last Judgment is painted together with a Passion.

Hankowice

Beginning of the seventeenth century. National Museum in Kraków, Ic 10. Tempera on wood. The village is now located in Ukraine, with the name Hankovychi. Kłosińska, *Ikony*, 161–2. Hordyns'kyi, *Ukrains'ka ikona*, pl. 159–60.

Horodok

End of sixteenth to beginning of seventeenth century. National Museum in Lviv, 33621/I-972. Tempera on linden. No image was available to me. Sydor, 'Reiestr ikon Strashnoho Sudu v kolektsii NML,' no. 18.

Izky

Seventeenth century. In situ in Church of St Nicholas. Tempera on wood. Crudely restored. Lohvyn, *Ukrainskie Karpaty*, illustration 54.

Jedlinka

1650s. The East Slovakian Museum in Košice. Tempera on wood. The attribution to Jedlinka is not certain (information from Vladislav Grešlík). The painter was Pavel of Muszyna. Biskupski, 'Sztuka kościoła prawosławnego i unickiego,' 357. Kovachovychova-Pushkar'ova and Pushkar, *Derev"iani tserkvy*, 188.

Kamianka Strumylova

1587. National museum in Lviv, 14537/I-1979. Tempera on three linden boards. Central board missing. *Istoriia ukrains'koho mystetstva*, 2:267, 269, illustration 186. Sydor, 'Reiestr ikon Strashnoho Sudu v kolektsii NML,' no. 9. Skrobucha, 'Zur Ikonographie des "Jüngsten Gerichts,"' 69. Helytovych, 'Datovani ikony,' 57–8. Svientsits'kyi, *Ikonopys'*, pl. 8, 86.

Klitsko

Sixteenth century. Branch of the Lviv Art Gallery in Olesko, Zh-4697. Tempera on wood. Right board of three.

Korytniki

Mid-sixteenth century. Castle Museum in Łańcut, 978 (heavenly Jerusalem and righteous) and 979 (paradise). Tempera on linden. Only the right board, in two parts, has survived. The icon was probably moved to Korytniki after the mid-sixteenth century. Giemza, 'Ikony XVI i XVII wieku,' 25-6, 28 n. 46, 44–5. Giemza, *O sztuce sakralnej*, 137, pl. 146–8.

Kožany

1790s. In situ in Church of the Encounter of Our Lord. Oil on canvas. Kovachovychova-Pushkar'ova and Pushkar, *Derev"iani tserkvy*, 177–8. Tkáč, *Ikony*, pl. 135.

Kožuchovce

1785. This no longer exists and is known only from reproductions. Mural. The church was moved from Kožuchovce to an open-air museum in

Košice in 1927. In the 1970s it was treated with chemical preservatives which destroyed the mural. (Information from Vladislav Grešlík, 7 July 2004.)

Krásny Brod

Late sixteenth or early seventeenth century. Museum of Ukrainian-Rusyn Culture in Svidník, 393/61. Tempera on wood. Lakata, 'Try "ostanni sudy."' Grešlík, 'Niekol'ko poznámok k ikonám 16. storočia,' 150. Sopolyha, *35 rokiv Muzeiu ukrains'koi kul'tury u Svydnyku*, 82.

Lipie

Late seventeenth century. Historical Museum in Sanok, S/3437 (old number 976). Tempera on wood. Kłosińska, 'Dwie ikony Sądu Ostatecznego.' Biskupski, *Ikony ze zbiorów Muzeum Historycznego w Sanoku*, pl. 69–71.

Lukov-Venecia

First half of sixteenth century. In situ in the Church of Ss Cosmas and Damian. Tempera on wood. The village Lukov-Venecia is the result of the union of two villages, Lukov and Venecia. Grešlík, 'Niekol'ko poznámok k ikonám 16. storočia,' 149–50. Tkáč, *Ikony*, pl. 58–67.

Mala Horozhanka

End of sixteenth–early seventeenth century. Branch of the Lviv Art Gallery in Olesko. Tempera on wood. Svientsits'ka and Otkovych, *Ukrains'ke narodne maliarstvo*, pl. 23.

Máramaros-Néprajzi

Seventeenth or eighteenth century. Budapest Museum of Ethnography (Néprajzi Múzeum), Sz239/a-b. Tempera on wood. Left board missing. Fejős, *Images of Time*, 143.

Medynychi

1662. National Museum in Lviv, 42413/I-2985. Pine. No image was available to me. Sydor, 'Reiestr ikon Strashnoho Sudu v kolektsii NML,' no. 24.

Moldavsko

1720. National Museum in Lviv, 13599/I-2007. Tempera on pine. Otkovych, *Narodna techiia*, 44–5, 55–9. Sydor, 'Reiestr ikon Strashnoho Sudu v kolektsii NML,' no. 29. Svientsits'ka and Otkovych, *Ukrains'ke narodne maliarstvo*, pl. 85.

Mshanets

Fifteenth century (third oldest). National Museum in Lviv, 34505/I-1181. Tempera on linden. Himka, 'The Last Judgment Icon of Mshanets.' Svientsits'ka and Sydor, *Spadshchyna vikiv*, 12–13. *Istoriia ukrains'koho mystetstva*, 2:231. Lohvyn et al., *Ukrains'kyi seredn'ovichnyi zhyvopys*, pl. XLVIII–XLIX. Dymytrii, *Ikonopys Zakhidnoi Ukrainy*, 241–50.

Museum of the History of Religion

Seventeenth century. Museum of the History of Religion in Lviv, L'v MA-2115, Zh-442. The right board is missing. Provenance uncertain, but internal evidence suggests the neighbourhood of Roztoka and Tiushka. Miasnikova et al., *L'vovskii muzei istorii religii i ateizma. Putevoditel'.* Himka, 'The Icon of the Last Judgment in the Village of Roztoka,' 364 n. 4, 366–73.

Nehrovets

1785. Stored in an attic not far from the church in Nehrovets when I visited in 2005, but it may have since been sold. Tempera on wood. Lohvyn, *Ukrainskie Karpaty*, 113, illustration 69. Syrokhman, *Tserkvy Ukrainy*, 481.

Nieznajowa/Rozstajne

1737. Regional Museum in Jasło, 96. Tempera on wood. Either from Nieznajowa or Rozstajne.

Nová Sedlica

End of seventeenth century. Slovak National Gallery in Bratislava, NL 15. Tempera on wood. Skrobucha, *Icons in Czechoslovakia*, pl. 44.

Novoselytsia

1676–79. In situ in Church of the Dormition. Mural. The mural has been restored by Halyna Druziuk and Lev Skop. Druziuk and Skop, 'Istoriia sozdaniia altarnoi pregrady,' 214–16. Lohvyn, *Po Ukraini*, 355, 369–70. *Istoriia ukrains'koho mystetstva*, 3:164.

Oleksandrivka

1779. In situ in Church of St Paraskeva. Mural. Only fragments are visible.

Paszowa

Sixteenth century. Museum of Folk Architecture in Sanok, 829. Tempera on wood. Central board only. Kłosińska, 'Dwie ikony Sądu Ostatecznego.' Czajkowski et al., *Ikona karpacka*, pl. 20.

Piilo

1778–94. This no longer exists and is known only from some artists' sketches. Mural. The old wooden church burned down in 1965, and the parishioners suspect politically motivated arson. Nothing was preserved from it. The parishioners tried to erect a new church shortly after the fire, but were denied permission. In fact, the authorities three times used tractors to demolish whatever structures the people put up there. Finally in 1988 a delegation sent to Moscow obtained permission and construction began in 1990. Zholtovs'kyi, *Monumental'nyi zhyvopys*, 117.

Plavie

Seventeenth century. National Museum in Lviv, 6492/I-1334. Tempera on linden. Sydor, 'Reiestr ikon Strashnoho Sudu v kolektsii NML,' no. 22. Zabolotnyi, *Narysy z istorii ukrains'koho mystetstva*, pl. 105–6 (not identified as Plavie). Zholtovs'kyi, *Ukrains'kyi zhyvopys XVII–XVIII st.*, 113.

Polana

Fifteenth century (second oldest). National Museum in Kraków, Ic 25. Tempera on wood. Kłosińska, *Ikony*, 156–7. Biskupski, *Ikony w zbiorach polskich*, pl. 22.

Popeli

Eighteenth century. National Museum in Lviv, 43037/I-3098. Oil on canvas. No image was available to me. Sydor, 'Reiestr ikon Strashnoho Sudu v kolektsii NML,' no. 35.

Powroźnik

1623. In situ at the Church of St James. Tempera on wood. This icon has recently been restored. Giemza and Szewczuk, 'Ikona Sąd Ostateczny.' Pieńkowska, 'Ikony sądeckie XVII i XVIII wieku (ze zbiorów Muzeum w Nowym Sączu),' 588–9. Giemza, *O sztuce sakralnej*, 137, pl. 145.

Przemyśl Land Museum

Sixteenth century. National Museum of the Przemyśl Land, M.P.H. 1134. Tempera on wood. Its provenance is unknown. Kurpik, 'Ikona Sądu Ostatecznego z Muzeum Ziemi Przemyskiej.' Biskupski, *Ikony w zbiorach polskich*, pl. 37.

Przemyśl Region

Beginning of seventeenth century. National Museum in Kraków, Ic 32. Tempera on wood. Only the central board is preserved. Provenance uncertain, but probably from the environs of Przemyśl. Kłosińska, *Ikony*, 158–9.

Radelychi

Second half of the sixteenth century. National Museum in Lviv, 22996/I-1698. Tempera on linden. Sydor, 'Reiestr ikon Strashnoho Sudu v kolektsii NML,' no. 8. Sydor, 'Ikona Strashnoho Sudu z Vil'shanytsi,' 87–8.

Rakovčík

1789. Museum of Ukrainian-Rusyn Culture in Svidník. Canvas.

Roztoka

Seventeenth century. Stored in the narthex of the new Church of the Presentation of the Mother of God when I visited in 2001, but may have since been sold. Tempera on wood. Himka, 'The Icon of the Last Judgment in the Village of Roztoka.' Lohvyn, *Ukrainskie Karpaty*, 86–90.

Ruská Bystrá

Mid-sixteenth century. Museum of Ukrainian-Rusyn Culture in Svidník, 1141/60. Tempera on wood. Attributed to Master Oleksii. Lakata, 'Try "ostanni sudy."' Grešlík, 'Niekol'ko poznámok k ikonám 16. storočia,' 148–9. Helytovych, '"Strashnyi sud" seredyny XVI st. peremyshl's'koho maliara Oleksiia Horoshkovycha.' Sydor, 'Ikony maistriv Oleksiia i Dymytriia,' 90. Tkáč, *Ikony*, pl. 49–57.

Shelestovo

Eighteenth century. Transcarpathian Museum of Folk Architecture in Uzhhorod. Tempera on wood.

Skole

Eighteenth century. Private collection of Rev. Rostyslav Hladiak. Tempera on pine. Only the left part of the icon has been reproduced. Sydor and Lozynskyi, *Ukrainian Icons*, 22, 221, pl. 157.

Skoryky

1754. National Museum in Lviv, 42822/I-3079. Oil on linden boards. Lohvyn, *Po Ukraini*, 295, 297. Sydor, 'Reiestr ikon Strashnoho Sudu v kolektsii NML,' no. 30.

Smilna

Eighteenth century. National Museum in Lviv, 10002. On wood? Information from Lilya Berezhnaya, who consulted the museum's *fototeka* (collection of photographs); for some reason this icon is not listed in Sydor, 'Reiestr ikon Strashnoho Sudu v kolektsii NML.' No image was available to me.

Stanylia

Second half of the sixteenth century. National Museum in Lviv, 36455/I-2123. Tempera on linden. Miliaieva, *Stinopys Potelycha*, 43. Sydor, 'Reiestr ikon Strashnoho Sudu v kolektsii NML,' no. 10.

Sukhyi Potik

End of sixteenth century. National Museum in Lviv, 13408/I1478. Tempera on pine. No image was available to me. Sydor, 'Reiestr ikon Strashnoho Sudu v kolektsii NML,' no. 17.

Świątkowa Mała

1687. In situ in the Church of St Michael the Archangel (Roman Catholic). Tempera on wood.

Świątkowa Wielka

Mid-eighteenth century. In situ in the Church of St Michael the Archangel (Roman Catholic). Tempera on wood. The dating is mine, because of its similarity to Nieznajowa/Rozstajne (dated 1737) and Bartne. The card catalogue at the Castle Museum in Łańcut dates it to the seventeenth century.

Sykhiv

1683. In situ in Church of the Holy Trinity in Sykhiv (now incorporated into Lviv). Mural. The mural was restored in the early 2000s. *Istoriia ukrains'koho mystetstva*, 3: 166.

Tiushka

Seventeenth century. City Museum: Spiritual Treasures of Ukraine, Kyiv. Tempera on three boards. The museum dated this icon to the sixteenth century, but many items in this newly established, private museum are dated too early and need to be corrected.

Topol'a

Seventeenth century. Museum of Ukrainian-Rusyn Culture in Svidník, 671/70. Canvas. Lakata, 'Try "ostanni sudy."' Kovachovychova-Pushkar'ova and Pushkar, *Derev"iani tserkvy*, 395.

Torky

1670. National Museum in Lviv, 6498/I-1975. Pine. Only a small reproduction was available to me. Sydor, 'Reiestr ikon Strashnoho Sudu v kolektsii NML,' no. 25.

Ročany

Seventeenth century. In situ in the Church of St Luke. Canvas. Kovachovychova-Pushkar'ova and Pushkar, *Derev"iani tserkvy*, 405.

Trostianets

Seventeenth century. National Museum in Lviv, 6441/1, 2/I-1310. Tempera on linden. No image was available to me. Sydor, 'Reiestr ikon Strashnoho Sudu v kolektsii NML,' no. 27.

Trushevychi

End of sixteenth century. National Museum in Lviv, 15812/I-1976. Tempera on linden. Sydor, 'Reiestr ikon Strashnoho Sudu v kolektsii NML,' no. 16. Svientsits'kyi, *Ikonopys'*, pl. 55, 79.

Vanivka

Fifteenth century (oldest). National Museum in Lviv, 34503/I-1179. Tempera on linden. The village is now called Węglówka. Svientsits'ka, 'Master ikon XV veka iz sel Vanivka i Zdvyzhen',' 280–2. Svientsits'kyi, *Ikonopys'*, pl. 52, 72.

Velyke

1590s. National Museum in Lviv, 42406/I-2982. Tempera on linden. Only central part preserved. No image was available to me. *Istoriia ukrains'koho mystetstva*, 2:261. Sydor, 'Reiestr ikon Strashnoho Sudu v kolektsii NML,' no. 15.

Vilshanytsia

First half of sixteenth century. National Museum in Lviv, 30675/I-1914. Tempera on linden. Sydor, 'Ikona Strashnoho Sudu z Vil'shanytsi.'

Volosianka

Second half of seventeenth century. Budapest Museum of Ethnography (Néprajzi Múzeum), 87 194. Tempera on wood. Puskás, 'Aktual'ni problemy vyvchennia davn'oho ikonopysu,' 73. Puskás, *Between East and West*, pl. 38. Fejős, *Images of Time*, 142.

Volytsia Derevlianska

Eighteenth century. National Museum in Lviv, 27844/I-3645. Oil on canvas. No image was available to me. Sydor, 'Reiestr ikon Strashnoho Sudu v kolektsii NML,' no. 33.

Vovche

Second half of sixteenth century. National Museum in Lviv, 25380/I-1743. Tempera on linden. Svientsits'kyi, *Ikonopys'*, pl. 54, 75.

Vyšný Orlík

1660–80. Šariš Museum in Bardejov. Tempera on canvas. Grešlík, *Ikony Šarišského Múzea*, 74–6, pl. 37.

Wola Wyżna

Second half of seventeenth century. Historical Museum in Sanok, S/4947 (old number 1106). Tempera on wood.

Yasinka Masova

Last third of sixteenth century. National Museum in Lviv, 29289/I-1904. Tempera on pine. Fragments of left board. No image was available to me. Sydor, 'Reiestr ikon Strashnoho Sudu v kolektsii NML,' no. 12.

Yezupil

Eighteenth century. National Museum in Lviv, 4686/I-1381. Oil on canvas. No image was available to me. Sydor, 'Reiestr ikon Strashnoho Sudu v kolektsii NML,' no. 34.

Zavadka

Last third of sixteenth century. National Museum in Lviv, 36569/1-6/I-1237/1-6. Tempera on linden. Six fragments. No image was available to me. Sydor, 'Reiestr ikon Strashnoho Sudu v kolektsii NML,' no. 14.

Zboj/Uličské Krivé

1660–80. Šariš Museum in Bardejov. Tempera on canvas. From either Zboj or Uličské Krivé. Grešlík, *Ikony Šarišského Múzea,* 75–6, pl. 38. Božová, Gutek, Grešlík, *Drevené kostolíky v okolí Bardejova,* 181–2.

Zhovkva

Mid-sixteenth century. National Museum in Lviv, 38484/I-2641. Tempera on wood. Right board only. Sydor, 'Reiestr ikon Strashnoho Sudu v kolektsii NML,' no. 4.

Bukovina

Berehomet, Kitsman raion

Second half of seventeenth century. In situ on the north wall in Church of the Transfer of the Relics of St Nicholas. Mural. At present the mural is covered over by plywood and a thick wallpaper. *Istoriia ukrains'koho mystetstva,* 3:166–7. Lohvyn, *Po Ukraini,* 342, 344–5.

Dubivtsi, Kitsman raion

Modern, twentieth-century. In situ on the south wall of the narthex in Church of the Dormition, built 1775. Fresco. I would date this to the interwar period. The fresco is disfigured by pipes or wiring running across it. This indicates that the fresco was in place before the Communists modernized and secularized the village.

Hlynytsia, Kitsman raion

Nineteenth-twentieth century. In situ on the north wall of the nave in Church of the Nativity of the Mother of God, constructed 1786. Oil on canvas.

Horecha, now part of Chernivtsi

1767. In situ on the west wall of Church of the Nativity of the Mother of God in Horecha Monastery. Fresco.

Kamianna, Storozhynets raion

1912. In situ on the north wall of the narthex of Church of St Michael, constructed in 1891. Oil on canvas. There is a Passion in the nave as well.

Kitsman

Nineteenth century, perhaps the interwar period. Chernivtsi Oblast Regional Museum, 28317-I 2563. Oil on canvas. Originally from the Church of the Three Holy Hierarchs.

Lukivtsi, Vyzhnytsia raion

The church elder who ordered the Last Judgment and Passion for Vyviz said he wanted them because he had seen such icons in nearby Lukivtsi.

Pohorilivka, Zastavna raion

Eighteenth century. Chernivtsi Oblast Museum of Art, Chernivtsi, 443. Canvas. Zholtovs'kyi, *Ukrains'kyi zhyvopys XVII–XVIII st.*, 285. After 1908. In situ on the east wall of the narthex of the Church of St Nicholas, built in 1870–81. Oil on canvas. There is also in the choir loft a Passion in oils very similar in size and format to the eighteenth-century Last Judgment that ended up in the Chernivtsi Oblast Museum of Art. It was evidently painted to match the eighteenth-century icon. Since the Passion is dated, to 1907–8, we can assume that the eighteenth-century Last Judgment was still in the church at that time. Therefore the replacement icon was painted sometime later in the twentieth century.

Putyla, Putyla raion

In situ in Church of St John the Baptist. A modern lithograph. A mountain village.

Roztoky, Putyla raion

Late nineteenth-twentieth century. In situ on the west wall of the nave in the Church of the Dormition. Oil on canvas with no inscriptions. A Passion is next to the Last Judgment. A mountain village.

Ust-Putyla, Putlya raion

Late nineteenth-twentieth century. In situ on the east wall of the narthex of Church of St Paraskeva, built 1891. Oil on canvas. The Last Judgment is placed to the north, a Passion to south. A mountain village.

Vyviz, Storozhynets raion

1990s or early 2000s. In situ high up on the east wall of the nave of Church of St George. Oil on canvas. The church was built in 1947, closed in 1957, and reopened in 1991. A Passion is on the west wall of the nave. Vyviz is a *khutir* near Kosovanka.

Maramureş

Note: The literature on Maramureş generally refers to the narthex as the 'pronaos,' and I follow that custom here.

Bârsana

1806. In situ on the south wall of the pronaos of what is now a Greek Catholic church. Small fragment of a mural. Painted by Toader Hodor. Pop-Bratu, *Pictura murală maramureşeană*, 73.

Borşa

1775. In situ on the east wall of the pronaos. Mural. Pop-Bratu, *Pictura murală maramureşeană*, 91.

Budeşti-Josani

Seventeenth century. In situ in the Orthodox church built in oak in 1643. Icon on three boards that seem to have had canvas glued to the surface.

Budeşti-Susani

Late nineteenth-early twentieth century. In situ on the north wall. Lithograph.

Călinești-Căieni

1754. In situ on the east and south wall of the pronaos. Mural. Painted by Alexandru Ponehalski. Pop-Bratu, *Pictura murală maramureșeană*, 27–8.

Cornești

Early nineteenth century. In situ throughout the pronaos. Mural. Painted by Toader Hodor. Pop-Bratu, *Pictura murală maramureșeană*, 62–4.

Cuhea

Mid-eighteenth century. In situ in the pronaos. Mural. Pop-Bratu, *Pictura murală maramureșeană*, 53–5.

Desești

1780. In situ in the pronaos of the church erected in 1770. Mural. Painted by Radu Munteanu 1780. Pop-Bratu, *Pictura murală maramureșeană*, 46–8.

Dragomirești

Turn of the nineteenth century. In situ on the west, south, and north walls of the pronaos. Mural. Perhaps by the same artist who painted Poenile Izei. Pop-Bratu, *Pictura murală maramureșeană*, 96,105.

Ferești

Late eighteenth century. In situ on the south, west, and east walls of the pronaos. Mural. Pop-Bratu, *Pictura murală maramureșeană*, 78–9.

Giulești-mănăstirea

Seventeenth or eighteenth century. In situ on the exterior west wall. Fragment of mural. Pop-Bratu, *Pictura murală maramureșeană*, 21–2, 105.

Ieud-Deal

1782. In situ throughout pronaos. Mural. Painted by Alexandru Ponehalski. Pop-Bratu, *Pictura murală maramureşeană*, 35–7, pl. 26, 30–1.

Onceşti

Eighteenth century. In situ on the west wall of the pronaos. Mural. Pop-Bratu, *Pictura murală maramureşeană*, 49–50, 105.

Poienile Izei

1793–4. In situ on the east, south, and north walls of the pronaos of the Church of St Paraskeva. Mural. Pop-Bratu, *Pictura murală maramureşeană*, 93–5, pl. 85.

Rogoz

1785. In situ in the pronaos of the Church of the Holy Archangels Michael and Gabriel. Mural. Painted by Radu Munteanu and Nicolae Mon de Fîntînele. Rogoz is located just south of Maramureş proper, in the Lăpuş region.

Rozavlea

1825. In situ in the pronaos. Remnants of a mural (only paradise, on the south wall, is well preserved). Painted by Ioan Plohod. Pop-Bratu, *Pictura murală maramureşeană*, 84–5.

Sat Şugătag

Late eighteenth century. In situ in pronaos. Mural. Costin, *Biserici de lemn din Maramureş*, 90.

Serednie Vodiane, Rakhiv Raion, Transcarpathia Oblast

Seventeenth or eighteenth century. In situ on the east wall dividing the pronaos and narthex in the Church of St Nicholas. Fragments of a mural. The inscriptions on the mural are in Slavonic, not Romanian, and Ukrainian art historians treat the murals in this church as part of Ukrainian art history. But this is a *Romanian* village in historical Maramureş that ended up on the Ukrainian side of the border. Inscriptions in Slavonic indicate the seventeenth rather than the early eighteenth century as proposed by Pavlo Zholtovsky. Zholtovs'kyi, *Monumental'nyi zhyvopys*, 98, 108, 153. Lohvyn, *Ukrainskie Karpaty*, 148.

Şieu

Late 1820s. In situ on the west, south, and north walls of the pronaos. Mural. Attributed to Ioan Plohod. Pop-Bratu, *Pictura murală maramureşeană*, 88–9.

Şurdeşti

Eighteenth century. In situ on the entrance walls to the nave. Mural. Costin, *Biserici de lemn din Maramureş*, 66.

Table 6.1
Carpathian Icons and Murals Known Only from Visitation Records

Locality	Deanery or Diocese	Type of Image	Placement	Source
Babuchów	Rohatyn	mural	left wall	Gronek, *Ikony Męki Pańskiej*, 15–25.
Bartatów	Obroszyn	mural	left wall	Gronek, *Ikony Męki Pańskiej*, 15–25.
Brzuchowice	Dunajów	icon on canvas	*babynets'*	Gronek, *Ikony Męki Pańskiej*, 15–25.
Bubszczane	Pomorzany	icon on canvas	left wall	Gronek, *Ikony Męki Pańskiej*, 15–25.
Chorościec	Kozłów	icon on canvas	right wall	Gronek, *Ikony Męki Pańskiej*, 15–25.
Czahrów	Żurawno	mural	–	Gronek, *Ikony Męki Pańskiej*, 15–25.
Czernichów (Czernichowce)	Tarnopol	icon on canvas	*babynets'*	Gronek, *Ikony Męki Pańskiej*, 15–25.
Daniłcze	Rohatyn	icon on canvas	–	Gronek, *Ikony Męki Pańskiej*, 15–25.
Glińsk	Żółkiew	icon on wood	right wall	Gronek, *Ikony Męki Pańskiej*, 15–25.
Gorzyce	Jarosław	–	–	AB GK 25, p. 29.
Hołowecke Górne	Stary Sambór	–	left wall	AB GK 52, p. 28.
Horodysławice	Bóbrka	icon on canvas	left wall	Gronek, *Ikony Męki Pańskiej*, 15–25.
Jarczowce	Zborów	icon on canvas	left wall	Gronek, *Ikony Męki Pańskiej*, 15–25.
Jawcze	Rozdół	mural	left wall	Gronek, *Ikony Męki Pańskiej*, 15–25.
Kozowa	Brzeżany	icon on canvas	left wall	Gronek, *Ikony Męki Pańskiej*, 15–25.
Kulawa	Żółkiew	mural	right wall	Gronek, *Ikony Męki Pańskiej*, 15–25.
Kulczyce Królewska	Sambór	–	north wall	AB GK 47, p. 45.
Lisowice	Bolechów	icon on canvas	left wall	Gronek, *Ikony Męki Pańskiej*, 15–25.
Mokrzany	Mokrzany	mural	right wall	Gronek, *Ikony Męki Pańskiej*, 15–25.
Moniłówka	Zborów	icon on canvas	left wall	Gronek, *Ikony Męki Pańskiej*, 15–25.
Nowosiółka	Zarwanica	mural	left wall	Gronek, *Ikony Męki Pańskiej*, 15–25.
Radziejowice	diec. kamieniecka	–	right wall	Gronek, *Ikony Męki Pańskiej*, 15–25.
Raków	Dolina?	icon on wood	left wall	Gronek, *Ikony Męki Pańskiej*, 15–25.
Remenów	Kulików	icon on wood	right wall	Gronek, *Ikony Męki Pańskiej*, 15–25.
Sarnki Dolne	Bursztyn	icon on canvas	–	Gronek, *Ikony Męki Pańskiej*, 15–25.
Sarnki Horiszne (Górne)	Bursztyn	mural	–	Gronek, *Ikony Męki Pańskiej*, 15–25.
Serafińce	Horodenka	icon on canvas	north wall	Gronek, *Ikony Męki Pańskiej*, 15–25.
Sielec	Mokrzany	–	below choir	AB GK 475, p. 526.

Table 6.1
Carpathian Icons and Murals Known Only from Visitation Records (*Continued*)

Locality	Deanery or Diocese	Type of Image	Placement	Source
Skniłów	Obroszyn	icon on canvas	*babynets'*	Gronek, *Ikony Męki Pańskiej*, 15–25.
Skwarzawa Nowa	Żółkiew	icon on canvas	right wall	Gronek, *Ikony Męki Pańskiej*, 15–25.
Stradcz	Obroszyn	mural	left wall	Gronek, *Ikony Męki Pańskiej*, 15–25.
Suchrów	Rozdół	mural	left wall	Gronek, *Ikony Męki Pańskiej*, 15–25.
Szczedrowa	diec. kamieniecka	icon on canvas	*babynets'*	Gronek, *Ikony Męki Pańskiej*, 15–25.
Tarnawska	Jarosław	icon on canvas	*babynets'*	AB GK 25, p. 117.
Tokarówka	diec. kamieniecka	icon on canvas	*babynets'*	Gronek, *Ikony Męki Pańskiej*, 15–25.
Trościaniec	Dolina	icon on wood	left wall	Gronek, *Ikony Męki Pańskiej*, 15–25.
Wierzbica	Rozdół	icon on canvas	left wall	Gronek, *Ikony Męki Pańskiej*, 15–25.
Wierzbiłowce	Rohatyn	mural	–	Gronek, *Ikony Męki Pańskiej*, 15–25.
Wola Kunińska	Żółkiew	icon on wood	left wall	Gronek, *Ikony Męki Pańskiej*, 15–25.
Wola Zołtaniecka	Kamionka Strumiłowa	icon on canvas	left wall	Gronek, *Ikony Męki Pańskiej*, 15–25.
Załuże	Rohatyn	icon on canvas	*babynets'*	Gronek, *Ikony Męki Pańskiej*, 15–25.
Zborów	Zborów	–	right wall	Gronek, *Ikony Męki Pańskiej*, 15–25.
Zubrzyca	Rozłucz	–	–	AB GK 6445, p. 3.

Notes

1. Introduction

1 Gellner, *Nations and Nationalism*, 124–5.

2 Himka, 'History, Christendom and Traditional Ukrainian Culture.'

3 Gould, *Wonderful Life*, 281.

4 Wuthnow, *Rediscovering the Sacred*, 52–5.

5 This is using 'icons for historians,' as called for by Woodsworth, 'The Venerated Image.'

6 Aleksandrovych, 'Rybotycki ośrodek malarski,' 341.

7 A Carpathian Last Judgment icon (Vyšný Orlík) is panned to great effect in the concluding scenes of Peter Kerekes's film *Murder Ballads and Legends from Ladomirova.*

8 Many of the illustrations to this book can also be found in colour on the internet, on the site of the Leopolis project (CIUS Research Programs>Last Judgment Iconography Project): http://www.leopolis-huri.org.ua/cambridge_face/external/campus02/go/horizon3/form004?id=1017.

9 Himka, 'Episodes in the Historiography of the Ukrainian Icon.'

10 Himka, 'What Constitutes a Ukrainian Cultural Artifact?'

11 I use this spelling as a compromise among its historical names: Bukowina (German), Bucovina (Romanian), and Bukovyna (Ukrainian).

12 For further information on the historical background and social conditions, see *Encyclopedia of Ukraine*; *Encyclopedia of Rusyn History and Culture*; Rozdolski, *Stosunki poddańcze w dawnej Galicji*; Mytsiuk, *Narysy z sotsiial'no hospodars'koi istorii*; Magocsi, *Galicia*; Magocsi, *Carpatho-Rusyn Studies.*

13 On the Syriac Ephraim, see Brock, *The Luminous Eye.*

14 Brock, 'Ephrem's Letter to Publius.'

15 Taylor, 'St. Ephraim's Influence on the Greeks,' 6. The texts on the Last Judgment are not included in the *Patrologia Graeca,* but Old Slavonic versions with the Greek originals and a German translation can be found in Bojkovsky and Aitzetmüller, *Paraenesis.* There are good and accessible Russian translations of the most important sermons in Ephraem Syrus, *Tvoreniia.* For an illustrated discussion on the impact of Ephraim the Syrian (Graecus) on Orthodox iconography of the Last Judgment, see Gavrilovic, 'St. Ephraim the Syrian's Thought and Imagery as an Inspiration to Byzantine Artists.' Sermons attributed to Ephraim appeared in Carpathian homiliary Gospels for Meatfare Sunday. See, for example, 'Poucheniie sviataho Iefrema o budushchem sudi,' Biblioteka Narodowa (Warsaw), manuscript division, Akc. 2740, microfilm 15353.

16 *The Lenten Triodion,* 150–65.

17 Ibid., 153.

18 Vilinskii, *Zhitie sv. Vasiliia Novago,* 1:315.

19 For full bibliographical details, please see the bibliography.

20 See Kots'-Hryhorchuk, 'Nove pro naidavnishi zrazky ukrains'koho ikonopysu,' and Ovsiichuk, 'Janina Kłosińska. Ikony.'

21 Czajkowski et al., *Ikona karpacka.* See the analysis in Himka, 'Episodes in the Historiography of the Ukrainian Icon,' 153–6.

22 He has written very good surveys of the literature on 'West Ruthenian' icons of the fifteenth and sixteenth centuries: Kruk, 'Stan badań nad atrybucjami warsztatowymi.' Kruk, 'Stan badań nad zachodnioruskim malarstwem ikonowym.'

23 Himka, '"Social" Elements in Ukrainian Icons of the Last Judgment.'

24 Svientsits'ka and Otkovych, *Ukrains'ke narodne maliarstvo XIII–XX stolit'.*

25 See Himka, 'Episodes in the Historiography of the Ukrainian Icon,' 160–6.

26 Magocsi, *Our People,* 111–43.

2. Origins

1 Himka, 'Episodes in the Historiography of the Ukrainian Icon,' 150–2, 154–5, 158–9, 167. Himka, 'What Constitutes a Ukrainian Cultural Artifact?' 232–3.

2 Icons in museums are commonly referred to by the names used by the museums themselves. Thus, although Vanivka came from a village now in Poland, it is held by the National Museum in Lviv and hence called by its Ukrainian name. Similarly, Polana, though from a village now in Ukraine, is held by the National Museum in Krakow and hence called by its Polish name.

3 Information from Romuald Biskupski, 2 June 2000.
4 Sydor, 'Reiestr ikon Strashnoho Sudu v kolektsii NML,' 90.
5 Skrobucha, 'Zur Ikonographie des "Jüngsten Gerichts,"' 61.
6 Helytovych, 'Datovani ikony,' 53, 57. A Volhynian icon was dated even earlier, in 1532.
7 Goldfrank, 'Who Put the Snake on the Icon and the Tollbooths on the Snake?' For another interpretation of the relationship between eschatological concerns and changes in iconography in northern Rus', see Flier, 'Till the End of Time.'
8 Węglówka (Vanivka) was founded in the first half, Poliana in the second half of the fifteenth century. Czajkowski, 'Dzieje osadnictwa historycznego na Podkarpaciu,' map 3. Mshanets was first mentioned in historical records in 1446. *Istoriia gorodov i sel Ukrainskoi SSR. L'vovskaia oblast'*, 637.
9 Sydor, 'Reiestr ikon Strashnoho Sudu v kolektsii NML,' 90.
10 Kłosińska, *Ikony*, 156. She does not mention the three boards, but they are visible in the photograph on the previous page.
11 Sydor, 'Reiestr ikon Strashnoho Sudu v kolektsii NML,' 90.
12 Brenk, *Tradition und Neuerung*, 89–90, 102–3.
13 The icon was originally published in Sotiriou, *Icones du Mont Sinaï*, vol. 1, pl. 151, but there is a larger and clearer black-and-white reproduction in Jónsdóttir, *An 11th Century Byzantine Last Judgement in Iceland*, ill. 6 (entire icon) and ill. 24 (detail of the personification of the sea). The Sotirious date the icon to the second half of the twelfth century on 2:131. Jónsdóttir describes the icon in on pp. 16 and 23–4. There is a colour reproduction and some commentary in Weitzmann, *The Icon*, 84–5, pl. 23. Heinz Skrobucha has also compared this icon with Russian icons of the Last Judgment in Skrobucha, 'Zur Ikonographie des "Jüngsten Gerichts."'
14 On the deesis, see Brenk, *Tradition und Neuerung*, 95–8, and Mazurkiewicz, *Deesis*.
15 Jónsdóttir only identified them as 'a group of five figures.' That they are condemned sinners is clear from the inscription: 'Depart from me, ye cursed, into the outer fire.' (This is a corruption of Mt 25:41 which reads 'into everlasting fire' *to pur to aiōnion* instead of, as in the icon inscription, *to pur to exōteron. Sto pur to exōteron* is the common modern Greek expression for 'Go to hell.') They may, in fact, be Jews. See below, n. 53.
16 See below, fig. 2.43.
17 It appears in the Last Judgment fresco of the Chora monastery painted in 1316–21. Underwood, *The Kariye Djami*, 3:389. It is also to be found in the sixteenth-century fresco in the Church of the Nativity in Arbanasi, Bulgaria.

18 'De exitu animi,' 1076 D. It is unlikely that the historical Cyril of Alexandria wrote this text.

19 Radelychi (second half of the sixteenth century), Mala Horozhanka (end of sixteenth-early seventeenth century), Dobroslava (second half of the seventeenth century), Drohobych-National Museum (1685), Moldavsko (1720).

20 Brenk, *Tradition und Neuerung*, 103, 163.

21 Patriarch Dymytrii (Yarema) discerns the signs of the zodiac in the land and sea beasts in the Mshanets resurrection scene. I do not. Dymytrii, *Ikonopys Zakhidnoi Ukrainy*, 248.

22 King James reads: 'Justice and judgment are the habitation of thy throne' (Ps 89:14). On the hetoimasia, see Brenk, *Tradition und Neuerung*, 71, 98, and Różycka-Bryzek, 'Bizantyńsko-ruskie malowidła ścienne w kaplicy Świętokrzyskiej,' 224–6.

23 For an interesting discussion of this theme in Byzantine theology and Ukrainian and Russian iconography, see Berezhnaya, 'Sub Specie Mortis,' 20–2.

24 This point was made by Sydor, 'Ikona Strashnoho Sudu z Vil'shanytsi,' 85.

25 Heinz Skrobucha calls this the earliest Russian icon of the Last Judgment. He states that it is usually dated to the first half of the fifteenth century, which he finds too early. Skrobucha, 'Zur Ikonographie des "Jüngsten Gerichts,"' 54, 54 n. 14. Below I will refer to another fifteenth-century Russian icon, from the Dormition Church in Moscow, that has more archaic features and is probably older. Mikhail Alpatov dates it to the mid-fifteenth century. Weitzmann et al., *The Icon*, 280–1.

26 Haustein-Bartsch, *Das Jüngste Gericht*, 4, 6, 8, 40, 50, pl. 1–2.

27 Ephraem Syrus, *Tvoreniia*, 217.

28 I am grateful to Mother Sophia Senyk for turning my attention to this. The first ten verses of chapter 3 of the Wisdom of Solomon are read on the Sunday of All Saints (the first Sunday after Pentecost) and on the feasts of St Theodosius the Cenobiarch (11 January), the Three Holy Hierarchs (30 January), and St George (23 April).

29 'De exitu animi,' 1081 C.

30 Kretzenbacher, *Die Seelenwaage*. Brandon, *The Judgment of the Dead*, 28–9, 47, 78–9, and ill. 1, 5, 8. Hegel mentions the weighing of souls in ancient Egypt in his *Philosophy of History*, 217: 'After the death of an Egyptian, judgment was passed upon him. – One of the principal representations on the sarcophagi is this judicial process in the realm of the dead. Osiris – with Isis behind him – appears, holding a balance, while before him stands the soul of the deceased.'

31 At Gračanica. Der Nersessian, 'Program and Iconography,' 331.

32 At the Church of the Holy Apostles in Salonika. Ibid. The hand of God has a much older lineage in Christian iconography, but it is not clear to me whether any of these earlier depictions included also the souls of the righteous. Kirschbaum, *Lexikon der christlichen Ikonographie*, s.v. 'Hand Gottes.' The hand of God with souls appears in a fresco from the 1370s-1380s in the Church of the Dormition in the Volotovo Field near Novgorod. Lazarev, *Drevnerusskie mozaiki i freski XI–XV vv.*, ill. 362. The image also appears as an illustration to Psalm 23 in the late fourteenth- or early fifteenth-century Munich Serbian psalter. The illumination depicts how the Lord founded the earth upon the seas (Ps 23:2). *Der Serbische Psalter. Faksimile*, folio 33.

33 Moscow Dormition has been dated differently, both from the second quarter and from the end of the fifteenth century. Goldfrank, 'Who Put the Snake on the Icon and the Tollbooths on the Snake?' 189.

34 Kretzenbacher, *Die Seelenwaage*, 152. Réau, *Iconographie de l'art chrétien*, 2:742.

35 Brenk, *Tradition und Neuerung*, 100–1.

36 Underwood, *The Kariye Djami*, 3:386.

37 For the purposes of this book, it does not matter whether the painting on the east wall of the narthex in Luzhany properly belongs to the set of Moldavian frescoes or not. Although I am including them here, I recognize that they are anomalous. These frescoes were restored only in the 1990s and demand more study. On the one hand, the church in Luzhany is shaped like a typical Moldavian church and even has traces of paint on the exterior, so typical of northern Moldavia. The style of the frescoes also suggests that they are Moldavian. The founder of the church was a court boyar of the Moldavian prince, Alexander I. On the other hand, these frescoes are much earlier than the others and also relatively far to the north of them. The boyar who built the church had the Rus'-Lithuanian name of Feodor Vitolt. Ukrainian scholars have concluded from the language of the inscriptions that the painters of the frescoes came from northern Volhynia, that is, Rus' territory under Lithuanian rule. (I would feel more comfortable if Romanian scholars had come to that conclusion on the language.) Pyvovarov, *Khrystyians'ki starozhytnosti*, 60–1. Nimchuk and Shynkaruk, 'Epihrafiia Voznesens'koi tserkvy.' Himka, 'What Constitutes a Ukrainian Cultural Artifact?' 232.

38 In Serbian Last Judgment frescoes in Dečani (1327–48) and Morača (1577–8) the scales are not held by an angel, but suspended from a segment of a circle representing the heavenly realm. Gavrilovic, 'St. Ephraim the Syrian's Thought and Imagery as an Inspiration to Byzantine Artists,' ill. 20.

Petković, *Morača*, 255. The Moldavian frescoes in Humor and Voroneţ combine the Serbian circle segment and the Rus' hand; Suceava: St Demetrius and Moldoviţa may also reflect Serbian influence.

39 This is also the view of Lilya Berezhnaya. She discusses the debate around the issue in 'Sub Specie Mortis,' 8–10. An icon painter in the mid-1650s wrote near the serpent and tollbooths: 'This is the serpent which for the devils led Adam and Eve in paradise into sin.' This would not be a survival of the original knowledge from a century and a half earlier, but an expression of how the iconographer understood the element. The icon with this inscription is Jedlinka.

40 An imaginative alternative explanation of the tollbooths on the serpent has been proposed by Patriarch Dymytrii (Yarema). He wrote that reports of near-death experiences recorded by physicians mention 'a terrible, dark corridor, or tube (the body of the serpent)' that souls passed through. 'Clearly, our ancestors also knew about the "corridor-tube" ...' Dymytrii, *Ikonopys Zakhidnoi Ukrainy*, 247. Also imaginative is V.K. Tsodikovich's attempt to demonstrate that the tollbooth rings on the serpent have a pre-Christian origin. Tsodikovich, *Semantika ikonografii 'Strashnogo Suda.'*

41 'De exitu animi.'

42 Vilinskii, *Zhitie sv. Vasiliia Novago.* A popular condensation of the Life is Antonii, *Sud za grobom.* A brief summary of the Life can be found in Appendix 3 of this book. On the tollbooths in the Life of St Basil the New, see also Every, 'Toll Gates on the Air Way.'

43 Vilinskii, *Zhitie sv. Vasiliia Novago*, 1:304–12. Podskalsky, *Christentum*, 102–3. There is an old, but still useful survey of the eschatological literature of old Rus': Sakharov, *Eskhatologicheskiia sochineniia i skazaniia.*

44 Vilinskii, *Zhitie sv. Vasiliia Novago*, 1:269–70.

45 Pokrovskii, 'Strashnyi sud v pamiatnikakh vizantiiskago i russkago iskusstva.' Goldfrank, 'Who Put the Snake on the Icon and the Tollbooths on the Snake?'

46 Brenk, *Tradition und Neuerung*, 193.

47 *The Hagiography of Kievan Rus'*, 143–4.

48 *Der Serbische Psalter. Fakismile*, folio 1v.

49 Himka, 'On the Left Hand of God,' 328.

50 Vilinskii, *Zhitie sv. Vasiliia Novago*, 1:43–5, 52–3 n. 4.

51 The translation here is from the Slavonic.

52 Vilinskii, *Zhitie sv. Vasiliia Novago*, 1:50.

53 Revel-Neher, *The Image of the Jew in Byzantine Art*, 80–1, states that Jews did not appear in Byzantine Last Judgments at all. Both Miltos Garidis and Eva Haustein-Bartsch write that the first appearance of the Jews in Last

Judgment iconography dates to the twelfth-century Mount Sinai icon that we examined above. Garidis, 'La représentation des "nations,"' 86. Haustein-Bartsch, *Das Jüngste Gericht*, 12. As we have seen above, n. 15, the five figures on the left-hand side are clearly identified as condemned sinners, but not specifically as Jews. Garidis and Haustein-Bartsch apparently based their opinion on the costumes. Sirarpie Der Nersessian makes a similar judgment with regard to the Last Judgment fresco in the Chora monastery of the fourteenth century. The fresco contains a 'group of old men above the lake of fire' who 'wear long mantles and scarfs [*sic*] that cover their heads and shoulders.' The costumes and a comparison with other images indicate, in his opinion, that these figures are Jews. Der Nersessian, 'Program and Iconography,' 328–9. See the reproduction: Underwood, *The Kariye Djami*, 3:390. The inscription again only identifies them as condemned sinners.

54 See above, n. 37.

55 *Kievskaia psaltir'*, fol. 180.

56 Sarab'ianov, '"Strashnyi Sud" v rospisiakh sobora Snetogorskogo monastyria,' 23–5.

57 Pokrovskii, 'Strashnyi sud v pamiatnikakh vizantiiskago i russkago iskusstva,' 314–15.

58 Garidis, 'La représentation des "nations,"' 86–8. A.N. Grabar, 'Ikonograficheskaia skhema piatidesiatnitsy,' 223–6, 232.

59 Lukov-Venecia also has the same peoples as Vanivka and Polana, but without Moses. I do not think, however, that this is additional testimony to the existence of the peoples as a separate element. This icon is clearly modelled on Vanivka, but it is a less competent piece of artistry which was unable to maintain Vanivka's proportions; the painter of Lukov-Venecia simply ran out of room for Moses. Hypothetically, both it and Vanivka could have been copied from an even earlier icon that lacked Moses and only depicted the peoples, but the placement of clearly labelled Jews as first in the troupe strongly suggests that this was modelled on an icon with the full complement of Moses, Jews, and other peoples.

60 Skrobucha, 'Zur Ikonographie des "Jüngsten Gerichts,"' 58.

61 See the comparisons in Himka, 'On the Left Hand of God,' 322–6.

62 Jarosław Giemza told me on 20 June 2000 that he visited the conservation site and saw 'the condemned peoples.'

63 Różycka-Bryzek, 'Bizantyńsko-ruskie malowidła ścienne w kaplicy Swiętokrzyskiej,' 182, 220.

64 Sarab'ianov, '"Strashnyi Sud" v rospisiakh sobora Snetogorskogo monastyria,' 25.

65 Haustein-Bartsch, *Das Jüngste Gericht*, 12, 14, pl. 17.

66 Podskalsky, *Byzantinische Reichseschatologie.* Nersesian, 'Videnie proroka Daniila.'

67 I consulted an example contained in a mid-sixteenth-century West Ukrainian miscellany, which identified the first beast as the Persian kingdom, the second as the Macedonian, the third as the Babylonian, and the fourth as the Roman. L'vivs'ka naukova biblioteka im. V. Stefanyka [LNB], Viddil rukopysiv, f. 77, op. 1, spr. 138, 45v–6, 167–71v.

68 Nersesian, 'Videnie proroka Daniila.' Sarab'ianov, '"Strashnyi Sud" v rospisiakh sobora Snetogorskogo monastyria,' 25–7. Briusova, *Andrei Rublev,* pl. 99.

69 Haustein-Bartsch, *Das Jüngste Gericht,* 14, pl. 18.

70 I thank Mother Sophia Senyk for pointing me in this direction.

71 'Nyni v nebesnykh obytelekh zhyvete veseliashcheshia, idizhe lykuiut' anhely.'

72 'Anhelov dostyhoste chyny.'

73 There is an English translation in Zenkovsky, *Medieval Russia's Epics, Chronicles, and Tales,* 153–60.

74 Franko, 'K istorii iuzhno-russkikh apokrificheskikh skazanii,' 427.

75 Franko, *Apokrify eskhatolohichni,* 151.

76 Mil'kov, *Drevnerusskie apokrify,* 613.

77 Nersesian, 'Voznesenie monakhov i padenie angelov.' For passages that appear to support this view, see Kazakova and Lur'ie, *Antifeodal'nye ereticheskie dvizheniia,* 319, 400. I am grateful to one of the anonymous reviewers for the latter reference.

Heinz Skrobucha connects the ascent of the monks with a vision of John Colobus on the basis of an inscription on the Recklinghausen icon from the second half of the seventeenth century. The main problem with this is that knowledge about iconographic elements declined over time; it did not improve. The monks flying into paradise made their appearance in the fifteenth century. The inscription linking it to the vision came two hundred years later. There is also a problem with dating: the earliest known Rus' version of the Colobus vision seems to come after the first appearance of the element in both Carpathian and northern Rus' icons. Furthermore, the Colobus vision has the monks with fiery wings specifically flying into the upper Jerusalem, and this is what is depicted on the Recklinghausen icon; but in the fifteenth-century icons, the monks fly into paradise with ordinary wings. I suggest that the text of the Colobus vision subsequently influenced and modified the image in Russian iconography of the Last Judgment, giving the monks red (fiery) wings and directing them to the heavenly Jerusalem on the top right rather than to paradise on the bottom right.

Skrobucha, 'Zur Ikonographie des "Jüngsten Gerichts,"' 59. See also Haustein-Bartsch, *Das Jüngste Gericht,* 38, 48, pl. 2.

78 Nersesian somehow overlooked Novgorod-Tretiakov (and the Carpathian icons) when he dated the appearance of the ascension of the monks to the middle of the sixteenth century. Perhaps he discounted it because the monks were flying into paradise, not into the heavenly Jerusalem. Nersesian, 'Voznesenie monakhov i padenie angelov,' 262.

79 Alekseev, '"Slovo o iskhode dushi" Kirilla Filosofa,' 15. LNB, Viddil rukopysiv, f. 77, op. 1, spr. 210, 35.

80 Stichel, *Studien zum Verhältnis von Text und Bild,* 17–48.

81 Kłosińska, *Ikony,* 161. Berezhnaya, 'Sub Specie Mortis,' 23, 23 n. 62 (references to possible prototypes in Polish art).

82 Stichel, *Studien zum Verhältnis von Text und Bild,* 19.

83 Smotryts'kyi, *The* Jevanhelije učitelnoje, fols 21v–2.

84 Berezhnaya, 'Sub Specie Mortis,' 24–5.

85 See those in Tiushka, Roztoka, and the Museum of the History of Religion. The first two of these icons definitely come from the Ukrainian-inhabited northern part of Máramaros/Maramureş. The provenance of the third is not documented, but details of the iconography convince me it is from the same region as the others.

86 LNB, Viddil rukopysiv, f. 77, op. 1, spr. 1: a sixteenth-century *Izmarahd* (it was being restored and I was unable to consult it); spr. 69, fol. 56–56v: a sixteenth-century *Zbornyk* composed of extracts from the *Izmarahd* and teachings of the Fathers; spr. 27, fols 497v–8v: a sixteenth-century *Proloh.* An early seventeeth-century Russian *Izmaragd* contains the tale as well and is available on the internet: 'Slaviansie rukopisy' (joint project of Russian State Library and St Sergius Trinity Monastery) http://www.stsl.ru/manuscripts/medium.php?col=1&manuscript=202 (accessed 11 November 2007). See the excellent treatment of the almsgiving fornicator in Berezhnaya, 'Sub Specie Mortis,' 17–20. She deals well with an erroneous interpretation advanced by Paslavs'kyi, 'Uiavlennia pro potoibichnyi svit.'

87 I am grateful to Spencer Young for calling my attention to this fact.

88 Mil'kov, *Drevnerusskie apokrify,* 589–90. Franko, *Apokrify eskhatolohichni,* 136, 146 (here in addition to slanderers are informers [*iabednyky*]).

89 Mil'kov, *Drevnerusskie apokrify,* 613. Franko, *Apokrify eskhatolohichni,* 138.

90 Mil'kov, *Drevnerusskie apokrify,* 591.

91 The inscription is partly illegible, but a cannibal probably appeared in the new hell in Dolyna, an icon from the 1560s.

92 Le Goff, *The Birth of Purgatory,* 36–7.

93 Garidis, *Études sur le Jugement dernier post-Byzantin,* 86–114.

94 Mijović, *Dečani,* 39, 41.
95 Brenk, *Tradition und Neuerung,* 81.
96 Garidis, *Études sur le Jugement dernier post-Byzantin,* pl. X.19.
97 Orosz, 'Gotycka polichromia,' 180.
98 Kliś, *Paruzja,* 234.
99 Orosz, 'Gotycka polichromia,' 176, 178.
100 Kłosińska, *Ikony,* 156.
101 In this I disagree with Patriarch Dymytrii (Yarema), who thought the Novgorod Last Judgments were no older than the Ukrainian ones. Dymytrii, *Ikonopys Zakhidnoi Ukrainy,* 257.
102 I am grateful to one of the anonymous reviewers for turning my attention to the significance of these differences.
103 Vilinskii, *Zhitie sv. Vasiliia Novago,* 1:233–4. A Life of St Basil the New, however, is in an early sixteenth-century miscellany of the former Library of the Zamoyski Ordination, now in the National Library in Warsaw. Zema, 'Eskhatolohichni motyvy,' 4.
104 Biskupski, *Król Chwały,* 7, 10–13. It is one of the failings of Mariia Helytovych's in many other ways exemplary catalogue of these icons in the National Museum in Lviv that she skirts entirely the issue of their connection with the iconography of northern Rus'. *Ukrains'ki ikony 'Spas u Slavi,'* 4. There is an English translation of the relevant passage in the book's summary: 'The appearance of "The Saviour in Glory" in Ukrainian iconography in the formative stages can be traced to the painting of the Church of The Holy Trinity in Lublin, Poland in 1415. It is more problematic to propose that this theme was brought in from Russia, after being presented by Theofan the Greek and developed by Andrei Rublev. In Ukrainian iconography it may have had a separate development.' No reason is advanced why this is 'more problematic.' Ibid., 24. Moreover, it is likely that the frescoes in Lublin were painted by iconographers from northern Rus'. Różycka-Bryzek, *Bizantyńsko-ruskic malowidła w kaplicy zamku lubelskiego.*
105 Gronek, *Ikony Męki Pańskiej,* 134–5, 138, 144.
106 Patriarch Dymytrii (Yarema) felt that there must have been an icon bridging the Novgorod and Galician Last Judgments, namely the Kyivan Last Judgment. He suggested that the Solvichegod Last Judgment was perhaps the work of Kyivan masters. But a comparison it with the Recklinghausen icon shows clearly that it is in the Russian tradition. Dymytrii, *Ikonopys Zakhidnoi Ukrainy,* 257–60. Haustein-Bartsch, *Das Jüngste Gericht.*
107 Inkin, *Sil'sk'e suspil'stvo Halyts'koho Prykarpattia,* 7, 12, 14.
108 Różycka-Bryzek, 'Bizantyńsko-ruskie malowidła ścienne w kaplicy Świętokrzyskiej.'

109 Rogov, 'Iz istorii kul'turnykh sviazei Galitsii i Moldavii,' 250–2.

110 Ibid., 235.

111 Information from Mariia Helytovych, 13 June 2005. She is the head of the department of old Ukrainian art at the National Museum and a native of Lavriv. She also sees a resemblance between inscriptions on the Lavriv frescoes and inscriptions on the icons of Master Oleksii, one of whose icons has been firmly dated to 1547. Helytovych, 'Datovani ikony,' 56.

112 Rogov, 'Iz istorii kul'turnykh sviazei Galitsii i Moldavii.'

113 Dvořáková et al., *Středkověká nástěnná malba na Slovensku*, 147–8.

114 Svinica was a village 'with significant Carpatho-Rusyn settlement' in 1806. Magocsi, *Carpatho-Rusyn Settlement.*

115 Inkin, *Sil'sk'e suspil'stvo Halyts'koho Prykarpattia*, 25–6.

116 Patterson, *Wooden Churches of the Carpathians*, 116.

117 Unfortunately, I omitted to record her name. This was during my visits on 22–3 June 2005.

118 Information from 13 June 2005.

119 Gronek, *Ikony Męki Pańskiej*, 37–8.

120 An agrotechnical crisis that began in the mid-seventeenth century hurt both the peasants and the landlords' *folwarks*. The size of peasant holdings declined over the course of the sixteenth through eighteenth centuries. Inkin, *Sil'sk'e suspil'stvo Halyts'koho Prykarpattia*, 35.

121 Miliaieva, *Stinopys Potelycha*, 125. For an account of how icon painters prepared the wood, see the appendix 'The Painting of Icons' by Richard Temple in Baggley, *Doors of Perception*, 102–3.

122 Grabar, *Die Freskomalerei der Dimitrij Kathedrale in Wladimir*, 32.

123 It graces the cover of Czajkowski et al., *Ikona karpacka.* Its technique is discussed in Grządziela, 'Twórczość malarza ikon z Żohatyna,' 61.

124 See also above n. 59.

125 Gronek, *Ikony Męki Pańskiej*, 163.

126 Senyk, *Women's Monasteries*, 55.

127 Krypiakevych, 'Serednevichni monastyri v Halychyni,' 70, 74–5, 96–101; there is a map on p. 105, but I have not been able to read it from the microfiche copy to which I had access.

128 Slobodian, *Tserkvy Ukrainy. Peremys'ka ieparkhiia*, 127. Vavryk, *Narys rozvytku i stanu Vasyliians'koho chyna*, 192, also dates the monastery to 1613. The Dobromyl monastery is not included in Krypiakevych's list of monasteries through the fifteenth century. Oleh Sydor has suggested that about thirty icons in the vicinity were produced by monks from Dobromyl, the so-called Master of Poliana and his school. The chronology does not work well, however, since Sydor has in mind icons of the fifteenth and sixteenth

century. See his introduction to Sydor and Lozynskyi, *Ukrainian Icons 13th–18th Centuries*, 17.

129 Shved, *Spas'kyi ta Lavrivs'kyi monastyri.*

130 Senyk, 'Ruthenian Monasticism in Decline: 1300–1600.'

131 Information from Yuriy Zazuliak, 4 August 2006.

132 Şandru and Viţega, *Made by Man, Created by God.*

133 *Encyclopedia of Rusyn History and Culture*, s.v. 'Hrushovo Monastery of St. Michael the Archangel' by Ivan Pop. Völkl, *Das rumänische Fürstentum Moldau und die Ostslaven*, 43.

134 Rusu et al. *Dicţionarul mănăstirilor*, 64.

135 Völkl, *Das rumänische Fürstentum Moldau und die Ostslaven*, 13–26.

136 Pereswetoff-Morath, *'Whereby We Know That It Is the Last Time,'* 80.

137 Völkl, *Das rumänische Fürstentum Moldau und die Ostslaven*, 91, 105.

138 In 1623 bishop and archimandrite Meletii Smotrytsky travelled from Vilnius to Constantinople and the Holy Land. 'He seems to have followed the normal route through Moldavia and onto the Black Sea at the mouth of the Danube, thence toward Bosporus and Constantinople.' He returned to Eastern Europe in 1625, but not to Vilnius. Instead, by 1627 he could be found in Derman Monastery in Volhynia. David Frick, 'Introduction,' Smotryts'kyi, *Rus' Restored*, l (quote), liii.

139 Senyk, 'Ruthenian Monasticism in Decline: 1300–1600,' 107.

140 'The royal mandate, issued by the king Sigismund I on April 2, 1511, ordered the Lviv Catholic archbishop to keep watch on *popones ritus Ruthenici*, who often traveled to Moldavia and were suspected by Poles of being Moldavian spies. (See: Corpus iuris Polonici, vol. 3, #71, datum Cracoviae, 2 Aprilis, a. 1511, p. 160.)' Personal communication from Yuriy Zazuliak, 4 August 2006.

141 Völkl, *Das rumänische Fürstentum Moldau und die Ostslaven*, 54–6.

142 A certain deacon Mihail 'was of Ukrainian origin (*Rusac*) and lived at Suceava' in the sixteenth century, perhaps at the archbishop's palace. Turdeanu, 'Centres of Literary Activity in Moldavia,' 116.

143 Völkl, *Das rumänische Fürstentum Moldau und die Ostslaven*, 45–6.

144 Turdeanu, 'Centres of Literary Activity in Moldavia,' 102.

145 'Under 6852 [1344] PSRL 15/1, 2nd ed., writes about Greek artists of metropolitan Theognost painting a church in Moscow. Theognost, like all the metropolitans of this period, although their principal residence was Moscow, actually moved around quite a bit, and Theognost spent a long period in Volyn' in particular. The Greek artists that he brought with him when he was named to Rus' weren't engaged the whole time in Moscow; they must have found commissions elsewhere in Rus' and also have had

native apprentices.' Letter from Mother Sophia Senyk to the author, 13 November 2001.

146 Różycka-Bryzek, 'Bizantyńsko-ruskie malowidła ścienne w kaplicy Swiętokrzyskiej,' 175.

147 Różycka-Bryzek, *Bizantyńsko-ruskie malowidła w kaplicy zamku lubelskiego.*

148 All the many inscriptions are in Greek.

149 Helytovych, 'Datovani ikony,' 53, 56. For further evidence of Moldavian connections with Ukrainan sacral art, see Petrov, 'Rumynskie khudozhestvennye pamiatniki.'

3. Further Elaboration

1 Sydor, 'Reiestr ikon Strashnoho Sudu v kolektsii NML,' no. 13. The village was called Dovhe and it was in the Drohobych region, but there are two villages that match those specifications, so I was unable to map it.

2 There is also a Torky near Przemyśl, closer to other sites of Last Judgment icons. I cannot help but wonder if an error has crept into Sydor, 'Reiestr ikon Strashnoho Sudu v kolektsii NML,' no. 25, upon whose information I have relied to situate the provenance of the Torky icon.

3 Giemza, 'Ikony XVI i XVII wieku,' 25.

4 Radwan, *Wizytacje generalne.*

5 For a vision of how the visitation records can expand historical knowledge, see Skochylias, *Heneral'ni vizytatsii*, xv–xxx.

6 Chlenova et al., *Shedevry ukrains'koho ikonopysu*, no. 30.

7 Haustein-Bartsch, *Ikonen*, 37–41.

8 Information from Halyna Hol'chuk, 11 June 1998. The catalogue of the Lutsk collection, Kot et al., *Volyns'ka ikona*, has no Last Judgment icon. There is a seventeenth-century Last Judgment icon in Volhynia, however, at the cemetery chapel in Ostroh. *Istoriia ukrains'koho mystetstva*, 2:286. I am not sure whether it is painted on wood or canvas.

9 *Ikony ta suchasne ukrains'ke mystetstvo.*

10 Konstantynovych, *Opisanie ikon.*

11 Helytovych, who has not to my knowledge ever mapped the surviving icons, nonetheless sees stylistic similarities among the icons of the Staryi Sambir (Mshanets-Poliana-Lavriv-Spas), Drohobych, and Dolyna regions. Helytovych, 'Datovani ikony,' 58.

12 Shepherds from the Sambir region and from Transcarpathia took their sheep to the same hills. Occasionally their interests clashed. Inkin, *Sil'sk'e suspil'stvo Halyts'koho Prykarpattia*, 26.

13 *Encyclopedia of Ukraine*, s.v. 'Krasný Brod [*sic*].'

14 Helytovych, '"Strashnyi sud" seredyny XVI st. peremyshl's'koho maliara Oleksiia Horoshkovycha.' I am not certain about this attribution, but I defer to Mariia Helytovych's judgment here. I do not accept as proven, however, the identification of this Oleksii with Oleksii Horoshkovych, a member of the Przemyśl goldsmith guild. The identification was originally proposed by Volodymyr Aleksandrovych. See Aleksandrovych, 'Ukrains'ke maliarstvo v Peremyshli,' 45, and Aleksandrovych, *Zakhidnoukrains'ki maliari XVI stolittia*, 64–70. Sydor, 'Ikony maistriv Oleksiia i Dymytriia,' 90, explains why this identification is problematic.

15 Sydor, 'Ikony maistriv Oleksiia i Dymytriia,' 99–116.

16 See above, p. 255 n111.

17 Sydor, 'Ikony maistriv Oleksiia i Dymytriia,' 91–5.

18 Information from Romuald Biskupski, 3 June 2000.

19 Otkovych, *Narodna techiia*, 43–4.

20 According to Jarosław Giemza, the curator of the icon collection in which Bartne is held, there was a bottom half to this icon, but it was taken by the Germans during the Second World War. Letter to the author, 6 April 2007. I would need to see the evidence before I could change my opinion on this matter.

21 Gronek, *Ikony Męki Pańskiej*, 215.

22 See the inflated view in Otkovych, *Narodna techiia*, 48–74. This account needs to be balanced by Aleksandrovych, 'Rybotycki ośrodek malarski.'

23 Puskás, 'Aktual'ni problemy vyvchennia davn'oho ikonopysu,' 73.

24 Gronek, *Ikony Męki Pańskiej*, 221.

25 Otkovych, *Narodna techiia*, 55.

26 Gronek, 'Ikona Męki Pańskiej z Lipia,' 29, 33. Gronek, *Ikony Męki Pańskiej*, 203.

27 Biskupski, 'Sztuka kościoła prawosławnego i unickiego,' 356.

28 Helytovych, 'Datovani ikony,' 53. Helytovych, 'Zakhidnoukrains'ki ta volyns'ki ikony XVI st. z vkladnymy tekstamy,' 34–5.

29 See also below, p. 152.

30 Biskupski, 'Sztuka kościoła prawosławnego i unickiego,' 356–7.

31 Patterson, *Wooden Churches of the Carpathians*, 116.

32 Aleksandrovych, 'Ukrains'ke maliarstvo v Peremyshli.'

33 *Istoriia ukrains'koho mystetstva*, 3:198–204.

34 Ibid., 2: 244. I was forced to the conclusion of the extinction of traditional icon painting in Lviv after looking up the references to Lviv in the index to vols 2 and 3 of *Istoriia ukrains'koho mystetstva.*

35 Such was the case in Maramureş. Patterson, *Wooden Churches of the Carpathians*, 45.

36 Cited in Gronek, 'Duchowieństwo wschodnie,' 85.

37 Bartrum, *German Renaissance Prints*, 9.

38 For example: Sydor, 'Ikona Strashnoho Sudu z Vil'shanytsi'; Kłosińska, 'Dwie ikony Sądu Ostatecznego'; Škoviera, 'Ikona Strašného súdu a jej text(y)'; Himka, 'The Icon of the Last Judgment in the Village of Roztoka.'

39 I am grateful to Mother Sophia Senyk for pointing out the scriptural source to me. The verse reads somewhat differently in the King James Bible: 'The memory of the just is blessed.'

40 Sydor, 'Ikona Strashnoho Sudu z Vil'shanytsi,' 88.

41 The heavenly Jerusalem can be found in Vilshanytsia, Lukov-Venecia, Zhovkva, Bahnovate, Dolyna, Drohobych-Elevation, Vovche, Krásny Brod, Radelychi, Kamianka Strumylova (?), Przemyśl Land Museum, Korytniki, and Wola Wyżna. The fall of the rebel angels can be found in Vilshanytsia, Lukov-Venecia, Bahnovate, Dolyna, Vovche, Klitsko, Krásny Brod, Radelychi, Kamianka Strumylova (?), Powroźnik, and Przemyśl Land Museum. Daniel can be found in Lukov-Venecia, Bahnovate, Krásny Brod, Mala Horozhanka, and Przemyśl Land Museum. The four evil beasts/kingdoms can be found in Vilshanytsia, Lukov-Venecia, Bahnovate, Krásny Brod, Paszowa, Radelychi, and Przemyśl Region. Monks flying into paradise can be found in Vilshanytsia, Drohobych-Elevation, Kamianka Strumylova, Krásny Brod, Mala Horozhanka, Przemyśl Land Museum, Korytniki, and Wola Wyżna.

42 The heavenly Jerusalem can be found in Drohobych-National Museum, Tiushka, and Moldavsko. The fall of the rebel angels can be found in Volosianka, Tiushka, and Moldavsko. Daniel can be found only in Roztoka. The four evil beasts/kingdoms can be found only in Moldavsko. Monks flying into paradise can be found only in Tiushka.

43 Tkáč, *Ikony*, 240, 242.

44 Lukov-Venecia, Paszowa, Vovche, Krásny Brod, Mala Horozhanka, Powroźnik, Przemyśl Region, and Przemyśl Land Museum.

45 Jedlinka, Wola Wyżna, and Volosianka.

46 Sydor, 'Ikona Strashnoho Sudu z Vil'shanytsi,' 82.

47 Vilshanytsia, Bahnovate, Ruská Bystrá, Stanylia, Radelychi, Trushevychi, and Hankowice.

48 Bogliarka, Lipie, Drohobych-National Museum, Shelestovo, Świątkowa Mała, Moldavsko, Bartne, Nehrovets, and Torky.

49 Lilya Berezhnaya suggests that both the booth and the zigzag form of the tollbooths were derived from the iconography of the ladder of John Climacus, but I fail to see the resemblance. Berezhnaya, 'Sub Specie Mortis,' 11–13.

50 Dolyna.

51 Tiushka, Roztoka, Skole, and Museum of the History of Religion.

52 Plavie, Izky, Nová Sedlica, Nieznajowa/Rozstajne, Świątkowa Wielka, Brzegi, Galicia-City Museum 1, and Galicia-City Museum 2.

53 That the peoples were enveloped by the river of fire did not actually signify that they were condemned; many texts testify to this. From one of the stichera for the vespers preceding Meatfare Sunday we read: 'The terrifying fiery river before your seat of judgment carries all' (vlechet vsikh). Cyril the Philosopher, in his 'Sermon on the Exit of the Soul,' wrote that the river of fire will go through the entire world of mankind (vsemu myru chelovicheskomu proity), through the entire human race (vsemu rodu chelovicheskomu proity). Sinners will be burned, but the righteous will feel coolness, not fire; the fire will clean and illumine them. Alekseev, '"Slovo o iskhode dushi" Kirilla Filosofa,' 18. 'Slovo sviatoho ottsa nasheho Kyrylla o iskhodi dushi,' LNB, f. 77, op. 1., spr. 210, 40. A West Ukrainian sermon from about 1600 also stated that 'the entire human people' (vshytkomu narodu chelovicheskomu) will feel the fire of the river. 'Pryslukhaizhesia pylno,' Biblioteka Narodowa (Warsaw), Akc. 2930 and 2584, microfilms 15620 and 14281, 28.

54 Carpathian icons in which the Orthodox are omitted are Dolyna, Stanylia, Przemyśl Land Museum, Hankowice, Bogliarka, Lipie, Tiushka, Shelestovo, and Skoryky.

55 Perhaps an icon from 1737, Nieznajowa/Rozstajne, also has its peoples in order of religion, but I am not sure. As I have deciphered the inscriptions, the peoples portrayed there are [Jews], Greeks, Rus', Serbs, Turks, Arabs, Muntenians (?), and Kalmyks (?). Perhaps what I am reading as Muntenians actually said Ishmaelites, which would then make the order fit religion. This icon was surely produced by a craftsman.

56 An icon with sixteenth-century lettering, once held by the Stauropegial Institute in Lviv but now lost, was reported to have portrayed Lutherans among the peoples. Svientsits'kyi, *Opis' muzeia Stavropigiiskago Instituta*, 185, no. 130.

57 Museum of the History of Religion.

58 Moldavsko and Bartne.

59 Roztoka and Museum of the History of Religion.

60 Świątkowa Mała, Bartne, and Skoryky.

61 Moldavsko, Nieznajowa/Rozstajne (probably), and Bartne.

62 'Mohylevs'ka khronika T.R. Surty i Iu. Trubnyts'koho,' chastyna 3, 'Lytovs'ko-bilorus'ki litopysy (PSRL t. XXXII; t. XXXV)' http://izbornyk.narod.ru/psrl3235/lytov30.htm (accessed 11 November 2007).

63 Vilshanytsia, Dolyna, Stanylia, Przemyśl Land Museum, Mala Horozhanka, Bogliarka, Plavie, Roztoka, Tiushka, Moldavsko, and Nieznajowa/Rozstajne.

64 Bahnovate, Bogliarka, Volosianka, Museum of the History of Religion (probably), Świątkowa Mała, and Bartne.
65 Vilshanytsia, Paszowa, Vovche, Stanylia, Przemyśl Land Museum, and Volosianka.
66 Kamianka Strumylova, Volosianka (probably), Tiushka, and Bartne. Also on the lost Stauropegial icon; see above, note 56.
67 Kamianka Strumylova and Roztoka.
68 Vilshanytsia. Also on the lost Stauropegial icon; see above, note 56.
69 Volosianka and Nieznajowa/Rozstajne (probably).
70 Vilshanytsia (Sydor here reads Bulgarians), Bahnovate, Volosianka, and Bartne. Sydor, 'Ikona Strashnoho Sudu z Vil'shanytsi,' 80.
71 Moldavsko, Nieznajowa/Rozstajne, and Bartne.
72 Volosianka.
73 Museum of the History of Religion. The restorer Yurii Ostrovsky told me on 13 December 2001 that he now reads the inscription *kozaky* as *kazakhy*. I think the original reading is the correct one.
74 Świątkowa Mała.
75 Bahnovate and Wola Wyżna (perhaps Vlachs).
76 On the lost Stauropegial icon; see above, note 56.
77 All these readings are from Sydor, 'Ikona Strashnoho Sudu z Vil'shanytsi,' 88. I had no access to Trushevychi and could not read any of the inscriptions on Kamianka Strumylova.
78 Trushevychi.
79 Kamianka Strumylova.
80 Vilshanytsia, Ruská Bystrá, Dolyna, Mala Horozhanka, Krásny Brod, Hankowice, Jedlinka, Plavie, Wola Wyżna, Lipie, Dobroslava, Świątkowa Mała, Roztoka, Moldavsko, Shelestovo, and Nehrovets.
81 Ginzburg, *The Cheese and the Worms*, 119.
82 Ruská Bystrá (*melnyk nepravdyvyi*).
83 Dolyna, Shelestovo, and Nehrovets.
84 Dolyna and Moldavsko.
85 Dolyna.
86 Plavie, Lipie, Roztoka, and Nehrovets.
87 Roztoka.
88 Lipie.
89 Himka, '"Social" Elements,' 238.
90 Peters, 'Between Catholicism and Orthodoxy: Wall Paintings,' 333.
91 Franko, *Apokrify eskhatolohichni*, 145–8.
92 Vilshanytsia, Roztoka, and Nehrovets.
93 Poienile Izei.

94 Franko, *Apokrify eskhatolohichni*, 146.

95 Stanylia (merciless rich man), Dobroslava, Lipie (merciless rich man), and Roztoka (twice).

96 Smotryts'kyi, *The* Jevanhelije učitelnoje, 27.

97 Vovche and Dolyna.

98 Moldavsko, Shelestovo, and Nehrovets.

99 Roztoka.

100 Franko, *Apokrify eskhatolohichni*, 149.

101 Ephraem Syrus, *Tvoreniia*, 225.

102 Inkin, *Sil'sk'e suspil'stvo Halyts'koho Prykarpattia*, 40.

103 Sorceresses: Vilshanytsia, Ruská Bystrá, Dolyna, Krásny Brod, Bogliarka, and Plavie (also holding a vessel for mixing potions). Infanticides: Przemyśl Region, Lipie, and Moldavsko.

104 Jedlinka (twice), Bogliarka, Wola Wyżna (the inscription reads 'vipers suck the childless woman'), Roztoka, Moldavsko, and Shelestovo. A childless woman also has her breasts attacked in the mural in Rogoz in Romanian Maramureş.

105 Dobroslava.

106 Roztoka. On the misunderstanding of the almsgiving fornicator, see Himka, 'The Icon of the Last Judgment in the Village of Roztoka,' 368.

107 Nehrovets.

108 Vilshanytsia and Ruská Bystrá.

109 Plavie, Roztoka, Shelestovo, and Nehrovets (in the latter two icons the couple seem to share one tongue and the depiction is almost identical).

110 Mil'kov, *Drevnerusskie apokrify*, 613. Franko, *Apokrify eskhatolohichni*, 138.

111 Medwidsky, 'Cantors and Godparents in Ukrainian Folkore,' 118–19.

112 Vilshanytsia (*otchaianyk*). Sydor, 'Ikona Strashnoho Sudu z Vil'shanytsi,' 81.

113 Nehrovets.

114 Jedlinka and Moldavsko.

115 Roztoka.

116 (*Svarlyvyi*) Przemyśl Land Museum.

117 Roztoka.

118 Roztoka.

119 Bahnovate, Dolyna, Vovche, Kamianka Strumylova, Trushevychi, Krásny Brod, Przemyśl Region, Jedlinka, Bogliarka, Dobroslava, Plavie, Lipie, Roztoka, Nová Sedlica, Museum of the History of Religion, Máramaros-Néprajzi, Moldavsko, and Skole.

120 Trushevychi, Lipie, and Bogliarka (here the devil's whispering is omitted, and the inscription just reads: 'the tavernmaid does not pour a full measure').

Berezhnaya, 'Sub Specie Mortis,' 27 n. 27, also mentions Przemyśl Region in this connection, but I see no such inscription on the icon.

121 Romuald Biskupski saw in Słopa Nowo (Poznań region) a Roman Catholic church that had, under the choir, a picture of a tavernmaid being pulled by a devil. The inscription read exactly as the formulas used on our icons: 'because she did not pour a full measure' (*bo nie dolewała*; Lipie: *zheby nedolyvala*, Bogliarka: *kachmarka nedolyvaie*).' Information from Romuald Biskupski, 2 June 2000.

122 Vilshanytsia, Ruská Bystrá, Dolyna (Ancient of Days only; inscription instead of depiction), Przemyśl Land Museum (Holy Spirit only), Stanylia, Mala Horozhanka, Trushevychi (Ancient of Days only), Hankowice, Przemyśl Region, Jedlinka, Moldavsko (Ancient of Days only), and Skole (Holy Spirit only).

123 Sarab'ianov, '"Strashnyi Sud" v rospisiakh sobora Snetogorskogo monastyria,' 26–7.

124 Haustein-Bartsch, *Das Jüngste Gericht*, 6, pl. 6.

125 Zlatohlávek et al., *Sąd Ostateczny*, 98.

126 Gormin and Yarosh, *Novgorod*, pl. 197. I am grateful to one of the anonymous reviewers for calling my attention to this.

127 Pătrăuţi, Probota, Humor, Suceava: St Demetrius, Moldoviţa, Arbore, Voroneţ, and Suceviţa.

128 Pătrăuţi, Probota, Humor, Voroneţ, Râşca, and Suceviţa.

129 Stichel, *Studien zum Verhältnis von Text und Bild*, 23.

130 *Kievskaia psaltir'*, 183.

131 The one exception is the icon that once belonged to George R. Hann and is now in a private collection in Munich. It is illustrated in Garidis, *Études sur le Jugement dernier post-Byzantin*, pl. XIX.38. The icon has both scenes. The reproduction in Garidis is too small to make out any inscriptions. Berezhnaya, 'Sub Specie Mortis,' refers to the scene depicted here as 'the Parable of Dives and Lazarus,' 24.

132 Vilshanytsia, Paszowa, Ruská Bystrá, Korytniki, Dolyna, Przemyśl Land Museum, Klitsko, Stanylia, Vovche, Radelychi, Bahnovate, Kamianka Strumylova, Trushevychi, Mala Horozhanka, Hankowice, Przemyśl Region, Powroźnik, Bogliarka, Volosianka, Wola Wyżna, Drohobych-National Museum, Jedlinka, Świątkowa Mała, Lipie, Tiushka, Roztoka, Moldavsko, Shelestovo, and Nehrovets.

133 Paszowa, Ruská Bystrá, Przemyśl Land Museum, Stanylia, Vovche, Mala Horozhanka, Hankowice, Przemyśl Region, Powroźnik, Wola Wyżna, Tiushka, and Shelestovo.

134 Vilshanytsia, Bahnovate, Radelychi, Dolyna, Kamianka Strumylova, Bogliarka, Volosianka, and Drohobych-National Museum.

135 This is the Septuagint reading. King James has: 'Evil shall slay the wicked' (Ps 34:21).

136 I had difficulty reading this at all. Patriarch Dymytrii (Yarema) read it as Proverbs 10:7: 'The memory of the righteous is with praises.' Dymytrii, *Ikonopys Zakhidnoi Ukrainy*, 256. This text is also on an icon of the Novgorod school. Ibid., 257.

137 Kamianka Strumylova, Mala Horozhanka, Jedlinka, Bogliarka, Volosianka, Wola Wyżna, Plavie, Lipie, Drohobych-National Museum, Świątkowa Mała, Museum of the History of Religion, Roztoka, Nová Sedlica, Máramaros-Néprajzi, Galicia-City Museum 1, Shelestovo, and Nehrovets.

138 Nehrovets.

139 Volosianka.

140 Shelestovo.

141 Inkin, *Sil'sk'e suspil'stvo Halyts'koho Prykarpattia*, 34–5, 152, 155.

142 Franko, *Apokrify eskhatolohichni*, 149.

143 Garidis, *Études sur le Jugement dernier post-Byzantin*, 109.

144 Dolyna, Kamianka Strumylova, Mala Horozhanka, Volosianka, Roztoka, Museum of the History of Religion, Tiushka, Galicia-City Museum 1, Shelestovo, Skoryky (the sinner is held upside down), and Nehrovets.

145 Roztoka and Museum of the History of Religion (two closely related icons).

146 Volosianka.

147 Roztoka.

148 Dolyna.

149 Volosianka.

150 Galicia-City Museum 1.

151 Shelestovo (probable reading).

152 Bahnovate, Jedlinka, Bogliarka, Plavie, Lipie, Drohobych-National Museum, Museum of the History of Religion, Roztoka, Nová Sedlica, and Máramaros-Néprajzi.

153 Bad confession only: Vilshanytsia, Radelychi, Przemyśl Land Museum, Wola Wyżna, Volosianka, Świątkowa Mała, Tiushka, Galicia-City Museum 1, Shelestovo, and Nehrovets. Sleeping in only: Dobroslava.

154 Alekseev, '"Slovo o iskhode dushi" Kirilla Filosofa,' 17. 'Slovo sviatoho ottsa nasheho Kyrylla o iskhodi dushi,' LNB, f. 77, op. 1., spr. 210, fol. 38–8v.

155 Cuhea. Pop-Bratu, *Pictura murală maramureşeană*, 55.

156 Mil'kov, *Drevnerusskie apokrify*, 589.

157 Garidis, *Études sur le Jugement dernier post-Byzantin*, 89.

158 Poienile Izei and Cuhea. Source for the latter: Pop-Bratu, *Pictura murală maramureşeană*, 55.

159 A list of preserved manuscripts can be found in Lebedeva, *Povest' o Varlaame i Ioasafe*, 294–5.

160 John Damascene, *Barlaam and Ioasaph*, 187, 189, 191. See also Lebedeva, *Povest' o Varlaame i Ioasafe*, 160–1.

161 I could not read it. Neither could Mariia Helytovych. None of the literature on this icon attempts it either.

162 Skrobucha, 'Zur Ikonographie des "Jüngsten Gerichts,"' 70–1.

163 Ibid., 70.

164 Réau, *Iconographie de l'art chrétien*, 2:747–8.

165 Goar, *Euchologion sive rituale graecorum*, 429. *Evkholohion abo Trebnyk Mytropolyta Petra Mohyly*, 629. I am grateful to Ihor Ševčenko, Jack Kollman, Tom Dykstra, and William Ryan for helping me to decipher this element.

166 *Der Serbische Psalter. Faksimile*, folio 2. *Textband*, 188–9.

167 Stichel, *Studien zum Verhältnis von Text und Bild*, 114–15.

4. Disintegration

1 Sydor, 'Reiestr ikon Strashnoho Sudu v kolektsii NML,' no. 27 (Trostianets), no. 28 (again Trostianets), and no. 30 (Skoryky).

2 Inkin, *Sil's'ke suspil'stvo Halyts'koho Prykarpattia*, 25.

3 Dolyna, Yasinka Masova, and Sukhyi Potik.

4 Medynychi, Torky, Drohobych-National Museum, Moldavsko, Dmytriie, and Skole.

5 Mytsiuk, *Narysy z sotsiial'no hospodars'koi istorii*, 1:170–1.

6 Sydor, 'Reiestr ikon Strashnoho Sudu v kolektsii NML,' no. 32 (Volytsia Derevlianska, tempera and oil on canvas, end of seventeenth century), no. 33 (Volytsia Derevlianska, oil on canvas, eighteenth century), no. 34 (Yezupil, oil on canvas, eighteenth century), no. 35 (Popeli, oil on canvas, eighteenth century), and no. 36 (Galicia, oil on canvas, nineteenth century).

7 Radwan, *Wizytacje generalne*: 'By the left [wall], an image of God [as] the terrible Judge, showing the last day of his judgment, also painted on canvas.' Kutiużyńce, 1791 (721). Last Judgment on canvas in Pryluka (city), left wall, 1791 (833). Sopin, 1791, left wall: 'the secret of St John the Theologian, of the Apocaypse, of the terrible judgment of the Lord, painted on canvas' (850). Samhorodek, 1791, right wall: '[the image] of St John the Theologian, or the Apocalypse, on canvas' (854). Turbów, 1791, right wall: 'the image of God [as] the terrible Judge, also painted on canvas' (869). The visitors wrote in Polish, using terminology that was more Latin than Eastern.

8 Sumtsov, 'K istorii ukrainskoi ikonopisi,' 134–5.

9 See above, p. 79.

10 Letnianchyn, 'Obraz sviatoho apostola Pavla,' 168, 171.

11 Information from Myroslav Marynovych.

12 Otkovych, 'Wyposażenie cerkwi p.w. świętego Mikołaja w Dmytrowicach,' 499.

13 Information from the pastor, Father Iosyp Hnatyshyn, 26 June 2005.

14 Jarosław Giemza, who supervised the restoration of the Chotyniec mural, disagrees with this interpretation. Letter to the author, 6 April 2006.

15 Information from Jarosław Giemza, 20 June 2000. The Kozachkovsky engraving originally appeared in a volume entitled *Akafisty i kanony*. Zapasko and Isaievych, *Pam"iatky knyzhkovoho mystetstva*, no. 1863.

16 Zholtovs'kyi, *Monumental'nyi zhyvopys*, 117.

17 In addition to the Last Judgment icon on glass illustrated here, another, also from the second half of the nineteenth century, is held by the Museum of Ethnography in Lviv. It was on display in July 1997.

18 Irimie and Focşa, *Romanian Icons Painted on Glass*, pl. 66–7, 87–8, 119–21. Szacsvay, *Üvegképek*, pl. 368.

19 Vasylyna Ushak and Ivan Hrechko, 'Icons on Glass,' in Zarivna and Loza, *Ukrainian Antiquities*, 328.

20 Andriy Tsybko and Taras Lozynsky, 'Tiles,' in Zarivna and Loza, *Ukrainian Antiquities*, 333.

21 Nehrovets and Novoselytsia; Dolyna, Piilo, and Yezupil.

22 Inventory no. 15959.

23 I am grateful to Vladislav Grešlík for giving me the key to the transcription.

24 So is the cross inscription on the Kožuchovce mural, but I am unable to make out any other inscriptions from the photograph I have.

25 Radwan, *Wizytacje generalne*, 14. Skochylias, *Heneral'ni vizytatsii*, xxvii.

26 Otkovych, *Narodna techiia*, 56.

27 Ibid., 52–3.

28 Cracraft, *The Church Reform of Peter the Great*, 212. The quotation is the words of Peter's decree in the translation of James Cracraft. The decree of 1722 was very much in the tradition of earlier state and ecclesiastical legislation concerning icon painting. Cracraft, *The Petrine Revolution in Russian Imagery*, 49–57, 296.

29 Ibid., 51.

30 Chyzhevs'kyi, *Poza mezhamy krasy*, 9.

31 Wawrzeniuk, *Confessional Civilising in Ukraine*.

32 *Nauky parokhial'nyia*, foreword [unpaginated], 278, 282. Copies are in the Basilian Monastery, Warsaw, starodruky 184 and 185; also in the Lviv Historical Museum, starodruk 231.

5. Conclusions

1 Himka, 'History, Christendom and Traditional Ukrainian Culture.'
2 *The Russian Primary Chronicle*, 110. *Litopys rus'kyi*, 59–60. See also the related tale about Bulgaria, in Mango, *Art of the Byzantine Empire*, 190–1.
3 I note that Gerold Vzdornov has posited that the illuminator was of northern Rus' origin. Vzdornov, *Issledovanie o Kievskoi Psaltiri*, 20–33. But see Himka, 'What Constitutes a Ukrainian Cultural Artifact?' 231–2.
4 Himka, 'Episodes in the Historiography of the Ukrainian Icon,' 153–6.
5 Notably Skrobucha, 'Zur Ikonographie des "Jüngsten Gerichts"'; and Goldfrank, 'Who Put the Snake on the Icon and the Tollbooths on the Snake?'
6 *Istoriia ukrains'koho mystetstva*, 2:286.
7 See above, p. 182.
8 Stepovyk, *Istoriia ukrains'koi ikony*, 52–73.
9 Ibid., 10, 73.
10 Putsko, 'Ukrains'kyi ikonopys XIII – pershoi polovyny XVII st.,' 309.
11 For example, Zholtovs'kyi, *Khudozhnie zhyttia*, 50.
12 It is now held by the National Museum in Kyiv, I–13.
13 Zholtovs'kyi, *Ukrains'kyi zhyvopys XVII–XVIII st.*, 284.
14 See also Himka, 'What Constitutes a Ukrainian Cultural Artifact?' 234–5.
15 Himka, 'History, Christendom and Traditional Ukrainian Culture.'

Appendix 4

1 An old but clear and useful introduction is Katajew, *Geschichte der Predigt in der russischen Kirche.*
2 On teaching Gospels, see Chuba, 'Do problemy typolohichnoho rozriznennia Uchytel'nykh Ievanhelii.' Chuba, 'Ukrains'ki uchytel'ni Ievanheliia.' Korzo, *Obraz cheloveka v propovedi XVII veka.* Korzo, 'Rukopisnye uchitel'nye evangeliia.'
3 Smotryts'kyi, *The* Jevanhelije učitelnoje. References in the text are to this edition.
4 Biblioteka Narodowa (Warsaw): Akc. 2797, pp. 5v–10v (early seventeenth century); Akc. 2795 mf. 15405, pp. 30–7v (1665–66). LNB, manuscript division: f. 77, spr. 30, pp. 3–9 (sixteenth century); f. 2, spr. 31 (first half of seventeenth century), pp. 8v–14v; f. 1, spr. 465, pp. 20v–6v (early seventeenth century).
5 Kharlampovich, *Malorossiiskoe vlianie*, 108–9.

6 Lviv Historical Museum, starodruk 215; Basilian Monastery in Warsaw, starodruk 1.
7 Radyvylovskii, *Vinets Khrystov.* I used the copy in the Historical Museum in Sanok, 9207.
8 See above, p. 191.

Bibliography

Aleksandrovych, Volodymyr [Wołodymyr Ałeksandrowycz]. 'Rybotycki ośrodek malarski w drugiej połowie XVII wieku.' In *Polska-Ukraina: 1000 lat sąsiedztwa.* Vol. 2, *Studia z dziejów chrześcijaństwa na pograniczu kulturowym i etnicznym*, ed. Stanisław Stępień, 341–50. Przemyśl: Południowo-Wschodni Instytut Naukowy w Przemyślu, 1994.

– 'Ukrains'ke maliarstvo v Peremyshli XIII – pochatku XVIII st.: Holovni problemy istorii.' In *Peremyshl' i peremys'ka zemlia protiahom vikiv: Zbirnyk naukovykh prats' i materialiv Mizhnarodnoi naukovoi konferentsii, orhanizovanoi Naukovym tovarystvom imeni T. Shevchenka v Pol'shchi 24–25 chervnia 1994 roku v Peremyshli*, ed. Stepan Zabrovarnyi, 38-52. Przemyśl and Lviv: NTSh v Pol'shchi, Vydavnycha rada v Peremyshli, 1996.

– *Zakhidnoukrains'ki maliari XVI stolittia. Shliakhy rozvytku profesiinoho seredovyshcha.* Lviv: Instytut ukrainoznavstva im. I. Kryp"iakevycha NAN Ukrainy, 2000.

Alekseev, A.I. '"Slovo o iskhode dushi" Kirilla Filosofa.' In *Opyty po istochnikovedeniiu: Drevenerusskaia knizhnost', arkheografiia, paleografiia, kodikologiia*, 8-18. St Petersburg: DB, 1999.

Antonii. *Sud za grobom ili mytarstva prepodobnoi Feodory: Strashnyi sud bozhii.* Izdanie Sviato-Vvedenskoi Optinoi Pustyni, 1996. Reprint of 10th ed., Moscow 1907.

Asieiev, Iu. S. *Mystetstvo Kyivs'koi Rusi.* Kyiv: Mystetstvo, 1989.

Baggley, John. *Doors of Perception – Icons and Their Spiritual Significance.* London and Oxford: Mowbray, 1987.

Bartrum, Giulia. *German Renaissance Prints 1490–1550.* London: British Museum Press, 1995.

Beneškovská, Klára, ed. *King John of Luxembourg (1296–1346) and the Art of His Era: Proceedings of the International Conference, Prague, September 16–20, 1996.* Prague: Koniasch Latin Press, 1998.

Berezhnaya, Lilya. 'Sub Specie Mortis: Ruthenian and Russian Last Judgement Icons Compared.' *European Review of History* 11, no. 1 (2004): 5–32.

Białopiotrowicz, Wojciech. 'Zagadnienia sztuki ludowej w malarstwie cierkiewnym w oparciu o wybrane zagadnienia terenu Karpat.' *Polska Sztuka Ludowa* (1986, no. 3-4): 171–8.

– 'Z problemów ikony karpackiej.' In *Chrześcijański Wschód a kultura polska*, ed. Ryszard Łużny, 347-64. Lublin: Redakcja wydawnictw Katolickiego Uniwersytetu Lubelskiego, 1989.

Bibliothèque Nationale, Département des manuscrits. *Évangiles avec peintures byzantines di XIe siècle: Reproduction des 361 miniatures du manuscrit grec 74 de la Bibliothèque Nationale.* 2 vols. Paris: Imprimerie Berthaud frères, n.d.

Biskupski, Romuald. 'Deesis na jednym podobraziu w malarstwie ikonowym XV i pierwszej połowy XVI wieku.' *Materiały Muzeum Budownictwa Ludowego w Sanoku* 29 (1986): 106–27.

– *Ikony w zbiorach polskich.* Skarby sztuki w Polsce. Warsaw: Wydawnictwa Artystyczne i Filmowe, 1991.

– *Ikony ze zbiorów Muzeum Historycznego w Sanoku.* Reproductions by Marek Brniak. Warsaw: Krajowa Spółdzielnia Artystyczno-Techniczna, 1991.

– *Król Chwały* – Spas w Siłach *z Nowosielec i Matka Boska Hodigitria z Doliny. Ikony z 2 połowy XV wieku.* Katalog zbiorów. Sanok: Muzeum Historyczne w Sanoku, 1999.

– 'Malarstwo ikonowe od XV do pierwszej połowy XVIII wieku na Łemkowszczyźnie.' *Polska Sztuka Ludowa* 39, no. 3-4 (1985): 153–76.

– 'Próba charakterystyki swoistych cech ukraińskiego malarstwa ikonowego od XV do pierwszej połowy XVIII wieku.' *Polska – Ukraina 1000 lat sąsiedztwa* 5 (2000): 157–64.

– 'Sztuka kościoła prawosławnego i unickiego na terenie diecezji przemyskiej w XVII i w pierwszej połowie XVIII wieku.' In *Polska–Ukraina. 1000 lat sąsiedztwa.* Vol. 2, *Studia z dziejów chrześcijaństwa na pograniczu kulturowym i etnicznym,* ed. Stanisław Stępień, 351–70. Przemyśl: Południowo-Wschodni Instytut Naukowy w Przemyślu, 1994.

– *Ukrzyżowanie z Owczar. Ikona z połowy XV wieku.* Katalog zbiorów. Sanok: Muzeum Historyczne w Sanoku, 2000.

Bojkovsky, Georg, and Rudolf Aitzetmüller, eds. *Paraenesis: Die altbulgarische Übersetzung von Werken Ephraims des Syrers.* 5 vols. Monumenta Linguae Slavicae Dialecti Veteris, Fontes et Dissertationes, 20, 22, 24, 26, 28. Freiburg: U.W. Weiher, 1984–90.

Božová, Jana, František Gutek, and Vladislav Grešlík. *Drevené kostolíky v okolí Bardejova.* Bardejov: Sajancy, 1997.

Brandon, S.G.F. *The Judgment of the Dead: The Idea of Life after Death in the Major Religions.* New York: Charles Scribner's Sons, 1967.

Brázdilová, Magdaléna. 'Kostol svätého Michala archanjela w Bodružali: Reštaurovanie nástenných malieb a historického mobiliára v interiéri.' *Pamiatky a Múzeá* (1999, no. 3): 18–22.

Brenk, Beat. *Tradition und Neuerung in der christlichen Kunst des ersten Jahrtausends: Studien zur Geschichte des Weltgerichtsbildes.* Wiener byzantinische Studien 3. Vienna: Österreichische Akademie der Wissenschaften, Kommission für Byzantinistik, Institut für Byzantinistik der Universität Wien, In Kommission bei Hermann Böhlaus Nachf., 1966.

Briusova, V.G. *Andrei Rublev.* Moscow: Izobrazitel'noe iskusstvo, 1995.

Brock, Sebastian P. 'Ephrem's Letter to Publius.' *Le Muséon: Revue d'Études Orientales* 89 (1976): 261–305.

– *The Luminous Eye: The Spiritual World Vision of St. Ephrem.* Cistercian Studies Series 124. Kalamazoo: Cistercian Publications, 1992.

Buslaev, F.I. *Sochineniia.* 2 vols. St Petersburg: Tipografiia Imperatorskoi akademii nauk, 1908–10.

Chlenova, Larysa, et al. *Shedevry ukrains'koho ikonopysu XII–XIX st.* Kyiv: Mystetstvo, 1999.

Chmelinová, Katarína, et al. *Monogramista C.Z.: Posledný Sud.* Bratislava: Slovenská národná galéria, 2002. Leaflet.

Chuba, Halyna. 'Do problemy typolohichnoho rozriznennia Uchytel'nykh Ievanhelii druhoi polovyny XVI – pershoi polovyny XVII st.' *Zapysky L'vivs'koi naukovoi biblioteky im. V. Stefanyka* 6 (1998): 70–81.

– 'Ukrains'ki uchytel'ni Ievanheliia.' In *Rukopysna ukrainika u fondakh L'vivs'koi naukovoi biblioteky im. V. Stefanyka NAN Ukrainy ta problemy stvorennia informatsiinoho banku danykh: Materialy mizhnarodnoi naukovo-praktychnoi konferentsii 20–21 veresnia 1996 roku,* ed. M.M. Trehub, et al., 294–302. Lviv: Natsional'na akademiia nauk Ukrainy, L'vivs'ka naukova biblioteka im. V. Stefanyka, 1999.

Chyzhevs'kyi, Dmytro. *Poza mezhamy krasy (do estetyky barokkovoi literatury).* New York: Ukrains'ko-amerykans'ke vydavnyche tovarystvo, 1952.

Costin, Emil. *Biserici de lemn din Maramureş.* Baia Mare: Editura Gutinul, 1999.

Cracraft, James. *The Church Reform of Peter the Great.* London: Macmillan, 1971.

– *The Petrine Revolution in Russian Imagery.* Chicago and London: The University of Chicago Press, 1997.

Cyril of Alexandria, Saint. 'De exitu animi, et de secundo adventu.' In *Patrologiae cursus completus, Series graeca* [*Patrologia Graeca*], 77:1071–90. Paris : Migne, 1844–66.

Czajkowski, Jerzy. 'Dzieje osadnictwa historycznego na Podkarpaciu i jego odzwiercedlenie w grupach etnograficznych.' In *Łemkowie w historii i kulturze*

Karpat, by Jerzy Czajkowski, pt. 1, 27–166. 2nd rev. ed. Sanok: Muzeum Budownictwa Ludowego w Sanoku, 1995.

Czajkowski, Jerzy, Romualda Grządziela, and Andrzej Szczepkowski. *Ikona karpacka*. Sanok: Muzeum Budownictwa Ludowego w Sanoku, 1998.

Der Nersessian, Sirarpie. 'Program and Iconography of the Frescoes of the Parecclesion.' In *The Kariye Djami*, vol. 4, ed. Paul A. Underwood, 303–49. London: Routledge & Kegan Paul, 1975.

Dionysios of Fourna. *The 'Painter's Manual' of Dionysius of Fourna*. Translated by Paul Hetherington. London: Sagittarius Press, 1974.

Domasłowski, Jerzy, Alicja Karłowska-Kamzowa, and Adam S. Labuda. *Malarstwo gotyckie na Pomorzu Wschodnim*. Warsaw and Poznań: Państwowe Wydawnictwo Naukowe, 1990.

Drăguţ, Vasile, and Petre Lupan. *Pictura murală din Moldova. Sec. XV–XVI*. Bucharest: Editura Meridiane, 1982.

Druziuk, Galina, and Lev Skop. 'Istoriia sozdaniia altarnoi pregrady v tserkvi Uspeniia bogoroditsy v s. Novoselitse na Zakarpat'e.' *Pamiatniki kul'tury. Novye otkrytiia. Pis'mennost'. Iskusstvo. Arkheologiia. Ezhegodnik* (1989): 204–18.

Druziuk-Skop, Galina, and Lev Skop. *Obraz galitskogo evreistva XIV–XVIII vv. v ukrainskoi ikonopisi*. Preprint. Moscow: Obshchestvo 'Evreiskoe nasledie,' 1996.

Dvořáková, Vlasta, Josef Krása, and Karel Stejskal. *Středověká nástěnná malba na Slovensku*. Photographs by Alexandr Paul st. Prague and Bratislava: Odeon, Tatran, 1978.

Dymytrii (Iarema), Patriarch. *Ikonopys Zakhidnoi Ukrainy XII–XV st*. Lviv: Drukars'ki kunshty, 2005.

Encyclopedia of Rusyn History and Culture, ed. Paul Robert Magocsi and Ivan Pop. Revised and expanded edition. Toronto: University of Toronto Press, 2005.

Encyclopedia of Ukraine, ed. Volodymyr Kubijovyč and Danylo Husar Struk. 5 vols, Toronto: University of Toronto Press, 1984–93.

Ephraem Syrus, Saint. *Tvoreniia*. Vol. 2. Moscow: Izdatel'skii otdel Moskovskogo Patriarkhata, 1993.

Every, George. 'Toll Gates on the Air Way.' *Eastern Churches Review* 8 (1976): 139–51.

Evkholohion abo Trebnyk Mytropolyta Petra Mohyly Kyiv 1646. Photoreproduction by Olexa Horbatsch [Oleksa Horbach]. Pratsi bohoslovs'koho fakul'tetu 66. Rome: Ukrains'kyi katolyts'kyi universytet im. sv. Klymenta papy, 1988.

Evseev, Ivan. *Kniga proroka Daniila v drevne-slavianskom perevode: Vvedenie i teksty*. Moscow: Otdelenie russkago iazyka i slovesnosti Imperatorskoi akademii nauk, 1905.

Fejős Zoltán, Lackner Mónika, and Wilhelm Gábor, eds. *Images of Time: Catalogue: Millenary Exhibition at the Museum of Ethnography 31 December2000 – 31 December 2001*. Budapest: Néprajzi Múzeum, 2001.

Flier, Michael S. 'Till the End of Time: The Apocalypse in Russian Historical Experience before 1500.' In *Orthodox Russia: Belief and Practice under the Tsars*, ed. Valerie A. Kivelson and Robert H. Greene, 127–58. University Park: Pennsylvania University Press, 2003.

Franko, Ivan. *Apokrify eskhatolohichni.* Vol. 4 of *Apokrify i liegendy z ukrains'kykh rukopysiv.* Pam"iatnyky ukrains'ko-rus'koi movy i literatury 4. Lviv: Arkheohrafichna komisiia NTSh, 1906.

– [Miron, pseud.]. 'K istorii iuzhno-russkikh apokrificheskikh skazanii.' *Kievskaia starina* 47 (1894): 425–44.

Freski Spasa-Nereditsy. Leningrad: Gosudarstvennyi russkii muzei, 1925.

Frický, Alexander. *Ikony z východného Slovenska.* Košice: Východnoslovenské vydatel'stvo, 1971.

Garidis, Miltiadis K. *Études sur le Jugement dernier post-Byzantin du XVe à la fin du XIXe siècle. Iconographie – esthetique.* Thessalonika: Etaireia Makedonikon Spoudon, 1985.

– 'La représentation des "nations" dans la peinture post-byzantine.' *Byzantion* 39 (1969): 86–103.

Gavrilovic, Zaga. 'St. Ephraim the Syrian's Thought and Imagery as an Inspiration to Byzantine Artists.' *Hugoye: Journal of Syriac Studies* [http://www.acad.cua.edu/syrcom/Hugoye] vol. 1, no. 2 (1998).

Gellner, Ernest. *Nations and Nationalism.* Ithaca: Cornell University Press, 1983.

Giemza, Jarosław. 'Ikony XVI i XVII wieku w zbiorach Muzeum – Zamku w Łańcucie.' In *Zachodnioukraińska sztuka cerkiewna*, ed. Jarosław Giemza, 17–52.

– 'Malowidła ścienne jako element wystroju drewnianych cerkwi w XVII wieku.' In *Sztuka cerkiewna w diecezji przemyskiej*, ed. Jarosław Giemza and Andrzej Stepan, 89–150.

– *O sztuce sakralnej przemyskiej eparchii. Słowem i obrazem.* Łańcut: Muzeum-Zamek w Łańcucie, 2006.

– 'Treści biblijne i apokryficzne w ikonach Sądu Ostatecznego.' *Peremys'ki dzvony* (1995, no. 2.19): 9–12.

– ed. *Zachodnioukraińska sztuka cerkiewna: Dzieła – twórcy – ośrodki – techniki: Materiały z międzynarodowej konferencji naukowej 10-11 maja 2003 roku.* Łańcut: Muzeum – Zamek w Łańcucie, 2003.

Giemza, Jarosław, and Andrzej Stepan, eds. *Sztuka cerkiewna w diecezji przemyskiej: Materiały z międzynarodowej konferencji naukowej 25–26 marca 1995 roku.* Łańcut: Muzeum Zamek w Łańcucie, Redakcja czasopisma 'Peremys'ki Dzwony,' Wydawnictwo 'STEPAN design,' 1999.

Giemza, Jarosław, and Maria Szewczuk. 'Ikona Sąd Ostateczny. Pawłentyj Radymskij 1623 r. z cerkwi p.w. Swiętego Jakuba Brata Pańskiego w Powroźniku.' Typescript: Muzeum-Zamek w Łańcucie, 1999.

Gieysztor, Aleksander. 'Z zagadnień historii kultury staroruskiej. Składniki rodzime i obce.' In *Studia Historica: W 35-lecie pracy naukowej Henryka Łowmiańskiego*, ed. Aleksander Gieysztor et al., 73–89. Warsaw: Państwowe Wydawnictwo Naukowe, 1958.

Ginzburg, Carlo. *The Cheese and the Worms: The Cosmos of a Sixteenth-Century Miller*. Translated by John and Anne Tedeschi. Baltimore: Johns Hopkins University Press, 1992.

Goar, Jacobus. *Euchologion sive rituale graecorum*. Graz: Akademische Druck- u. Verlagsanstalt, 1960. Reprint of Vienna 1730.

Goldfrank, David M. 'Some Reflections on Moldavian, Ukrainian, and Russian Last Judgment Iconography in the "Long" Sixteenth Century: Preliminary Draft for Oral Presentation with Slides.' Paper presented at the National Convention of the American Association for the Advancement of Slavic Studies, 18–21 November 1999, St Louis, Missouri. Typescript.

– 'Who Put the Snake on the Icon and the Tollbooths on the Snake? – A Problem of Last Judgment Iconography.' *Harvard Ukrainian Studies* 19 (1995): 180–99.

Gormin, Vladimir, and Luidmila Yarosh. *Novgorod: Art Treasures and Architectural Monuments 11th–18th Centuries*. Leningrad: Aurora Art Publishers, 1984.

Gould, Stephen Jay. *Wonderful Life: The Burgess Shale and the Nature of History*. New York and London: W.W. Norton, 1989.

Grabar, A.N. 'Ikonograficheskaia skhema piatidesiatnitsy.' *Seminarium Kondakovianum* 2 (1928): 223–39.

Grabar, Igor. *Die Freskomalerei der Dimitrij Kathedrale in Wladimir*. Berlin: Petropolis Verlag, Der Schmiede, n.d. [1920s].

Grešlík [Hreshlyk], Vladislav [Vladyslav]. 'Do stanu doteperishnikh doslidzhen' ikonopysu na Skhidnii Slovachchyni.' *Pravoslávny Teologický Zborník* 20.5 (1997): 244–78.

– *Ikony Šarišského Múzea v Bardejove*. Bratislava: Ars Monument, 1994.

– *Ikony 17. storočia na Východnom Slovensku*. Prešov: Akcent Print, 2002.

– 'Niekol'ko poznámok k ikonám 16. storočia na východnom Slovensku.' In [Jarosław Giemza,] *Zachodnioukraińska sztuka cerkiewna*, ed. by Giemza, 141–55.

– *Ukrains'ka ikona Skhidnoi Slovachchyny XV–XIX st....Avtoreferat dysertatsii...* Lviv: Ministerostvo osvity ukrainy, L'vivs'ka akademiia mystetstv, 1996.

Gronek, Agnieszka. 'Duchowieństwo wschodnie wobec przemian zachodzących w malarstwie ikonowym na Ukrainie w wieku XVII.' In *Harmonijne współistnienie kultury Wschodu i Zachodu na Ukrainie*, ed. Włodzimierz Mokry, 79–104. Biblioteka Fundacji św. Włodzimierza 3. Kraków: Wydawnictwo 'Szwajpolt Fiol,' 2000.

– 'Ikona Męki Pańskiej z Lipia w Muzeum Historycznym w Sanoku. Ze studiów nad przemianami XVII-wiecznego malarstwa ukraińskego.' M.A. diss., Jagiellonian University, 1997.

– *Ikony Męki Pańskiej: O przemianach w malarstwie cerkiewnym ukraińsko-polskiego pogranicza.* Biblioteka Tradycji 58. Kraków: Collegium Columbinum, 2007.

– 'Ikony Męki Pańskiej: O przemianach w malarstwie ukraińskim w wiekach XVI–XIX.' PhD diss., Jagiellonian University, 2003.

– 'On the Dependence of Western Ruthenian Passion Presentations on Western Graphics in the 16th to 18th Centuries.' *Series Byzantina* 1, (2003): 159–78.

Grządziela, Romualda. 'Prowieniencja i dzieje malarstwa ikonowego po północnej stronie Karpat w XV i na pocz. XVI w.' In *Łemkowie w historii i kulturze Karpat,* pt. 2, ed. Jerzy Czajkowski, 207–67. Sanok: Muzeum Budownictwa Ludowego w Sanoku, 1994.

– 'Twórczość malarza ikon z Żohatyna.' *Folia Historiae Artium* 10 (1974): 51–80.

Grządziela, Romualda, Jadwiga Malinowska, and Łucja Turczak. *Ikony w muzeach województwa rzeszowskiego.* Rzeszów: Muzeum okręgowe w Rzeszowie, 1968.

Gurevich, Aaron. 'Historical Anthropology and the Science of History.' In *Historical Anthropology of the Middle Ages,* by Aaron Gurevich, ed. Jana Hewlett, 3–49. Chicago: University of Chicago Press, 1992.

The Hagiography of Kievan Rus'. Translated with an introduction by Paul Hollingsworth. Harvard Library of Early Ukrainian Literature, English Translations 2. Cambridge, MA: Distributed by Harvard University Press for the Ukrainian Research Institute of Harvard University, 1992.

Haustein-Bartsch, Eva. *Ikonen: Eine Stiftung für das Ikonen-Museum Recklinghausen, Museen der Stadt Recklinghausen, Kunsthalle Recklinghausen, 3.10–22.10.1995.* Recklinghausen: Bitter KG, 1995.

– *Das Jüngste Gericht: Eine Ikone im Ikonen-Museum Recklinghausen. Mit einem Beitrag über die Randinschriften von Thomas Daiber.* Monographien des Ikonen-Museums Recklinghausen 2. Recklinghausen: Bitter KG, 1963.

Hegel, Georg Wilhelm Friedrich. *The Philosophy of History.* Translated by J. Sibree. New York: Dover, 1956. Reprint of 1899 Colonial Press edition.

Helytovych, Mariia. *Bohorodytsia z Dytiam i pokhvaloiu. Ikony kolektsii Natsional'noho muzeiu).* L'viv: Svichado. 2005.

– 'Datovani ikony peremyshl's'koi, volyns'koi ta l'vivs'koi shkil ukrains'koho maliarstva XVI stolittia.' In *Pam"iatky sakral'noho mystetstva Volyni na mezhi tysiacholit': Pytannia doslidzhennia, zberezhennia ta restavratsii. Naukovyi zbirnyk. Materialy VI mizhnarodnoi naukovoi konferentsii po volyns'komu ikonopysu, m. Luts'k, 1–3 hrudnia 1999 roku,* ed. Anatolii Syliuk et al., 53–60. Lutsk: Nazustrich, 1999.

– 'Ikony kintsia XVI stolittia z Vovcha.' *Rodovid* 17 (1999): 32–7.

– '"Strashnyi sud" seredyny XVI st. peremyshl's'koho maliara Oleksiia Horoshkovycha z tserkvy Perenesennia moshchei sv. Mykoly s. Rus'ka Bystra v Muzeiu ukrains'ko-rus'koi kul'tury v Svydnyku.' *Pravoslávny teologický zborník* 22, no. 7 (1999): 321–32.

– *Ukrains'ki ikony 'Spas u Slavi.'* Lviv: Vydavnytstvo 'Drukars'ki kunshty,' Natsional'nyi muzei u L'vovi, 2005.

– 'Zakhidnoukrains'ki ta volyns'ki ikony XVI st. z vkladnymy tekstamy.' *Sakral'ne mystetstvo Volyni: Naukovyi zbirnyk* 9 (2002): 33–5.

Himka, John-Paul. 'Episodes in the Historiography of the Ukrainian Icon.' *Journal of Ukrainian Studies* 29, nos. 1–2 (summer–winter 2004): 149–67.

– 'History, Christendom and Traditional Ukrainian Culture: Towards a Mental Archeology.' Maria and Vasyl Petryshyn Memorial Lecture in Ukrainian Studies, Ukrainian Research Institute, Harvard University, 11 April 1997. Unpublished. There is, however, a published Ukrainian translation: 'Istoriia, khrystyians'kyi svit i tradytsiina ukrains'ka kul'tura: Sproba mental'noi arkheolohii.' *Ukraina Moderna* 6 (2001): 7–24.

– 'The Icon of the Last Judgment in the Village of Roztoka, Transcarpathia.' In *Zachodnioukraińska sztuka cerkiewna*, pt. 2: *Materiały z międzynarodowej konferencji naukowej Łańcut-Kotań 17–18 kwietnia 2004 roku*, ed. Jarosław Giemza, 363–80. Łańcut: Muzeum-Zamek w Łańcucie; Narodowy Naukowo-Badawczy Ośrodek Konserwatorski Ukrainy, Oddział we Lwowie, 2004.

– 'The Last Judgment Icon of Mshanets.' *Journal of Ukrainian Studies.* Forthcoming.

– 'On the Left Hand of God: "Peoples" in Ukrainian Icons of the Last Judgment.' In *State, Societies, Cultures East and West: Essays in Honor of Jaroslaw Pelenski*, ed. Janusz Duzinkiewicz et al., 317–49. New York: Ross, 2004.

– '"Social" Elements in Ukrainian Icons of the Last Judgment (through the Eighteenth Century).' In *Letters from Heaven: Popular Religion in Russia and Ukraine*, ed. John-Paul Himka and Andriy Zayarnyuk, 235–50. Toronto: University of Toronto Press, 2006.

– 'What Constitutes a Ukrainian Cultural Artifact? The Case of Images of the Last Judgment.' In *Ukraine's Re-integration into Europe: A Historical, Historiographical and Politically Urgent Issue*, ed. Giovanni Brogi Bercoff and Giulia Lami, 227–41. Alessandria: Edizioni dell'Orso, 2005.

Hordyns'kyi, Sviatoslav. *Ukrains'ka ikona 12–18 storichchia.* Philadelphia: Provydinnia, 1973.

Hoshko, Iu. H. *Naselennia Ukrains'kykh Karpat XV–XVIII st. Zaselennia. Mihratsii. Pobut.* Kyiv: Naukova dumka, 1976.

Hunt, Priscilla. 'A Novgorod Last Judgment Icon and Hesychast Spirituality.' Typescript, 2001.

Hyhlík, Vladimír. *Košice*. Introduction by Ladislav Cselényi. Martin: Osveta, 1959.

Iarema, Volodymyr [Włodzimierz Jarema]. 'O pracowniach w Galicji w XIV–XVI wieku.' In *Sztuka cerkiewna w diecezji przemyskiej*, ed. Jarosław Giemza and Andrzej Stepan, 26–48.

Ikony ta suchasne ukrains'ke mystetstvo z kolektsii Pereiaslav-Khmel'nyts'koho istoryko-kul'turnoho zapovidnyka ta Dyrektsii khudozhnikh vystavok Ukrainy. Kyiv: no publisher, 1994.

Inkin, Vasyl'. *Sil'sk'e suspil'stvo Halyts'koho Prykarpattia u XVI–XVIII stolittiakh. Istorychni narysy*. Lviv: L'vivs'kyi natsional'nyi universytet imeni Ivana Franka, Instytut istorychnykh doslidzhen', 2004.

Irimie, Cornel, and Marcela Focşa. *Romanian Icons Painted on Glass*. Bucharest: Meridiane, 1968.

Istoriia gorodov i sel Ukrainskoi SSR. L'vovskaia oblast'. Kyiv: Institut istorii Akademii nauk USSR, Glavnaia redaktsiia Ukrainskoi Sovetskoi Entsiklopedii, 1978.

Istoriia ukrains'koho mystetstva v shesty tomakh. Vol. 2, *Mystetstvo XIV-pershoi polovyny XVII stolittia*. Kyiv: Akademiia Nauk Ukrains'koi Radians'koi Sotsialistychnoi Respubliky, Holovna redaktsiia Ukrains'koi Radians'koi Entsyklopedii, 1967.

Istoriia ukrains'koho mystetstva v shesty tomakh. Vol. 3, *Mystetstvo druhoi polovyny XVII–XVIII stolittia*. Kyiv: Akademiia Nauk Ukrains'koi Radians'koi Sotsialistychnoi Respubliky, Holovna redaktsiia Ukrains'koi Radians'koi Entsyklopedii, 1968.

John Damascene, Saint. *Barlaam and Ioasaph*. Translated by G.R. Woodward and H. Mattingly. London: William Heinemann; New York: Macmillan, 1914.

Jónsdóttir, Selma. *An 11th Century Byzantine Last Judgement in Iceland*. Reykjavik: Almenna Bókafélagið, 1959.

Karger, M.K. *Drevnerusskaia monumental'naia zhivopis' XI–XIV v.v.* Moscow and Leningrad: Izdatel'stvo 'Sovetskii Khudozhnik,' [1963].

Katajew, N. *Geschichte der Predigt in der russischen Kirche: Eine kurze Darstellung ihrer Entstehung und Entwickelung bis auf das XIX. Jahrhundert*. Stuttgart: W. Kohlhammer, 1889.

Kazakova, N.A., and Ia. S. Lur'ie. *Antifeodal'nye ereticheskie dvizheniia na Rusi XIV-nachala XVI veka*. Moscow and Leningrad: Izdatel'stvo Akademii nauk SSSR, 1955.

Kerekes, Peter. *Murder Ballads and Legends from Ladomirova*. Slovakia, 1998. (Documentary film.)

Kharlampovich, K.V. *Malorossiiskoe vlianie na velikorusskuiu tserkovnuiu zhizn'*. 1914. Reprint, The Hague and Paris: Mouton, 1968.

Kievskaia psaltir' 1397 goda iz Gosudarstvennoi Publichnoi biblioteki imeni M.E. Saltykova-Shchedrina v Leningrade [OLDP F6]. Moscow: Iskusstvo, 1978.

Kilesso, T.S. *Vydubyts'kyi monastyr.* Kyiv: Tekhnika, 1999.
Kirschbaum, Engelbert, ed. *Lexikon der christlichen Ikonographie.* 8 vols. Rome: Herder, 1968–76.
Kiwała, Bronisława, and Janina Burzyńska. *Ikony ze zbiorów Muzeum Okręgowego w Przemyślu.* Kraków: Krajowa Agencja Wydawnicza w Krakowie, 1981.
Kliś, Zdzisław. *Paruzja. Przedstawienie Sądu Ostatecznego w sztuce średniowiecznej Europy Srodkowej.* Kraków: Wydawnictwo Naukowe PAT, 1999.
Kłosińska, Janina. 'Dwie ikony Sądu Ostatecznego w zbiorach Sanockich.' *Materiały Muzeum Budownictwa Ludowego w Sanoku* 6 (December 1967): 30–45.
– *Ikony.* Muzeum Narodowe w Krakowie, Katalogi zbiorów, 1. Kraków: Muzeum Narodowe w Krakowie, 1973.
Komashko, Natalia. 'Ukrainian Icon Painting.' In *A History of Icon Painting: Sources Traditions Present Day*, ed. Lilia Evseyeva et al., trans. Kate Cook, 189–96. Moscow: 'Grand-Holding,' 2005.
Konstantynovych, Ioann. *Opisanie ikon po tserkvakh ruskykh u stolychnom hradi L'vovi.* Lviv: Typom instytuta Stavropyhian'skoho, 1858.
Korzo Margarita. *Obraz cheloveka v propovedi XVII veka.* Moscow: Rossiiskaia Akademiia Nauk, Institut filosofii, 1999.
– 'Rukopisnye uchitel'nye evangeliia iz sobranii LNB v traditsii tserkovno-uchitel'noi literatury Rechi Pospolitoi XVII veka: Tolkovanie pritchi o bogache i Lazare.' In *Rukopysna ukrainika u fondakh L'vivs'koi naukovoi biblioteky im. V. Stefanyka NAN Ukrainy ta problemy stvorennia informatsiinoho banku danykh: Materialy mizhnarodnoi naukovo-praktychnoi konferentsii 20–21 veresnia 1996 roku*, ed. M.M. Trebub et al., 302–20. Lviv: Natsional'na akademiia nauk Ukrainy, L'vivs'ka naukova biblioteka im. V. Stefanyka, 1999.
Kos, Hanna. '"Strashnyi sud" v ukrains'komu maliarstvi.' *Kyivs'ka tserkva* (2000, no. 2.8): 105–7.
Kot, Serhii, et al. *Volyns'ka ikona XVI–XVIII st. Kataloh ta al'bom.* Kyiv and Lutsk: Tov. 'Spadshchyna,' 1998.
Kots'-Hryhorchuk, Lidiia. 'Napysy na tvorakh ukrains'koho seredn'ovichnoho maliarstva (Linhvistychne ta paleohrafichne doslidzhennia).' *ZNTSh*, vol. 221, *Pratsi filolohichnoi sektsii* (1990): 210–36.
– 'Nove pro naidavnishi zrazky ukrains'koho ikonopysu.' *Narodna tvorchist' ta etnohrafiia* (1991, no. 4): 59–68.
Kovachovychova-Pushkar'ova, Blanka, and Imrikh Pushkar. *Derev"iani tserkvy skhidn'oho obriadu na Slovachchyni.* Naukovyi zbirnyk Muzeiu ukrains'koi kul'tury v Svydnyku 5. Prešov: Svydnyts'kyi muzei ukrains'koi kul'tury, 1971.
Kretzenbacher, Leopold. *Die Seelenwaage: Zur religiösen Idee vom Jenseitsgericht auf der Schichsalswaage in Hochreligion, Bildkunst und Volksglaube.* Buchreihe des Landesmuseums für Kärnten 4. Klagenfurt: Verlag des Landsemuseums für Kärnten, 1958.

Kruk, Mirosław P. 'Stan badań nad atrybucjami warsztatowymi zachodnioruskiego malarstwa ikonowego XV–XVI wieku.' *Polska Akademia Umiejętności. Prace Komisji Wschodnioeuropejskiej* 5 (1997): 163–77.

– 'Stan badań nad zachodnioruskim malarstwem ikonowym XV–XVI wieku.' In *Sztuka kresów wschodnich*, vol. 2, ed. J.K. Ostrowski, 29–55. Kraków: Instytut Historii Sztuki, Uniwersytetu Jagiellońskiego, 1996.

– *Zachodnioruskie ikony Matki Boskiej z Dzieciątkiem w wieku XV i XVI.* Kraków: Wydawnictwo Uniwersytetu Jagiellońskiego, 2000.

– 'Związki południowe malarstwa ikonowego XV–XVI wieku z obszaru północnych Karpat na przykładzie tematu ukrzyżowania.' In *Sztuka cerkiewna w diecezji przemyskiej*, ed. Jarosław Giemza and Andrzej Stepan, 49–72.

Krypiakevych, Ivan. 'Serednevichni monastyri v Halychyni.' *Zapysky Chynu sv. Vasyliia Velkykoho* 2 (1926): 70–105.

Kurpik, Wojciech. 'Ikona Sądu Ostatecznego z Muzeum Ziemi Przemyskiej.' *Rocznik Przemyski* 11 (1967): 229–41.

Lakata, Vasyl'. 'Try "ostanni sudy" v fondi Muzeiu ukrains'koi kul'tury.' *Naukovyi zbirnyk Muzeiu ukrains'koi kul'tury v Svydnyku* 6, no. 1 (1972): 289–309.

Latukha, Tetiana. 'Fresky Uspens'koho soboru v Chernihovi.' *Siverians'kyi litopys* (1998, no. 1): 60–9.

Lazarev, V.N. *Drevnerusskie mozaiki i freski XI–XV vv.* Moscow: Iskusstvo, 1973.

Lebedeva, I.N. *Povest' o Varlaame i Ioasafe. Pamiatnik drevnerusskoi perevodnoi literatury XI–XII.* Leningrad: Nauka, 1985.

Le Goff, Jacques. *The Birth of Purgatory.* Translated by Arthur Goldhammer. Chicago: University of Chicago Press, 1984.

The Lenten Triodion. Translated by Mother Mary and Archimandrite Kallistos Ware. London and Boston: Faber and Faber, 1978.

Letnianchyn, Lesia. 'Obraz sviatoho apostola Pavla v tserkovnomu zhyvopysi drohobyts'kykh khramiv sv. Iura ta Vozdvyzhennia Chesnoho Khresta.' In *Drohobyts'ki khramy Vozdvyzhennia ta Sviatoho Iura u doslidzhenniakh: Druhi chytannia. Materialy vystupiv 9 kvitnia 2000 r.*, ed. L. Skop, 166–75. Drohobych: Vidrodzhennia, 2000.

Likhachev, D.S., ed. *Slovar' knizhnikov i knizhnosti Drevnei Rusi.* Vyp. 1: *(XI - pervaia polovina XIV v.).* Leningrad: Izdatel'stvo 'Nauka,' leningradskoe otdelenie, 1987.

Litopys rus'kyi za ipats'kym spyskom. Translated by Leonid Makhnovets'. Kyiv: Dnipro, 1989.

Lohvyn, Hryhorii. *Po Ukraini: Starodavni mystets'ki pam"iatky.* Kyiv: Mystetstvo, 1968.

– *Ukrainskie Karpaty.* Moscow: Iskusstvo, 1973.

– *Z hlybyn. Hraviury ukrains'kykh starodrukiv XVI–XVIII st.* Kyiv: Dnipro, 1990.

Lohvyn, Hryhorii, Lada Miliaieva, and Vira Svientsits'ka. *Ukrains'kyi seredn'ovichnyi zhyvopys.* Kyiv: Mystetstvo, 1976.

Lykhach, Lidiia, and Mykola Korniienko. *Ikony Shevchenkovoho kraiu.* Kyiv: Rodovid, 2000.

Magocsi, Paul Robert. *Carpatho-Rusyn Settlement at the Outset of the 20th Century with Additional Data from 1881 and 1806.* 2nd, rev. ed. [Orwell, VT]: Carpatho-Rusyn Research Center, 1998.

– *Carpatho-Rusyn Studies: An Annotated Bibliography.* New York: Garland Press, 1988- .

– *Galicia: A Historical Survey and Bibliographic Guide.* Toronto: University of Toronto Press, 1983.

– *Our People: Carpatho-Rusyns and Their Descendents in North America.* 3rd, rev. ed. Toronto: Multicultural History Society of Ontario, 1994.

Mango, Cyril. *The Art of the Byzantine Empire 312–1453: Sources and Documents.* Medieval Academy Reprints for Teaching 16. Toronto: University of Toronto Press in association with the Medieval Academy of America, 1986.

Marek, Anna, et al., eds. *Losy cerkwi w Polsce po 1944 roku.* Rzeszów, 1997.

Marholina, Iryna. *Kyrylivs'ka tserkva v istorii seredn'ovichnoho Kyieva.* Kyiv: Natsional'nyi zapovidnyk 'Sofiia Kyivs'ka'; Natsional'na Akademiia nauk Ukrainy, Viddilennia relihiieznavstva; Instytut filosofii im. Hryhoriia Skovorody, 2001.

Mazurkiewicz, Roman. *Deesis. Idea wstawiennictwa Bogarodzicy i św. Jana Chrzciciela w kulturze średniowiecznej.* Kraków: Universitas, 1994.

Medwidsky, Bohdan. 'Cantors and Godparents in Ukrainian Folklore.' In *From* Chantre *to* Djak*: Cantorial Traditions in Canada,* ed. Robert B. Klymasz, 109–23. Mercury Series, Canadian Centre for Folk Culture Studies 73. Hull, Quebec: Canadian Museum of Civilization, 2000.

Miasnikova, L.M., O.B. Sin'kevich, M.M. Sitarchuk, Iu.M. Matiukhin. *L'vovskii muzei istorii religii i ateizma. Putevoditel'.* Lviv: Kameniar, 1988.

Miclea, Ion, and Radu Florescu. *Probota.* Bucharest: Editura Meridiane, 1978.

Mijović, Pavle. *Dečani.* 3rd ed. Belgrade: Jugoslavija, 1970.

Miliaieva, Liudmyla. *Stinopys Potelycha. Vyzvol'na borot'ba ukrains'koho narodu v mystetstvi XVII st.* Kyiv: Mystetstvo, 1969.

Mil'kov, V.V. *Drevnerusskie apokrify.* Pamiatniki drevnerusskoi mysli, Issledovaniia i teksty 1. St Petersburg: Izdatel'stvo Russkogo khristianskogo gumanitarnogo instituta, 1999.

Milošević, Desanka. *Das Jüngste Gericht.* Recklinghausen: Verlag Aurel Bongers, 1963.

Mytsiuk, Oleksander. *Narysy z sotsiial'no hospodars'koi istorii b. Uhors'koi nyni Pidkarpats'koi Rusy.* 2 vols. Uzhhorod, Prague: published by the author, 1936–8.

Nauky parokhial'nyia na nedili i S[via]ta urochystyia tsiloho roku ... z Slavensko-Ruskaho na prostyi, i pospolytyi iazyk Ruskii. Pochaiv, 1794.

Nersesian, L.V. 'O nekotorykh istochnikakh russkoi ikonografii "Strashnogo Suda" XV–XVI vekov.' Moscow: Moscow State University, Fedorovo-Davydovskie cheniia, 1999. Typescript.

– 'Videnie proroka Daniila v russkom iskusstve XV–XVI vekov.' *Mir istorii* (2000, no. 3). Available on internet: http://nesusvet.narod.ru/ico/books/ners.htm.

– 'Voznesenie monakhov i padenie angelov. Ob odnom ikonograficheskom motive v russkikh ikonakh "Strashnogo Suda" XVI veka.' *Iskusstvoznanie* (1998, no. 2): 262–70.

Nimchuk, Vasyl,' and Vasyl' Shynkaruk. 'Epihrafiia Voznesens'koi tserkvy XV st. u s. Luzhany na Bukovyni.' *Bukovyns'kyi zhurnal* 1 (1998): 101–7.

Orosz, Anna. 'Gotycka polichromia w kościele w Strzelcach Swidnickich.' *Kwartalnik Opolski* (1956, no. 1): 172–90. Files.

Otkovych, Vasyl'. *Narodna techiia v ukrains'komu zhyvopysu XVII–XVIII st.* Kyiv: Naukova dumka, 1990.

Otkovych [Otkowycz], Vasyl' [Wasyl]. 'Wyposażenie cerkwi p.w. świętego Mikołaja w Dmytrowicach koło Sądowej Wiszni.' In *Zachodnioukraińska sztuka cerkiewna*, ed. Jarosław Giemza, 497–503. Muzeum – Zamek w Łańcucie.

Otkovych, Vasyl', and Vasyl' Pylyp"iuk. *Ukrains'ka ikona XIV–XVIII st. Iz zbirky Natsional'noho muzeiu u L'vovi. Ukrainian Icon XIV–XVIII Cent.: From the Collection of the National Museum in Lviv.* Lviv: Svitlo i tin', 1999.

Ouspensky, Leonid, and Vladimir Lossky. *The Meaning of Icons.* Translated by G.E.H. Palmer and E. Kadloubovsky. Crestwood, NY: St Vladimir's Seminary Press, 1983.

Ovsiichuk, Volodymyr. 'Janina Kłosińska. Ikony – Kraków, 1973 – 312 s.' *Zapysky NTSh*, vol. 227, Pratsi Sektsii mystetstvoznavstva (1994): 471–8.

– *Ukrains'ke maliarstvo X–XVIII stolit': Problemy kol'oru.* Lviv: Instytut narodoznavstva Natsional'noi akademii nauk Ukrainy, 1996.

– *Ukrains'ke mystetstvo XIV–pershoi polovyny XVII stolittia.* Kyiv: Mystetstvo, 1985.

Paslavs'kyi, Ivan. 'Uiavlennia pro potoibichnyi svit i formuvannia poniattia chystylyshcha v ukrains'kii serednovichnii narodnii kul'turi.' *Zapysky NTSh. Pratsi Istorychno-filosofs'koi sektsii* 228 (1994): 343–56.

Patterson, Joby. *Wooden Churches of the Carpathians: A Comparative Study.* Boulder, CO: East European Monographs, 2001.

Pereswetoff-Morath, A.I. *'Whereby We Know That It Is the Last Time': Musings on Anti-Messiahs and Antichrists in a Ruthenian Textual Community.* Slavica Lundensia Supplementa 3. Lund: Department of East and Central European Studies, Lund University, 2006.

Peters, Christin[e]. 'Between Catholicism and Orthodoxy: Wall Paintings and Devotional Interaction in Mediaeval Transilvania and Moldovia.' In

Christianity in East Central Europe: Late Middle Ages, ed. Jerzy Kłoczowski, Paweł Kras, and Wojciech Polak, part 2, 328–36. Lublin: Instytut Europy Środkowo-Wschodniej, 1999.

Petković, Sreten. *Morača*. Belgrade: Prosveta, 1986.

Petrov, N.I. 'Rumynskie khudozhestvennye pamiatniki v Rossii i vozmozhnost' vliianiia ikh na russkoe iskusstvo.' In *Trudy chetyrnadtsatago arkheologicheskago s"ezda v Chernigove 1908*, vol. 14, pt. 2, 89–95. Moscow, 1911.

Piaskowski, Tadeusz, and Józef Poklewski 'Malowidło "Sąd Ostateczny" w kaplicy Św. Anny we Fromborku.' *Komentarze Fromborskie* (1972): 45–55. Files.

Pieńkowska, Hanna. 'Ikony sądeckie XVII i XVIII wieku (ze zbiorów Muzeum w Nowym Sączu).' *Rocznik Sądecki* 12 (1971): 573–618.

Plokhy, Serhii. *Tsars and Cossacks: A Study in Iconography*. Harvard Papers in Ukrainian Studies. Cambridge, MA: Distributed by Harvard University Press for the Harvard Ukrainian Research Institute, 2002.

Podlacha, Władysław. *Malowidła ścienne w cerkwiach Bukowiny*. Archiwum Naukowe, wydawnictwo Towarzystwa dla Popierania Nauki Polskiej, Dział 1, Tom V, Zeszyt 2. Lviv: Nakładem Towarzystwa dla Popierania Nauki Polskiej, 1912.

Podskalsky, Gerhard. *Byzantinische Reichseschatologie: Die Periodisierung der Weltgeschichte in den vier Grossreichen (Daniel 2 und 7) und dem tausendjährigen Friedensreiche (Apok. 20): Eine motivgeschichtliche Untersuchung*. Munich: W. Fink, 1972.

– *Christentum und theologische Literatur in der Kiever Rus' (988–1237)*. Munich: C.H. Beck'sche Verlagsbuchhandlung, 1982.

Pokrovskii, N.V. 'Strashnyi sud v pamiatnikakh vizantiiskago i russkago iskusstva.' In *Trudy VI arkheologicheskago s'ezda*, 3:295–381. Odessa, 1887.

Pop-Bratu, Anca. *Pictura murală maramureşeană: Meşteri zugravi şi interferenţe stilistice*. Bucharest: Editura Meridiane, 1982.

Puškár, Ladislav. 'Ikony posledných súdov zo zbierok MURK vo Svidníku.' *Pamiatky a múzeá* (2000, no. 4). http://www.snm.sk/old/pamiatky/index.htm.

Puskás [Pushkash], Bernadett [Bernadet]. 'Aktual'ni problemy vyvchennia davn'oho ikonopysu.' In *Ukrains'ke sakral'ne mystetstvo: Tradytsii, suchasnist', perspektyvy:Materialy mizhnarodnoi naukovoi konferentsii (L'viv, 4–5 travnia 1993 r.)*, ed. Emmanuil Mys'ko et al., 69–76. Lviv: Monastyr Monakhiv Studiis'koho Ustavu, Vydavnychyi viddil 'Svichado,' 1994.

– *Between East and West: Icons in the Carpathian Region in the 15th–18th Centuries*. Budapest: Magyar Nemzeti Galéria, 1991.

Putsko, V.G. 'Nekotorye zamechaniia o rospisiakh Uspenskogo sobora vo Vladimire (K ikonografii Strashnogo suda).' In *Drevnerusskoe iskusstvo XV–XVII vekov*, ed. V.N. Sergeev, 118–27. Moscow: Iskusstvo, 1981.

– 'Ukrains'kyi ikonopys XIII – pershoi polovyny XVII st. iak istoryko-kul'turna problema.' *Krakowskie Zeszyty Ukrainoznawcze* 7-8 (1998–9): 299–312.

Pyvovarov, Serhii. *Khrystyians'ki starozhytnosti v mezhyrichchi Verkhn'oho Prutu ta Seredn'oho Dnistra.* Chernivet'skyi Natsional'nyi Universytet imeni Iuriia Fed'kovycha, Bukovyns'kyi tsentr arkheologichnykh doslizhen' pry ChNU. Chernivtsi: Zelena Bukovyna, 2001.

Radwan, Marian, ed. *Wizytacje generalne parafii unickich w województwie kijowskim i bracławskim po 1782 roku.* Lublin: Towarzystwo Naukowe Katolickiego Uniwersytetu Lubelskiego, 2004.

Radyvylovskii, Antonii. *Vinets Khrystov z propovidii nedelnykh.* Kyiv, 1688.

Réau, Louis. *Iconographie de l'art chrétien.* 3 vols in 6. Paris: Presses universitaires de France, 1955–9.

Revel-Neher, Elisabeth. *The Image of the Jew in Byzantine Art.* Translated by David Maizel. Studies in Antisemitism. Oxford: Published for the Vidal Sassoon International Center for the Study of Antisemitism (SICSA), The Hebrew University of Jerusalem by Pergamon Press, 1992.

Rogov, A.I. 'Iz istorii kul'turnykh sviazei Galitsii i Moldavii s balkanskimi stranami (freski Lavrova).' In *Iugo-Vostochnaia Evropa v srednie veki,* ed. Ia. S. Grosul et al., 235–54. Kishinev: Shtiintsa, 1972.

Rozdolski, Roman. *Stosunki poddańcze w dawnej Galicji.* 2 vols. Warsaw: Państwowe Wydawnictwo Naukowe, 1962.

Różycka-Bryzek, Anna. 'Bizantyńsko-ruskie malowidła ścienne w kaplicy Świętokrzyskiej na Wawelu.' *Studia do Dziejów Wawelu* 3 (1968): 175–293.

– *Bizantyńsko-ruskie malowidła w kaplicy zamku lubelskiego.* Warsaw: Państwowe Wydawnictwo Naukowe, 1983.

– 'Bizantyńsko-ruskie malowidła w Polsce wczesnojagiellońskiej: Problem przystosowań na gruncie kultury łacińskiej.' In *Polska-Ukraina. 1000 lat sąsiedztwa.* Vol. 2, *Studia z dziejów chrześcijaństwa na pograniczu kulturowym i etnicznym,* ed. Stanisław Stępień, 307–26. Przemyśl: Południowo-Wschodni Instytut Naukowy w Przemyślu, 1994.

– 'Malarstwo cerkiewne w polskiej tradycji historycznej i w badaniach naukowych.' In *Sztuka cerkiewna w diecezji przemyskiej,* ed. Jarosław Giemza and Andrzej Stepan, 11–25.

– 'Sztuka w Polsce piastowskiej a Bizancjum i Ruś.' In *Polska-Ukraina. 1000 lat sąsiedztwa.* Vol. 2, *Studia z dziejów chrześcijaństwa na pograniczu kulturowym i etnicznym,* ed. Stanisław Stępień, 295–305. Przemyśl: Południowo-Wschodni Instytut Naukowy w Przemyślu, 1994.

The Russian Primary Chronicle: Laurentian Text. Translated and edited by Samuel Hazzard Cross and Olgerd P. Sherbowitz-Wetzor. Cambridge, MA.: The Mediaeval Academy of America, 1973.

Rusu, Adrian Andrei, et al. *Dicționarul mănăstirilor din Transilvania, Banat, Crișana și Maramureș*. Cluj-Napoca: Presa universitară, 2000.

Sakharov, V. *Eskhatologicheskiia sochineniia i skazaniia v drevne-russkoi pis'mennosti i vliianie ikh na narodnye dukhovnye stikhi.* Tula: Tipografiia N.I. Sokolova, 1879.

Șandru, Ionuț, and Mihai Vițega. *Made by Man, Created by God.* Suceava: Cygnus, 2004. Multimedia CD-ROM.

Sarab'ianov, Vladimir. '"Strashnyi Sud" v rospisiakh sobora Snetogorskogo monastyria v Pskove i ego istoricheskaia osnova.' *Problemy na izkustvoto* 30.2 (1996): 23–30.

Senyk, Sophia. 'Ruthenian Monasticism in Decline: 1300-1600.' *Studi sull' Oriente Cristiano* 8, no. 2 (2004): 79–119.

– *Women's Monasteries in Ukraine and Belorussia to the Period of Suppressions.* Orientalia Christiana Analecta 222. Rome: Pont. Institutum Studiorum Orientalium, 1983.

Der Serbische Psalter: Faksimile-Ausgabe des Cod. Slav. 4 der Bayerischen Staatsbibliothek München. Textband, ed. Hans Belting. Wiesbaden: Dr. Ludwig Reichert Verlag, 1978. *Faksimile,* 1983.

Ševčiková, Eva. 'Ikony z drevených kostolíkov a ich reštaurovanie.' *Pamiatky a Múzeá,* (1999, no. 3): 47–51.

Shevzov, Vera. 'Miracle-Working Icons, Laity, and Authority in the Russian Orthodox Church, 1861–1917.' *Russian Review* 58, no. 1 (January 1999): 26–48.

Shved, Mykhailo. *Spas'kyi ta Lavrivs'kyi monastyri – oseredky dukhovnosti i kul'tury v Halychyni.* Lviv: Misioner, 2000.

Sinigalia, Tereza, and Voica Maria Pușcașu. *Mânăstirea Probota.* Bucharest: Editura Meridiane, 2000.

Skochylias, Ihor. *Heneral'ni vizytatsii Kyivs'koi uniinoi mytropolii XVII–XVIII stolit'. L'vivs'ko-Halyts'ko-Kam"ianets'ka ieparkhiia.* Vol. 2, *Protokoly heneral'nykh vizytatsii.* Lviv: Vydavnytstvo Ukrains'koho Katolyts'koho Universytetu, 2004.

Škoviera, Andrej. 'Ikona Strašného súdu a jej text(y).' *Ročenka Slovenskej národnej galérie* (2002): 137–54.

Skrobucha, Heinz. *Icons in Czechoslovakia.* London: Hamlyn, 1971.

– 'Zur Ikonographie des "Jüngsten Gerichts" in der russischen Ikonenmalerei.' *Kirche im Osten. Studien zur osteuropäischen Kirchengeschichte und Kirchenkunde* 5 (1962): 51–74.

Slobodian, Vasyl'. *Tserkvy Ukrainy. Peremys'ka ieparkhiia.* Lviv: Instytut ukrainoznavstva, 1998.

Smirnova, E.S. *Moskovskaia ikona XIV–XVII vekov.* Leningrad: Avrora, 1988.

Smorąg Różycka, Małgorzata. 'Sztuka cerkiewna Rusi Halicko-Wołyńskiej. Artystyczna symfonia tradycji bizantyńsko-ruskiej i romańskiej.' *Sztuka Kresów Wschodnich* 4 (1999): 7–32.

[Smotryts'kyi, Meletii.] *The* Jevanhelije učitelnoje *of Meletij Smotryc'kyj.* Introduction by David Frick. Harvard Library of Early Ukrainian Literature, Texts, 2. Cambridge, MA: Distributed by the Harvard University Press for the Ukrainian Research Institute of Harvard University, 1987.

– *Rus' Restored: Selected Writings of Meletij Smotryc'kyj 1610–1630,* trans. and annotated with an introduction by David Frick. Harvard Library of Early Ukrainian Literature, English Translations, 7. Cambridge, MA: Distributed by Harvard University Press for the Harvard Ukrainian Research Institute, 2005.

Sopolyha, Myroslav. *35 rokiv Muzeiu ukrains'koi kul'tury u Svydnyku.* Bratislava and Prešov: Slovats'ke pedahohichne vydavnytstvo v Bratislavi, Viddil ukrains'koi literatury v Priashevi, 1990.

Sotiriou, G., and M. Sotiriou. *Icones du Mont Sinaï.* Collection de l'Institut Français d'Athènes, 100, 102. 2 vols. Athens: [Institut Français d'Athènes], 1956–8.

[Stavrovetskii], Kyryll Trankvylionn. *Ievanheliie uchytel'noie albo kazania na nedilia prez rok i na praznyky hospodskiie.* Rokhmaniv, 1619.

Ştefănescu, I.D. *L'évolution de la peinture religieuse en Bucovine et en Moldavie depuis les origines jusqu'au XIXe siècle.* 2 vols (*Texte* and *Album*). Paris: Libraire orientaliste Paul Geuthner, 1928.

Stepovyk, Dmytro. *Istoriia ukrains'koi ikony, X–XX st.* Kyiv: Lybid', 1996.

Stichel, Rainer. *Studien zum Verhältnis von Text und Bild spät- und nachbyzantinischer Vergänglichkeitsdarstellungen: Die Anfangsminiaturen von Psalterhandschriften des 14. Jahrhunderts, ihre Herkunft, Bedeutung und ihr Weiterleben in der griechischen und russischen Kunst und Literatur.* Byzantina Vindobonensia 5. Vienna: In Kommision bei Hermann Böhlaus Nachf., 1971.

Sumtsov, N.F. 'K istorii ukrainskoi ikonopisi.' *Sbornik Khar'kovskogo istoriko-filologicheskoho obshchestva* 16 (1905): 131–41.

Svientsits'ka [Sventsitskaia], Vera. 'Master ikon XV veka iz sel Vanivka i Zdvyzhen'.' In *Drevnerusskoe iskusstvo. Problemy i atributsii,* ed. O.I. Podobedova, 273–90. Moscow: Nauka, 1977.

– 'Pro deiaki ikonohrafichni analohii ta paraleli v zobrazhenni Strashnoho Sudu v zakhidnoukrains'kykh ikonakh XV–XVI stolit' ta ikonakh khudozhnykiv novhorods'koho kola.' *Zapysky NTSh* vol. 236, *Pratsi Komisii obrazotvorchoho ta uzhytkovoho mystetstva* (1998): 85–93.

Svientsits'ka, V.I., and V.P. Otkovych. *Ukrains'ke narodne maliarstvo XIII–XX stolit'. Al'bom.* Svit ochyma narodnykh myttsiv. Kyiv: Mystetstvo, 1991.

Svientsits'ka, V.I., and O.F. Sydor. *Spadshchyna vikiv. Ukrains'ke maliarstvo XIV–XVIII stolit' u muzeinykh kolektsiiakh L'vova.* Lviv: Kameniar, 1990.

Svientsits'kyi, Ilarion *Ikonopys' halyts'koi Ukrainy XV–XVI. vikiv.* Zbirky Natsional'noho muzeiu u L'vovi. Lviv: Ukrains'kyi natsional'nyi muzei, 1928.

Svientsitskyi-Sviatyts'kyi [*sic*], Ilarion. *Ikony halyts'koi Ukrainy XV–XVI. vikiv.* Zbirky Natsional'noho muzeiu u L'vovi. Lviv: Ukrains'kyi natsional'nyi muzei, 1929.

Svientsits'kyi [Sventsitskii], Ilarion *Opis' muzeia Stavropigiiskago Instituta vo L'vove.* Lviv: Tipografiia Stavropigiiskago Instituta, 1908.

Svientsitskyi, Ilarion. *Tematychnyi uklad stinopysu tserkvy sv. Iura v Drohobychi.* Vidbytka z 'Litopysu Boikivshchyny' ch. 10. N.p., n.d. Reprint (without illustrations): Svientsits'kyi, Illarion [*sic*]. 'Tematychnyi uklad stinopysu tserkvy sviatoho Iura v Drohobychi.' In *Drohobyts'ki khramy Vozdvyzhennia ta Sviatoho Iura u doslidzhenniakh. Pershi chytannia. Materialy vystupiv 23 chervnia 1998 r. m. Drohobych*, 65–7. Drohobych: Vidrodzhennia, 1998.

Sydor, Oleh. 'Ikona Strashnoho Sudu z Vil'shanytsi. Z materialiv do zvedenoho kataloha zbirok NML.' *Litopys Natsional'noho muzeiu u L'vovi*, no. 2 (7) (2001): 79–89.

– 'Ikony maistriv Oleksiia i Dymytriia v kolektsii Natsional'noho muzeiu u L'vovi. Z materialiv do zvedenoho kataloha zbirok NML.' *Litopys Natsional'noho muzeiu u L'vovi*, no. 1 (6) (2000): 89–152.

– 'Reiestr ikon Strashnoho Sudu v kolektsii NML.' *Litopys Natsional'noho muzeiu u L'vovi*, no. 2 (7) (2001): 90–6.

Sydor, Oleh, and Taras Lozynskyi, eds. *Ukrainian Icons 13th–18th Centuries from Private Collections.* Introduction by Oleh Sydor. Kyiv: Rodovid in association with the Prairie Centre for the Study of Ukrainian Heritage (St Thomas More College, University of Saskatchewan, Canada), 2003.

Syrokhman, Mykhailo. *Tserkvy Ukrainy. Zakarpattia.* Lviv: Vydavnytstvo 'Ms,' 2000.

Szacsvay, Éva. *Üvegképek.* Budapest: Néprajzi Múzeum – Vízió Művészeti Alkotóközösség, 1996.

Szanter, Zofia. 'Ruskie i mołdawskie wzory architektury cerkiewnej – ich wpływ na obszar północnego odcinka łuku Karpat.' In *Sztuka cerkiewna w diecezji przemyskiej*, ed. Jarosław Giemza and Andrzej Stepan, 207–32.

Taylor, David G.K. 'St. Ephraim's Influence on the Greeks.' *Hugoye: Journal of Syriac Studies* [http://www.acad.cua.edu/syrcom/Hugoye] vol. 1, no. 2 (1998).

Tkáč, Štefan. *Ikony zo 16.–19. storočia na severovýchodnom Slovensku.* Bratislava: Tatran, 1982.

Trajdos, Tadeusz. 'Początki osadnictwa Wołochów na Rusi Czerwonej.' In *Łemkowie w historii i kulturze Karpat*, ed. Jerzy Czajkowski, pt. 1, 199–210. 2nd, rev. ed. Sanok: Muzeum Budownictwa Ludowego w Sanoku, 1995.

Tserkovni starozhytnosti XVI–XVII stolit'. U zibranni Natsional'noho kyievo-pechers'koho istoryko-kul'turnoho zapovidnyka. Kataloh vystavky. Kyiv: Vydavnytstvo 'Aktsent,' 1999.

Tsodikovich, V.K. *Semantika ikonografii 'Strashnogo Suda.'* Ulianovsk: Ul'ianovskoe oblastnoe gazetnoe izdatel'stvo, 1995.

Turdeanu, Emil. 'Centres of Literary Activity in Moldavia, 1504–1552.' *Slavonic and East European Review* 34 (1955–6): 99–122.

Underwood, Paul A. *The Kariye Djami.* Vols 1-3. Bollingen Series 70. New York: Bollingen Foundation, 1966. Vol. 4. London: Routledge & Kegan Paul, 1975.

Uspenskii, B.A. '"Pravoe" i "levoe" v ikonopisnom izobrazhenii.' In his *Semiotika iskusstva,* 297–303. Moscow: Shkola 'Iazyki russkoi kul'tury,' 1995.

Vavryk, Mykhailo M. *Narys rozvytku i stanu Vasyliians'koho chyna XVII–XX st. Topohrafichno-statystychna rozvidka.* Analecta OSBM, Series 2, Sectio 1: Opera, 40. Rome: PP. Basiliani 1979.

Vilinskii, S.G. *Zhitie sv. Vasiliia Novago v russkoi literature.* 2 parts. *Zapiski Imperatorskogo Novorossiiskogo universiteta. Istoriko-filologicheskii fakul'tet* 6–7. Odessa: Tipografiia 'Tekhnik,' 1911, 1913.

Völkl, Ekkehard. *Das rumänische Fürstentum Moldau und die Ostslaven im 15. bis 17. Jahrhundert.* Veröffentlichungen des Osteuropa-Institutes München, Reihe: Geschichte, 42. Wiesbaden: In Kommission bei Otto Harrassowitz, 1975.

Vysotskaia, N.F. *Ikanapis Belarusi XVI–XVIII stahoddziau.* 6th ed. Minsk: Belarus', 2001.

Vzdornov, G. *Issledovanie o Kievskoi Psaltiri.* Moscow: Iskusstvo, 1978.

Wawrzeniuk, Piotr. *Confessional Civilising in Ukraine: The Bishop Iosyf Shumliansky and the Introduction of Reforms in the Diocese of Lviv 1688–1708.* Huddinge: Södertörns högskola, 2005.

Weitzmann, Kurt. *The Icon: Holy Images – Sixth to Fourteenth Century.* New York: George Braziller, 1978.

Weitzmann, Kurt, Gaiané Alibegašvili, Aneli Volskaja, Manolis Chatzidakis, Gordana Babić, Mihail Alpatov, and Teodora Voinescu. *The Icon.* New York: Dorset Press, 1987.

Woodsworth, Cherie. 'The Venerated Image among the Faithful: Icons for Historians.' *Kritika: Explorations in Russian and Eurasian History* 8, no. 2 (spring 2007): 389–408.

Wuthnow, Robert. *Rediscovering the Sacred: Perspectives on Religion in Contemporary Society.* Grand Rapids, MI: William B. Eerdmans, 1992.

Zapasko, Iakym, and Iaroslav Isaievych. *Pam"iatky knyzhkovoho mystetstva. Kataloh starodrukiv, vydanykh na Ukraini.* Book 2, part 1: *1701–1764.* Lviv: Vydavnytstvo pry L'vivs'komu derzhavnomu universyteti vydavnychoho ob"iednannia 'Vyshcha shkola,' 1984.

Zarivna, Teodoziia, and Olha Loza, eds. *Ukrainian Antiquities in Private Collections: Folk Art of the Hutsul and Pokuttia Regions.* Kyiv: Rodovid, 2002.

Zema, Valerii. 'Eskhatolohichni motyvy v rus'kykh propovidiakh na m"iasopust (XVI – persha polovyna XVII st.).' Typescript.

Zenkovsky, Serge A., ed. and trans. *Medieval Russia's Epics, Chronicles, and Tales.* Rev. and enlarged ed. New York: E.P. Dutton, 1974.

Zholtovs'kyi, P.M. *Khudozhnie zhyttia na Ukraini v XVI–XVIII st.* Kyiv: Naukova dumka, 1983.

– *Monumental'nyi zhyvopys na Ukraini XVII–XVIII st.* Kyiv: Naukova dumka, 1988.

– *Ukrains'kyi zhyvopys XVII–XVIII st.* Kyiv: Naukova dumka, 1978.

Zlatohlávek, Martin; Christian Rätsch, and Claudia Müller-Ebeling. *Sąd Ostateczny. Freski, miniatury, obrazy.* Trans. Anna Kleszcz. Kraków: Wydawnictwo WAM, 2002.

Index

www.ingramcontent.com/pod-product-compliance
Lightning Source LLC
LaVergne TN
LVHW090805070826
844660LV00022B/1081

* 9 7 8 1 4 8 7 5 2 3 4 1 1 *